RACIAL DISCRIMINATION IN THE UNITED STATES

EDITED BY

THOMAS F. PETTIGREW

HARVARD UNIVERSITY

HARPER & ROW

Publishers

, EVANSTON, SAN FRANCISCO, LONDON

To
my mother and
Miss Mildred Adams
who both in their own
ways have combatted
racial discrimination
all their lives.

Sponsoring Editor: Ronald K. Taylor
Project Editor: William B. Monroe
Production Supervisor: Stefania J. Taflinska

RACIAL DISCRIMINATION IN THE UNITED STATES
Copyright © 1975 by Thomas F. Pettigrew. All rights
reserved. Printed in the United States of America. No
part of this book may be used or reproduced in any manner whatsoever without written permission except in the
case of brief quotations embodied in critical articles and
reviews. For information address Harper & Row, Publishers, Inc., 10 East 53rd Street, New York, N.Y. 10022.

Library of Congress Cataloging in Publication Data

Pettigrew, Thomas F   comp.
    Racial discrimination in the United States.

    (Readers in social problems)
    Includes index.
    1.   Negroes—Civil rights—Addresses, essays,
lectures.   2.   Race discrimination—United States—
Addresses, essays, lectures.   3.   United States—Rac
question—Addresses, essays, lectures.   I.   Title.
E185.615.P44   301.45'19'6073   74-23900
ISBN 0-06-045183-1

Contents

Part III / DISCRIMINATION IN
   EMPLOYMENT, EDUCATION, AND
   INCOME: THE BARRIERS TO STATUS

Part IV / DISCRIMINATION IN CRIME,
   POLITICS, AND OTHER AREAS

Part V / THE HUMAN COST OF RACIAL DISCRIMINATION

Part VI / PROPOSED REMEDIES

Preface

"You don't have to love me—just get your foot off my neck!" This exclamation to white America has been voiced by black spokesmen as varied as James Baldwin and the late Dr. Martin Luther King, Jr. Prejudice and face to face abuse are painful and difficult to confront. But it is *racial discrimination* that delimits life chances and constrains human existence. This volume attempts to provide a succinct social science analysis of this persistent and major social problem in American life.

I. FOUR WORKING DEFINITIONS

Racial discrimination, confided a black respondent to a *Newsweek* interviewer, "feels like being punished for something you didn't do."[1] This candid description serves as an initial definition of the focus of this book, for racial discrimination actually *is* racist punishment for "something" black Americans "didn't do."

More technically, we must distinguish between the concepts of prejudice and individual racism, on the one hand, and discrimination and institutional racism, on the other hand.[2]

[1] "The Negro in America," *Newsweek*, July 29, 1963, *62*, 15–34.

[2] A more detailed discussion is provided in T. F. Pettigrew, "Racism and the Mental Health of White Americans: A Social Psychological View." In C. V. Willie, B. M. Kramer, and B. S. Brown (eds.), *Racism and Mental Health*. Pittsburgh: University of Pittsburgh Press, 1973; pp. 269–298.

Prejudice is a broader term than racism. More formally, we can define *prejudice as an affective, categorical mode of mental functioning that involves rigid prejudgment and misjudgment of human groups.*[3] By contrast, *individual racism involves both prejudicial beliefs and discriminatory behavior of individuals specifically directed against black Americans.*[4] Its antiblack orientation is *fundamentally based on superiority-inferiority assumptions of race* that trace straight back to Count Arthur de Gobineau's *Essai sur l'inégalité des races humaines,* published in the nineteenth century. Over the years the arguments of de Gobineau have changed surprisingly little in racist thought despite repeated efforts to dress them up with pseudoscientific respectability.[5]

Prejudice and individual racism are phenomena of *individuals.* But this volume must necessarily concentrate less on the individual level than on the *societal* level. *Racial discrimination is basically an institutional process of exclusion against an outgroup on largely ascribed and particularistic grounds of group membership rather than on achieved and universalistic grounds of merit.* A useful distinction can be made, too, between direct and indirect discrimination. Direct discrimination results from restrictions within an institution, such as the schools, leading to impaired opportunities in that realm, such as less advanced training. Important as this phenomenon is in American race relations, indirection discrimination is even more common for it refers to restrictions in one realm, such as employment, created by direct discrimination in another realm, such as education.

Gunnar Myrdal pointed out a generation ago in his *An*

---

[3] For the definitive discussion of the concept of prejudice, see G. W. Allport, *The Nature of Prejudice.* Reading, Mass.: Addison-Wesley, 1954.

[4] "Racism" can, of course, apply to a range of outgroups who are perceived to be racially distinct from the ingroup. Thus anti-Semites are more likely than others to perceive Jews as a race, and, hence, their feelings against Jews might be described as racist. But we are here using the term in its narrow and current U.S. application to black Americans

[5] T. F. Pettigrew, *A Profile of the Negro American.* New York: Van Nostrand Reinhold, 1964; chaps. 3–6.

American Dilemma that racial discrimination in the United States forms a vicious circle, with restrictions in housing, politics, employment, education, or any one realm complexly interwoven with restrictions in all others.[6] Thus authorities in each realm can point to the "true" core of the problem as lying elsewhere. In reality each institution's constraints contribute to the web of direct and indirect discrimination that has encircled black Americans for years. But Myrdal also pointed out an interesting property of vicious circles of causation: They can be broken at any point and can evolve in time into self-correcting benign circles of affirmative racial change.

We shall see in the following pages that the past three decades bear out Myrdal's contentions with one vital qualification. Racial change does not come evenly across all realms; rather, discrimination is alleviated in some areas faster than in others, with the retarded areas acting through indirect discrimination to slow progress generally. During the 1940s and 1950s direct discrimination in employment proved to be the primary barrier to general improvement. More recently, direct discrimination in housing and in education have become especially crucial.[7] Yet remedial efforts in a given realm are most effectively fashioned against the direct discrimination involved rather than the indirect discrimination stemming from other realms.[8] More effective still, of course, are broad-scaled antidiscrimination efforts that attack systematically the whole process across institutions.

Closely allied with this conception of racial discrimination is that of *institutional racism*. It can be usefully defined as *that complex of institutional arrangements that restrict the life choices of black Americans in comparison to those of white Americans*. Such a definition can rightfully be chal-

[6] Gunnar Myrdal, *An American Dilemma*. New York: Harper & Row, 1944.

[7] T. F. Pettigrew, *Racially Separate or Together?* New York: McGraw-Hill, 1971.

[8] Ibid.; and R. Fein, "An Economic and Social Profile of the Negro American." In T. Parsons and K. B. Clark (eds.), *The Negro American*. Boston: Houghton Mifflin, 1966.

lenged as too all-encompassing, since it covers virtually all of the nation's institutions and their operations. But is this the fault of the definition, or is it a reasonably accurate picture of American society? This volume contends that the latter is the case, and its material will demonstrate the utility of the broad definition.

Three general observations need to be made about racial discrimination and institutional racism. First, institutional racism avidly supports individual racism as if it were a fifty-two-week-a-year antibrotherhood reminder. Attacks upon discrimination and institutional racism are needed more than all the brotherhood sermons and dinners conceivable. Prejudice does not operate in a social and institutional vacuum; it requires a contaminated environment of ingroup privilege and outgroup exclusion.

Second, racist institutions need not be operated by racists nor designed with racist intentions to limit black choice. Prejudice and discrimination are by no means perfectly correlated, and institutional racism can easily result as an unintended consequence of nonracial arrangements. But it makes little difference to black Americans what the formal intentions are when the constraining consequences are the same.

Finally, discrimination and institutional racism are extremely difficult to combat effectively. One reason for this, as we have already noted, is that discrimination is a vast, interlocking system that spans all of the various institutions of American society. Robert Friedman, in the final selection of this volume, further elucidates this complexity and organizes our understanding of it as a system. A second reason for the difficulty of antidiscrimination efforts concerns the positive functions of institutional arrangements with racist effects. Many of these arrangements, perhaps even most of them, were originally designed and established to serve positive functions for the institution without thought of their racial implications. They have been nurtured and maintained precisely because they do in fact accomplish these positive functions. The problem, then, is not simply to eliminate racist arrangements, difficult as that in itself would be, but to replace these arrangements with others that serve the same positive functions equally well without the racist consequences.

II. A SOCIAL CONCEPTION OF RACE

One more concept must be examined before we pursue our topic—race, "man's most dangerous myth." Scientifically, races signify only subspecies of the one species of mankind; more technically, races are relatively isolated mating groups with distinctive gene frequencies. Modern authorities hold that there are no pure races in the world today, that there is little reason to believe that interracial mixing is genetically harmful, that the precise number of races in existence depends on the particular scheme of the classifier, and that there is little support for the ranking of races as genetically superior or inferior.[9]

Extensive racial intermixture has taken place from ancient times to the present. Modern technology has made geographic isolation almost an impossibility and has so altered man's environment as to render racial adaptations to older environments largely obsolete. This means that the purity of races is even more impossible to achieve than before. On the American scene specifically, miscegenation over the past three and a half centuries has resulted in roughly one-fourth of the black American gene pool's consisting of genes of Caucasian origin. And about three-fourths of all black Americans have some Caucasian ancestry. Likewise a minority of white Americans possess some Negroid ancestry. In law, parts of the United States long defined a "Negro" as anyone with one known black ancestor—regardless of how Caucasian his genes may be in origin. Clearly "race" is more socially than biologically

[9] Pettigrew, *A Profile of the Negro American*, op. cit., chap. 3.

defined in the United States. Black Americans are those citizens who are socially recognized as "black," a definition that only loosely relates to the scientific conception of race.

In spite of its severe limitations, this social conception of "race" is employed throughout this book for two compelling reasons. First, for reasons of practicality: The relevant research on racial discrimination has been forced to use the concept in this loose fashion. The studies of "blacks" contained in these pages actually utilized data on socially defined black people, many of whom were at least partly Caucasian in ancestry. Second, the nation's problems of racial discrimination are posed in these terms. Institutional restrictions against black Americans constitute a basically social, not genetic, problem.

A full exposition of *racial* discrimination in the United States would ideally include restrictions against all of the nation's minority racial groups. But we shall have to be content with an exclusive concentration upon black Americans. There are four reasons for this limitation: (1) Black people comprise over 90 percent of the nation's "nonwhites"; (2) by far the bulk of research on discrimination has been conducted on black Americans; (3) many of the basic principles of how racial discrimination operates against black Americans apparently apply in large measure to discrimination against the other racial minorities; and (4) space limitations militate for a more focused treatment on discrimination against black Americans alone.

III. AN OVERVIEW OF THE VOLUME

The book is organized into six parts. The Introduction opens with a brief historical perspective by W. E. B. Du Bois, a major black spokesman who spanned both the late nineteenth and twentieth centuries. Not only have the forms of racial discrimination changed over this century, but so has the social science study of them. From armchair analysis to sophisticated computer models, the trends of social research in this realm are chronicled in the second selection of the Introduction.

As the United States has increasingly become an urban industrial society, the role of housing segregation and discrimination has become ever more central in the whole racial system of societal restrictions. Hence Part II begins our analysis with an in-depth look at housing discrimination. We shall note the complicity of federal and local government as well as that of the housing industry itself in the establishment and maintenance of the problem; that the problem is still widespread and not necessarily improving; that discrimination in housing against black people far exceeds that against other minorities; and that the attitudes of blacks and whites toward race and housing are not as far apart as the actual housing situation today might lead one to expect.

Part III applies this analysis of housing to discrimination in employment, education, and income. Now we begin to learn how the various realms interlock. The first selections show how housing segregation in the central city relates to unemployment and underemployment. Next, the U.S. Commission on Civil Rights provides us with documented evidence of how job discrimination is practiced against blacks even by state and local governments. The final two selections on employment make use of modern computer methodology on refined census data. Otis Dudley Duncan demonstrates that at least prior to 1962 the social origins of black males were a far less important factor in the explanation of racial differences in occupational achievement than inequalities within the process of mobility itself. More encouraging are the computer calculations of Stanley Lieberson and Glenn V. Fuguitt. Their model suggests that if all employment discrimination suddenly and miraculously ceased, over half of the racial occupational differences would disappear in one generation despite the indirect effects of discrimination in such other sectors as education.

Two selections on education follow. First, Robert Crain reveals the apparent occupational gains that accrue to blacks who received an interracial education as children. Next, the editor employs the work of Crain and others in a discussion of public school integration. Part III closes with two selections on income. The first outlines the intricate and direct relationship between racial discrimination and the poverty of many black people. The second summarizes the educational, occupational, and purchasing power gains of blacks between 1960 and 1970, but it emphasizes that "very large racial differences remain."

Discrimination in both the administration of justice and in political power are the focus of Part IV. Marvin Wolfgang and Bernard Cohen reveal how racial discrimination marks each step in the judicial process from arrest to parole and that black people are more likely to be victims of crime than other Americans.

Many observers convincingly argue that basic to all of these patterns of racial discrimination is the relative powerlessness of blacks in the American political system. This vast and critical topic, of course, deserves far more space than this volume can provide. But we outline the issue with the second selection of Part IV on the underrepresentation of blacks in positions of power in Milwaukee, Wisconsin. While the reader is undoubtedly aware of the problem, the virtual exclusion of blacks from policy-making roles in a major northern city may still surprise you. Part IV concludes with another summary article, which compares changes over the past generation not only in the status dimensions of income, education, and occupation but in such matters as mortality and marital condition.

Until this point, impersonal census statistics and large-scale social processes have dominated the discussion. Part V remedies this imbalance by reminding us that there is a tragic human cost of racial discrimination. We learn how black people are rapidly losing their faith in American government, how Harlem's drug addicts view their defeated lives, and how a young black man of unusual promise struggling to rise in Chicago's tough West Side is gunned down.

The book closes with a discussion of proposed remedies. Specific examples are provided to illustrate the type of structural changes that will be necessary if racial discrimination is ever to be eradicated from American society. Robert Friedman concludes the volume by summarizing the findings on racial discrimination under four different types of institutional racism. His original analysis should stimulate further thinking about needed remedies. Indeed, as you read through the grim facts that together sketch out the enormous scope of racial discrimination, try to ask yourself continually: Given these facts, what needs to be changed about the United States in order to eliminate this process forever? This effort will be a critical task for your generation.

Acknowledgments

The past decade has witnessed a spate of books and articles on American race relations. Some of these volumes have been useful collections of articles on the field in general. Yet, surprisingly enough, there have been no such collections specifically on the critical topic of racial discrimination against black Americans. This "reader," drawing on the rich contributions of recent years, aims to fill this need.

I am indebted to the distinguished series editor, Dean Donald R. Cressey, for suggesting the volume to me and for his and the publisher's patience in awaiting its completion. Appreciation is due also Susan Heidel Lutz, whose initial help launched the effort, and Professor J. Michael Ross of Boston University, whose suggestions proved invaluable. There would be no volume at all were it not for the careful and efficient assistance of Sharon Cronan over the past year. And my wife Ann, and son, Mark, provided the support and encouragement that I have come to need and expect.

My sincere gratitude is also extended to the many authors and original publishers of the articles included in this volume for their prompt and courteous permission to reprint their material. Their names and the original sources appear with each article. As a reprinted author myself, I realize the imposition such requests represent and therefore am particularly appreciative of their extensive and necessary cooperation.

Finally, I must acknowledge the two ladies to whom this book is dedicated. My mother, Mrs. Janet G. Pettigrew, and lifelong friend, Miss Mildred Adams, have both cared about and resisted racial discrimination all their lives. I hope they will find this effort to be a similar contribution.

THOMAS F. PETTIGREW

PART I

INTRODUCTION

THIS *volume focuses on the social science analysis of discrimination against black Americans. We begin with two historical overviews, one of the treatment of black Americans over three centuries and the other of the treatment by social science of the subject over the past seven decades.*

W. E. B. Du Bois, the author of the initial statement, was one of the most remarkable leaders in black American history. A brilliant man of unyielding purpose, Du Bois's writings constitute the most important single body of work on the black American's long struggle for justice. Together with such important volumes as The Philadelphia Negro, The Souls of Black Folk, *and* Black Reconstruction, *his*

All footnotes appear in the Notes section, grouped by article, at the end of this book. Bibliographies follow each of the four parts of this book.

1

writings include numerous novels, magazine articles and editorials, and policy statements. "Three Centuries of Discrimination," reproduced here, is drawn from Du Bois's forthright introduction to an appeal for redress that the National Association for the Advancement of Colored People made in 1947 to the then new United Nations. Already 79 years of age when he wrote it, Du Bois was uniquely equipped to author such a piece. And it still provides a perspective needed for this volume.

The second introductory article, by the editor, outlines the past trends in the social science study of racial discrimination in the United States. In addition the article optimistically projects four positive trends for future research in this realm, which hopefully this volume will help further.

Three Centuries of Discrimination*

W. E. B. DU BOIS

There were in the United States of America, 1940, 12,865,-518 native-born citizens, something less than a tenth of the nation, who form largely a segregated caste, with restricted legal rights, and many illegal disabilities. They are descendants of the Africans brought to America during the sixteenth, seventeenth, eighteenth and nineteenth centuries and reduced to slave labor. This group has no complete biological unity, but varies in color from white to black, and comprises a great variety of physical characteristics, since many are the offspring of white European-Americans as well as of Africans and American Indians. There are a large number of white Americans who also descend from Negroes but who are not counted in the colored group nor subjected to caste restrictions because the preponderance of white blood conceals their descent.

The so-called American Negro group, therefore, while it is in no sense absolutely set off physically from its fellow Americans has nevertheless a strong, hereditary cultural unity, born of slavery, of common suffering, prolonged proscription and curtailment of political and civil rights; and especially because of economic and social disabilities. Largely from this fact have arisen their cultural gifts to America—their rhythm, music and folk-song; their religious faith and customs; their contribution to American art and literature;

* Slightly abridged from W. E. B. Du Bois, "Three Centuries of Discrimination," *The Crisis*, December 1947, *54*, 262–264, 379–380. Reprinted with permission of the Crisis Publishing Company.

their defense of their country in every war, on land, sea and in the air; and especially the hard, continuous toil upon which the prosperity and wealth of this continent has largely been built.

The group has long been internally divided by dilemma as to whether its striving upward should be aimed at strengthening its inner cultural and group bonds, both for intrinsic progress and for offensive power against caste; or whether it should seek escape whenever and however possible into the surrounding American culture. Decision in this matter has been largely determined by outer compulsion rather than inner plan; for prolonged policies of segregation and discrimination have involuntarily welded the mass almost into a nation within a nation with its own schools, churches, hospitals, newspapers and many business enterprises.

The result has been to make American Negroes to wide extent provincial, introvert, self-conscious and narrowly race-loyal; but it has also inspired them to frantic and often successful effort to achieve, to deserve, to show the world their capacity to share modern civilization. As a result there is almost no area of American civilization in which the Negro has not made creditable showing in the face of all his handicaps.

COLOR CASTE SYSTEM

If, however, the effect of the color caste system on the North American Negro has been both good and bad, its effect on white America has been disastrous. It has repeatedly led the greatest modern attempt at democratic government to deny its political ideals, to falsify its philanthropic assertions and to make its religion to a great extent hypocritical. A nation which boldly declared "That all men are created equal," proceeded to build its economy on chattel slavery; masters who declared race-mixture impossible, sold their own children into slavery and left a mulatto progeny which neither law nor science can today disentangle; churches which excused slavery as calling the heathen to God, refused to recognize the freedom of converts or admit them to equal communion. Sectional strife over the profits of slave labor and conscientious revolt against making human beings real estate led to bloody civil war, and to a partial emancipation of slaves which nevertheless even to this day is not complete. Poverty, ignorance, disease and crime have been forced on these unfortunate victims of greed to an extent far beyond any social necessity; and a great nation, which today ought to be in the forefront of the march toward peace and democracy, finds itself continuously making common cause with race-hate, prejudiced exploitation and oppression of the common man. Its high and noble words are turned against it, because they are contradicted in every syllable by the treatment of the American Negro for three hundred and twenty-eight years.

Slavery in America is a strange and contradictory story. It cannot be regarded as mainly either a theoretical problem of morals or a scientific problem of race. From either of these points of view, the rise of slavery in America is simply inexplicable. Looking at the facts frankly, slavery evidently was a matter of economics, a question of income and labor, rather than a problem of right and wrong, or of the physical differences in men. Once slavery began to be the source of vast income for men and nations, there followed frantic search for moral and racial justifications. Such excuses were found and men did not inquire too carefully into either their logic or truth.

The twenty Negroes brought to Virginia in 1619 were not the first who had landed on this continent. For a century small numbers of Negroes had been arriving as servants, as laborers, as free adventurers. The southwestern part of the present United States was first traversed by four explorers of whom one was an African Negro. Negroes accompanied early explorers like D'Ayllon and Menendez in the southwestern United States. But just as the earlier black visitors to the West Indies were servants and adventurers and then later began to appear as laborers on the sugar plantations, so in Virginia, these imported black laborers in 1619 and after, came to be wanted for the raising of tobacco which was the money crop.

In the minds of the early planters, there was no distinction as to labor whether it was white or black; in law there was at first no discrimination. But as imported white labor became scarcer and more protected by law, it became less profitable than Negro labor which flooded the markets because of European slave traders, internal strife in Africa; and because in America the Negroes were increasingly stripped of legal defense. For these reasons America became a land of black slavery, and there arose first, the fabulously rich sugar empire; then the cotton kingdom, and finally colonial imperialism.

FREE V. SLAVE LABOR

Then came the inevitable fight between free labor and democracy on the one hand, and slave labor with its huge profits on the other. Black slaves were the spearhead of this fight. They were the first in America to stage the "sitdown" strike, to slow up and sabotage the work of the plantation. They revolted time after time and no matter what recorded history may say, the enacted laws against slave revolt are unanswerable testimony as to what these revolts meant all over America.

The slaves themselves especially imperiled the whole slave system by escape from slavery. It was the fugitive slave more than the slave revolt, which finally threatened investment and income; and the organization for helping fugitive slaves through Free Northern Negroes and their white friends, in the guise of an underground movement, was of tremendous influence.

Finally it was the Negro soldier as a co-fighter with the whites for independence from the British economic empire which began emancipation. The British bid for his help and the colonials against their first impulse had to bid in return and virtually to promise the Negro soldier freedom after the Revolutionary War. It was for the protection of American

Negro sailors as well as white that the war of 1812 was precipitated and, after independence from England was accomplished, freedom for the black laboring class, and enfranchisement for whites and blacks, was in sight.

In the meantime, however, white labor had continued to regard the United States as a place of refuge; as a place for free land; for continuous employment and high wage; for freedom of thought and faith. It was here, however, that employers intervened; not because of any moral obliquity but because the Industrial Revolution, based upon the crops raised by slave labor in the Caribbean and in the Southern United States, was made possible by world trade and a new and astonishing technique; and finally was made triumphant by a vast transportation of slave labor through the British slave-trade in the eighteenth and early nineteenth centuries.

This new mass of slaves became competitors of white labor and drove white labor for refuge into the arms of employers, whose interests were founded on slave labor. The doctrine of race inferiority was used to convince white labor that they had the right to be free and to vote, while the Negroes must be slaves or depress the wage of whites; western free soil became additional lure and compensation, if it could be restricted to free labor.

On the other hand the fight of the slave-holders against democracy increased with the spread of the wealth and power of the Cotton Kingdom. Through political power based on slaves they became the dominant political force in the United States; they were successful in expanding into Mexico and tried to penetrate the Caribbean. Finally they demanded for slavery a part of the free soil of the West, and because of this last excessive, and in fact impossible effort, a Civil War to preserve and extend slavery ensued.

THE FREE NEGRO

This fight for slave labor was echoed in the law. The free Negro was systematically discouraged, disfranchised and reduced to serfdom. He became by law the easy victim of the kidnapper and liable to treatment as a fugitive slave. The Church, influenced by wealth and respectability, was predominately on the side of the slave owner and effort was made to make the degradation of the Negro, as a race, final by Supreme Court decision.

But from the beginning, the outcome of the Civil War was inevitable and this not mainly on account of the predominant wealth and power of the North; it was because of the clear fact that the Southern slave economy was built on black labor. If at any time the slaves or any large part of them, as workers ceased to support the South; and if even more decisively, as fighters they joined the North, there was no way in the world for the South to win . . .

Victory, however, brought dilemma; if victory meant full economic freedom for labor in the South, white and black; if it meant land and education, and eventually votes, then the slave empire was doomed, and the profits of Northern industry built on the Southern slave foundation would also be seriously curtailed . . .

The result was an attempt at Reconstruction in which black labor established schools; tried to divide up the land and put a new social legislation in force. On the other hand, the power of Southern land owners soon joined with Northern industry to disfranchise the Negro; keep him from access to free land or to capital, and to build up the present caste system for blacks founded on color discrimination, peonage, intimidation and mob-violence . . .

DEMOCRATIC PROCESS CRIPPLED

In 1876 the democratic process of government was crippled throughout the whole nation. This came about not simply through the disfranchisement of Negroes but through the fact that the political power of the disfranchised Negroes and of a large number of equally disfranchised whites was preserved as the basis of political power, but the wielding of that power was left in the hands and under the control of the successors to the planter dynasty in the South.

Let us examine these facts more carefully. The United States has always professed to be a Democracy. She has never wholly attained her ideal, but slowly she has approached it. The privilege of voting has in time been widened by abolishing limitations of birth, religion and lack of property. After the Civil War, which abolished slavery, the nation in gratitude to the black soldiers and laborers who helped win that war, sought to admit to the suffrage all persons without distinction of "race, color or previous condition of servitude." They were warned by the great leaders of abolition, like Sumner, Stevens and Douglass, that this could only be effective if the Freedmen were given schools, land and some minimum of capital. A Freedmen's Bureau to furnish these prerequisites to effective citizenship was planned and put into partial operation. But Congress and the nation, weary of the costs of war and eager to get back to profitable industry, refused the necessary funds. The effort died, but in order to restore friendly civil government in the South the enfranchised Freedman, seventy-five per cent illiterate, without land or tools, was thrown into competitive industry with a ballot in his hands. By herculean effort, helped by philanthropy and his own hard work, the Negro built a school system, bought land and cooperated in starting a new economic order in the South. In a generation he had reduced his illiteracy by half and had become a wage-earning laborer and share-cropper. He still was handicapped by poverty, disease and crime, but nevertheless the rise of the American Negro from slavery in 1860 to freedom in 1880 has few parallels in modern history.

However, opposition to any democracy which included the Negro race on any terms was so strong in the former slave-holding South, and found so much sympathy in large parts of the rest of the nation, that despite notable improvement in the condition of the Negro by every standard of social measurement, the effort to deprive Negroes of the right to vote succeeded. At first he was driven from the polls in the South by mobs and violence; and then he was openly cheated; finally by a "Gentleman's agreement" with the North, the Negro was disfranchised in the South by a series of laws, methods of administration, court decisions and general public policy, so that today three-fourths of the Negro population of the nation is deprived of the right to vote by open and declared policy.

SITUATION SERIOUS

Most persons seem to regard this as simply unfortunate for Negroes, as depriving a modern working class of the minimum rights for self-protection and opportunity for progress. This is true as has been shown in poor educational opportunities, discrimination in work, health protection and in the courts. But the situation is far more serious than this: the disfranchisement of the American Negro makes the functioning of all democracy in the nation difficult; and as democracy fails to function in the leading democracy in the world, it fails in the world. . . .

This paradox and contradiction enters into our actions, thoughts and plans. After the First World War, we were alienated from the proposed League of Nations because of sympathy for imperialism and because of race antipathy to Japan and because we objected to the compulsory protection of minorities in Europe, which might lead to similar demands upon the United States . . .

But today the paradox again looms after the Second World War. We have recrudescence of race hate and caste restrictions in the United States and of these dangerous tendencies not simply for the United States itself but for all nations. When will nations learn that their enemies are quite as often within their own country as without? It is not Russia that threatens the United States so much as Mississippi; not Stalin and Molotov but Bilbo and Rankin; internal injustice done to one's brothers is far more dangerous than the aggression of strangers from abroad.

Finally it must be stressed that the discrimination of which we complain is not simply discrimination against poverty and ignorance which the world by long custom is used to see: the discrimination practiced in the United States is practiced against American Negroes in spite of wealth, training and character. One of the contributors of this statement happens to be a white man but the other three and the editor himself are subject to "jim-crow" laws, to denial of the right to vote, to unequal chance to earn a living; of the right to enter many places of public entertainment supported by their taxes. In other words our complaint is mainly against a discrimination based mainly on color of skin, and it is this that we denounce as not only indefensible but barbaric. . . .

[2]

Trends in Research
on Racial Discrimination

THOMAS F. PETTIGREW

The study of race relations in the United States has traditionally been a ghetto itself. Ironically this field of intellectual inquiry mirrored its subject matter in that it was an insulated domain within social science, typically viewed with disdain, granted meager status and research funds, and cut off from many of the principal trends and advances in both theory and method. Not surprisingly, then, the technical literature in the field prior to 1960 is in general disappointing; while it contains many entries, it all too often reflects the field's insulation.

TRENDS FROM 1900 TO 1960

To be sure, there were important studies in American race relations written during the 1930s and 1940s that come down to us now as classics. An "armchair theory" approach characterized the race literature through the 1920s, much of it openly antiblack. This pattern was disturbed only occasionally by such exceptional works as W. E. B. Du Bois's *The Philadelphia Negro* (1899). But the decade of the Great Depression witnessed the emergence of a number of significant studies. Klineberg's (1935) research on black intelligence and Dollard's (1937) Mississippi community study are particularly noteworthy. The 1940s occasioned Davis and the Gardners' *Deep South* (1941), Gunnar Myrdal's *An American Dilemma* (1944), and Drake and Cayton's *Black Metropolis* (1945). Myrdal's work attracted far wider popular acclaim and attention than any earlier social science work on the subject. Note, however, that all of the early classics, save for Klineberg's field experiment, were essentially descriptive works.

Major field experiments representing a departure from the descriptive past began to be published in the late 1940s and early 1950s. The most influential of these studies concerned interracial contact and relative deprivation, were conducted in the U.S. Army during World War II, and were published by Samuel Stouffer and his colleagues in *The American Soldier* (1949). Social psychologists centered at New York University also conducted a series of experiments on interracial contact in such natural settings as department stores and public housing developments. Their work appeared in numerous articles of the period (e.g., Saenger & Gilbert, 1950; Jahoda & West, 1951; and Harding & Hogrefe, 1952) and in two books (Deutsch & Collins, 1951, and Wilner, Walkley & Cook, 1955). Though this work later became influential, it was ahead of its time as indicated by the fact that the articles were disproportionately published in *The Journal of Social Issues*, one of the few activist journals of the period, and the volumes were issued in limited editions by a university press.

On the personality level, at this same time, the field took a major step forward with the publication of a series of psychoanalytically influenced studies of prejudice sponsored by the American Jewish Committee, particularly Adorno, Frenkel-Brunswick, Levinson, and Sanford's *The Authoritarian Personality* (1950), Bettelheim and Janowitz's *Dynamics of Prejudice* (1950), and Ackerman and Jahoda's *Anti-Semitism and Emotional Disorder* (1950). While brilliantly exploring the depth personality implications of intergroup prejudice, these works gave little attention to the institutional supports of prejudice and discrimination. Their overemphasis on the individual level reflected the period. The human relations emphasis of the 1940s and 1950s, fueled by the rejection of Hitler's Aryan theories, centered on inducing bigoted individuals to "accept" minority group individuals by means of speeches, movies, advertisements, and "Brotherhood Dinners." Little focus was placed on an institutional view of intergroup discrimination.

There was a second reason why the series received such widespread attention within the disciplines of social science. The chief volume of the series, *The Authoritarian Personality*, published four easily administered Likert-type scales: authoritarianism (the F Scale), ethnocentrism (the E Scale), anti-Semitism (the A-S Scale), and "politico-economic conservatism" (the PEC Scale). Soon professional journals in psychology, sociology, and political science were deluged with empirical articles employing these measures—especially the F Scale. It almost appeared that the F Scale was significantly correlated with everything tested against it (Christie & Jahoda, 1954; Titus & Hollander, 1957; Christie & Cook, 1958), though this all-embracing quality was later shown to be related to problems of both response set and multidimensionality of the F Scale (Camilleri, 1959; Couch & Keniston, 1960; Krug, 1961; Krug & Moyer, 1961).

Major change in the insularity of the field of race relations, however, awaited the mid-1950s. The U.S. Supreme Court's historic ruling in 1954 against the *de jure* racial segregation of the public schools brought the field to the forefront of attention. Moreover, two new texts introduced at this point brought the various theoretical and empirical trends of the field into a coherent focus: for social psychology, Allport's *The Nature of Prejudice* (1954), and for sociology, Simpson and Yinger's *Racial and Cultural Minorities* (1953); (now in its fourth edition). In 1956 systematic attention to survey research data on racial attitudes over time was introduced in a *Scientific American* paper by Hyman and Sheatsley (1956). And from 1948 to 1956 the Cornell Studies in Intergroup Relations, headed by Robin Williams, conducted intensive survey and community research in four small cities throughout the nation. This work was not reported in book form until 1964 (Williams, 1964a). The Cornell group was approached at the time of the Supreme Court desegregation ruling by a major foundation to plan an expansion of their work in order to study in detail the racial change process as it unfolded. But after funding a substantial planning grant, the foundation suddenly rejected the idea.

The failure of private and public funding agencies to support systematic, widespread, and over time research of the racial desegregation process as it occurred is undoubtedly one of the most tragic setbacks the study of American race relations has experienced. The process presented an ideal and rare opportunity to understand the complex structure of racial discrimination, and it had to be studied as it happened or not at all. Large-scale interdisciplinary studies, employing longitudinal designs in a variety of carefully chosen communities, were urgently needed. Only an empirical attack of such magnitude could have captured the emerging pattern of highly diverse accommodations to the court-ordered alterations. This urgent point was repeatedly made in articles by Cook (1957), Pettigrew (1961), and others, but to little avail.

Lacking the necessary financial support, low-budget reports on a single community became the rule. Many of the studies were theses or seminar projects; many remained at the descriptive level; most sampled only one time period; and there was almost no comparability of instruments and approach. Ironically, the first nationwide sampling of black Americans and their racial attitudes, long sought by specialists in the field, was finally executed in the summer of 1963 by a commercial survey agency financed by *Newsweek* magazine (Brink & Harris, 1964).

Why such funding timidity? Two speculations can be ventured. First, organized pressure against such funding was apparently enormous. Southern congressmen of prosegregationist persuasion openly threatened federal agencies at appropriations hearings while menacingly reviewing government financing of all types of social research. These same legislators also angrily threatened to withdraw the valued tax-free status from private foundations because of such research support. Organized pressure was also brought to bear through local boycotts carried out by segregationists against products popularly identified with the foundations.

The second factor was more subtle. As Pettigrew and Back (1967) describe it:

No simple mechanical device or single research breakthrough is likely to provide simple solutions for the peculiarly complex problems of desegregation. In a topic similarly laden with controversy and conflict, birth control, it has proven possible to appropriate large amounts for the study of the purely technical aspects of reproduction and the development of pills which may aid in easing the population problem. No comparable hope for a pill or similar gadget has ever been suggested for desegregation, and so funding agencies are less able to avoid the emotionally charged aspects of the issue on such purely technical aspects.

The lost opportunity to study the desegregation process both deeply and widely from its inception casts its shadow to this day. But it does not represent the only lost opportunity. Social scientists have themselves alone to blame for the fact that a narrow range of topics and emphases was consistently considered in intergroup relations research until the 1960s. Consider the data of Table 1, adapted from Back (1963). This table provides a content breakdown of the 255 research papers

TABLE 1. *Research in Intergroup Relations Reported in Major Social Science Journals*

Focus on Factors Favoring:	INDIVIDUAL						SOCIAL					
	Attitudes			Action			Static			Change		
	Integration	Segregation	Both	Integration	Segregation	Both	Integration	Segregation	Both	Integration	Segregation	Both
Time period												
1900–1910	1							7				
1910–1920							2	4		2	2	
1920–1930	3	3	2		1	2	3	2		1	3	
1930–1940	3	3		2	2	1	7	8	1	1		1
1940–1950	6	20	4	4			14	10	6	8	13	
1950–1958	5	39	7	4	8	3	7	9	4	3	14	
Total:	18	65	13	10	11	6	33	40	11	15	32	1

on intergroup relations published from 1900 through 1958 in 20 of the most relevant social science journals, most of them sociological.

The first distinction made in Table 1 is between the individual and social systems. Note that almost half of the papers concentrate on the individual level even in these largely sociological journals. The second distinction concerns the purely static approach of attitudes and stable institutional structures as opposed to individual actions and social change. Here Back finds 71 percent (180 of 255) of the papers focused on static elements; at the individual level, 78 percent of the papers focused on attitudes rather than action. The third distinction drawn in Table 1 divides the publications according to whether they focused on integration, segregation, or both. Here 58 percent (149 of 255) of the papers dealt exclusively with segregation processes compared to only 30 percent (76 of 255) that dealt exclusively with integration processes. Note, too, that the data by decade do not show wide differences, with all of these imbalances in emphasis still apparent in the 1950s. Out of the 103 papers recorded from 1950 through 1958, 64 percent were at the individual level, 69 percent were static in focus, and 68 percent concentrated exclusively on segregation processes. Indeed, 38 percent of these 103 publications fall in only one of Table 1's twelve cells—individual, static, and segregation in orientation.

TRENDS DURING THE SIXTIES AND EARLY SEVENTIES

The decade of the 1960s finally witnessed the start of a basic break with the past in race relations research. A number of factors seem to have coalesced during the height of the Civil Rights Movement to create this change. First, new personnel and even new disciplines were attracted into the field. They brought with them new theories and new methodological tools and thereby eroded the field's nagging problem of insularity within social science. Second, the work of social scientists in race relations began to be seen in Washington, the mass media, and elsewhere as policy-relevant. This shift eroded the field's low status and separation from significant decision-making. Consequently, too, research funds slowly began to become available. Third, the dramatic racial events of the decade forced social scientists to realize belatedly that a more dynamic focus on institutional change than had typified earlier work was necessary. Let us briefly explore each of these three coalescing factors.

The attraction of new researchers and points of view into the field occurred in a number of ways. Primarily, of course, new Ph.D.'s entering social science began choosing race relations as an exciting and promising area of relevance. Many of these new recruits were mathematically inclined and introduced new methods to the field. Most of them were heavily influenced by the Civil Rights Movement and its successes; some had as undergraduates personally participated in demonstrations or gone south during the interracial days of the Student Non-Violent Coordinating Committee. Not surprisingly, then, these new Ph.D.'s were interested in studying racial change directly rather than continuing to study static factors maintaining racial oppression. By the late sixties, Marxist thought returned to an important place in the theories of American race relations. This was not an entirely new development, to be sure, for Du Bois in *Black Reconstruction* (1935) and Cox in *Caste, Class and Race* (1948) had long before successfully applied Marxist theorizing to the field.

Equally valuable for the swift development of the field in the sixties was the interest shown in it by leading social scientists and by whole disciplines that had not previously focused on the subject. The 1966 volume organized by the American Academy of Arts and Sciences, *The Negro American* (Parsons & Clark, 1966), best illustrates this trend. In addition to such long-time specialists as Kenneth Clark, St. Clair Drake, and John Hope Franklin, this significant effort also enlisted such figures as Talcott Parsons, Erik Erikson, and James Tobin. The inclusion of Tobin is especially noteworthy, since economics as a discipline has only recently become involved in the study of American race relations. (See Thurow, 1969; Becker, 1971; Pascal, 1972.)

At the same time the study of race relations began to attract more interest within social science, it also began to be taken more seriously outside the field. Indeed, these years witnessed far greater receptivity of policy makers toward social science in general. To be sure, limited use of social science had prevailed in previous decades. There had been surveys and consultings for presidents since Roosevelt (Cantril, 1967), citation of race relations sources in the famous footnote 11 of the 1954 Supreme Court ruling against *de jure* public school segregation, and considerable use of the advice of economists. But it was during the sixties that social science came into style in Washington and subsequently in the mass media. The new prominence, in fact, often involved unrealistically high expectations of what the present state of social science knowledge could do to solve the nation's domestic problems. Nevertheless, modern economic theory had its chance to prove itself practically in the heralded tax cut of 1965. Talk of social indicators (Bauer, 1966) became widespread; and sociological analyses of public education were called for in the 1964 Civil Rights Act and supplied in the massive volume *Equality of Educational Opportunity* (Coleman et al., 1966), popularly known as the Coleman report (Caldwell, 1970).

The Coleman report in particular brought race relations research into serious policy consideration. The report covered many aspects of unequal access to quality education, but its implications for the education of black Americans gained special notice and scrutiny. In its *Racial Isolation in the Public Schools* the U.S. Commission on Civil Rights (1967) reanalyzed those Coleman data most relevant for considerations of racial school desegregation in a directly policy-oriented report. And extensive theoretical discussions and empirical reanalyses have been published continually since the Coleman report appeared in 1966, such as Mosteller and Moynihan's *On Equality of Educational Opportunity* (1972). Though finding numerous data errors caused by haste, these intensive reexaminations did not substantially alter the chief conclusions of Coleman's work.

Research on school desegregation, however, has received far greater policy and mass media attention than other realms of race relations. Though extensive data and analyses exist on such critical realms as racial discrimination in employment and housing, they have not generally entered the public discussion of these issues. The National Advisory Commission on Civil Disorders, for example, utilized disappointingly few social science insights and analyses in its "Kerner Commission Report" (1968), and even summarily dismissed many of its social science staff members midway through its existence.

Together with the field's new personnel and greater prominence, the dramatic nature of racial change and resistance during the sixties also required a shift in social science perspective. The headlined racial events of the decade centered around institutions—the schools, business corporations, unions, the political system, the construction and real estate industries, etc.—and this led to greater interest in institutional change apart from individual prejudice. Realization of the need for a different emphasis came in two parts. First, the desegregation process itself began to make clear that institutional barriers, not prejudice, constituted the chief obstacles to sweeping racial alterations. As the neglected intergroup contact studies had indicated over a decade earlier, it became obvious that bigotry itself was most effectively alleviated by first changing social structures. Second, the leadership of the Civil Rights Movement by blacks and the black community invited more attention to black insistence on racial change, and not just on white resistance to it. Later the renewal of the black cultural emphasis, a recurrent theme in black American history, gave added impetus to view blacks not merely as helpless objects of oppression but as vibrant reactors to oppression as well.

The significance of this shift of emphasis, both for theory and research, is difficult to overemphasize. Back's data, shown earlier in Table 1, demonstrated how imbalanced the work in this field had been prior to the 1960s. Statics were stressed over dynamics; prejudiced attitudes over institutional discrimination; segregation over desegregation. But a definite righting of this imbalance has occurred recently.

PROJECTED TRENDS FOR THE LATE SEVENTIES AND EIGHTIES

These past trends combine with the recent course of American race relations to allow a crude projection of four trends that may well characterize future research on race relations in general and on racial discrimination in particular.

These four trends are already discernible, even if still somewhat tenuous at this time. First, there will continue to be a growing interest in developing *systematic theory* in intergroup relations, with the emphasis placed upon middle-range theories consisting of interdependent, empirically testable hypotheses. Second, there will be a growing interest in *longitudinal survey studies* involving shifting racial attitudes toward racial discrimination in their social contexts. Third, there will be further, and hopefully rapid, development of *mathematical models and simulations* of racial discrimination. Finally, there will be an increasing stress placed upon detailed *process studies of institutional racial change*. Let us examine these projected trends.

Systematic Theory

Allport (1954) noted that the study of prejudice and race relations has been plagued with "monistic" theories, simple and sovereign one-variable explanations for the whole complex range of intergroup phenomena. Initially Myrdal (1944), Simpson and Yinger (1953), and Allport (1954) countered this trend by adopting eclectic approaches that gave weight to a variety of largely unrelated explanations. But there was little attempt to generate systematic, testable, middle-range theory. A striking exception to this situation, however, was provided by Williams (1947), who advanced a systematic list of 102 research "propositions" centered on "the reduction of intergroup tensions."

But the sixties saw a change in this situation, too. Lieberson (1961) advanced a broad "societal theory of race and ethnic relations." Williams (1964b, 1965) again demonstrated his talent in this domain by presenting a systematic list of 61 factors hypothesized to relate to community acceptance of or resistance to the racial desegregation of public schools. Blalock (1967) followed with a more general theoretical effort that placed major emphasis upon status, competition, and power. Admitting to his having "been frustrated by the lack of systematic theory in the field of minority-group relations," Blalock did not claim to have formulated an all-encompassing theoretical framework. Yet the consistent focus on power running through his 97 interrelated hypotheses represents a significant step forward for the field, for he unites both microlevel, social psychological considerations with macrolevel, sociological ones.

A more recent effort extends this search for systematic theory in intergroup relations to the comparative international level. LeVine and Campbell's volume, *Ethnocentrism: Theories of Conflict, Ethnic Attitudes and Group Behavior* (1972), grew directly out of their extensive cross-cultural study of ethnocentrism at Northwestern University. LeVine, an anthropologist, and Campbell, a social psychologist, combine their talents to consider the spectrum of theoretical perspectives ranging from evolutionary to reinforcement doctrines. They, too, specify numerous testable hypotheses that can be directly derived from each of these doctrines. They close with a brief 19-page summary chapter on the "concord and discord" among the theories, a highly suggestive statement despite its brevity.

Longitudinal Survey Studies

Many of the central and unresolved issues of intergroup relations discussed by LeVine and Campbell will require diachronic studies to untangle. Yet longitudinal research is even rarer in this field than in most areas of social science. Nowhere is this fact more conspicuous than in research on racial attitudes, a domain that virtually begs for over time studies.

Hyman and Sheatsley (1956) opened up this research methodology by comparing white attitudes toward racial segregation and discrimination in 1956 with those of 1942 and 1944. They found that sharp national improvements had occurred, including positive changes in the racial opinions of white Southerners. Two follow-up studies noted further improvements (Hyman & Sheatsley, 1964; Greeley & Sheatsley, 1971). Shifting black attitudes about race relations were also recorded in three national surveys sponsored by *Newsweek* magazine in 1963, 1966, and 1969 (Brink & Harris, 1964, 1967; Goldman, 1970).

The shifting marginals in both of these longitudinal series

are of considerable importance. They both sternly counter the prevailing mass media notion that the 1960s witnessed a massive "white backlash" in the growth of antiblack opinions and a massive turn by black Americans away from integrationist goals toward racial "separatism." To be sure, the rate of improvement in white attitudes slowed considerably during the late sixties compared to the previous generation; and a significant minority of young blacks did begin to explore goals other than integration. But the media grossly exaggerated both of these phenomena. Surveys of a variety of agencies employing diverse questions, samples, and methodologies all agree that white racial attitudes in the aggregate have recently reached their most positive recorded levels and that black attitudes in the aggregate remain overwhelmingly pro-integrationist. (See also Campbell & Schuman, 1968; Campbell, 1971.) Thus longitudinal survey data provide a valuable corrective to popular mythology about American race relations.

But how does this predicted trend toward more over time research coincide with the trend away from attitude work and toward institutional research? If the longitudinal survey work is placed carefully in its social context, the two trends can be complementary. For example, Hyman and Sheatsley (1964) found that white attitudes toward desegregation tended to become more favorable in Southern communities after, and not before, the public schools had actually been racially desegregated. Only time-series data could have uncovered this empirical link between change at the individual and the societal levels, a link consistent with other research demonstrating the attitude-changing potential of institutional alterations. Likewise Ross has analyzed an 18-survey series over the sixties on one Gallup question asking respondents if they believe the presidential administration in office is "pushing integration" too fast, too slow, or about right. He has derived a model of shifting black and white responses to this question that systematically relates to the dramatic events and institutional changes of this momentous period (Pettigrew, Riley, & Ross, 1975).

Mathematical Models and Simulations

Both of these projected trends—more systematic theory and longitudinal survey research—can be importantly furthered by the continued development of mathematical models and simulations of racial phenomena.

The entry of economics into the study of American race relations has been critical for this development, as many of the examples of this trend come from this discipline. The interests and tools of economists center on problems of discrimination in employment and income, but their ideas and analyses often generalize to other types of discrimination. Gary Becker (1957) pioneered this work with a theory drawn from international trade. Discrimination for Becker is a restrictive practice that interferes with the free trade between two independent societies, black and white. If free trade existed, blacks would export labor and whites capital until the marginal products of labor and capital were roughly equal in both groups so as to maximize their incomes. But discrimination results from the fact that whites have "tastes" against working with blacks and thus attempt to maximize both their income and physical distance from blacks. Unlike the case with South Africa, whites in the United States are so numerically and economically predominant that this discrimination costs them in money terms relatively little. The gains from unrestricted interracial "trade" are proportionately much greater for black Americans, however, and consequently discrimination lowers their incomes by a relatively large percentage.

Becker's model launched the problem within economics, demonstrated the utility of quantifying a nonpecuniary motivation, antiblack "tastes," and raised some intriguing ideas. But more recent economic models of discrimination have challenged Becker's position. Thurow (1969), for example, questions the notion that whites generally forfeit income in order to discriminate and argues that more typically majorities lift their money incomes through discrimination at the expense of minorities. He further argues that racial discrimination in the United States occurs within one society, not two independent ones. And it is one society "where much of the impact of discrimination comes from the monopoly powers of the discriminator rather than from his ability to distort perfect competition with trade barriers." Blacks have few options and must trade, for, Thurow insists, they live in a white supremacist society and not just a segregated one. Discrimination, then, involves the monopolistic power of whites to specify the trade relationships between the two races.

Thurow's "monopoly" model of racial discrimination leads to radically different policy recommendations. Where Becker would stress that white "tastes" concerning contact with blacks be altered and whites be bribed to mingle with blacks, Thurow calls for direct governmental intervention to lessen the monopoly powers of whites. Since "the coercive powers of the white community flow through local, state, and federal government institutions," Thurow believes that the elimination of governmental discrimination "may be one of the most effective means of eliminating the effects of discrimination throughout the economy."

Kenneth Arrow, the Nobel Prize winner, questions Becker's neoclassical approach on three counts (Pascal, 1972). First, the hypotheses generated lack specificity, and Arrow observes that the concept of interracial contact must be broken down into its several dimensions. Second, Arrow wonders if Becker's "tastes" against association with blacks as an explanation of racial discrimination is not simply referring the problem back to an unanalyzed realm. Racial discrimination and these anti-black "tastes" may both well be tools of economic exploitation. Finally, Arrow argues that the hypothesis of competitive elimination has special force for racial discrimination; that is, he finds it "hard to understand how discriminatory behavior could persist in the long run in the face of competitive pressures."

Why, then, do racial wage differentials persist? Arrow proposes a mathematical model with two primary elements: the employer's investment of personnel capital that will be lost if the employee fails; and the employer's uncertainty about the employee's qualifications and probable success. The employer does, however, know the job applicant's race and may well believe that blacks are not as good workers as whites. One need not, therefore, have to assume a conscious exploitation of blacks by a conspiracy of 170 million whites. Rather, Arrow maintains, investment risks and internalized attitudes of black inferiority are central. This reasoning leaves open the question of whether racial discrimination is in fact profitable or costly to whites. In agreement with Thurow, Arrow suspects that it is indeed often beneficial for whites.

There are, then, a range of economic models of discrimination from which to choose—Becker's anticontact "taste" theory, Thurow's monopoly exploitation theory, and Arrow's investment risk theory. And there will undoubtedly soon be many more economic models of discrimination, most of which, like Arrow's attempt, will probably focus on a more delimited portion of the problem. Economists, moreover, will increasingly apply their skills in developing mathematical models and simulations to nonpecuniary discrimination issues not traditionally studied by the discipline. Schelling (1971), for example, has presented a simulation of housing segregation in which individuals define their own neighborhoods as the areas within a given distance from themselves. Schelling has also published a model of the process of neighborhood "tipping" in residential segregation (Pascal, 1972).

Other simulations of the racial segregation process in housing have been advanced by sociologists. The most interesting by Freeman and Sunshine (1970) employs market-income, economic-interest, racial prejudice, and ethnic-proximity-proportion factors. It fits closely to what is known of the process and contributes several interesting insights. Thus the model suggests that the critical succession pattern is not much influenced by the purchasing power differentials of the two races. It also suggests that a stable interracial neighborhood could be maintained under conditions of moderately low prejudice, high white demand, moderate black demand, and black buying power realistically set at 72 percent that of whites. In the simulated experiment reaching this equilibrium, blacks enter the neighborhood from the beginning. Some are pushed out, but most remain. Those whites with the highest prejudice levels leave and prices drop somewhat. Unprejudiced whites still buy into the neighborhood, internal segregation does not develop, prices recover much of their lost ground, and the black proportion stabilizes. Interestingly, Bradburn and his colleagues (1970) uncovered a surprisingly large number of such stable interracial residential areas throughout the United States, many of which may have repeated a pattern not unlike that simulated by Freeman and Sunshine.

The Freeman-Sunshine work is the forerunner of many similar efforts by sociologists and social psychologists in the race relations area. The growing trend toward the use of mathematical models is a general one in sociology, social psychology, and political science. The trend, then, is fully underway and holds out high promise for the study of racial discrimination.

Process Studies of Institutional Racial Change

Advances in mathematical models would also encourage process studies of institutional change. From protest to riots, we have considerable work on the pressures which are applied to institutions in order to have them alter their racial practices. And we have a growing body of research on the effects of these structural changes once achieved. But, surprisingly, we lack both theoretical insights and research data on precisely the *processes* of change that link the cross-sectional alterations with the later observed effects. Indeed, as the shift from attitudes and individual bigots to institutional mechanisms and societal resistance occurs within social science, the need to study process becomes more conspicuous.

Consider, as an illustration, the school desegregation issue. We know in detail how the country came to make this issue a primary element in the overall national program of racial change. Furthermore, since the issuance of the Coleman report in 1966, we have accumulated considerable information of the various effects of racial school desegregation upon both black and white children. Yet we know little or nothing about the processes going on in desegregated classrooms over the country that actually mediate these effects, positive and negative. Our ignorance, moreover, is not caused by a dearth of promising leads. Rosenthal and Jacobson's (1968) work on teacher expectations, Entwisle and Webster's (1972) on student expectations, Rotter's (1966) on fate control, and Pettigrew's (1967, 1969) on social evaluation may all be in operation as mediators of "the desegregation effects." But the process research to test such leads has seldom been conducted. (For a rare exception, see Katz, 1964, 1967.)

The absence of process research in American race relations has a dangerous political significance. In its absence, arguments can be put forward by the politically motivated to justify or damn racial change on simple grounds of presumed effects without attention to the interracial context which produced the effects. The much-publicized antidesegregation paper by Armor (1972), which purported to review "the evidence on busing" but was in reality a highly selected treatment of available data, provides a particularly blatant example of how this weakness can be exploited (Pettigrew, Useem, Normand & Smith, 1973). Armor argued only effects and neither studied nor discussed process.

Armor and many others confuse means with ends in assigning final policy importance to effects data. The nation, through its courts and political system, decides policy goals, not social scientists and their studies. But social science can be of aid in revealing *how* various policy goals may best be achieved. (This is not to exempt scientists from all concern with policy goals; it is just to maintain that their research data are not in themselves determining.) And it is process research that is needed to determine *how* racial change might best be effected for all concerned. Ironically, then, the type of social research that is most needed for policy guidance is precisely the type of race relations research in shortest supply.

One example of process research illuminates the point. Mayhew (1968), in his study of the actual operations of the Massachusetts Commission Against Discrimination, demonstrated that the principal reason why the antidiscrimination state laws of Massachusetts had not proven particularly effective was basically structural. He showed how racial discrimination in housing and employment was largely a patterned, systemic process; but the efforts to combat it relied upon individual complaints which were so unstrategic as to leave the basic discriminatory system virtually untouched. His conclusion was straightforward. If the policy goal was truly to eliminate racial discrimination root and branch, then an enforcement effort that was not dependent on complaints but was a patterned response to fit the problem was essential.

There are reasons to believe that Mayhew's type of incisive process research on institutional change will become more common in the future. As increasing interest is generated for institutional studies, process research will become necessarily more into vogue. And recent retardation in racial progress makes the vast and complex web of interinstitutional racism and discrimination more obvious.

"MORAL OUTRAGE AND DISPASSIONATE ANALYSIS"

Finally, responsible scientific work on racial discrimination during the last fourth of the twentieth century must be guided by a clear understanding of the place of values in such research. Arrow states it well (Pascal, 1972, p. 100), and his position offers a needed moral perspective from which to view the chapters that follow:

I have chosen a topic on which many of us feel the greatest moral outrage and have analyzed it most dispassionately. Neither the moral indignation nor the cool analysis is misplaced; their juxtaposition is one of those paradoxes inherent in the nature of human society of which only the naive are ignorant. Our mastery of ourselves as social beings needs all the reinforcement it can get from study of ourselves in all contexts. Indeed, in the absence of analysis from a self-imposed and sometimes painful distance, our moral feelings can lead us to actions whose effects are the opposite of those intended. This is not intended to imply that social action must wait on adequate analysis. Inaction may be, and in this case surely is, as dangerous as any likely alternative. Indeed, social action may be indispensable to increasing our knowledge when the consequences are subjected to adequate study. But a firm commitment to ends must not preclude a tentative questioning attitude to particular means of achieving them.

BIBLIOGRAPHY

N. W. Ackerman and M. Jahoda, *Anti-Semitism and Emotional Disorder*. New York: Harper & Row, 1950.

T. W. Adorno, E. Frenkel-Brunswik, D. J. Levinson, and R. N. Sanford, *The Authoritarian Personality*. New York: Harper & Row, 1950.

G. W. Allport, *The Nature of Prejudice*. Reading, Mass.: Addison-Wesley, 1954.

D. J. Armor, "The Evidence on Busing," *The Public Interest*, Summer 1972, 90–126.

K. W. Back, "Sociology Encounters the Protest Movement for Desegregation," *Phylon*, 1963, 24, 232–239.

R. A. Bauer (ed.), *Social Indicators*. Cambridge, Mass.: M.I.T. Press, 1966.

G. S. Becker, *The Economics of Discrimination*. Second edition. Chicago: University of Chicago Press, 1971 (1st ed., 1957).

J. Berger, M. Zelditch, Jr., and B. Anderson, *Sociological Theories in Progress*. Vol. I. Boston: Houghton Mifflin, 1966.

B. Bettelheim and M. Janowitz, *Dynamics of Prejudice*. New York: Harper & Row, 1950.

H. M. Blalock, Jr., *Toward a Theory of Minority-Group Relations*. New York: Wiley, 1967.

N. M. Bradburn, S. Sudman, and G. L. Gockel, *Racial Integration in American Neighborhoods*. Chicago: National Opinion Research Center, 1970.

W. Brink and L. Harris, *The Negro Revolution in America*. New York: Simon & Schuster, 1964.

W. Brink and L. Harris, *Black and White*. New York: Simon & Schuster, 1967.

C. Caldwell, "Social Science as Ammunition," *Psychology Today*, September 1970, *4*, 38–41, 72–73.

S. Camilleri, "A Factor Analysis of the F Scale," *Social Forces*, May 1959, 37, 316–323.

A. Campbell, *White Attitudes Toward Black People.* Ann Arbor, Mich.: Institute for Social Research, 1971.

A. Campbell and H. Schuman, "Racial Attitudes in Fifteen American Cities." In The National Advisory Commission on Civil Disorders, *Supplemental Studies.* Washington, D.C.: GPO, 1968.

H. Cantril, *The Human Dimension.* New Brunswick, N.J.: Rutgers University Press, 1967.

R. Christie and M. Jahoda (eds.), *Studies in the Scope and Method of "The Authoritarian Personality."* New York: Free Press, 1954.

R. Christie and P. Cook, "A guide to Published Literature Relating to the Authoritarian Personality Through 1956," *Journal of Psychology*, 1958, *45*, 171–199.

J. S. Coleman, E. Q. Campbell, C. J. Hobson, J. McPartland, A. M. Mood, F. D. Weinfeld, and R. L. York, *Equality of Educational Opportunity.* Washington, D.C.: GPO, 1966.

S. W. Cook, "Desegregation: A Psychological Analysis," *American Psychologist*, 1957, *12*, 1–13.

A. Couch and K. Keniston, "Yeasayers and Neasayers: Agreeing Response Set as a Personality Variable," *Journal of Abnormal and Social Psychology*, March 1960, *60*, 151–174.

O. C. Cox, *Caste, Class and Race: A Study in Social Dynamics.* Garden City, N.Y.: Doubleday, 1948.

A. W. Davis, B. B. Gardner, and M. R. Gardner, *Deep South.* Chicago: University of Chicago Press, 1941.

M. Deutsch and M. E. Collins, *Interracial Housing: A Psychological Evaluation of a Social Experiment.* Minneapolis: University of Minnesota Press, 1951.

J. Dollard, *Caste and Class in a Southern Town.* New Haven, Conn.: Yale University Press, 1937.

S. C. Drake and H. R. Cayton, *Black Metropolis.* New York: Harcourt Brace Jovanovich, 1945.

W. E. B. DuBois, *Black Reconstruction.* New York: Harcourt Brace Jovanovich, 1935.

D. R. Entwisle and M. Webster, Jr., "Raising Children's Performance Expectations," *Social Science Research*, 1972, *1*, 147–158.

L. C. Freeman and M. H. Sunshine, *Patterns of Residential Segregation.* Cambridge, Mass.: Schenkman, 1970.

P. Goldman, *Report from Black America.* New York: Simon & Schuster, 1970.

A. M. Greeley and P. B. Sheatsley, "Attitudes Toward Racial Integration," *Scientific American*, 1971, 225, No. 6, 13–19.

J. Harding and R. Hogrefe, "Attitudes of White Department Store Employees Toward Negro Co-workers," Journal of Social Issues, 1952, 8, 18–28.

H. H. Hyman and P. B. Sheatsley, "Attitudes Toward Desegregation," Scientific American, 1956, 195, 35–39.

H. H. Hyman and P. B. Sheatsley, "Attitudes Toward Desegregation," Scientific American, 1964, 211, 16–23.

M. Jahoda and P. West, "Race Relations in Public Housing," Journal of Social Issues, 1951, 7, 132–139.

I. Katz, "Review of Evidence Relating to Effects of Desegregation on the Performance of Negroes," American Psychologist, 1964, 19, 381–399.

I. Katz, "The Socialization of Competence Motivation in Minority Group Children." In D. Levine (ed.), Nebraska Symposium on Motivation, 1967. Lincoln: University of Nebraska Press, 1967.

O. Klineberg, Negro Intelligence and Selective Migration. New York: Columbia University Press, 1935.

R. Krug, "An Analysis of the F Scale: I. Item Factor Analysis," Journal of Social Psychology, April 1961, 53, 285–291.

R. Krug and K. E. Moyer, "An Analysis of the F Scale: II. Relationship to Standardized Personality Inventories," Journal of Social Psychology, April 1961, 53, 293–301.

R. A. LeVine and D. T. Campbell, Ethnocentrism: Theories of Conflict, Ethnic Attitudes and Group Behavior. New York: Wiley, 1972.

S. Lieberson, "A Societal Theory of Race and Ethnic Relations," American Sociological Review, December 1961, 26, 902–910.

L. H. Mayhew, Law and Equal Opportunity: A Study of the Massachusetts Commission Against Discrimination. Cambridge, Mass.: Harvard University Press, 1968.

F. Mosteller and D. P. Moynihan (eds.), On Equality of Educational Opportunity. New York: Random House, 1972.

G. Myrdal, An American Dilemma. New York: Harper & Row, 1944.

National Advisory Commission on Civil Disorders, Report. Washington, D.C.: GPO, 1968.

T. Parsons and K. Clark (eds.), The Negro American. Boston: Houghton Mifflin, 1966.

A. H. Pascal (ed.), Racial Discrimination in Economic Life. Lexington, Mass.: Heath, 1972.

T. F. Pettigrew, "Social Psychology and Desegregation Research," American Psychologist, 1961, 16, 105–112.

T. F. Pettigrew, "Social Evaluation Theory: Convergences and Applications." In D. Levine (ed.), Nebraska Symposium on

Motivation, *1967*. Lincoln: University of Nebraska Press, 1967; pp. 241–311.

T. F. Pettigrew, "The Negro and Education: Problem and Proposals." In I. Katz and P. Gurin (eds.), *Race and the Social Sciences*. New York: Basic Books, 1969; pp. 47–94.

T. F. Pettigrew, "When a Black Candidate Runs for Mayor: Race and Voting Behavior." In H. Hahn (ed.), *Urban Affairs Annual Review, 1972*. Beverly Hills, Calif.: Sage, 1972.

T. F. Pettigrew and K. W. Back, "Sociology in the Desegregation Process: Its Use and Disuse." In P. F. Lazarsfeld, W. H. Sewell, and H. Wilensky (eds.), *The Uses of Sociology*. New York: Basic Books, 1967; pp. 692–722.

T. F. Pettigrew, R. T. Riley, and J. M. Ross, *Understanding Racial Change: Studies in American Race Relations*. Cambridge, Mass.: Harvard University Press, 1975.

T. F. Pettigrew, E. Useem, C. Normand, and M. Smith, "A Critique of 'The Evidence on Busing,'" *The Public Interest*, Winter 1973, 88–118.

R. Rosenthal and L. Jacobson, *Pygmalion in the Classroom*. New York: Holt, Rinehart & Winston, 1968.

J. B. Rotter, "Internal Versus External Control of Reinforcement," *Psychological Monographs*, 1966, *80*, No. 609.

G. Saenger and E. Gilbert, "Customer Reactions to the Integration of Negro Sales Personnel," *International Journal of Opinion and Attitude Research*, 1950, *4*, 57–76.

T. C. Schelling, "Dynamic Models of Segregation," *Journal of Mathematical Sociology*, 1971, *1*, 146–186.

G. E. Simpson and J. M. Yinger, *Racial and Cultural Minorities*. Fourth edition. New York: Harper & Row, 1972 (1st ed., 1953).

S. A. Stouffer, E. A. Schuman, L. C. DeVinney, S. A. Star, and R. M. Williams, Jr., *Studies in Social Psychology in World War II*. Vol. 1, *The American Soldier: Adjustment During Army Life*. Princeton, N.J.: Princeton University Press, 1949.

L. C. Thurow, *Poverty and Discrimination*. Washington, D.C.: Brookings, 1969.

H. E. Titus and E. P. Hollander, "The California F Scale in Psychological Research: 1950–1955," *Psychological Bulletin*, 1957, *54*, 47–64.

United States Commission on Civil Rights, *Racial Isolation in the Public Schools*. Vols. I and II. Washington, D.C.: GPO, 1967.

R. M. Williams, Jr., *The Reduction of Intergroup Tensions*. New York: Social Science Research Council, 1947.

R. M. Williams, Jr., *Strangers Next Door*. Englewood Cliffs, N.J.: Prentice-Hall, 1964a.

R. M. Williams, Jr., "Factors Affecting Reaction to Public School Desegregation." In New York State Education Department, *State of Knowledge Conference*. Albany, N.Y.: State Education Department, 1964b.

R. M. Williams, Jr., "Social Change and Social Conflict: Race Relations in the United States, 1944–1964," *Sociological Inquiry*, 1965, *35*, No. 1, 8–25.

D. M. Wilner, R. P. Walkley, and S. W. Cook, *Human Relations in Interracial Housing*. Minneapolis: University of Minnesota Press, 1955.

PART II

HOUSING
DISCRIMINATION:
A CRITICAL
ILLUSTRATION

Racial discrimination in the Southern United States did not traditionally depend upon residential separation. Prior to the historic U.S. Supreme Court ruling in May 1954 striking down de jure racial segregation in the public schools, the South had relied during the twentieth century upon formal state laws of racial separation and exclusion. A virtually complete system of legal repression of black Southerners went undisturbed by patterns of interracial neighborhoods. These patterns, often remnants of slave quarters behind handsome mansions, are still discernible in such Old South cities as Charleston, South Carolina, New Orleans, Louisiana, and Macon, Georgia.

The North, without such traditions and with few such

formal racial statutes, based its system of racial dis-
crimination primarily upon separate housing areas. This
trend began to emerge in Chicago, Detroit, and New York
as early as the 1920s—just a few years after the mass
migration of black Southerners to the urban North was
initiated in 1915. This "Northern plan of discrimination"
separates blacks off and discriminates by geographical
area without directly harsh laws. In other words, housing
segregation became in large part the functional equivalent
for the North of state segregation laws in the South.

American law came to recognize this structural fact by
distinguishing between so-called de facto *and* de jure
segregation, though it was believed until recently that
Northern de facto *patterns were somehow "natural" and*
therefore beyond the reach of the Fourteenth Amendment
of the United States Constitution. This view never received
empirical support, as research has repeatedly demonstra-
ted that governmental action created housing separation
just as surely as if there had been laws requiring it. The
federal courts, from Denver and Minneapolis to Detroit
and Boston, are beginning to agree. The following selec-
tions provide some of the evidence underlying this new
view of misnamed de facto *housing segregation.*

Continued urbanization and industrialization together
with the striking down of segregation statutes as uncon-
stitutional have made residential separation by race in-
creasingly the key to racial discrimination throughout
the United States. Hence it is appropriate to begin our
analysis with an intensive look at housing discrimination.

It is also appropriate to begin with a succinct statement
of the problem by the leading authority on the subject, the
late Charles Abrams. He organizes his discussion in
Selection 3 around five "fictions": that the housing prob-
lem of blacks is largely that of deficient, slum housing;
that the best way to deal with this issue is to tear down the
slums; that blacks and whites do not mix, with blacks
spoiling any neighborhood they enter; that the federal
government has always been the champion of equal

*rights in housing; and that state and local antibias laws
can end discrimination. In the course of disposing of
these "fictions," Abrams bluntly indicts the federal government as a major contributor to our present plight. But
his proposed remedies lean heavily on affirmative inter-
ventions by the United States government. Though a weak
federal antidiscrimination-in-housing statute was enacted
in 1968 after this article was written, it is apparent that
the situation has not fundamentally changed.*

*Karl and Alma Taeuber provided in 1965 the most
definitive research to date on racial residential patterns in
urban America.[1] Their analyses of central city data from
the U.S. censuses of 1940, 1950, and 1960 led to some
stark conclusions. By 1960, seven out of every eight
urban "nonwhite" families would have had to move to a
white residential area before a random racial pattern
would exist in central cities. Housing segregation during
the 1940s increased throughout the country, and during
the 1950s continued to spread in the South while receding
slightly outside the South.*

*Have these patterns changed since 1960? Selection 4,
written by Theodore Clemence of the U.S. Census Bureau,
updates the Taeuber analysis through the mid-sixties with
the latest data available on selected cities. He finds a general trend of increasing "polarization rather than dispersion of the nonwhite population," with black areas
becoming larger and more racially distinct in cities ranging from Buffalo to Shreveport and Providence to
Sacramento.*

*Why? The Taeubers state flatly that: "Economic factors
cannot account for more than a small portion of observed levels of racial residential segregation."[2] Abrams,
we have seen, cited a combination of federal government actions and local initiatives by the real estate industry. Selections 5 and 6 provide convincing empirical
support for Abrams's contentions. First, Theodore Lowi
presents us with a case study of the racial effects of two
federal programs in a Southern city. The devastating con-*

sequences of the programs may impress the reader as extreme; yet, unfortunately, Lowi's dramatic findings can be duplicated in many cities, North as well as South. Residential separation by race does not simply "happen," de facto; its structural roots have to be carefully planned and implemented.

Once established, the apartheid pattern is typically maintained by a vigilant exclusion of prospective black residents in predominantly white areas. Daniel Johnson and his colleagues in Selection 6 demonstrate in a field experiment how this vigilant exclusion operates in apartment rentals in Los Angeles despite both state and federal antidiscrimination housing statutes. Mexican-American couples were discriminated against in comparison to white couples, and black American couples received even more discriminatory treatment. Note how the differential treatment to minority applicants takes several forms: availability of apartments denied as well as higher rents and fees quoted. Laws which require the victim of discrimination to file a complaint are seldom effective precisely because these acts of discouragement are difficult to prove as discriminatory without an experimental design comparable to Johnson's. Thus Leon Mayhew has demonstrated that antidiscrimination legislation proves a valuable tool only when it provides a well-staffed, assertive enforcement agency with the power and willingness to initiate broad remedial action beyond specific complaints.[3] We shall return to this critical point when we discuss proposed remedies in Part VI.

The finding that Mexican-Americans also face rental discrimination in Los Angeles raises the comparative question of how distinctive is the residential segregation of black people. Do white immigrant groups not often live in separate areas, sometimes from choice? So what, then, is so special about the racially separate pattern? The Taeubers answer these queries in Selection 7. They find in Chicago, for example, that such recently arrived minorities as Puerto Ricans, Mexican-Americans, and Japanese-

Americans had dispersed more in a few years despite discrimination than black Americans in two generations. Clearly the force of racial discrimination in housing practiced against blacks has no parallel in the United States.

Finally, Selection 8 by the editor presents a collation of the available survey evidence of black and white attitudes toward race and housing. The evidence is quite consistent across a variety of survey agencies and samples. Attitudes are at least as derivative from social structure as they are creators of it. Consequently it is interesting to observe that the attitudes of the two races toward housing are apparently not as far apart as the actual housing situation might lead one to expect. There are, to be sure, some differences. Whites tend to think of ideal interracial neighborhoods as involving only token numbers of black families; blacks prefer mixed areas with substantial black concentration. Moreover, those black respondents most able to locate in interracial areas—the young and educated with higher incomes—are precisely those who tend to perceive the greatest barriers to living in such neighborhoods.

Finally, black respondents repeatedly view better housing as one of their most pressing needs. Inspection of the relevant census data explains why.[4] While black housing conditions did improve during the 1960s, a sharp racial disparity in the quality of shelter persists. Thus black home ownership edged up from 38 to 42 percent of all units during the decade but still lagged far behind the 1970 white figure of 65 percent. Home ownership among blacks is especially restricted in such large Northern cities as New York (16%), Newark (16%), and Boston (18%). In addition, among these owner-occupied units, only half as many of the black units (30%) were valued at $15,000 or more in 1970 compared to white units (61%). The 1970 median value of the black-owned units ($12,000) was only 61 percent that of white-owned units ($19,600). The black-owned units were also older, *with 59 percent of them built before 1950 compared to 45 percent of the white-owned units. Black renters also live in older housing stock; 70 percent of black rental units were built prior to 1950 compared to 59 percent of white rental units. And while black renters paid in 1970 a smaller median gross rent ($89 to $112 per month), this required a larger percentage of their smaller incomes.*

A dramatic improvement was noted between 1960 and 1970 in the percentage of black housing units with full plumbing facilities (from 59% to 83%), but it still trailed the white figure (95% in 1970) largely because of the racial differences in the South. Overcrowding also improved but still remained a problem. Roughly a fifth of all black housing units in 1970 were "overcrowded" by the census definition (1.01 or more persons per room), and one in every fourteen (7%) were "seriously overcrowded" (1.51 or more persons per room). The same figures for all white housing units in 1970 were only 7 percent and 2 percent. We turn now to our six selections to learn why and how these racial disparities in shelter developed and persist.

❪ 3 ❫

The Housing Problem
and the Negro*

CHARLES ABRAMS

When Hell broke loose in the Watts area of Los Angeles taking 36 lives and injuring close to 1,000 people, reporters were astonished and reformers shocked to find that the area . . . was hardly a slum in the usual sense. Instead of rat-infested crumbling tenements on littered streets, the section was made up of small homes mostly about twenty-five years old, many of them surrounded by lawns, and only 20 per cent of them actually dilapidated. In the public mind, the Negro housing problem was therefore discounted as one of the causes of the eruption in favor of hoodlumism, anti-white emotionalism, and poverty.

The rioting in Los Angeles highlighted one of the five fictions that surround the Negro housing problem and still condition federal housing policy. One reason these fictions persist is that officials are not eager to probe too thoroughly into the Negro housing issue, while the vocal Negro leadership has relegated the issue to a low priority in the fight for Negro rights. Yet, until these fictions are put to rest, the Negro's housing problem will remain one of the conspicuous failures in the nation's effort to elevate his status in American life.

* Slightly abridged from C. Abrams, "The Housing Problem and the Negro." In T. Parsons and K. Clark (eds.), *The Negro American*. Boston: Houghton Mifflin, 1966, pp. 512–524. Reprinted by permission of *Daedalus*, Journal of the American Academy of Arts and Sciences, Boston, Mass. Winter 1966, *The Negro American*.

The fiction which the Watts area exposed is that the primary aspect of the Negro's housing problem is the slum, that is, insanitary or structurally deficient housing. The fact is that many Negroes do live in slums and some do not. The accelerated movement of whites to the suburbs has been providing Negroes with a wider choice among the leavings, while improved income has enabled others to venture into neighborhoods once inhabited by middle-class whites; thus the houses Negroes occupy are no longer all on the other side of the tracks but are now part of a mixed inventory. Despite this, the housing problem persists for most Negro families, and in many places it is becoming worse. About half the nonwhite renters in California, for example, and two-fifths of the nonwhite homeowners live in substandard houses in contrast to only one-fifth of white renters and one-tenth of white homeowners. The physical condition of the Negro's homes, however, is only one aspect of the Negro's housing conditions. The neighborhoods are run-down; officialdom is less concerned with their maintenance, and their general atmosphere is demoralizing; the schools are segregated and inferior, and so are the recreational, hospital, and social facilities; there are also fewer new buildings erected in Negro areas, even for those who can afford them. Above all, the Negro is discriminated against in almost every aspect of housing and neighborhood life, and he feels it. Urbanization and suburbanization have recast the American scene and redistributed the population into areas inhabited by a new white "élite" and a black unwanted. If poor housing was not the mainspring that touched off the rioting, it certainly has not been a force for advancing interracial harmony—in California or elsewhere.

The 1961 report on "Housing" by the United States Commission on Civil Rights is punctuated by references to housing discrimination in California. Builders refuse to sell Federal Housing Administration and Veterans Administration homes to Negroes, and lenders are chary of lending them money on mortgages. Negroes have been refused access to houses repossessed by the VA, and the Los Angeles Realty Board has consistently rejected Negro applications for membership. The

California Advisory Committee of the U.S. Commission on Civil Rights said it was "almost impossible" for minorities to buy homes in new subdivisions. In Northern California, fewer than 100 nonwhites have been able to buy houses in unsegregated tracts in a period during which 350,000 new homes were built. In a check on 117 advertisements for apartment rentals in Northern California, only two were available to Negroes and both were in Negro areas.

Far more serious, however, are the overcrowding within the buildings the Negro occupies and the high proportion of income he pays for rent. A sixth of Los Angeles Negroes, for example, were crowded into the Watts area in conditions four times as congested as those in the rest of the city. A U.S. census survey in March 1965 in the renewal areas of 132 cities showed 36 per cent of the Negroes paying 35 per cent or more of their incomes for their shelter. Moreover, the isolation of the Negro from the main stream of community life keeps resentment well-kindled and gives Negro mischiefmakers little trouble in churning up hate of the white man on the ghetto fringe.

Because official policy still views the slum as a building instead of a condition, a second fiction has worked its way into official housing policy, that the best way to solve the Negro's housing problem is to tear down his slums. Because many of the houses are deteriorated, they have been the primary targets for slum clearance. In the United States, from 60 to 72 per cent of those who have been displaced from their homes by urban renewal projects have been Negroes, while only a tiny fraction of the new houses built on the sites have been open to them. Through May 1962, 5,105 Negro families were evicted by renewal projects in California and 58 per cent of those displaced were nonwhite. In the Western Addition redevelopment area in San Francisco, which had a population of 13,000, about 90 per cent of the children among the evicted families were nonwhite.

The renewal program is not the only or even the main culprit, for code enforcement and displacement for public works have taken an even greater toll of Negro homes. Whatever the motivation, these evictions have been disrupting neighborhood life before it has had a chance to mature. In Stockton, California, a renewal project not only leveled a whole Negro neighborhood but destroyed 32 Negro churches in the process. Negro displacement cannot always be avoided, and renewal of central sections is often necessary to salvage the economies of the beleaguered central cities; but as M. Justin Herman, Executive Director of San Francisco's Redevelopment Agency, told the U.S. Commission on Civil Rights: "Much of the problem is a matter of economics—the inability of families to afford such housing as can be made available in the market today. The biggest problem is the discrimination that exists with respect to non-white persons." Thus, low income, coupled with high housing costs and anti-Negro bias, has been at the root of the Negro's housing problem not only in California but throughout the nation. In 1963, the median Negro income was $3,465, compared with $6,548 for white families, and the Negro unemployment rate was twice as high; as a result, many Negro families have found it difficult to secure decent housing even if builders were ready to offer it to them.

Instead of expanding the number of houses available to the Negro, demolitions have been shrinking the housing supply in sections in which he has established footholds, thereby intensifying his overcrowding. The Negro, crowded into his shelter and paying more than he can afford or facing eviction, continuously eyes the white areas on the borders of his ghetto. This does little to enhance his popularity with his white neighbors—which brings us to *a third fiction, that Negroes and whites do not mix and that Negroes will spoil any neighborhood and destroy its social status.* This fiction is usually supplemented by claims that, once the Negro establishes a beachhead, more Negroes will follow—which is often the case—causing real-estate values to topple—which may or may not be the case.

As long as the Negro had been a small and docile minority in the North, the feeling that Negroes always destroy social status and market values never gained widespread acceptance. "Where the Negro pitches his tent," wrote Jacob Riis in 1902, "he pays more rent than his white neighbor next door and is a better tenant." In Washington, D.C., Baltimore, and Philadelphia, Negroes lived in small clusters near the better white dwellings, and, before 1915, they lived in almost every section in Chicago—a third of the city's Negroes living in areas that were less than 10 per cent Negro-occupied. The Negro's presence in cities rarely caused a white exodus; it would in fact have disturbed the equanimity of the whites in those days if their maids and butlers moved too far from the town houses.

The situation changed in the thirty years following 1910 when 1,750,000 Negroes moved northward. By 1960 the central cities of the twelve largest metropolitan areas accounted for 24 per cent of all United States Negroes. They were then 29 per cent of Detroit's population; 35 per cent of Baltimore's; a quarter of Cleveland's and Philadelphia's; 34 per cent of Newark's; and 55 per cent of Washington, D.C.'s. As the Negroes moved to the cities, they accelerated the white movement to the burgeoning suburbs so that by 1960 less than a third of the urban and suburban whites were living in the central cities. Though they constituted only a ninth of the national population, 78 per cent of all Negroes in the nation's 212 metropolitan areas lived in the central cities compared to only 52 per cent of the whites.

As the Negro's numbers increased and as he moved into the adjoining sections or made inroads into white sections, the whites moved out in droves. Homes were often offered at bargain prices. Since cause was confused with effect, the Negroes were always blamed for declines in values.[1]

As opposition crystallized, racial zoning became the main device to keep the Negro in his place and, when the courts struck it down as unconstitutional, the restrictive covenant was thereafter written into deeds in the effort to maintain white supremacy in neighborhoods. About 80 per cent of the vacant land in Los Angeles was at one time covered by such covenants. When the courts held racial covenants unenforceable, subtler devices were ushered in, including overrigid zoning ordinances sternly enforced against Negroes but relaxed for whites. Condemnation for incinerator dumps or other public works is another current device, while building inspectors and other petty officials are always on hand to harass the Negro who ventures where he is not wanted. When, for example, a private builder announced he would sell a few of his houses to Negroes in Deerfield, Illinois, his site was promptly condemned for a park. When the Ford Motor Company moved its plant from Richmond, California, to Milpitas, and when the union tried to build houses for its Negro workers, the area was promptly rezoned for industrial use. Thereafter came a sudden strengthening of building regulations, followed by a hike of sewer connection costs to a ransom figure. It is not surprising, therefore, that discrimination in housing also reduces the chances of Negro employment; many suburban firms refuse to hire Negroes either for fear of offending the local community or because they know the Negroes will have trouble finding housing.

The big city has thus been performing its historic role as a refuge for minorities, while the Northern and Western suburbs have become the new Mason-Dixon lines of America; of the total suburban population of metropolitan areas with a population of half a million or more, barely 4 per cent are Negroes and a substantial number of these live either in the South or in little fringe ghettos that have precariously survived suburban engulfment.

A fourth fiction is that the federal government is and always has been the prime protagonist of equal rights in housing. One gathers this impression from hearing so often of the law of 1866 which supposedly guarantees the Negro the right to own and lease real property, or the protections of the 14th Amendment, or the recent liberal rulings of the Supreme Court. But the law of 1866 was soon a dead letter; the 14th Amendment, enacted to protect Negroes, was long used primarily to protect corporations; as for the Supreme Court, up to 1948 it supported the use of the racial restrictive covenant as a private prerogative, and so did the highest courts of twelve states. Although the Supreme Court after

1948 became the spearhead in the drive for expanding the Negro's civil rights, and although general economic improvement has helped raise the Negro's sights, he has made little gain in housing.

One of the reasons is that the federal government, during the New Deal period, not only sanctioned racial discrimination in housing but vigorously exhorted it.[2] From 1935 to 1950, discrimination against Negroes was a condition of federal assistance. More than 11 million homes were built during this period, and this federal policy did more to entrench housing bias in American neighborhoods than any court could undo by a ruling. It established a federally sponsored mores for discrimination in the suburban communities in which 80 per cent of all new housing is being built and fixed the social and racial patterns in thousands of new neighborhoods.

In 1962, two years after he had made the promise to do so, President Kennedy signed an executive order outlawing discrimination in federally aided housing. By that time, seventeen states and fifty-six cities had passed laws or resolutions against housing discrimination. This movement at the state and local levels originated in New York in the 1940's and spread elsewhere partly as a liberal protest against discrimination in publicly assisted undertakings and partly because the minority numbers were beginning to become more politically significant. But the Executive Order was hardly a prophylactic against the virus that now afflicted American neighborhoods. In the first place, it embraced only about 23 per cent of all new housing construction and only 13 per cent of the housing not already covered by state or local action. In the second place, it explicitly excluded the federally regulated and federally assisted savings and loan associations which are the principal mortgage lenders in the nation. It was hardly surprising, therefore, that the order could not crack the vitrified prejudices and fears that had become impacted during the sixteen years of concerted federal anti-Negro policy. Nor has the enforcement of the order done much to secure equal rights to housing in American suburbs. At best, the order manifests a shift from officially sponsored prejudice to an invertebrate morality.

The rising tide of state and local anti-bias laws in housing has insinuated a fifth fiction into the housing issue, that such state and local anti-bias laws provide the means for ending discrimination. These laws have had educational value, have helped create a better moral climate in some areas, have secured housing for a few upper-income Negro families, and have demonstrated that such laws do not adversely affect property values. But they have brought no solution to the Negro's housing troubles. City anti-bias laws cannot affect the suburbs where most of the exclusionary practices exist. As for state-wide laws, it is all but impossible to buck the concerted power of the suburbs to which the political balance has shifted. Proceedings before anti-discrimination commissions are protracted and costly, and, when a Negro complainant wins a favorable ruling, he must be ready after the long delays to brave the pressures of his hostile landlord, neighbors, and local officials. He must be willing to have his child be the lone Negro child in an all-white school. Most important, he must be financially poised to pay the suburban rents or, if he buys a house, to get a mortgage on it—which is still all but impossible.

The slender hope these laws offer the Negro family is again illustrated in the case of California, where there were two state laws, the Hawkins Act which banned discrimination in publicly assisted housing and the Unruh Act which prohibited discrimination in "all business establishments of any kind whatsoever" and therefore applied to discriminatory practices by real-estate brokers. One reason for the existence of these laws is that the state by 1960 had 1.3 million nonwhites and another 1.4 million of the Spanish-speaking minority, composing a formidable force of voters.

The two laws were hardly strictures which a real-estate owner should have viewed with trepidation. But California has had a long history of anti-racial activities dating from the anti-Chinese campaign of the 1870's and the anti-Japanese outbursts in the decade that followed. Moreover, California's real-estate boards, which compose one of the most formidable lobbies in the state, have continuously favored race segregation. When, for example, the Supreme Court ruled against the racial covenant, the Los Angeles Board was the first to broadcast eight ways of evading the decision. It simultaneously sought a state constitutional amendment to validate the covenant but did not succeed.

The situation changed in 1963 when a local ordinance was introduced in the city of Berkeley—a community generally considered liberal—which proposed to ban racial discrimination by property owners. Largely because the bill carried a possible prison penalty, it was defeated. The defeat lent courage to California's real-estate interests and, shortly after the Berkeley fiasco, the California Real Estate Association, representing 173 local boards, announced its plan to initiate a constitutional amendment barring any anti-bias laws in housing. The proposed amendment, cleverly framed, provided that

Neither the State nor any subdivision or agency thereof shall deny, limit or abridge, directly or indirectly, the right of any person, who is willing or desires to sell, lease or rent any part or all of his real property, to decline to sell, lease or rent such property to such person or persons as he, in his absolute discretion, chooses.

The California Real Estate Association was soon backed by the powerful National Association of Real Estate Boards which not only gave its nationwide support to its affiliate but also joined the campaign and helped finance it. An advertising agency was hired to guide the campaign, and a fund reported to run well over one million dollars was raised to assure victory.

California now became the battle ground for a nationwide campaign to end, once and for all, the long struggle for equal access to shelter. Anti-Negro propaganda circulated freely, and fear of Negro invasion of white neighborhoods was whipped up throughout the state. As a prominent industrialist put it: "In the real estate industry there were a number who were motivated by racial bigotry, others by their concern for property values and some who won't buck the stream. But at the bottom of it all is racial bigotry."

Proposition 14 rolled up a surprising 4.5 million votes in its favor to less than 2.4 million against it. The votes for the proposition exceeded those polled by President Johnson by more than 350,000. President Johnson received almost 1.8 million more votes than those cast against the proposition, indicating that many voters saw no conflict in voting against Goldwater while protecting their own neighborhoods against the Negro scourge. "People just voted their prejudice" was Governor Brown's private comment.

Proposition 14 was also a great victory for the National Association of Real Estate Boards. Its official code of "ethics" up to 1950 had barred its member realtors from "introducing into a neighborhood members of any race or nationality, or any individual whose presence will clearly be detrimental to property values in the neighborhood.[3] The association had grudgingly modified its code of ethics in 1950 on the advice of counsel who may have feared that the Board could be charged with conspiring against the Civil Rights Laws. But despite the modification, there was little evidence that the official view had altered, and, nine days after Proposition 14 was approved, the NAREB Annual Convention in Los Angeles openly resolved that "government should not deny, limit or abridge, directly or indirectly, the fundamental right of every person to sell, lease, or rent any part or all of his real property." The Convention called the California victory to the attention of other states "where the freedom of real estate practices may be imperilled."

The battle lines were thus drawn for a nationwide campaign. Detroit and Akron have followed California's example, while in 1965 Ohio, Rhode Island, and Indiana adopted the other course of banning race bias in private home selling and renting, with Maine barring discrimination in apartments only. This mixed record of victories and defeats suggests that, while the average voter will acquiesce when moral leadership is given to an anti-bias law by his legislators or Governor, he will vote his property rights against his moral scruples when put to the test in person. As long as ethical leadership is lacking, the supporters of property rights are in a position to win the tests, particularly if put to the people themselves, as in California.

Access of the Negro to decent housing is becoming the vortex around which his other rights revolve. Without housing in areas of his choice, the right of his child to an unsegregated school is meaningless; his right to a job will be impaired; his right to move and to secure shelter in a decent neighborhood will be an empty shell. The vote on Proposition 14 indicates that racial prejudice is still a potent political commodity in the nation, and it is not at all unlikely that the device may become the legal instrument for pitting the issue of property rights against civil rights in the years to come.

The extent to which the heated contest over Proposition 14 contributed to the anti-white emotions that burst forth into the Watts riot will be hard to assess. But this is certain: housing has and will continue to play a part, if not in Negro outbreaks against the whites, then in white outbreaks against the Negro. American history reveals a long string of such riots, dynamitings, and other forms of violence from the time Negroes began moving North in greater numbers. The toll in deaths and injuries is in the thousands, and property damage is in the hundreds of millions—the Watts riot alone destroyed $50 million in property . . .

The Negro is only 11.6 per cent of the nation's population, and about half of the American Negroes still live in the South. Although the presence of Negroes appears formidable because of exclusion and their concentration in the major cities, they would hardly be noticed in Northern and Western cities if the suburbs were opened to them, for there simply are not enough Negro families in the country to threaten white areas, even if the Negroes and other low-income families were subsidized to make their move possible.

— To deal with the Negro's housing problem—as well as with school segregation—a meaningful housing program is needed for low-income families at costs they can afford. Despite official claims to the contrary, present programs cannot accomplish this. The public housing program hardly scratches the surface, and the local housing authorities that build the projects are generally located in the cities and lack the power to build beyond their legal boundaries. The states which could build without regard to local boundaries will not do so because of suburban opposition. FHA mortgage insurance is designed mostly for builders in suburban areas; besides, the housing it produces is too costly for most Negro families . . .

The real answer is for the federal government to build directly wherever there is racial exclusion and housing needs for minorities are demonstrated. The federal government should not only insist that equal access to housing be provided in all federally assisted private subdivisions, but it should also combine direct building with rent supplements in order to bring the dwellings in suburbs as well as in cities within the means of lower-income families. Federal home building has a precedent in the housing constructed during World War I by the United States Housing Corporation and in the building of public housing and new towns during the New Deal. After their completion, the houses and new towns were sold as they should be under the formula proposed. Until Congress is ready to move in that direction, Negro slum life and neighborhood and school segregation will persist.

Simultaneously, the federal government must also meet the predicament facing the central cities. The migration into their centers of millions of low-income Negroes, combined with the presence of poor elderly families, is confronting these cities with social and economic problems with which they can no longer cope. Unlike the federal government, these cities cannot go beyond their boundaries in search of new levies to meet their rising costs. Since 1946 their debts per capita have trebled while federal debt per capita has actually gone down. The money which the federal government has given them for public housing and urban renewal is of small help when measured against the new burdens they have had to assume. Nor can they expect much help from the states whose debts have also rocketed and who are similarly limited to their taxing ability . . .

Urbanization has confronted these cities with new tasks

that are national in scope and origin. The Negro housing problem is only one of these concerns, and it involves much more than housing. It is also undeniably linked with making neighborhoods livable, safe, and socially solvent; creating schools, playgrounds, and social facilities which are better and more ample; providing homes that are within a reasonable distance of areas of employment and are within the means of low-income families. In short, the poverty of people and the poverty of cities are parts of the same problem. The plight of the city's people can be dealt with only if the cities are enabled to deal with them.

If the Los Angeles rioting reveals the underlying weaknesses of the current federal approach to segregation, poverty, and housing, and if it stimulates some fresh thinking on these problems, it may compensate at least in part for the terrible havoc it wreaked.

[4]

Residential Segregation in the Mid-Sixties*

THEODORE G. CLEMENCE

A high degree of racial segregation is universal in American cities. Whether a city is a metropolitan center or a suburb; whether it is in the North or South; whether the Negro population is large or small in every case, white and Negro households are highly segregated from each other. Negroes are more segregated resi-

* Abridged from T. G. Clemence, "Residential Segregation in the Mid-Sixties," *Demography*, 1967, *4*, 562–568. Reprinted with permission of the publisher and author.

dentially than are Orientals, Mexican Americans, Puerto Ricans, or any nationality group. In fact, Negroes are by far the most residentially segregated urban minority group in recent American history. This is evident in the virtually complete exclusion of Negro residents from most new suburban developments of the past fifty years as well as in the block-by-block expansion of Negro residential areas in the central portions of many large cities.[1]

This statement, made by Karl and Alma Taeuber in their recent book, *Negroes in Cities*, is amply supported by their analysis. Much of their data was drawn from the 1960 Census. Most would agree that residential segregation remains both a fact and a problem in the mid-sixties, though it is still several years until substantiating data will be available from the 1970 Census.

Interim data are available for a few large cities from special censuses taken by the Census Bureau. Since 1960, approximately 26 million of the nation's inhabitants have been enumerated in a special census. Approximately 1,200 censuses have been conducted, of which about 100 were in cities of 50,000 or more people. Statistics for the population by age, race, and sex for census tracts are published for these cities, and these reports provide the means for comparisons with 1960.

To examine some of the trends in the white and nonwhite populations as affected by residential segregation, ten cities have been selected for study, all of which had 100,000 or more inhabitants at mid-decade. Four of the cities are in the Northeast, the others in the South and West. The criteria for selection were that (1) census tract boundaries in the central portion of the city remained unchanged since 1960; (2) a special census was conducted in 1964, 1965, or 1966; and (3) considered as a group, the cities are geographically scattered . . .

Table 1 shows average annual changes in this decade compared to the 1950–60 decade, expressed as absolute numbers. The four cities in the Northeast continue to experience the types of change evident during the decade 1950–60. White people are moving out of these cities faster than nonwhites

TABLE 1. *Average Annual Change in the White and Nonwhite Population for Ten Selected Cities, 1950–60 and 1960 to Date of Special Census*
(Figures Rounded to Nearest Hundred)

CITY	WHITE Increase, 1960 to Special Census	WHITE Increase, 1950–60	NONWHITE Increase, 1960 to Special Census	NONWHITE Increase, 1950–60
Buffalo	−10,300	− 8,300	1,800	− 3,600
Cleveland	−18,300	−14,200	5,200	10,400
Providence	− 4,700	− 4,400	600	300
Rochester	− 5,200	− 3,000	2,000	1,600
Louisville	− 2,400	900	2,000	1,300
Raleigh	1,500	2,400	500	400
Shreveport	− 700	2,300	− 100	1,400
Des Moines	− 500	2,900	100	200
Evansville	400	1,200	100	100
Sacramento	8,700	4,000	2,200[a]	800[a]

[a] Negroes only; excludes other races.

are moving in. (Higher Negro birth rates do not account for all of the shift in percent nonwhite in the central cities.) Moreover, the decreases in the white population of these four cities have accelerated since 1960. In Buffalo and Cleveland, the nonwhite population continues to increase rapidly, but at a slower pace now than during the 1950's. In Providence and Rochester, on the other hand, nonwhites are increasing, and at an accelerated rate.

In Buffalo, whites decreased at a rate of 8,300 per year during the decade 1950–60. This rate of change has accelerated to more than 10,000 per year since 1960. Nonwhites increased by 3,600 a year during the 1950's, but only by about one-half that rate during the 1960's. The same pattern is observed in Cleveland. In Des Moines and Evansville, moreover, the nonwhite population is increasing at a slower pace than in the previous decade. In the remaining cities, the nonwhite population is increasing, and at an accelerated rate.

Gross changes do not, of course, reveal patterns of residential change within these cities; they merely point to the general concentration of nonwhites in the central cities. In the 212 Standard Metropolitan Statistical Areas as a group, from 1960 to 1965, the central cities experienced a decline of 0.6 percent in the white population and a 20.3 percent increase in nonwhites. As of 1965, four out of five metropolitan nonwhites lived in the central cities, compared to less than two out of every five white people.[2]

In order to examine these trends with reference to segregated areas within the ten cities in this comparison, census tracts were studied to reveal the rate of dispersion or concentration which had taken place within the central city since 1960. The established Negro area in each city was defined simply as those census tracts in 1960 in which more than half of the nonwhites lived. The identical area is used in presenting post-census data. Generally this is a compact area of neighboring tracts comprising less than a dozen of the city's census tracts . . .

Table 2 shows the concentration of nonwhites in 1960

TABLE 2.   *Nonwhite Population Living in Established Negro Area, for Ten Selected Cities 1960, and Special Census Date*

CITY AND YEAR OF SPECIAL CENSUS	PROPORTION OF ALL NONWHITES IN CITY LIVING IN ESTABLISHED NEGRO AREA	
	1960	*1964–66*
Buffalo, 1966	85.8	88.4
Cleveland, 1965	80.5	65.2
Providence, 1965	73.8	76.2
Rochester, 1964	62.8	56.0
Louisville, 1964	83.2	82.2
Raleigh, 1966	82.3	75.3
Shreveport, 1966	79.3	81.6
Des Moines, 1966	74.5	77.4
Evansville, 1966	79.1	80.9
Sacramento, 1964[a]	62.6	49.6

[a] Negroes only.

and in the special census year. One would expect, for example, that perhaps where whites are moving out more rapidly than nonwhites are moving in (as in Buffalo), dispersion of nonwhites would occur. Actually, the proportion of the city's nonwhites who live in the established Negro area of Buffalo has risen since 1960 from 85.8 to 88.4 percent—74,000 nonwhites living in ten of the city's 75 census tracts. This trend, in which the increasing nonwhite population of the central cities tends to concentrate in areas already predominantly nonwhite, might be termed the "polarization" of the Negro. But, this phenomenon is not true for all ten cities. In Cleveland, Rochester, Sacramento, Louisville, and Raleigh the proportion of the city's nonwhites living in established Negro areas is lower now than in 1960, and this suggests that some dispersion has taken place. When census-tract maps for these cities are examined, it becomes apparent that some of the dispersion results from a shift from the tracts of highest concentration of nonwhites to tracts with a lower initial concentration. This has occurred chiefly where slum clearance and the construction of interstate highways or office buildings have brought about a relocation of Negro families from one section to another.

A different and perhaps more direct way to see the changes in residential segregation is through examining the extent to which the nonwhite neighborhoods have become more or less racially mixed. Table 3 presents this comparison. For example, in Buffalo, most nonwhites in 1960 lived in an area which was almost one-half white. In 1966, the same census tracts are now nonwhite by a ratio of three-to-one. In all of the ten cities, the developments since 1960 indicate that Negro predominance has increased in the established areas or, conversely, racial segregation in housing has been maintained. One would not expect to observe this pattern if all of the city housing were equally accessible to nonwhites. The increases in the percent nonwhite in the established Negro areas are most dramatic in Buffalo, Rochester, and Louisville. Even in Des Moines and Providence, where Negroes constitute a small minority in the area where most live, the proportion

TABLE 3.   *Percent of the Population in Established Negro Area Which Is Nonwhite, for Ten Selected Cities, 1960 and Special Census Date*

CITY	PERCENT NONWHITE		NUMBER OF TRACTS IN NEGRO AREA	(1960) NUMBER OF TRACTS IN CITY
	1960	1964–66		
Buffalo	55.3	73.2	10	75
Cleveland	82.6	88.5	37	205
Providence	17.7	27.6	9	37
Rochester	55.9	71.2	8	90
Louisville	67.5	80.1	21	128
Raleigh	91.6	94.7	12	43
Shreveport	88.9	93.3	12	41
Des Moines	28.1	37.3	7	47
Evansville	51.4	59.4	4	38
Sacramento[a]	22.4	31.1	8	54

[a] Negroes only.

of the area which is now nonwhite has increased. Many of the census tracts where Negroes are concentrated are declining in total population, and the growing concentration of Negroes in such areas reflects the movement of white families out of those tracts as well as restrictions on the housing market for Negroes.

Special censuses do not usually provide economic statistics for the population. For Cleveland, however, the publication of sample data from the 1965 test census permits a comparison of Negro neighborhoods with the 1960 Census.[3] The report shows that nearly all Negro neighborhoods in Cleveland have suffered economic decline since 1960. This is reflected most obviously by decreases in family income when measured in constant dollars.

A more indirect indication of the impact of population change on the central cities may be observed through changes in age distribution. Buffalo is used for illustration. Whites 24–44 years old account for almost one-half of the decrease in the city's white population; but these age groups comprise only one-fourth of the total white population. Thus, they are disproportionately represented in the movement of white people out of the city. These white adults, together with their small children, make up the great urban stream to suburbia. Among nonwhites, on the other hand, about four-fifths of the increase in population is in the ages 5–24 years. This age group comprised only 35 percent of the nonwhites in 1960 (40 percent in 1966). White adults in their prime working years are leaving the city and being replaced by nonwhite children and by young adults who have not yet reached their most productive working years.

A review of recent special census data for ten large cities offers little assurance that patterns of residential segregation are giving way to a racially integrated urban society. On the contrary, it is evident from these observations that established Negro areas are becoming more, rather than less, racially distinct, and that the general trend is toward polarization rather than dispersion of the nonwhite population.

⟦ 5 ⟧

Apartheid U.S.A.*

THEODORE J. LOWI

What follows is a simple case study of the implementation of the two major federal urban programs in a single city. The case goes far toward explaining why the national regime in the United States is no longer taken to be legitimate by so

* Published by permission of Transaction, Inc. from transaction/ SOCIETY, Vol. 7, No. 4 (1970). Copyright © 1970 by Transaction, Inc. This article, slightly abridged here, is a revised version of a chapter in Theodore J. Lowi's *The End of Liberalism* published by W. W. Norton, 1969.

many black people and why this sense of illegitimacy was so likely to spread eventually to whites. Legitimacy, that elusive but vital underpinning of any stable regime, is that sense of the rightness of the general political order. It is that generalized willingness to view public error or corruption as the result of bad administration. There is probably no way practicably to measure legitimacy as such, but one can usually assess roughly the extent to which a regime is less legitimate today than yesterday—just as a doctor may not say precisely what a healthy body is but can know whether it is less healthy now than before.

In this spirit, one can fairly clearly detect a decline in the legitimacy of the regime by noting the rise of instances of repression of Left and Left-sounding activities; one can also detect it by noting the increasing number of political trials and political prisoners, and, more palpably still, the increased infiltration of Left organizations by paid informers. But other indications are not limited to the Left, as for example the increasing numbers of instances of defiance of federal laws— something Southerners have been leading the country in at least since 1954. One can therefore speak of problems of national legitimacy when he begins to sense a general unwillingness to submit political disputes to recognized channels of political settlement, when he sees mediation replaced by direct action.

This case suggests the extent to which the policies of the liberal state are producing its own downfall, and along with that the failure to achieve even a modicum of social justice. Also, in its perverse way, the case also illustrates the effectiveness of planning when governments do define their goals clearly and guide administrators firmly. Tragically the plan was for implementation of an evil policy, apartheid. But through the case perhaps liberals could learn a little something about how to plan for good ends.

Iron City is an urban-industrial area whose corporate boundary surrounds nearly 60,000 residents and whose true metropolitan area includes about 100,000. The history of the development plan of Iron City presents a single, well-documented case of the implementation of explicit racial goals. More than that, the nature of Iron City's official development plans and proposals upon which federal allocations were based serve to document beyond doubt the extraordinary permissiveness of federal urban policy.

HOUSING POLICY IN IRON CITY

The name of the city has been changed to protect the guilty. They are guilty as charged, but no more so than thousands of mayors, councilmen, planners, realtors and builders all over the country. The Iron City situation is extreme and unrepresentative, but it will soon be clear that it provides an ideal laboratory for discovering the nature and limitations of modern federal enabling legislation. Iron City is a southern city, and its development plan fostered racist goals, namely, apartheid, but in doing so its officials only stated the awful truth about the goals of land use development plans in cities all over the country.

In 1950 over 20 percent of Iron City's population was Negro, and they did *not* live in a ghetto. There were neighborhoods of Negroes in virtually every section of town. There was a narrow strip along the river, and there were several strips in the west central and western sections in easy walking distance from the steel and textile mills. There was a largely black neighborhood in the south central section, and there was a larger concentration in the north central section, "across the tracks." (Note the shadings on the map.) There was no Harlem; the implications of the very word suggest the nonsouthern origin of systematic housing discrimination.

Iron City's has been the typical Negro residential pattern in stable, middle-size southern cities. Rather than a single Negro section, there were interwoven neighborhoods of black and white. This patchwork pattern began in the 1920s with the slow but steady immigration of Negroes from outlying areas to the growing city. Access to industry and the needs of the wealthier whites for domestic servants made "close

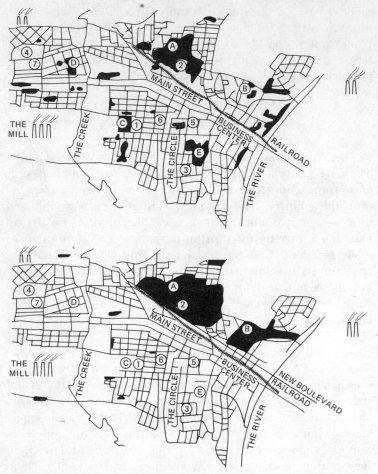

Iron City in 1950. Iron City in 1962

quarters" a desired condition. For example, the Negro neighborhoods east and north of The Circle were surrounded on three sides by the wealthiest homes in Iron City. But while the residents tolerated and encouraged in many ways the proximity of the races, it could not be said that Iron City constituted an integrated community. Each neighborhood was distinctly monochromatic. There were no black-white-black-white house patterns, although there were a number of instances when several Negro families lived directly across the street from or alley-to-alley with a larger number of white families.

THEY "KNEW THEIR PLACE"

Negroes seemed to accept their back-of-the-bus status and the questionable privileges they had which were unavailable to whites. Crimes committed within the race were not, as a rule, investigated or prosecuted with utmost vigor. Black bootleggers (legal sale of liquor has for years been forbidden in the county) had freer rein to cater to the blacks and the insatiably thirsty white middle class. The raising of a pig or a goat was usually allowed, in violation of public health regulations. The rents tended to run considerably lower. And merchants and newsboys were more permissive in granting or extending petty credit to Negroes. This was the dispersed and highly status-bound social situation as recently as 1950.

Early in that decade, however, most Southerners could see a racial crisis approaching, and for them the problems inherent in the residential pattern were immediately clear. In Iron City each of the major public schools was within walking distance of at least one strip of Negro housing and its complement of school-age children. The map serves to make this graphically clear.

Central High School (1 on the map) offered 9th–12th grade education to the white children who lived east of The Creek. Rebel High (4) served white children living west of The Creek, including some areas not shown on the map. Washington High School (2) taught both junior and senior high school grades (7th–12th) to Negro children from both the entire city and the surrounding county. Note the proximity of Negro neighborhoods, hence eligible children, to the white high schools. Most vulnerable to any impending court order for integration would be Central High, attended by virtually all of the children of upper-middle and middle-class families. Note also how far a good half of the Negro children commuted to Washington High and also how many of them actually crossed the paths to Rebel and Central in the course of their journey. The same problem existed for the junior high (3 and 7) and elementary schools (5, 6 and 7).

THE PLAN

Into this situation stepped the Iron City Planning Commission in 1951. First, the commission analyzed housing, land uses, economic facilities and deterioration. In 1952 they produced a handsome and useful Master Plan, the emphasis of which was upon the need for measures ". . . for arresting beginning blight and correcting advanced blight." On the basis of the Master Plan, a more intensive investigation was ordered toward ultimate production of a Rehabilitation Plan to guide actual implementation and financing. The result of this careful study was a professionally designed, fully illustrated, three-color, glossy paper booklet entitled *Iron City Redevelopment*. The focus of this publication was three areas, designated A, B and E on the map, in which blight had made urban redevelopment necessary.

Upon closer scrutiny, however, the plan reveals itself less a scheme for urban renewal as much as a script for Negro removal. All of the projects proposed in the plan are explicit on this point. The underlying intent to create a ghetto is further highlighted by the inconsistences between the design for Area E, which had relatively few Negroes, and that for Area A, which was predominantly Negro. The latter housing was as blighted as Area E, but, curiously, the standard of blighting was not applied. There the plan called for intensification of use rather than renewal.

The plan identified Area E as:

occupied by Negroes, but the number is too few to justify provisions of proper recreational, school and social facilities. . . . The opportunity to reconstitute the area as a residential district in harmony with its surroundings was the main reason for its selection as the number one redevelopment site.

The second, Area B, was chosen because "a relatively small amount of housing—standard and substandard—exists there"; therefore it would serve as a companion project to ". . . [Area E] . . . thus affording home sites for those occupants of [Area E] who are not eligible for relocation in public housing or who, for reasons of their own, prefer single-family or duplex dwellings." Area A, as shown by the intensive survey and the maps published with the plan, contained as much dilapidated and blighted housing as Area E; but Area A was *not* designated an urban redevelopment area in the plan. Although "blighted and depreciating," it was the "center part of the area . . . growing as the focal point of Negro life." Along the main street of this area, extending into Area B, the plan proposed the building of an auditorium, a playfield and other public facilities "to serve [Iron City's] Negro community." Sites were inserted for the three Negro churches which would be removed by the redevelopment of Area E.

Before completion of *Iron City Redevelopment*, implementation projects had begun and were expanding as financing allowed. It was to be a showcase program, and enthusiasm ran high. The first steps, quite rationally, were to acquire housing for those families who were to be displaced. It was perfectly consistent with the city's view of these people that this housing would be public housing. There had been some public housing projects built under depression legislation, but the only meaningful projects were those begun in 1952 under The Housing Act of 1949. On the map the letters A, B, C and D represent the actual locations of these projects. There was never any controversy over the racial distribution of the occupants. Projects A and B were 100 percent Negro; Projects C and D were 100 percent white. By 1955 they were completed and occupied.

Public Housing Projects in Iron City

PROJECT	SIZE (NO. OF UNITS)	% NEGRO IN PROJECT	ORIGINAL COMPOSITION OF AREA	DEVELOPMENT COST
A	160	100	Negro	$1,491,000
B	224	100	Mixed	$2,491,000
C	146	0	Negro	$1,595,000
D	220	0	Negro	$2,300,000

Each public housing project was placed carefully. Project A was built in the middle of the largest Negro area. Project B was built in a sparse area, about 50 percent Negro, but marked out in the plan as the area for future expansion of the Negro community. In the area around Project B, the plan proposed sites for the three new "colored churches" and the "colored auditorium."

Project C, an exclusively white project, was built literally on top of the Negro area around it. While it was relatively inexpensive and contained the fewest number of units, it occupied an eight-square-block area due to its design. According to the executive director of the Greater Iron City Housing Authority, it was "a rather unique design, known in the architectural trade as a crankshaft design, thus providing both front and rear courtyards." This project was cited professionally as an outstanding example of good design. And no wonder! Its maximum utilization of space, although a low-rent project, made it a combination public housing, urban renewal and Negro removal plan par excellence. Project D was also built on top of a blighted Negro neighborhood. While it was a relatively large project, it was not solely responsible for eliminating every Negro from the area, as was Project C.

Meanwhile, renewal of the central city was proceeding at a slower pace; it wasn't until 1956 that implementation projects were fully designed. Two areas, designated by the shaded areas around B and E on the map, were selected for intensive renewal. Most important was Area E, a 56-acre area relatively tightly packed with rickety frame houses, outside toilets, corn or potato plots and Negroes. In the official plan, Area E included the unconnected Negro neighborhood just north of The Circle, as well as the entire shaded area due east of The Circle. Area B was relatively sparsely populated, containing a few shacks which needed removing. In some of these shacks were white unemployables.

Within three years the two urban renewal projects were declared 100 percent accomplished. In the official report to the Urban Renewal Administration, the results were as follows:

Completed Urban Renewal Projects in Iron City

ACCOMPLISHMENT	ACTIVITY	FOR AREA E	FOR AREA D
100%	Land Acquisition, No. of Parcels Acquired	168	39
100%	No. of Families Relocated	176	24
100%	No. of Structures Demolished (Site Clearance)	236	33

In Area E every trace of Negro life was removed. As the executive director of the Greater Iron City Housing Authority put it, "In this project, all of the then existing streets were vacated and a new land use map was developed." One entirely new street was put in, several of the narrow lanes (e.g., Saint James' Alley) were covered over, and through connectors were built for a dead-end street or two.

All of Area E has now become prime property. One large supermarket, several neighborhood businesses and two apartment complexes are operating on renewal land purchased from the authority. To serve the 95 percent white area, an elementary school was constructed, as a consolidation of schools No. 5 and No. 6 which no longer exist. Its large playground and lighted ball field occupy most of the eastern sec-

tor of Area E. The renewal effort resulted in an equally im-
pressive campus for the nearby junior high, No. 3. But most
of the area was zoned for single family residences, and, as
of 1968, the boom in construction of houses in the $25,000–
$40,000 range was still in progress.

Area B now enjoys a new elementary school with a field
house, lighted ball field, tennis court·and playground. The
city also built a swimming pool here, but it and the original
municipal pool on The River were closed for several years to
avoid integration of public facilities. Moreover, though redevelopment sites had been set aside in Area B for the three
churches demolished in the redevelopment of Area E, each of
the congregations chose locations elsewhere in the Negro
community. Similarly, most of the relocating Negroes rejected
Area B in favor of Area A, even though it was more densely
populated and blighted. Except for the 224 units of new public
housing, Area B remains underutilized. Furthermore, the
major part of Area B extends north of Project B toward the
mountain, where *Iron City Redevelopment* reports that although

some of the terrain is steep, much of it is gently rolling and well
drained. . . . In most southern cities there is a scarcity of vacant
land located close to schools and churches and shopping districts
and served by city utilities and transportation, land that is suitable
and desirable for expansion of Negro neighborhoods or creation
of new ones. [Area B] is such an area.

Apparently the Negroes do not agree, and most of the area
remains a graded, but raw, expanse of red southern earth on
the side of the mountain. This was the one part of the plan
that went wrong; this was the voluntary part, not financed by
federal agencies.

Yet, as a whole, the plan was an overwhelming success.
Well before the 1960 census the large Negro contingent in
Area E had been reduced to 5.1 percent of the entire census
tract, and this was comprised of a few shanties behind the
bottling works and the western edge of the area along The

River. In Area C the removal process immediately around Central High was completed with Public Housing Project C. After 1960 some 10 percent of the area was still nonwhite, but this was drying up still further. Removal from Area D was approaching totality. By 1964 removal from all areas west of The Creek was given further assistance by the completion of one federally supported artery running east-west through the city and the inauguration of Iron City's portion of the new north-south Interstate Highway. That brought the nonwhite proportion in the western sectors of the city down to about 3 percent of the total population of those areas.

This is how the situation stood by the end of 1967: west of The Creek and north of Main Street (all around Area D), there remained six Negro families. When a nearby textile mill was closed down some years before, they, as employees, were given the right to buy their houses, and they have chosen to remain. West of The Creek and south of Main Street (the area including The Mill), fewer than 5 percent of the housing units were occupied by Negroes. Virtually every one of these houses is located in isolated and sparse sections along The Creek and behind The Mill, where one can still plant a plot of sorghum, catch a catfish, and, undisturbed, let a 1948 Chevrolet corrode into dust. Closer to the center of things, east of The Creek and south of Main Street, the 1960 distribution of Negroes continues to be reduced. Every last shack is gone from Area E and the entire central section of the white city. Three small pockets remain in the western portion near Area C, and that is all that remains in all of the white city. The last remaining Negro neighborhood of any size, a group of shanties running along The River south of Main Street, was removed by the construction of a City Hall-Police Department-YMCA complex. Area B remains completely nonwhite and underdeveloped. Area A now fills the entire triangle pointing north. It is a ghetto.

The plan enjoyed strong consensus among officials and white citizens. It enjoyed at least the acquiescence and tacit consent of the Negroes whose landlords, in any case, were white. Consensus or not, the plan would have had little chance of success without outside financial assistance. That assistance came, abundantly, from federal programs. And, most importantly, the federal personnel who allocated these funds, and still do, also had access to all the project plans, including the Master Plan and the Renewal Plan. Despite Iron City's open approach to apartheid—nothing was kept secret—federal assistance was never in question. Relative to the population of Iron City and the size of its annual public sector budget, federal aid was quite substantial—amounting to 20 percent of the municipal budget for a few years. What we have seen here is an honest, straightforward job of federally sponsored physical and social planning. And the results were dramatic. Perhaps only New Haven, Connecticut, a city famous for its redevelopment, has had a higher per capita success ratio.

Direct federal assistance for public housing in Iron City amounted to slightly over $280,000 for the single fiscal year 1966. Each year since the completion of the four projects the city received a similar amount. This varying figure cannot be broken down among the four projects because it is computed on the basis of the "development costs" given above and granted as a lump sum. The Public Housing (recently changed to Housing Assistance) Administration of Housing and Urban Development (HUD) is authorized by law to grant *each year* to any housing authority the difference between expenses (governed by development costs) and income from public housing. Such a subsidy arrangement enabled authorities like Iron City's to borrow from private banks and to refinance through sale of relatively cheap Housing Authority bonds. What is even more significant is that, under the formula, Iron City is authorized to receive a maximum grant of nearly $305,000 per annum. It is a point of pride at the Greater Iron City Housing Authority that the full amount available under the law was never needed or requested. At a minimum estimate of $250,000 per year, federal grants to help carry the public housing have amounted to $3,000,000.

And federal public housing grants are never-ending. Each year the total to Iron City goes up another $250,000 or more.

SUBSIDIZING THE RICH

Federal assistance for urban renewal, as differentiated from housing assistance, was another indispensable part of the plan. Between 1957 and 1961, by which time virtually everything but land disposition was completed, Iron City received just short of $1,600,000 from the federal government under the urban redevelopment laws. This amounts to an additional subsidy of $400,000 per annum.

The federal housing assistance was at least $300,000 for each year between 1954 or 1955 and 1957. Together with the urban renewal allotments, the total was at least $700,000 during the years of peak planning activity, 1957–1962. This money is the key to the plan's success.

But to this we must also add the resources made available through various other federal agencies. Federal highway assistance added an undetermined amount for new arteries and, incidentally, forced Negroes to move from the western edge of Iron City. The Federal Housing Authority and the Veterans Administration help to finance the lovely homes being built in Area E . . .

TARNISHED LEGITIMACY

First, the case bears out what many people have been saying for two decades, that slum removal meant Negro removal. But it goes further. It supports the even more severe contention that the ultimate effects of federal urban policies have been profoundly conservative or separatist, so much so as to vitiate any plans for positive programs of integration through alteration of the physical layout of cities.

Second, it supports the general thesis that a policy of

delegation of powers without rule of law will ultimately come to ends profoundly different from those intended by the most libertarian and humanistic of sponsors. Moreover, it supports the unfashionable contention that some of the most cherished instruments of the liberal state may be positively evil—and that a criterion by which this evil can be predicted is the absence of public and explicit legislative standards by which to guide administrative conduct.

Third, the case of Iron City, especially the explicit nature of its racial policy, shows precisely how and why federal policy is ill equipped to govern the cities directly. The permissiveness of federal enabling legislation could do no greater harm to the social future of the cities than if harm were intended. The present disorder in the cities is explained properly by the failure of government and politics, rather than by the inferiority of Negro adjustment. The case demonstrates how national legitimacy can be tarnished to the degree that it is loaned to the cities for discretionary use and how the crisis of public authority is inevitable as long as a political process unguided by law climaxes in abuses such as those catalogued in Iron City. In sum, it helps show why liberal government based on current principles of delegation cannot achieve justice.

Every Negro in Iron City knew what was happening. Every Negro in Chicago and New York and Cleveland and Detroit knows the same about his city too. But since northern Negroes are not as docile, does that mean that federal imperium was used completely differently outside the South? True, planning authorities would never so deliberately pursue such obviously racial planning. It is also true that few social plans could be as relatively extensive or as successful as Iron City's. Nonetheless, it is undeniable that misuse of federal programs in ways indistinguishable in principle from the Iron City misuse has been widespread.

Martin Anderson, for example, estimated in 1964 that about two-thirds of all displacements resulting from urban renewal were Negro, Puerto Rican or some other minority group. In public housing the record is even more somber. First, because the pattern is even clearer, and second, because these projects stand as ever-present symbols of the acts of discrimination by which they were created.

A study by Bernard Weissbrourd for the Center for the Study of Democratic Institutions concluded that ". . . most cities have followed a deliberate program of segregation in public housing. . . ." Until July 1967, many housing administrators followed a rule of "free choice" allowing eligible tenants to wait indefinitely for an apartment, which allowed them also to decline a vacancy on racial grounds. Still more recently it was revealed that the Chicago Housing Authority, with the full knowledge of federal agencies, cleared all proposed public housing sites with that member of the Board of Aldermen whose ward would be affected. Thus, while the whole story cannot be told from official statistics, we may conclude what every urban Negro knows—Iron City is not unique.

SEPARATE BUT EQUAL?

According to HUD reports of 1965, only three of New York City's 69 public housing projects were officially listed as all nonwhite or all white in occupancy; but ten of Philadelphia's 40 projects were all nonwhite, and 21 of Chicago's 53, five of Detroit's 12, four of Cleveland's 14 and all of Dallas' ten projects were listed as either all nonwhite or all white. The rest of reality is hidden, because the Public Housing Administration defines an "integrated project" as one in which there are "white and more than one nonwhite, including at least one Negro family." Not only does this system of reporting make it impossible to determine the real number of truly integrated projects, it also serves to maintain local racial policies and prejudices.

The Civil Rights Act of 1964 was supposed to have put an end to such practices, but there is little evidence that it can or will improve the situation in public housing in particular or city housing in general. It was not until July of 1967 that the rule of "free choice" was replaced with a "rule of three," a plan whereby an applicant must take one of the first three available units or be dropped to the bottom of the eligible lists. All of this is undeniable testimony that the practices all along had constituted a "separate but equal" system of federally supported housing.

In June 1967, three years after the 1964 Civil Rights Act and after strenuous efforts by the Johnson Administration, two of Detroit's five segregated projects became "integrated" when one white family moved into each of two totally black projects. At the same time, at least 11 of New York's projects were classified as "integrated" when, in fact, fewer than 15 percent of the units were occupied by families of some race other than the race of the 85 percent majority in that project.

For 33 years the Federal Housing Authority has insured over $110 billion of mortgages to help whites escape, rather than build the city. This confession was made when the FHA instituted a *pilot* program to increase FHA support for housing finance in "economically unsound" areas. And it took the belated 1967 directive on public housing to get them to do that much. These remedial steps came five years after President Kennedy's famous "stroke of the pen" decision aimed at preventing discrimination in publicly supported housing and three years after the first applicable Civil Rights Act. Yet no such legislation or executive decisions can erase the stigma of second-class citizenship placed upon the residents of federal housing programs. Nor can more skillful administration of essentially separatist programs remove the culpability of federal participation in the American local government policy of apartheid. Rather, all of these efforts merely suggest that remedies and correctives are never going to help bad organic laws, because bad organic laws are, quite literally, congenitally defective . . . [T]hese programs will produce no lasting social benefit without the rule of law that states unmistakably what administrators can and cannot do, what is to be forbidden, and what is to be achieved. That is the moral of the Iron City story.

⟦ 6 ⟧

Racial Discrimination
in Apartment Rentals*

DANIEL A. JOHNSON, RICHARD J. PORTER,
AND PATRICIA L. MATELJAN

. . . The purposes of this study were threefold: (a) to evaluate the extent of racial housing discrimination in a large Southern California city, (b) to provide information for possible use in remedying the problem, and (c) to demonstrate the applicability of behavioral science techniques for detection and measurement of racial segregation due to racial discrimination.

METHOD

Subjects

The subject population consisted of managers of 25 apartment houses. Twenty-four of the apartments were managed by Caucasians, and one apartment was managed by a Negro. Approximately 70% of the subjects were females. There was no reason to believe that the subjects became aware of their participation in the study.

* Abridged from D. A. Johnson, R. J. Porter, and P. L. Mateljan, "Racial Discrimination in Apartment Rentals," *Journal of Applied Social Psychology*, 1971, *1*, 364–377. Reprinted by permission of V. H. Winston & Sons, Inc., and the authors.

Observers

The observers were comprised of six couples, with two male-female couples representing each ethnic group—Negro, Mexican-American, and Caucasian. The age range of the Negroes was 20 to 23 years, and that of the Mexican-Americans was 18 to 21. All were college students, articulate, spoke English fluently, and lived in nearby communities . . . The two male-female couples representing the Caucasian ethnic group consisted of the three experimenters plus an additional white female volunteer; their age range was 25 to 33.

All observers were well dressed in an informal manner; that is, all wore cleaned and pressed dress clothes, although no ties or jackets were worn. Males wore dress slacks, shirts, and shoes, while females wore dresses, or skirts and blouses, and shoes. Wedding rings were supplied to those females having none.

Each observer couple supplied their own automobile, which ranged in age from a 13 year old sedan (used by one of the Caucasian couples) to late model sedans.

Selection of Apartments

Twenty-four apartment buildings were initially selected for observation using the following criteria:

1. The apartment building was in the boundaries of the target city.

2. An advertisement in the previous day's newspaper indicated the availability of an apartment for rent.

3. Each apartment facility contained more than two individual apartments, as evidenced by indication of multiple apartments in the advertisement itself, or by telephone conversations with the manager on the day before the investigation.

Apparatus

Twelve numbered dots, each indicating the location of a selected apartment building, were placed onto each of six

street maps. Attached to each map was a list of the addresses
of these apartments in the order that they were to be visited
by the observer couple. Numbers by the dots also indicated
this order . . .

Procedure

During a briefing session just before the observation period,
each couple was instructed to assume the roles of a man and
wife with no children or pets. If asked by a subject, the male
observer was told to say that he worked in the general locale
at a middle economic level (e.g., engineer employed at a
particular company, assistant manager in a specific department store, etc.).

Each observer couple was told to obtain the following information from every subject: (a) whether or not there was
an apartment available for rent, (b) if none was now available, when a vacancy could be expected, (c) the amount of
rent for a two-bedroom, unfurnished apartment, and (d) the
amount of any miscellaneous fees (e.g., cleaning deposit, key
charges, etc.). The observers were also told not to fill out
any form that could be construed as a promise to rent.

Each couple was randomly assigned to one of two teams;
each team, made up of a couple from each of the three ethnic
groups was assigned to visit 12 of the selected apartment
buildings. The other team was assigned to the remaining 12
apartments.

A basic assumption underlying the order in which the observers visited the apartment houses was that for those apartments which advertised vacancies, there would be more
apartments available for rent in the morning following the
advertisement than in the afternoon. The rationale for this
assumption was that: (a) managers would not advertise a
vacancy unless one was available; and (b) during the course
of the day following the advertisement, there would be a
smaller number of current renters giving notice of vacating
any one apartment building than the number of prospective
renters applying for a vacancy at the same apartment. There-

fore, there should have been at least as many, and perhaps more, apartments available for rent in the early part of the day, than in the latter part.

A prospective renter would be told that no apartment was available to him for at least two reasons: (a) there was in reality no vacancy at that particular apartment, or (b) the manager did not care to have that particular applicant as a renter. The latter reason would indicate racial discrimination if it was only given to the minority applicants. Then in order to reduce, or eliminate, the former reason (no vacancy) for minority groups being told no apartments were available, the minority couples visited the apartments only in the morning hours, when a maximum number of apartments should have been available. In addition, the Caucasians visited the apartments only in the afternoon of the same day. In this way, if the reason, "no vacancy," was the sole determinate of whether an observer couple was told an apartment was or was not available, the minority couples should have had as many, or more, apartments available to them than the Caucasian couples. Conversely, if more apartments were available to Caucasian couples than to the minority couples, racial discrimination may have been the prime cause. This particular order in apartment visiting produced a conservative test for racial discrimination.

The minority observers started visiting their assigned apartment buildings at the same time (approximately 9:30 A.M.) on a Saturday. The schedule for visiting apartments was established in such a way that each apartment was visited by a Mexican-American couple and a Negro couple, with a 2 hour separation between visits. Half of the apartments were visited in the order, Mexican-American, Negro; the remaining apartments in the reverse order. Observers were allowed 20 minutes to visit the apartment building, return to their cars, record the data, and travel to the next assigned apartment.

In the case when a "no vacancy" sign was displayed, or when the manager was not on the premises, the observers called the coordination office, reported this fact, and received the location of a nearby apartment building, the address of which was drawn from the advertising section of the local phone book. The standby address was relayed to the second observer couple when they called in at a prearranged time.

After completing the route, each minority couple was debriefed. Debriefing consisted of an experimenter reviewing each record sheet entry with the observer couple in order to eliminate any ambiguities.

In the afternoon of the same day, a Caucasian observer couple visited every apartment at which a subject had been interviewed by a minority couple. The Caucasian couple asked for the same information asked for by the minority couples.

In every case, the subject interviewed was found in the "office" building or in an apartment indicated as the "manager's apartment." The subject questioned was the person who was at the office desk or who answered the door to the manager's apartment. Married couples many times manage an apartment complex; in the present study all three observer couples interviewed the same subject at 68% of the apartment buildings. In some instances both the man and wife manager team were interviewed by an observer couple, while a follow-up couple interviewed only one spouse of the team.

The situation arose where one minority couple interviewed a couple at a scheduled apartment and the second minority couple failed to find the manager on the premises. This latter couple was then given the address of, and visited, a standby apartment. Later the Caucasian couple interviewed subjects at both apartments, thus resulting in 25 (rather than the scheduled 24) total number of apartments visited in this study. One team visited 13 apartments, the other team 12.

Because of "no vacancy" signs and managers not on the premises, subjects at only 15 apartment houses were interviewed by all three observer couples. Ten other apartment houses were visited by two couples only. The number of apartments visited by a Negro couple and Mexican-American couple only was two; three apartments were visited by only Negro and Caucasian observer couples; and the number visited by Mexican-American and Caucasian couples only was five. Thus, Negro observers interviewed subjects at 20 apartments; Mexican-Americans successfully visited 22 apartments; while Caucasians interviewed subjects at 23 apartments.

Criteria of Discrimination

Racial discrimination could be evidenced by differential treatment according to race in terms of apartment availability, rental costs, or amount of miscellaneous fees.

Availability discrimination. This was judged to occur if either of the two following criteria were met:

1. A subject told one or two observers that an apartment was available, but denied such availability to the remaining couple(s).

2. A subject gave one or two couples a date of apartment availability more than one-half week later than he gave to the other couple(s).

Rental costs. Discrimination was judged to occur if one or two couples were quoted rents higher than those quoted at the same apartment to the other observer couple(s) for an apartment of the same size.

Miscellaneous fees. If the cumulative fees (other than rent) quoted to an observer couple were higher than those quoted to the other couple(s), the former couple was judged to have been discriminated against.

RESULTS

Availability Discrimination

At the 15 apartments visited by all three observer couples of a team, there were more apartments available to the Caucasians than to the minority couples combined ($p < .05$) (see Table 1).

TABLE 1.   *Comparison of Number of Apartments Available to Caucasian and Minority Observer Couples at 15 Apartments Visited by Three Observer Couples*

NUMBER OF APARTMENTS	CAUCASIANS	MINORITY COUPLES (COMBINED)
Available	12	13
Not available	3	17

Note. $-\chi^2 = 4.06$; $p < .05$.

Examination of the 20 apartments visited by both Mexican-Americans and Caucasians revealed that there were fewer apartments available to the Mexican-American couples than to the Caucasian couples ($p = .05$) (see Table 2). Similar results were found at the 18 apartments visited by both Negro and Caucasian couples ($p < .02$) (see Table 3). However, there was no reliable difference between Negroes and Mexi-

TABLE 2.   *Comparison of Number of Apartments Available to Caucasian and Mexican-American Observer Couples at 20 Apartments Visited by Both*

NUMBER OF APARTMENTS	CAUCASIANS	MEXICAN-AMERICANS
Available	16	9
Not available	4	11

Note. $-\chi^2 = 3.84$; $p = .05$.

TABLE 3.   *Comparison of Number of Apartments Available to Caucasian and Negro Observer Couples at 18 Apartments Visited by Both*

NUMBER OF APARTMENTS	CAUCASIANS	NEGRO
Available	14	6
Not available	4	12

Note. $-\chi^2 = 5.51$; $p < .02$.

can-Americans in terms of availability at the 17 apartments visited by both.

Of the 25 apartments visited, four managers made no apartments available to any of the observers who visited them, presumably because no vacancies existed. One additional manager made an apartment available to the first visiting minority couple, but not to the second minority couple or to the follow-up Caucasian couple; while the vacancy was probably filled between the first and second observers' visits, this was conjecture, and the latter two couples were judged to have been discriminated against according to the established criteria.

Negroes were discriminated against 9 times out of the 20 apartments visited (45%); for Mexican-Americans and Caucasians the percentage of times discriminated against were 36% and 4% respectively. In comparing the two teams, it is apparent that no significant differences existed between like ethnic groups. This suggests that there probably was no large difference between couples of the same race in terms of demeanor when interviewing the subjects.

Apartment Rental Costs

Negroes were quoted rents higher than one or both of the other groups five times. Mexican-Americans and Caucasians were each quoted rents higher than one or both of the other groups twice. No Caucasian couple was ever given a rent quotation higher than that given a Negro, although Negroes were given quotations higher than Caucasians four times (binomial test, 1 tail, $p = .0625$). No other comparisons approached significance. The five high quotes given to Negroes ranged from $5 to $35 with a mean of $12 for each high quote. The Mexican-Americans were given two high quotes of $5 and $10, while Caucasians were given two high quotes of $3 and $5.

Miscellaneous Fees

Negroes were quoted five miscellaneous fees higher than those quoted to Caucasians, though no Caucasian couple was quoted a miscellaneous fee higher than the fee quoted to the Negro couple (binomial test, 1 tail, $p = .031$). No other comparisons were significant. Negroes were quoted high fees ranging from $5 to $50, with a mean of $20.83, over the fees quoted to one or both of the other ethnic groups. Mexican-Americans were quoted five high fees, ranging from $5 to $100, with a mean of $58, over those quoted to the other groups. Caucasians were quoted two fees that were $5 and $20 higher than quoted to one or both of the minority groups. The differences within ethnic groups across teams were not significant.

Combined Discrimination

In some instances, subjects used more than one of the three forms of discrimination described above. Nine subjects used two forms against some observer couples, while one subject used all three forms against one Negro couple. Of the 15 comparisons where all three observers were successful in interviewing a single subject only two subjects showed no discrimination. Of the 10 remaining comparisons, four of the subjects showed no discrimination. That is, of the 25 apartment managers visited 19 (76%) showed some discrimination. When all three forms of discrimination were considered, it was found that Negroes were discriminated against by 15 of the 20 subjects that they visited, Mexican-Americans were discriminated against by 11 of the 22 subjects visited, while Caucasians were discriminated against by 4 of the 23 subjects that they visited.

DISCUSSION

The results of this study indicate that the complaint, registered by many minority group members, of considerable racial discrimination in obtaining living accommodations, is not without basis. Judging from the present study, a Negro couple can expect to be discriminated against in a majority of apartment houses visited, while a Mexican-American may expect some type of discrimination in perhaps as high as 50% of the apartments visited.

The Justice Department of the U.S. government has been successful in prosecuting housing discrimination suits under the 1968 Fair Housing Act. In one recent suit, covering 8000 apartment units in the Los Angeles area, some novel steps against racial bias were taken.

These steps required that the operators: (a) include non-whites as well as whites in advertising that depicts persons; and (b) place at least one-third of their advertising for apartments with less than 10% Negro occupancy in a predominately Negro newspaper. Since most apartment house owners are probably aware that racial discrimination is illegal this could be a possible reason why the minority observer couples in this study had less success in interviewing managers, as indicated by the smaller number of apartments visited by those groups. It is possible that some managers refused to open the door to a minority couple, thereby eliminating the possibility of any legal repercussions that could occur from not renting available apartments to minority groups . . .

A separate check of the accuracy of information recording by the observers should perhaps be carried out in the future by having the observers interview a confederate of the experimenters, who would be acting as an apartment manager. Then the accuracy of the observer could be determined and in addition, a posttest interview with the manager could reveal any possible differences between the observers in terms of behavior during the interview.

The probability of experimenter bias in future studies should be decreased by insuring that the Caucasian and minority couples are not aware of the true purpose of the study. The use of separate facilities for the pretest briefing, and adequate cover stories, could keep the observers unaware of their part in a racial discrimination study.

Managers may have lowered the rental and/or miscellaneous fees during the course of the day, accounting for some apparent economics discrimination. To control for this possibility in the future, Caucasian couples should visit each apartment both before and after the minority couples. This will allow a check on the stability of economic costs.

The difference in ages between the minority couples (mean = 21.9 years) and Caucasians (mean = 28.2 years) may have contributed in part to the discrimination found in this study. If one makes the assumption that some apartment managers would discourage prospective renters in their early 20s but not those in their late 20s, then the relationship between race and discrimination could be spurious. It is not believed, however, that this factor alone could account for the magnitude of discrimination found. It definitely would not account for the apparently greater discrimination practiced against Negroes than against Mexican-Americans, since the Negroes were 2 years older on the average than the Mexican-Americans . . .

A review of the study was prominently placed in a widely read newspaper in the Southern California area. Interest in the results of this study was expressed by, among others, the California State Attorney General's Office, the U.S. Justice Department, and the Federal Bureau of Investigation. These organizations have indicated that, since both California and federal civil rights laws may have been broken, more intensive legal investigations should be carried out. An additional effect has been the interest expressed by the local Apartment House Owners Association. This group has initiated recent meetings dealing with discrimination, the purpose of which was to help the local owners and managers overcome their reluctance to renting apartments to minority groups. While no follow-up study has yet been initiated, it is possible that publicizing in the mass media the results of a study such as the present one, which attempted only to measure discriminatory behavior, may act as an agent of change of that very behavior.

That is, if an apartment manager was made aware that several apartments in the community had been evaluated and were found to be discriminating along racial lines, then he

or she may infer that this same event could recur. If the
manager had engaged in racial discrimination, it is possible
that the threat of legal repercussions, made possible following detection, might act to inhibit further racial discrimination. Future research should attempt to determine if the mere
act of measuring discrimination, and publishing the results,
can cause a significant reduction in racial discrimination, or
whether more positive steps on the part of social scientists
and public officials are needed to gain that result.

(7)

Are the Housing Patterns of Blacks
Like Those of Immigrants?*

KARL E. AND ALMA F. TAEUBER

The large-scale migration of Negroes to Northern cities
began during the first World War. In a very real sense
Negroes served as a native-born substitute to fill in the labor
gap created by the cessation of large-scale immigration from
abroad, at first due to the war, and then as a result of newly
imposed restrictions on immigration. Like the immigrants
from abroad, the Negro migrants from the South moved to
urban industrial centers where they filled the lowest occupational niches and rapidly developed a highly segregated pattern of residence.

Viewing the obvious analogies between the Northern urban

* Karl E. Taeuber and Alma F. Taeuber, "Is the Negro an Immigrant
Group?" *Integrated Education*, June 1963, *1*, 25–28. Reprinted by permission of the publisher and authors.

Negro populations and the European immigrant populations which preceded them, some sociologists have concluded that the Negroes will undergo a similar process of "assimilation," and that it is only a matter of time until social and economic progress is translated into their residential dispersion. Other sociologists believe that the Negroes in Northern cities are not following the immigrant pattern of socio-economic advancement and residential dispersion, but rather that the second-generation urban Negroes are occupying the same relative position in the society as did their parents.

The question of whether or not a Northern urban Negro population can fruitfully be viewed as an immigrant population, comparable to the immigrant populations of earlier decades with respect to the nature and speed of assimilation, is the underlying theme in our consideration of recent trends in race and ethnic segregation in Chicago. In historical perspective, it appears that the economic status of immigrant groups went hand in hand with decreasing residential segregation. In contrast, Negro residential segregation from whites has increased steadily over past decades until it has reached universally high levels in cities throughout the United States, despite significant advances in the socio-economic status of Negroes.

The pattern of decreasing residential concentration of immigrant groups and increasing residential concentration of Negroes is not what would have been expected from the fact that many nationality groups worked hard at maintaining the ethnic colonies, whereas most of the major Negro organizations strive for residential dispersal. Furthermore, there were declines in the residential concentration of the immigrant groups almost from the initial formation of the ethnic colonies, and this dispersion was going on during the periods of rapid increase in immigrant populations. These observations tend to discredit the argument that a major barrier to residential dispersion of the Negro population in Chicago is its continuing rapid increase. However, the size of the Negro population and the magnitude of its annual increase are larger than for any single ethnic group in the past, and comparisons with smaller groups are not completely convincing. That rapid increase of Negro population does not necessarily lead to increasing residential segregation, however, has been demonstrated in another phase of our research. Considering all cities with large Negro populations, there was no definite relationship between increase in Negro population and change in the value of a segregation index. Indeed, during the 1950–60 decade, there appeared to be some relationship in the opposite direction.

It has been suggested that considerable time is required for Negroes to make the transition from a "primitive folk culture" to "urbanism as a way of life." Several types of data indicate that large and increasing proportions of the Negro urban population are city-born and raised. For instance, there is a rapidly decreasing color differential in the percentage of the Chicago population born in the state of Illinois. In 1960, 44 per cent of the native-born nonwhite residents of Chicago were born in Illinois, as contrasted to 66 per cent of the white population. National estimates for 1958 showed that of all males age 45–64 living in metropolitan places of 500,000 or more population, 65 per cent of the nonwhites as compared to 77 per cent of the whites had lived in this size of city for 20 years or longer. Estimates of the components of growth of the nonwhite population of Chicago indicate that between 1950 and 1960 natural increase was as important as net immigration, and that natural increase will in the future account for rapidly increasing proportions of the growth of nonwhite population.

That many of the "first generation" Negro migrants to Northern cities have lived there for 20 years and more and that in the younger adult ages there are sizable numbers of "second generation" urban Negroes suggests to us that there has been ample time for whatever adjustments to urban living may be necessary, at least for large proportions of the Negro population. It is also clear that if Northern Negroes remain inadequately educated for urban living and fail to participate fully in the urban economy, the "primitive folk culture" of the South can less and less be assigned responsibility, and Northern cities will be suffering from the neglect of their own human resources.

The "visibility" of Negroes due to skin color and other features which make the large majority of 2nd, 3rd, and later generation descendants readily identifiable as Negroes is often cited as a basic factor in explaining the distinctive position of Negroes in our society. It is exceedingly difficult to assess the significance of visibility. For instance, there is no other group which is strictly comparable to Negroes regarding every factor except visibility. It is not completely irrelevant, however, to note that nonwhite skin color, by itself, is not an insurmountable handicap in our society. The socioeconomic status of the Japanese population of Chicago in 1950 substantially exceeded that of the Negro population, and their residential segregation from whites, although high, was considerably lower than that between Negroes and whites. Unfortunately there are no trend data available on the characteristics of the Japanese in Chicago. A more appropriate Japanese population for comparison, however, is the much larger one in the San Francisco area. A recent study there affirmed that "ethnic colonies of Japanese are gone or rapidly going," and documented their rapid socio-economic advance.

In the traditional immigrant pattern, the more recent immigrants displaced the older groups at the bottom socioeconomic levels. How do the Negroes compare with the other "newer" immigrant groups, the Mexicans and the Puerto Ricans? The limited data now available suggest that the Negroes may soon be left alone at the bottom of the social and economic scale. The "newer" groups were in 1950 of very low status compared to the other immigrant groups, and their residential segregation from the native whites of native parentage was the highest of all the immigrant groups. For 1960, census data are available showing the distribution within Chicago of persons from those born in the U.S. of Puerto Rico parentage. Comparison between the residential patterns of the first generation and the second generation indicate that residential dispersion was already begun for the Puerto

Ricans. This difference actually understates the amount of dispersion, since the second generation consists in large proportion of children still living with their first generation parents.

Selected socio-economic measures for the Puerto Rican and the nonwhite populations of the city of Chicago in 1960 show that on every measure, the Puerto Rican population is less well off—it is less educated, of lower income, more crowded, less likely to be home-owners, less well-housed, and living in older buildings. Yet, Puerto Ricans are significantly less segregated than Negroes.

Thus far we have been making comparisons between Negroes and immigrant groups. With respect to the relationship between socio-economic status and residential segregation, it is appropriate to pursue a more direct approach. Since Negroes are disproportionately represented in low status groups, it might be argued that on this basis alone we would expect some segregation between whites and Negroes. To the extent that this is the case, future economic advances on the part of the Negro population should be translated into lowered residential segregation. In 1950, the white-nonwhite residential segregation index expected on the basis of income was 11, compared to the actual segregation index of 79. (The higher the index, the greater the degree of segregation.) Thus in 1950 income differentials can account for 11/79, or 14 per cent, of the observed racial segregation. In 1960, the expected segregation index was 10 and the actual 83, so that income differentials can account for only 12 per cent of the observed racial segregation.

It is not Negroes' inability to pay for housing that accounts for their residential segregation. In fact, in Chicago in 1960 Negroes paid as much as whites for housing, regardless of their lower incomes. Median rents for both groups were $88, but Negroes obtained much poorer housing for their money. To a very real extent, there exists a separate housing market for Negroes in Chicago, so that their economic status cannot be used except in exceptional circumstances to obtain unsegregated housing. Regardless of their assimilation to urban living and their advancing economic position, therefore, Negroes have been unable to achieve the residential dispersion undergone by the second and third generation immigrant groups.

We find ourselves in general agreement with the view that it is misleading to regard Negroes as another immigrant group. Even adopting a very simple formulation of assimilation as involving socio-economic advancement and residential dispersion, we do not think that data for Negroes can be interpreted as fitting the pattern. The second generation persons from several countries, in fact, are of higher socioeconomic status than the total native whites of native parentage. Relatively few Negroes in Chicago have white collar jobs or have incomes above the median level for whites and yet there are large numbers of adult Negroes who were born in the city. Basic differences between the Negroes and the immigrant groups seem to us implicit in the failure of residential desegregation to occur for Negroes, while it has continued to take place for the immigrant groups.

In view of the fundamental impact of residential segregation on extra-legal segregation of schools, hospitals, parks, stores, and numerous other facilities, the failure of residential dispersion to occur strikes us as an especially serious social problem. Although socio-economic advance and residential dispersion occurred simultaneously for the various immigrant groups, a causal relationship cannot be assigned. Nevertheless, it is apparent that the continued residential segregation of the Negro population will act as an impediment to the continued "assimilation" of Negroes into full and equal participation in the economy and the society at large.

⟦ 8 ⟧

Black and White Attitudes
Toward Race and Housing*

THOMAS F. PETTIGREW

The attitudes of white Americans on race and housing have changed fundamentally over the past three decades. This clear trend emerges regardless of the type of question asked or the survey agency conducting the study (Table 1). Coupled with survey data concerning discrimination in other realms, these results indicate that a basic shift toward favoring black rights evolved between World War II and the mid-1950's. This shift was fueled in all probability by economic prosperity over these years together with the resounding decision of the U.S. Supreme Court in 1954 against *de jure* segregation of public schools. In any event, the race and housing opinions of white Americans appear to have remained relatively stable into the sixties, only to become more pro-desegregation between 1963 and 1965 (see items b, c, d, n, o of Table 1). This was the fateful period of the assassination of President John Kennedy followed by the passage of the sweeping Civil Rights Act of 1964.

The much publicized "white backlash" of the mid- and late-1960's did not, in fact, materialize in survey data in any manner similar to its lurid descriptions in the mass media of the period (Pettigrew, 1971). Neither is it to be noted in the

* Abridged from T. F. Pettigrew, "Attitudes on Race and Housing: A Social Psychological View." In A. H. Hawley and V. P. Rock, *Segregation in Residential Areas*. Washington, D.C.: National Academy of Sciences, 1973; pp. 21–84. Reprinted with permission of the publisher.

data shown in Table 1, except possibly for the 1966 results
of item d; rather, these and other opinion findings covering
this period indicate that possibly some polarization occurred
with whites of many different persuasions adopting stronger
positions in the direction they already leaned, but that the
overall effect led to little change in racial views similar to the
1958–1963 period. Indeed, the most recent results on items a
and f suggest the possible resumption of the trend since 1968,
the year of the murder of Dr. King and the issuance of the
Kerner Commission Report.

Within these broad trends, Table 1 enables us to obtain a

TABLE 1.   *White American Attitudes Toward Race and Housing**

a.   If a Negro, with just as much income and education as you
have, moved into your block, would it make any difference to
you?
      Survey Agency: NORC

DATE	WHITE SAMPLE	PERCENTAGE OF AGREEMENT
		Yes, make a difference
June 1942	National	62
June 1956	National	46
May 1963	National	39
Dec 1963	National	35
May 1964	National	36
June 1965	National	32
Apr 1968	National	21

b.   If colored people came to live next door, would you move?
      Survey Agency: AIPO, Gallup

DATE	WHITE SAMPLE	PERCENTAGE OF AGREEMENT
		Yes, definitely, or might move
Oct 1958	National	46
June 1963	National	45
May 1965	National	35
July 1966	National	34
Aug 1967	National	35

TABLE 1.   (*Continued*)

c. Would you move if colored people came to live in great numbers in your neighborhood?
    Survey Agency: AIPO, Gallup

DATE	WHITE SAMPLE	PERCENTAGE OF AGREEMENT
		Yes, definitely, or might move
Sept 1958	National	77
May 1963	National	78
May 1965	National	69
July 1966	National	70
Aug 1967	National	71

d. . . . tell me if you personally would or would not object to: Having a Negro family as your next door neighbor.
    Survey Agency: Harris

DATE	WHITE SAMPLE	PERCENTAGE OF AGREEMENT
		Would object
Aug 1963	National	55
Oct 1963	National	51
Oct 1965	National	37
Aug 1966	National	51

e. Do you think [that] (i) there should be laws compelling Negroes to live in certain districts; or (ii) there should be an unwritten understanding, backed up by social pressure, to keep Negroes out of the neighborhood where white people live; or (iii) Negroes should be allowed to live wherever they want to live, and there should be no laws or social pressure to keep them from it?
    Survey Agency: Roper

DATE	WHITE SAMPLE	PERCENTAGE OF AGREEMENT		
		Alternatives		
		(i)	(ii)	(iii)
1939	National	41	42	13

f. White people have a right to keep Negroes out of their neigh-
    borhoods if they want to, and Negroes should respect that right.
        Survey Agency: NORC

DATE	WHITE SAMPLE	PERCENTAGE OF AGREEMENT
		Agree that whites have right to exclude
Dec 1963	National	56
Apr 1968	National	54
Apr 1970	National	43

g. Which of these statements would you agree with: (i) white
    people have a right to keep Negroes out of their neighborhoods
    if they want to; (ii) Negroes have a right to live wherever they
    can afford to, just like white people.
        Survey Agency: Survey Research Center

DATE	WHITE SAMPLE	PERCENTAGE OF AGREEMENT	
Sept–Oct 1964	National[a]	Alternatives	
		(i)	(ii)
		Strongly	*Strongly*
		24	28
		Not strongly	*Not strongly*
		6	22
		Alternative	
Jan–March 1968	15 key central cities[b]	(i)	(ii)
		30	62

h. Negroes are not ready to live in better neighborhoods.
        Survey Agency: Harris

DATE	WHITE SAMPLE	PERCENTAGE OF AGREEMENT
		Agree
July 1963	National	61

TABLE 1.   (*Continued*)

i. Would you favor a Federal law forbidding discrimination in housing against Negroes?
   Survey Agency: Harris

DATE	WHITE SAMPLE	PERCENTAGE OF AGREEMENT
		Oppose law
Oct 1963	National	56
Aug 1966	National	52
Oct 1966	National	51
June 1967	National	63

j. Do you favor or oppose laws to prevent discrimination against Negroes in . . .
   Survey Agency: Survey Research Center

DATE	WHITE SAMPLE	PERCENTAGE OF AGREEMENT		
Jan–March 1968	15 key central cities[b]			
		Favor	*Oppose*	*Don't know*
job hiring and promotion		67	23	10
buying or renting houses and apartments		40	51	9

k. In your own words, what is "open housing"—what does this term mean? [If answers correctly] Would you like to see Congress pass an "open housing" bill or reject it?
   Survey Agency: AIPO, Gallup

DATE	WHITE SAMPLE	PERCENTAGE OF AGREEMENT		
		Answers correctly		
Apr 1967	National	59		
		Pass	*Reject*	*No opinion*
		35	54	11

l. Would you be willing to live in the same general neighborhood with members of the other race?
   Survey Agency: Gaffin

DATE	WHITE SAMPLE	PERCENTAGE OF AGREEMENT		
		Yes	*No*	*No opinion*
May 1958	National[c]	52	44	4

m. Would it make any difference to you if a Negro family moved in next door to you?
Survey Agency: NORC

DATE	WHITE SAMPLE	PERCENTAGE OF AGREEMENT		
				Qualified or
		Yes	*No*	*no opinion*
May 1944	National	69	22	9

n. Would you be willing to live next door to members of the other race?
Survey Agency: Gaffin

DATE	WHITE SAMPLE	PERCENTAGE OF AGREEMENT		
		Yes	*No*	*No opinion*
May 1958	National°	41	53	6

o. Suppose a Negro family moved next door to you. What would you do?
Survey Agency: AIPO, Gallup

DATE	WHITE SAMPLE	PERCENTAGE OF AGREEMENT	
		Would dislike, move, or wouldn't socialize	*Depends on family*
June 1965	National	24	9

p. As far as your own personal feelings go, would you be personally concerned or not if a Negro neighbor moved in next door?
Survey Agency: Harris

DATE	WHITE SAMPLE	PERCENTAGE OF AGREEMENT
		Concerned
Oct 1966	National	56

q. Now I want to give you a list of groups and institutions. Do you think [real estate companies] have tended to help Negroes or have tended more to keep Negroes down?
Survey Agency: Harris

TABLE 1. (*Continued*)

DATE	WHITE SAMPLE	PERCENTAGE OF AGREEMENT		
		Helping	*Keeping down*	*Not sure*
Aug 1963	National	22	44	34
Aug 1966	National	30	34	36

r. Now on each of the following I'd like to ask you, if you were in the same position as Negroes, would you think it justified or not to protest against discrimination in:
Survey Agency: Harris

DATE	WHITE SAMPLE	PERCENTAGE OF AGREEMENT		
		Justified	*Not justified*	*Not sure*
Aug 1966	National			
jobs		59	30	11
education		60	30	10
housing		49	36	15

s. Do you think that in [central city] many, some, or only a few Negroes miss out on good housing because white owners won't rent or sell to them?
Survey Agency: Survey Research Center

DATE	WHITE SAMPLE	PERCENTAGE OF AGREEMENT		
		Many	*Some*	*Few or none*
Jan–March 1968	15 key central cities[b]	38	30	26

t. On the average, Negroes in [central city] have worse jobs, education, and housing than white people. Do you think this is due mainly to Negroes having been discriminated against, or mainly due to something about Negroes themselves?
Survey Agency: Survey Research Center

DATE	WHITE SAMPLE	PERCENTAGE OF AGREEMENT		
		Discrimination	*Themselves*	*Both*
Jan–March 1968	15 key central cities[b]	19	56	19

u. If a Negro family with about the same income and education as you moved next door to you, would you mind it a lot, a little, or not at all?

Survey Agency: Survey Research Center

DATE	WHITE SAMPLE	PERCENTAGE OF AGREEMENT		
		Mind		
		A lot	*A little*	*Not at all*
Jan–March 1968	15 key central cities[b]	19	25	49

v. Suppose there are 100 white families in a neighborhood. One white family moves out and a Negro family moves in. Do you think it would be a good idea to have some limit on the number of Negro families that move there, or to let as many move there as want to?

Survey Agency: Survey Research Center

DATE	WHITE SAMPLE	PERCENTAGE OF AGREEMENT		
		Some limit	*No limit*	*Don't know*
Jan–March 1968	15 key central cities[c]	48	40	12

[a] Data adjusted slightly from those published by Survey Research Center to correct for inclusion of nonwhites in sample.

[b] The fifteen cities sampled include, with few exceptions (e.g., Los Angeles and Dayton, Ohio), all of the larger cities outside of the South with significant black populations: Baltimore, Boston, Chicago, Cincinnati, Cleveland, Detroit, Gary, Milwaukee, Newark, New York City (Brooklyn only), Philadelphia, Pittsburgh, San Francisco, St. Louis, and Washington, D.C.

[c] Gaffin provided data by regions only; thus, the national data shown represent an extrapolation based on the fact that southern respondents represent roughly one fourth of the nation's white adults.

*SOURCES: Schwartz (1967), Erskine (1967, pp. 482–498), Brink & Harris (1967), Sheatsley (1966, pp. 303–324), Campbell & Schuman (1968, pp. 1–67).

sense of the order of magnitude of present white opposition to open housing. About a fourth of the nation's white adults object to a Negro family of the same social class as themselves moving into their block (item a), and this proportion rises to over two fifths if the Negro family were to move into a house immediately next door (items d, o, p, u). Indeed, one third claim that if Negroes of unspecified class background moved next door, they would move (item b). And the fear of "great numbers" of black families coming to the neighborhood causes seven in ten to report that they would move, a percentage that has declined only slightly in recent years (item c, 77 percent in 1958 and 71 percent in 1967). In key central cities of the North and West, this fear leads half of the white respondents to favor limits being placed on the number of Negro families who could come to a single, previously white neighborhood (item v).

Most white Americans are well aware that racial discrimination in housing exists. Two thirds of the urban northern respondents realize that at least "some Negroes miss out on good housing" because of discrimination (item s). And in a list of 14 white institutions, ranging from "Congress" and "local government" to "retail stores" and "labor unions," "real estate companies" comprise the *only* institution rated by whites in 1966 as "keeping Negroes down" more than "helping Negroes" (item q). Moreover, half the whites believe black protest against housing discrimination to be "justified," though this proportion is 10 percent below that thinking protests against job and education discrimination are justified (item r). Yet only a minority of whites favored laws against housing discrimination prior to the passage of such federal legislation in 1968 (items i, j, k). In the urban northern results (item j), while only 40 percent favored antidiscrimination legislation for housing, two thirds did so for employment. This huge difference would seem to point to a joint function of how employment and housing differ in racial opinions (also in item r) as well as the *fait accompli* effect. In 1968, at the time of this 15 city survey, federal legislation against job discrimination was 4 years old and gaining increasing acceptance, but such legislation for housing was under debate at that point with prestigious national figures opposing it with such seemingly legitimate and nonracial arguments as its constitutionality.

A conflict in two widely held beliefs undergird these white attitudes on race and housing. On the one hand, many whites feel strongly that they should have the right to restrict Negroes from their areas (items e, f, g). On the other hand, a rapidly growing number of whites believe that Negroes as American citizens have a right to live where they wish and can afford (items e, g). What is more, many of the same white Americans hold *both* of these beliefs. One study in a New Jersey suburb set out to confront directly its middle-class survey respondents with this conflict, and found both the conflict and similar means of handling it to be widespread (Friedrichs, 1959). Often white Americans assume that their values are different from those of Negroes: 61 percent in 1963 thought "Negroes are not ready to live in better neighborhoods" (item h), and 75 percent of urban Northerners in 1968 believed that Negroes have "worse jobs, education, and housing than white people" at least in part because of "something about Negroes themselves" (item t).[1]

The millennium, then, has not arrived. Despite steady erosion of white attitudinal resistance to interracial residential patterns over the past generation, there remains an enormous degree of fear, reluctance, and downright opposition. Part of this resistance stems from not having experienced interracial living, for attitudes often follow behavior rather than precede it.[2] Table 2 reveals how few white respondents in 1965 report ever having lived on a block together with a Negro family. Observe that while there is a regional difference there is little or no difference by education.

A closer look at white attitudes on interracial housing can be achieved by seeing how they range across geographic and demographic categories. Two of the most important controls are region and education. Whites in the South are consistently more opposed to housing desegregation than other whites. This fact, of course, is consistent both with other racial at-

TABLE 2.   *Percentages of Whites with Experience on Interracial Blocks, 1965[a]*

Negro Family Lived on Same Block	REGION AND EDUCATION (%)					
	South			North		
	Grade School	High School	College	Grade School	High School	College
Yes, live there now	6	3	5	15	10	15
Yes, used to	21	27	14	24	25	22
No, never	73	70	81	61	65	63

[a] Adapted from Schwartz (1967, p. 61).

titudes of southern whites and with the greater degree of residential segregation in the urban South.[3] More surprising, however, is the relationship with education. As Figure 1 illustrates, there was little or no association between education

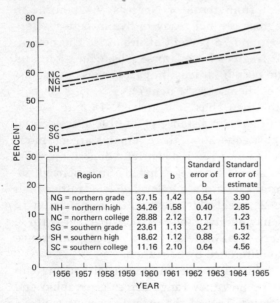

FIGURE 1.   *Least squares trend lines by region and education in percent who would not mind if Negro with same education and income moved on same block, 1956–1965. Adapted from Schwartz (1967, p. 56).*

and housing opinions in 1956, especially in the North. But the shift in attitudes by 1965 had created significant differences between the college-educated in both regions and other whites, though high-school-trained Southerners remained the most opposed to accepting equal status Negroes on their block. In short, while Figure 1 shows that all six regional and educational groups participated in the increasing favorable white attitudes toward interracial living from 1956 to 1965, the college-educated throughout the country disproportionately contributed to the shift.

Campbell and Schuman (1968, p. 35) unravel this phenomenon in their 1968 study of 15 northern cities by relating both age and education to two measures of white racial attitudes concerning housing. Figure 2 supplies the results for white males. Witness the virtually flat education percentage line for those 40 years or older on both graphs. By contrast, see the remarkably more favorable opinions on both graphs of those under 40 who had attended at least a few years of college . . . Schools at all levels through World War II accepted the prevailing culture in race relations and possessed little or no potential for changing the racial opinions of their products . . . But the colleges appear to have changed as noted by Campbell and Schuman (1968, p. 35):

Since World War II those white students who have gone on to college have evidently been exposed to influences which have moved their attitudes away from the traditional pattern in the directions we have observed. We cannot say whether this resulted from specific instruction regarding questions of race or from a general atmosphere of opinion in the college community but it is clear that a sizable proportion of these postwar generation college students were affected.

In other words, age seems to be critical only for the college-educated as a predictor of racial housing attitudes. Even sex is not a critical predictor. In general, white women are only slightly less in favor of neighborhood integration than white men. Similarly, Bradburn and his colleagues could find *no* consistent relation between the belief that whites have the right to keep Negroes out of their neighborhood (item f of

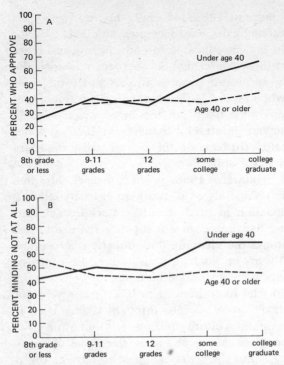

FIGURE 2.   *Relation of racial housing attitudes to educational levels among white men. A: "How about laws to prevent discrimination against Negroes in buying or renting houses and apartments? Do you favor such laws?" B: "If a Negro family with about the same income and education as you moved in next door to you, would you mind a lot, a little, or not at all?" From Campbell & Schuman (1968, p. 35).*

Table 1) and such variables as central city versus suburbs, size of metropolitan area, and ownership (Bradburn *et al.*, 1970). There was some evidence to suggest that renters and those living in "open neighborhoods," with two or more Negro families but less than 1 percent Negro, were more likely to disagree with the right of whites to exclude Negroes (Bradburn *et al.*, 1970) . . .

In sum, significant shifts in white American opinions on racial residential mixing have come about over the past generation. Despite the growing percentage of those who favor open desegregated housing, however, there remains a large and critical minority who oppose it. A number of related phenomena seem to underlie this pattern. First, the shift in opinion, while reflected in all regional and educational groups, is particularly strong among those who have received their college training since World War II. Second, this leaves particularly intense opposition to interracial neighborhoods among many white Southerners, relatively homogeneous groups of ethnic Northerners, the old, and the poorly educated. Third, opposition to black neighbors is often just one part of a conflict with national and religious values of fair play and equal opportunity for all. On the abstract level of what is "right," an overwhelming number of white Americans believe a black family should be able to live where it wishes and can afford. But, in the face of their own block and the house next door, many of these same whites shift ground and believe whites have the right to exclude blacks. It is more than a simple fear of lowered property values that motivates this threatened response on the concrete level. Many white Americans assume "blacks aren't ready yet," that they are typically of a different and lower social class . . . Few whites have ever experienced interracial neighborhoods in their past, and this adds to their unease and fear.

BLACK ATTITUDES

Table 3 summarizes a variety of survey findings concerned with black attitudes. When presented with a meaningful choice between an all-black neighborhood and a mixed neighborhood (items a, e, g, h, k), black respondents overwhelmingly favored the latter. This trend is clearest for respondents outside of the South; yet, in 1969, 63 percent of even low-income black Southerners favored desegregated residential areas. Those who favored mixed areas made it clear that they did so for positive reasons of racial harmony even more than for the obvious advantages of good neighborhoods (items b and f). Similarly, those who preferred all-black areas made it

TABLE 3.   *Black American Attitudes Toward Race and Housing**

a.   In living in a neighborhood, if you could find the housing you want and like, would you rather live in a neighborhood with Negro families, or in a neighborhood that had both whites and Negroes?

Survey Agency: Newsweek

DATE	BLACK SAMPLE	PERCENTAGE OF AGREEMENT		
		Negro	*Both Negro and white*	*Not sure*
Aug 1963	National	20	64	16
Aug 1966	National	17	68	15
May 1969	National	16	74	10
	By Category			
1963	South	27	55	18
1966		26	57	17
1969		21	67	11
1963	Non-South	11	75	14
1966		8	79	13
1969		11	80	9
	South			
1969	Low income	24	63	14
1969	Low middle	20	69	11
1963	Middle income	6	69	25
1966		17	70	13
1969		23	69	8
	Non-South			
1963	Low income	19	75	6
1966		10	79	11
1969		10	76	14
1963	Low middle	11	75	14
1966		7	78	15
1969		9	84	7
1963	Middle income	12	69	19
1966		6	80	14
1969		11	81	8
1966	Under 35 yr	12	75	13
1969		18	71	7
1966	35–49 yr	17	67	16
1969		15	73	11
1966	50+yr	21	63	16
1969		16	75	10

b. [Of those who answered item a "both whites and Negroes"]
    Why do you feel this way?
    Survey Agency: Harris

DATE	BLACK SAMPLE	PERCENTAGE OF AGREEMENT		
		Races should mix	*Quieter, cleaner, etc.*	*Other*
Aug 1963	National	49	26	25

c. [Of those who answered item a "Negro families"] Why do you
    feel this way?
    Survey Agency: Harris

DATE	BLACK SAMPLE	PERCENTAGE OF AGREEMENT		
		Get along better	*Less tension, conflict*	*Can't get used to rival groups*
Aug 1963	National	52	14	24

d. If both neighborhoods were equally well kept up, would you
    rather live in a neighborhood that was mostly Negro or mostly
    white?
    Survey Agency: Marx

DATE	BLACK SAMPLE	PERCENTAGE OF AGREEMENT		
		Mostly Negro	*Mixed or no difference*	*Mostly white*
Fall 1964	Non-southern metropolitan areas[a]	55	38	4
	New York	52	35	9
	Chicago	68	25	5
	Atlanta	74	18	5
	Birmingham, Ala.	69	27	1
	Total	62	31	4

TABLE 3.   (*Continued*)

e. Would you personally prefer to live in a neighborhood with all Negroes, mostly Negroes, mostly whites, or a neighborhood that is mixed half and half?
    Survey Agency: Survey Research Center

DATE	BLACK SAMPLE	PERCENTAGE OF AGREEMENT				
		All Negro	Mostly Negro	Mostly white	Mixed half and half	No difference
Jan–March 1968	15 key central cities[b]	8	5	1	48	37

f. [Of those who answered item e "mixed half and half"] Why do you feel that way?
    Survey Agency: Survey Research Center

DATE	BLACK SAMPLE	PERCENTAGE OF AGREEMENT			
		Learn to get along together	Less crime, quieter, etc.	Better services	Other
Jan–March 1968	15 key central cities[b]	44	24	10	22

g. Would you be willing to live next door to members of the other race?
    Survey Agency: Gaffin

DATE	BLACK SAMPLE	PERCENTAGE OF AGREEMENT		
		Yes (whites)	No (whites)	No opinion (whites)
May 1958	National[c] Total	87	5	8
		(41)	(53)	(6)
	South only	79	8	13
		(19)	(78)	(3)
	Non-South only	97	1	2
		(48)	(45)	(7)

h. Would you be willing to live in the same general neighborhood with members of the other race?
Survey Agency: Gaffin

DATE	BLACK SAMPLE	PERCENTAGE OF AGREEMENT		
		Yes (whites)	*No* (whites)	*No opinion* (whites)
May 1958	National Total	91 (52)	4 (44)	5 (4)
	South only	86 (32)	6 (65)	8 (3)
	Non-South only	98 (59)	1 (37)	1 (4)

i. Do you think that most Negroes want to live in white neighborhoods, or in Negro neighborhoods, or that it doesn't matter to them?
Survey Agency: Gaffin

DATE	BLACK SAMPLE	PERCENTAGE OF AGREEMENT		
		Negro neighborhoods (whites)	*White neighborhoods* (whites)	*Doesn't matter* (whites)
May 1958	National Total	17 (52)	8 (18)	68 (23)
	South only	24 (74)	3 (12)	65 (10)
	Non-South only	9 (44)	13 (20)	73 (26)

j. Would you prefer to live on a block with people of the same race or of every race?
Survey Agency: Center for Urban Education

DATE	BLACK SAMPLE	PERCENTAGE OF AGREEMENT
Summer 1968	Bedford-Stuyvesant (Brooklyn, N.Y.)	*Every race* 80

TABLE 3.   (*Continued*)

k.   Would you rather live in a neighborhood with only Negro families or in a neighborhood that had both Negro and white families?

   Survey Agency: Meyer

DATE	BLACK SAMPLE	PERCENTAGE OF AGREEMENT		
		Negro Only	*Both Negro and white*	*Don't know*
Aug 1967	Detroit	17	61	22
Sept 1968	Detroit	13	75	12

l.   Which do you think is more important now—to get more and better housing in and around where Negroes already live, or to open housing for Negroes in other parts of the city and suburbs?

   Survey Agency: Meyer

DATE	BLACK SAMPLE	PERCENTAGE OF AGREEMENT			
		More and better housing	*Open up interracial housing*	*Both equally vital*	*Don't know*
Sept 1968	Detroit	44	41	14	1

m.   An owner of property should not have to sell to Negroes if he doesn't want to.

   Survey Agency: Marx

DATE	BLACK SAMPLE	PERCENTAGE OF AGREEMENT		
		Agree	*Disagree*	*Don't know*
Fall 1964	Non-southern metropolitan areas[a]	50	47	3
	New York	33	64	3
	Chicago	58	37	5
	Atlanta	50	47	3
	Birmingham, Ala.	53	43	4

n. An owner of property should not have to sell to Negroes if he
    doesn't want to.
    Survey Agency: Meyer

DATE	BLACK SAMPLE	PERCENTAGE OF AGREEMENT		
		Agree	Disagree	Don't know
Sept 1968	Detroit	38	54	8

o. On the whole, would you say you are satisfied or dissatisfied
    with your housing situation?
    Survey Agency: Gallup

DATE	BLACK SAMPLE	PERCENTAGE OF AGREEMENT		
		Satisfied (whites)	Dissatisfied (whites)	No opinion (whites)
1949	National	59 (67)	32 (28)	9 (5)
Oct 1963	National	43 (76)	54 (21)	3 (3)
Sept 1965	National	29 (77)	66 (20)	5 (3)
Nov 1966	National	51 (77)	44 (19)	5 (4)
May 1969	National	50 (80)	48 (18)	2 (2)

p. Let me read you some situations you might find yourself in.
    Suppose in each situation you had to see a white person. Tell
    me . . . if you think you would be likely to be given a hard
    time by the white person or not.
    Survey Agency: Harris

DATE	BLACK SAMPLE	PERCENTAGE OF AGREEMENT		
		Hard time	Not a hard time	Not sure
Feb–March 1970 National				
Looking for new housing		66	25	9
Applying for a job in a big company		59	26	15
Applying for a loan in a bank		48	38	14
Enrolling child (self) in integrated school		33	49	18

TABLE 3.   (*Continued*)

q. In general, if you were to get a house or apartment (flat) the same as a white person, do you feel you would pay more rent or the same as the white person would pay?
    Survey Agency: Harris

DATE	BLACK SAMPLE	PERCENTAGE OF AGREEMENT		
		More rent	*Same rent*	*Not sure*
Aug 1963	National	53	30	17

r. Believe "many" or "some" Negroes in this city miss out on good housing because of racial discrimination.
    Survey Agency: Survey Research Center

DATE	BLACK SAMPLE	PERCENTAGE OF AGREEMENT
Jan–March 1968	15 key central cities[b]	76

s. Believe there are "many" places in this city where they could not rent or buy a house because of discrimination.
    Survey Agency: Survey Research Center

DATE	BLACK SAMPLE	PERCENTAGE OF AGREEMENT
Jan–March 1968	15 key central cities[b]	43

t. Believe that racial discrimination in housing is increasing or not changing.
    Survey Agency: Survey Research Center

DATE	BLACK SAMPLE	PERCENTAGE OF AGREEMENT
Jan–March 1968	15 key central cities[b]	54

u. As far as your being able to live in neighborhoods with whites, if you want to, do you feel you are better off today than you were three years ago, worse off, or about the same as you were then?

Survey Agency: Harris

DATE	BLACK SAMPLE	PERCENTAGE OF AGREEMENT			
		Better off	*Worse off*	*About the same*	*Not sure*
Aug 1966	National				
	Total	50	4	32	14
	By Category				
	South	54	4	25	17
	Non-South	44	5	40	11
	Under 35 yr	44	6	36	14
	35–49 yr	49	4	33	14
	50+ yr	56	3	28	13

v. As far as your housing accommodations go, do you feel you are better off today than you were three years ago, worse off, or about the same as you were then?

Survey Agency: Harris

DATE	BLACK SAMPLE	PERCENTAGE OF AGREEMENT			
		Better off	*Worse off*	*About the same*	*Not sure*
Aug 1963	National	43	11	42	4
Aug 1966	National	43	8	44	5
Feb–March 1970	National	41	11	46	2
	By Category				
1963	South	45	11	41	3
1966		45	8	41	6
1970		47	9	42	2
1963	Non-South	41	11	44	4
1966		39	9	47	5
1970		35	12	50	3
1966	Under 35 yr	44	8	43	5
1966	35–49 yr	40	9	47	4
1966	50+yr	45	6	44	5
1970	Rural	47	10	38	5
1970	Small urban	45	9	44	2
1970	Large urban	35	12	51	2
	Family income				
1970	< $3,000	44	12	41	3
1970	$3,000–6,999	39	12	48	1
1970	$7,000–9,999	36	10	52	2
1970	> $10,000	47	7	43	3

TABLE 3. (*Continued*)

w. As far as you personally are concerned, what do you feel are the two or three biggest problems facing Negro people that you feel something should be done about?
    Survey Agency: Gallup

DATE	BLACK SAMPLE	PERCENTAGE OF AGREEMENT		
		Jobs and pay	*Schools*	*Housing*
May 1969	National	60	38	33

x. Do you or does any member of your immediate family now have contact or not with a white person who is (listed below)? And do you feel this relationship with this white is generally pleasant and easy, or is there sometimes trouble due to difference in race?
    Survey Agency: Harris

DATE	BLACK SAMPLE	PERCENTAGE OF AGREEMENT	
		Yes, Contact	*Pleasant and easy*
Feb–March 1970 National			
A friend socially		39	88
A neighbor		29	81
Employer or supervisor at work		68	66
Co-worker at work		59	69
A landlord or rent collector where you live		22	67
A policeman in the neighborhood		24	59

y. Now I want to give you a list of different people and groups that are run by white people. Do you think real estate companies have been more helpful or more harmful to Negro rights?
    Survey Agency: Newsweek

DATE	BLACK SAMPLE	PERCENTAGE OF AGREEMENT		
		Helpful	*Harmful*	*Not sure*
Aug 1963	National	15	44	41
Aug 1966	National	22	29	49
May 1969	National	22	43	35

z. In your neighborhood, do you think that the merchants in the following kinds of businesses treat Negroes fairly or unfairly?
Survey Agency: Meyer

DATE	BLACK SAMPLE	PERCENTAGE OF AGREEMENT	
		Unfair	
Aug 1967	Detroit		
Sept 1968	Detroit	1967	1968
Real estate		47	34
Home improvement		47	42
Furniture stores		40	43
Insurance		39	27
Grocery		54	57
Loan offices		48	41

aa. People have different ideas about what causes riots like the one in Detroit last summer. Let me read you a list of possible riot causes. . . . Please tell me whether it might have a great deal to do with causing a riot, something to do with causing a riot, or nothing at all to do with causing a riot.
Survey Agency: Meyer

DATE	BLACK SAMPLE	PERCENTAGE OF AGREEMENT	
		A great deal to do with causing a riot	
Aug 1967	Detroit		
Sept 1968	Detroit	1967	1968
Police brutality		57	71
Poor housing		54	61
Poverty		44	60
Lack of jobs		45	57
Overcrowded living conditions		55	55
Dirty neighborhoods		44	43

bb. Which of the following do you think is a "big problem" for Negroes here?
Survey Agency: Meyer

TABLE 3.   (*Continued*)

DATE	BLACK SAMPLE	PERCENTAGE OF AGREEMENT	
		Big Problem	
Feb–March 1968 Miami			
May–July 1968 Miami		Winter 1968	Summer 1968
Too many school dropouts		80	82
Rents too high		63	78
Poor housing		57	75
Overcrowded living conditions		58	75
Too much crime		71	74
Dirty neighborhoods		67	73
Poverty		41	73

[a] The "non-southern metropolitan area" sample of blacks was drawn by the National Opinion Research Center apart from the special probability samples of blacks drawn for the four cities studied in detail and listed separately.

[b] The fifteen cities sampled include, with few exceptions (e.g., Los Angeles and Dayton, Ohio), all of the larger cities outside of the South with significant black populations: Baltimore, Boston, Chicago, Cincinnati, Cleveland, Detroit, Gary, Milwaukee, Newark, New York City (Brooklyn only), Philadelphia, Pittsburgh, San Francisco, St. Louis, and Washington, D.C.

[c] Gaffin provided data by regions only; thus, the national data shown represents an extrapolation based on the fact that southern respondents represent slightly over half of the nation's black adults.

* SOURCES: Erskine (1967), Brink & Harris (1967), Campbell & Schuman (1968), Marx (1969), Goldman (1970), Gallup (1969, p. 11), Harris (1970), Meyer (1967, 1968, 1969).

equally clear that their reasons center around a desire to avoid interracial tension and strife (item c).

Where, then, is the turn to black separatism heralded by the mass media as the chief black shift of the late 1960 s? These housing data are actually consistent with a host of other survey data that demonstrate the media have grossly exaggerated this trend. Campbell and Schuman (1968), for example, show that the basic black ideological shift stresses cultural emphasis far more than racial separatism. They show that what little attention is given to separatism is concentrated among young Northerners, though even for them integration was the overwhelming choice. This trend is evident in the present results in an age and region interaction (Goldman, 1970). In the 1969 survey, young respondents in the North were the strongest segment in their desire for all-black neighborhoods—though this still came to only 17 percent compared to 77 percent desiring *mixed* neighborhoods.

These black attitudes favoring interracial housing do not appear in the aggregate to be declining. Indeed, the results for item a in Table 3 suggest that, if any trend is occurring, it is toward greater willingness to live in mixed areas. It is also clear, however, that there is no widespread desire among black Americans to live in "mostly" or overwhelmingly white areas. Marx (1969) asked his question d of Table 3 by giving only the two alternatives, "mostly Negro" and "mostly white." Although this inadequate wording greatly enhances the percentages selecting "mostly Negro," two remarkable findings emerge from his results. First, relatively large percentages of his black respondents said "mixed" or "it does not matter," even though these alternatives were not even offered by the question. Second, the percentages favoring "mostly Negro" for the four cities are almost linearly related to the Taeubers' 1960 indices of racial segregation by block for these central cities. New York, of the four sampled, has, by far, the lowest index (79.3) and the lowest percentage wanting "mostly Negro" areas, while Chicago (92.6) and Birmingham, Alabama (92.8), are relatively intermediate and Atlanta is the most segregated (93.6) (Taeuber & Taeuber, 1966, p. 39–41). This suggests that there is a "reality" factor involved: Separatist attitudes are often formed *after* the harsh facts of racial discrimination and segregation in housing.

Such a conclusion is supported by a special survey of black opinion conducted in 1968 in Bedford-Stuyvesant in New York City (Center for Urban Education, 1968). As item j shows, four fifths of the respondents in this relatively dense ghetto area would prefer to live on a multiracial, rather than a uniracial, block. Significantly, however, the most favorable group to heterogeneous living in the entire sample were the black residents of a still-desegregated public housing development, 88 percent of whom favored multiracial blocks . . .

Naturally, a desire for better housing undergirds these data. This becomes apparent as soon as we compare the findings of items a, j, and k with l in Table 3. When the choice is simply between all-black or genuinely mixed areas, roughly four-to-one majorities preferred the latter. But when the hard policy choice is presented between improving ghetto housing and opening up housing for blacks outside of the ghetto, a clear split in the Detroit sample (item l) occurs with a seventh of the respondents who realistically argued for both even though the question did not list this response alternative. The findings of item i bear this out further. Whites in both the North and South tended to comfort themselves with the idea that "most Negroes want to live in . . . Negro neighborhoods," but the overwhelming majority of blacks in both regions believed that it "does not matter."

Conservative notions about property rights are not limited to white Americans. As the data for items m and n reveal, close majorities of urban blacks, save for New York City and Detroit, believed in the 1960's that "an owner of property should not have to sell to Negroes." This finding is made all the more remarkable when we inspect the results for item o in Table 3. About half of the nation's blacks remained dissatisfied with their housing throughout the 1960's. This situation contrasts sharply with white dissatisfaction with housing, which has steadily declined from 28 percent in 1949 to only 18 percent in 1969. Note, too, that black dissatisfaction with housing *increased* sharply between 1949 and 1963—from 32 percent to 54 percent—even though we know from considerable census data that black housing significantly improved in the aggregate throughout the 1950's. This interesting situation affords yet another example of the phenomenon of rising aspirations and *relative* deprivation as a source of growing dissatisfaction; beyond survival levels, the difference between aspiration and achievement is socially and psychologically more critical than *absolute* deprivation itself (Pettigrew, 1964, Ch. 8, 1968; Geschwender, 1964; Runciman, 1966; Hyman & Singer, 1968).

One might naively ask at this point why blacks do not

seek better housing in presently white areas now that many of them have rising incomes. One answer, of course, is that blacks are keenly aware of the discrimination and possible abuse they face in such efforts. Item p shows that blacks throughout the nation anticipated "a hard time" from whites more in "looking for new housing" than in any of twelve situations offered by the Harris survey question. Only "applying for a job in a big company" and ". . . for a loan in a bank" rival the search for new housing, and looking for a suitable mortgage from a bank is itself likely to be involved in seeking to purchase new housing. By contrast, only one third of the black respondents anticipated "a hard time" over seeking integrated schooling, conflict-ridden as that process has been, compared to the two thirds who anticipated it in the house-hunting process.

Additional data round out this view of black perceptions of housing discrimination. A definite majority were correctly aware in 1963 of the "race tax" they must pay in higher rents compared to those paid by whites (item q in Table 3).[4] In their 15-city study for the Kerner Commission (items r, s, and t), Campbell and Schuman (1968) found in 1968 that three in four blacks believed that numbers of blacks "miss out on good housing" because of racial discrimination; and three in seven believed that many parts of their cities were closed to them because of discrimination—a proportion that might have well been higher had "suburbs" been included in the item wording. Roughly half believed that the pervasive pattern of racial discrimination in housing is not eroding (items t and u)—a belief that, apart from its validity, probably acts to discourage black attempts to grapple with white officials and real estate dealers for housing outside of the ghetto. A policy implication of this possibility immediately emerges: *Successful efforts at decreasing racial discrimination in housing must, among other things, be made widely known among black Americans.* It should be observed, too, in the results for item u, that it is the young and northern blacks who are the most skeptical—the very segments who otherwise are the most likely to take advantage of new interracial housing opportunities.

Black estimations of how they are personally faring in the housing market did not change in the aggregate much over the 1960's (item v of Table 3). When these data are disaggregated, however, we find diverse trends by region, which, again, suggest the operation of the relative deprivation process. Black Southerners consistently perceived more progress in their housing conditions than black Northerners, whose percentage reporting "better off" declined 6 percent over the 7 years from 1963 to 1970. Furthermore, in 1970, rural and small city blacks reported far greater housing improvements than big city blacks, and both the poorest and richest blacks reported more progress than the middle-income ($3,000–9,999). Finer analyses unravel these findings. The poor blacks who saw advances in their personal accommodations are found largely on the farm and in smaller communities in the South—a phenomenon that is a comment on the incredibly bad living conditions for these Americans in the past rather than a comment on the status of their present living conditions. The well-off blacks who saw advances in their personal accommodations are found largely in the larger cities of both regions, a phenomenon that largely reflects their ability to rent and purchase housing in the central city vacated by suburban-bound whites.

Housing, together with schools, was rated by a national sample of blacks as one of the "biggest problems facing Negro people that . . . something should be done about" (item w). Yet, 60 percent listed "jobs and pay," compared to only one third listing housing. This difference probably reflects the pressing immediacy of economic problems for many blacks as well as the prior need for greater income in order to seek better accommodations.

Two questions on interracial contact (item x) provide suggestive results. Only 29 percent of a 1970 national sample of blacks reported family contact with a white neighbor. But 81 percent of those with such contacts reported them to be "pleasant and easy"—the second highest percentage of twelve types of contact presented by Harris and surpassed only by that for "a friend socially." At the other end of the scale, 22 percent reported family contact with a white landlord or rent collector, and only 67 percent of these contacts were described as "pleasant and easy"—a percentage reflecting tension surpassed only by contact with an "employer or supervisor at work" or "a policeman in the neighborhood." These findings, though hardly surprising, bear reflection, too, by those who are concerned about generating greater racial harmony in our torn society. Interracial contact on a neighborly basis is reported by blacks themselves as typically achieving the type of interaction necessary for reducing intergroup prejudice. The contact with landlords and collectors is understandably often unpleasant and likely to generate greater intergroup intolerance and conflict . . .

The next two items of Table 3 (y and z) narrow this point further. By 1969, two out of every three blacks with an opinion on the subject think real estate companies were more harmful than helpful "to Negro rights." If Rose Helper's research (1969) on the real estate industry can be generalized nationally, this dominant black view is correct. Indeed, of the twelve white groups and institutions employed in the *Newsweek* surveys, real estate companies were rivaled only by "the local police" for a negative black view. Again, this negative view is held strongest by those segments of black population most likely otherwise to seek housing in interracial areas: i.e., Northerners, those under 30 years of age, and those with higher incomes (Goldman, 1970, p. 255–256).

Item z illustrates with 1967 and 1968 survey data from Detroit how real estate dealers in the neighborhood were viewed relative to five other types of business. Local grocery stores drew particular fire as "unfair" both years. While there is some improvement as more time passes after the 1967 Detroit race riot, four types of businesses—related, in part, to housing—all continued to be rated as "unfair" by sizable minorities of black respondents: real estate brokers, home improvement companies, furniture stores, and loan offices.

The six leading causes of race riots cited by Detroit blacks from a list of 25 are shown under item aa (Meyer, 1968). "Police brutality," as might be expected, leads the list in both surveys. But three of the six perceived chief causes of race riots relate directly to housing: "poor housing," "overcrowded living conditions," and "dirty neighborhoods." Clearly, in the minds of Detroit's blacks, housing needs have a high priority in assessing the conditions underlying the type of racial riot they witnessed.

The final item of Table 3 (bb) attempts to show changes among Miami's blacks over the brief and tragic spring of 1968 that saw Dr. Martin Luther King assassinated, a new rash of race riots, and the issuance of the forthright report of the National Advisory Commission on Civil Disorders (the Kerner Commission Report) (Meyer, 1969). Interestingly, some of the biggest shifts in rating the issues that are "a big problem" involve housing. "Rents too high" rose from 63 percent to 78 percent over the spring of 1968; "poor housing," from 57 percent to 75 percent; "overcrowded living conditions," from 58 percent to 75 percent; and "dirty neighborhoods," from 67 percent to 73 percent. By the summer of 1968, then, four of the seven issues considered by Miami blacks as "big problems" for them involved housing—yet another indication of the special importance granted this realm by black Americans.

In summary, black Americans rate better housing as one of their most pressing needs. They would be more than willing to obtain it in racially mixed neighborhoods if they could, though typically, they do not wish to reside in an overwhelmingly white area. In fact, their willingness to move to genuinely interracial neighborhoods appears motivated by a desire to live in racial harmony as well as to achieve better housing and services. As it is, blacks are far more dissatisfied with their present housing situation than whites; and only a minority feel "better off" personally from recent improvements in the housing stock of blacks. Yet they are reluctant to seek housing in presently white areas, in part, because of the discrimination and abuse they anticipate they would suffer. Furthermore, it is precisely those blacks—the young, well-off, and living in the North—who otherwise are most likely to seek interracial housing, who most often harbor these fears as well as the belief that residential discrimination is not receding.

In conclusion, one important dimension must be added. Although we are concentrating on the factor of *race* for both whites and blacks, race is only one of many factors involved in residential choice—one that is often not critical to either whites or blacks. Thus, we should not let our focus on race cause us to overlook the many other factors that people do actively take into account in housing selection. This point is underlined by data from Bradburn and his colleagues (1970, p. 242–244, 261–263). They sought information on what families thought were the chief advantages causing them to move to their present home. When they compared these factors for whites and blacks who had moved into either integrated or segregated neighborhoods, extremely similar patterns emerged for both groups. Of these, four dominant advantages emerged: convenience to work; the dwelling unit was of appropriate size; specific features of the dwelling other than size (e.g., a garage); and financial advantages. Mention of these essentially nonracial, but often decisive, factors impresses on us the need to place the attitude data just reviewed in their socially meaningful context.

THE SOCIAL CONTEXT OF ATTITUDES ON RACE AND HOUSING

The attitudes of both whites and blacks are more derivative than causal in the total process of how shelter, as a resource, is distributed by race in the United States.

The survey results just reviewed provide evidence for this contention. Recall that whites are far more likely to move into an interracial neighborhood if they have experienced integration previously as a child or as an adult—particularly, if both. Recall, too, that blacks across four cities preferred all-black neighborhoods in direct relation to the degree of residential segregation by race within these cities and that the most pro-desegregation blacks in the Bedford-Stuyvesant study were those who resided in one of the few remaining interracial developments in the area. These findings coincide with those of a 1966 survey study of the urban North and West designed by the U.S. Commission on Civil Rights (1967, Vol. I, 108–113; Vol. II, 221–241) to test this phenomenon explicitly. It found that white adults who had attended interracial schools as children expressed more willingness to reside in an interracial neighborhood, as well as other more positive attitudes toward blacks, and were, in fact, more likely to be living in interracial neighborhoods and to have close black friends than comparable whites. Also, it found that black adults who had attended interracial schools as children were more trusting of whites than comparable blacks, more eager for their children to attend desegregated schools, and more willing to live in an interracial neighborhood, even if they would have to "pioneer" to do so. What is more, the biracially educated blacks were more likely to be living in mostly white neighborhoods, to be sending their children to desegregated schools, and to have close white friends. Thus, interracial experience is a cumulative process for both races and even spans generations.

According to this model, then, behavior change typically precedes, rather than follows from, attitude change. There is considerable social psychological evidence to support this principle (Pettigrew, 1971), although it is almost precisely the opposite process from that popularly assumed to be true. One practical corollary of this thesis is that *an effective way to alter opposition, white and black, to interracial housing is to have them live successfully in such housing.* Extensive research in social psychology supports this contention (Pettigrew, 1971).

Increasing interaction, whether it be of groups or individuals, intensifies and magnifies the processes already under way. Hence, more interracial contact can lead either to greater prejudice and rejection or to greater respect and acceptance, depending on the situation in which it occurs. The basic issue, then, concerns the types of situations in which contact leads to distrust and those in which it leads to trust.

Gordon Allport, in his review of the relevant research (1954), concludes that four characteristics of the contact situation are of utmost importance. Prejudice is lessened when the two groups (1) possess equal status, (2) seek common goals, (3) are cooperatively dependent on each other, and (4) interact with the positive support of authorities, laws, or custom.

To sum up, interracial living itself will effectively erode racial opposition to open housing to the degree that it is characterized by Allport's four key criteria. The rapidly changing neighborhood, with whites selling low in panic, is a classic urban housing situation that grossly violates all of Allport's factors and generates intense hostility on both sides of the color line. Stable interracial neighborhoods—which are far less publicized, but were found by Bradburn (1970) to be more numerous than many thought—illustrate the positive operation of Allport's factors and are, in fact, characterized by greater interracial acceptance and tolerance.

BIBLIOGRAPHY

G. W. Allport, *The Nature of Prejudice*. Reading, Mass.: Addison-Wesley, 1954, Chapter 16.

N. M. Bradburn, S. Sudman and G. L. Gockel, *Racial Integration in American Neighborhoods*. Chicago: National Opinion Research Center, 1970.

W. Brink and L. Harris, *Black and White*. New York: Simon & Schuster, 1967.

A. Campbell and H. Schuman, "Racial attitudes in fifteen American cities." In *Supplemental Studies for National Advisory Commission on Civil Disorders*. Washington, D.C.: GPO, 1968.

Center for Urban Education, "Survey of the residents of Bedford-Stuyvesant." Unpublished paper of the Center for Urban Education, New York, 1968.

B. Duncan and P. M. Hauser, *Housing a Metropolis—Chicago*. New York: Free Press, 1960.

H. G. Erskine, "The polls: Negro housing," *Public Opinion Quarterly*, 1967, *31*, 482–498.

R. W. Friedrichs, "Christians and residential exclusion: An empirical study of a northern dilemma," *Journal of Social Issues*, October 1959, *15*, 14–23.

Gallup International, Inc., *Gallup Opinion Index*. Report No. 47. Princeton, N.J., May 1969.

J. A. Geschwender, "Social structure and the Negro revolt: An examination of some hypotheses," *Social Forces*, 1964, 43, 248–256.

P. Goldman, *Report From Black America*. New York: Simon & Schuster, 1970.

L. Harris, "Harris overlay on *Time* black poll." Unpublished paper of Study No. 2014, March 1970.

R. Helper, *Racial Policies and Practices of Real Estate Brokers*. Minneapolis: University of Minnesota Press, 1969.

H. H. Hyman and E. Singer (eds.), *Readings in Reference Group Theory and Research*. New York: Free Press, 1968.

G. T. Marx, *Protest and Prejudice*. (Revised edition) New York: Harper & Row, 1969.

P. Meyer, *The People Beyond 12th Street: A Survey of Attitudes of Detroit Negroes After the Riot of 1967*. Detroit: The Detroit Urban League and the Detroit Free Press, 1967.

P. Meyer, *Return to 12th Street: A Follow-up Survey of Attitudes of Detroit Negroes, October 1968*. Detroit: The Detroit Free Press, 1968.

P. Meyer, "Aftermath of martyrdom: Negro militancy and Martin Luther King," *Public Opinion Quarterly*, Summer 1969, 33, 160–173.

T. F. Pettigrew, *A Profile of the Negro American*. New York: Van Nostrand Reinhold, 1964.

T. F. Pettigrew, "Social evaluation theory: Convergences and applications." In D. Levine (ed.), *Nebraska Symposium on Motivation, 1967*. Lincoln: University of Nebraska Press, 1968.

T. F. Pettigrew, *Racially Separate or Together?* New York: McGraw-Hill, 1971.

W. G. Runciman, *Relative Deprivation and Social Justice*. London: Routledge & Kegan Paul, 1966.

M. A. Schwartz, *Trends in White Attitudes Toward Negroes*. Chicago: National Opinion Research Center, 1967.

P. B. Sheatsley, "White attitudes toward the Negro." In T. Parsons and K. Clark (eds.), *The Negro American*. Boston: Houghton Mifflin, 1966, pp. 303–324.

K. E. Taeuber and A. F. Taeuber, *Negroes in Cities*. Chicago: Aldine, 1965.

U. S. Commission on Civil Rights, *Racial Isolation in the Public Schools*. Washington, D.C.: GPO, 1967. 2 Vols.

PART III

DISCRIMINATION IN EMPLOYMENT, EDUCATION, AND INCOME: THE BARRIERS TO STATUS

Two *centuries of slavery and another of segregation effectively closed to blacks the many avenues to status and opportunity open to most other Americans. Racial differentials in employment, education, and income are the most glaring results of this racist legacy; and discrimination in these interrelated realms has therefore received the most attention from social science. This section presents nine incisive papers from this extensive research literature.*

Two popular if inconsistent myths surround this domain. The first maintains that since black Americans enjoy one of the highest absolute *standards of living of any black people on the globe, they should be happy and* satisfied. The second denies the variety of status and social conditions found among blacks. It simply equates poor with black and assumes that the vast majority of the group are menially employed, ill-educated, and on welfare. Let us briefly examine these misconceptions.

One veteran senator from the deep South is fond of comparing the living conditions of black Americans with those of black Africans and proclaiming bewilderment at why blacks in the United States dare to protest. From his perspective of absolute standards, they should be grateful for what they have. Indeed, black Americans have an aggregate buying power similar to that of Canadians and a larger percentage of its youth receive higher education than the youth of the United Kingdom. But such comparisons are psychologically meaningless. Blacks in America no more compare their lot with those of blacks in Africa, Canadians, or Britishers than the senator compares his lot with that of Englishmen. Of necessity, black Americans utilize the living conditions of their fellow Americans as the relevant standard. And by this standard, absolute black gains in jobs, schooling, and finances often pale relative to white gains. Social psychologists refer to this phenomenon as "relative deprivation"; and this concept has proved useful in understanding black unrest over the past two decades.[1] Consequently, most of the selections use white data as the comparison for black data—a practice that not only makes theoretical sense but psychological sense as well.

The second myth, which equates blacks as a group with poverty, has been badly outdated by the gains of the past generation.[2] True, substantial racial differentials in status remain. But the rapid development of a genuine black middle class has been one of the primary racial accomplishments of the post-World War II era in the United States. If one adopts a rough definition of middle-class status in terms of employment, education, and income, then about two-fifths of blacks are middle-class contrasted with about two-thirds of whites. Hence, 38.5 percent of employed blacks in 1972 were either in white-collar or skilled blue-collar occupations; 63.8 percent of employed whites held such positions.[3] The percentages of adults who are high school graduates are similar. Likewise about 40 percent of black families had incomes over $8000 during 1971 compared to about 65 percent of white families.

In short, there is now a sizable and expanding black middle class for the first time in our national history, in spite of the persistence of large racial discrepancies in status. Any explanation of the status discrepancies, however, must separate out the operation of two types of handicaps: those common to all Americans related to background or misfortune, and those specific to racial discrimination against black people. This requirement raises difficult methodological issues, but it is necessary to distill out general problems in order to isolate the specific racial problem.

EMPLOYMENT

"If a social condition is bad, blacks have twice as much of it as whites" goes a useful aphorism of race relations specialists. "And if a condition is good, blacks have only half as much of it." Crude, to be sure, but this rule of thumb is unfortunately seldom too far off the mark. Consider unemployment. For the 13 years from 1960 through 1972, the U.S. Labor Department's recorded rate of unemployment for nonwhites varied between 1.8 and 2.2 times that for whites. Indeed the crude rule holds even when the specific rates for teen-agers, adult women, and adult men are examined separately. In 1972, for example, nonwhite teen-agers had a soaring recorded unemployment rate of 33.5 percent contrasted to the white figure of 14.2 percent; and nonwhite adult males and females had rates of 6.8 and 8.8 percent contrasted with white rates of 3.6 and 4.9 percent. Concludes one economist:

". . . whites fluctuate between prosperity and recession but Negroes fluctuate between depression and great depression."[1]

The aphorism also predicts the occupational distributions of the two races. Thus in 1972, 25.2 percent of employed whites were either professionals, managers, or administrators, compared to only 13.2 percent of employed nonwhites. But at the low-status and poorly paid end of the job hierarchy, 27.2 percent of employed nonwhites were service workers compared to 11.8 percent of employed whites. Yet there has been a substantial upgrading of black employment in recent years. The percentage of employed nonwhites who hold white-collar occupations almost doubled in 12 years, rising from 16.1 percent in 1960 to 29.8 percent in 1972. The equivalent white percentages only edged up over these same years from 46.6 to 50.0 percent. Moreover, younger blacks in white-collar jobs are earning salaries more comparable to those of younger whites than older blacks. Some of this improvement is directly attributable to the minority-hiring efforts of the federal government, the biggest employer in the nation. By May 1972 there were 388,000 blacks in federal employment (excluding the armed services), and they constituted over 15 percent of the federal work force.

W. Clark Roof begins our analysis of employment discrimination in Selection 9 by demonstrating its direct link with residential segregation in Southern cities. The black ghetto, he argues, is "instrumental in institutionalizing inequalities." Roof presents an interesting model that connects the findings of Part II on housing with discrimination not only in occupations but in education and income as well. He shows first how both a city's age and percentage of blacks relate to housing segregation, which in turn shapes status inequities. Note that employment inequality is directly shaped in Roof's model both by residential separation and educational inequality. This model is crude and approximate; yet it presents the reader with a useful tool for ordering much of this volume's material, and it *reveals some of the complexity of how the various societal realms intermesh.*

Section 10 succinctly discusses the problem of ghetto unemployment. It shows how the employment situation of blacks is actually worse than even the recorded rates indicate. Black unemployment is twice that of whites under the traditional index of those located respondents who are actively seeking work but unable to find it. But Selection 10 introduces the more sophisticated "subemployment index." This new indicator not only includes those traditionally recorded as "unemployed" but also part-time workers who desire full-time jobs and those with jobs whose meager earnings still result in poverty, as well as estimates of those who want a job but have given up hope of finding one and those males unavailable to be recorded. With this measure the perpetual black crisis in employment comes into more realistic focus. "Subemployed" black rates reach almost half of the ghettos in such cities as Cleveland, New Orleans, and San Antonio, and they are typically three and a half times those of white rates.

We have noted the importance of federal employment. But state and local governments have lagged far behind. Selection 11, based on data assembled by the United States Commission on Civil Rights, provides case-by-case insight into how racial discrimination operates in promotion procedures at this level. Little wonder that ambitious blacks rarely consider state and local government careers.

Turning from the concrete example to broad assessments, Otis Dudley Duncan presents in Selection 12 an analysis of occupational change over a generation for black and nonblack men. The full force of employment discrimination across generations is starkly revealed. For black males there was only a slight occupational advantage to having grown up in a family whose head was either a professional or manager. For nonblack (overwhelmingly white) males, such an upbringing bestowed an enormous occupational advantage. Thus black men *who originated in lower-status families were likely to remain there, while white men were likely to move up. Black men who originated in upper-status families tended to slide down, but white men tended to remain. Duncan points out that these results indicate that social origins are not the principal cause of racial differences in occupational achievement. Rather, the more important explanation lies in the racially discriminatory results of the mobility process itself. His work is based on special 1962 census data. The results may well be somewhat more favorable for cohorts of young blacks who have since entered the labor market during a period of general upgrading in black employment.*

Selection 13 attempts to answer the intriguing question: What would happen to the occupational differences between blacks and whites if discrimination were suddenly and totally eradicated? Utilizing a Markov model,[5] Stanley Lieberson and Glen Fuguitt ingeniously demonstrate that within the limitations of their assumptions racial equality in jobs could not be attained in a few years or even a decade. Yet the direct elimination of employment discrimination would reduce the racial differences in occupational distribution by two-thirds in one generation and virtually end them in two generations. Interestingly, the elimination of educational discrimination would have only a slight effect on occupational differences despite the close link between education and occupation. Though necessarily technical in its methodology, Selection 13 is worth careful study by students interested in modern social science research and in effective remedial action to counter discrimination.

EDUCATION

Similar to other realms, solid gains in education have been registered by blacks in absolute terms; but wide educational differences remain relative to whites. Black illiteracy, for instance, declined by over half between 1959 and 1969 (7.5% to 3.6%) but remained five times that of whites (0.7%). Black school enrollment percentages are now up to their highest levels, and black drop-out rates have declined. The percentage of black high school dropouts fell from 22.8 to 17.5 percent between 1967 and 1972 but was still higher than the 11.3 percent of whites.

The major gains, however, invlove markedly higher percentages of black youth now completing high school and entering college. Among blacks in their twenties, 41 percent had finished four years of high school in 1960 as against 65 percent in 1972. The comparable white percentages over these same years rose from 65 to 83 percent. Black college enrollments have risen more recently. Among blacks in their twenties, 15 percent had completed at least one year of college in 1967 as against 23 percent by 1972. Since the comparable white percentages for these years are 24 and 39 percent, the black college figure by 1972 is actually farther behind the white one despite the absolute increases. However, the higher education shift represents more than an increase in absolute numbers; the majority of blacks in college by 1970 were in predominantly white institutions compared with less than a fourth of earlier black college graduates.

But if educational desegregation has advanced in higher education, its progress at the elementary and secondary levels has been stormy and slow. It was no accident that the post-World War II protest movement of black America singled out school segregation as its first major target for change. Separate educational facilities had traditionally been the means of administering racially unequal educational opportunity. And this discrimination during the formative years made discrimination in other realms all the easier on the ostensibly "objective" grounds of lower academic achievement. The historic ruling of the United States Supreme Court on May 17, 1954, striking down de jure segregation by race in the public schools appeared at the time to be the culmination of black efforts.

But it proved to be only the opening shot in a struggle that still continues.

Selections 14 and 15, therefore, focus on the segregation issue, the institutional key to educational discrimination. First, Robert Crain demonstrates that the long-held black belief in the strategic importance of establishing interracial schools is basically valid. In a unique survey of black adults, he found that those who had attended desegregated public schools as children have better jobs and higher incomes as adults. Crain employs some ingenious analysis to suggest that these apparent benefits of interracial schooling are less strictly "educational" than they are based on "contacts" with the larger society.

Next, the editor discusses the present status of public school desegregation, the chief causes of urban segregation, and the myths that persist as part of the effort to reverse the process. A sharp process distinction is made between mere desegregation and genuine integration. The former term refers to an interracial mix without reference to the quality of the interaction, while the latter implies cross-racial acceptance under optimal conditions. Eight specific structural factors are discussed that appear to relate to this crucial dimension.

INCOME

As a direct result of racial discrimination, a disproportionate share of black America suffers from poverty. One-fourth of all black families received public assistance in 1971 contrasted with one in twenty of white families. And the U.S. Census lists 29 percent of all black families "below the low-income level." This figure contrasts with only 7 percent of white families; it is down from 48 percent in 1959, but it has not declined at all since the Nixon Administration took office.

Throughout the 1950s the median income of black families remained at slightly over half that of white families (the old rule of thumb again!). But this ratio rose *sharply from 52 percent in 1959 to 61 percent in 1969. By 1973 it had declined to 58 percent; $7,270 for black families to $12,600 for white families. Yet even this discrepancy understates the problem of black income. Francis Tucker has shown that when age differences between blacks and whites are controlled, income differences between the races are still larger.[6] Andrew Brimmer, the first black member of the Federal Reserve Board, has demonstrated, too, that there is a growing income dichotomy within the black community.[7] Thus a disproportionate share of the black "income gains" have accrued to the already financially comfortable families, while the poorest families benefit little if at all. In 1947 the poorest two-fifths of "nonwhite" families received 15 percent of all "nonwhite" income, but in 1960 they received only 13.5 percent. This split between a rising upper-middle class and a persisting sector of poverty is reflected in 1971 data: 37 percent of black families grossed less than $5,000 while 30 percent grossed over $10,000.*

What experiences differentiate these families? We learned from Crain's work that desegregated schooling can make a difference in jobs and income. Other investigators have found that service in the armed forces can have a similar effect. While white nonveterans report higher incomes than white veterans, black and Mexican-American veterans report higher incomes than minority nonveterans.[8] Indeed, James Coleman and his colleagues have found that blacks are apparently led by initially low incomes to adopt a different employment strategy than whites.[9] In a study of men during their first 10 years of work after leaving full-time education, blacks were found typically to maximize income at the expense of status while whites typically maximized status at the expense of income. Many black workers probably have no choice, since they do not have the accumulated family means to adopt the status strategy. Yet the white strategy of deferring income for status often leads to far greater income at later stages of occupational careers.

But are the large black-white differences in income

actually due to racial discrimination or to a "culture" and "inheritance" of poverty? The latter explanation became so fashionable during the 1960s that Otis Dudley Duncan attempted to answer the question empirically.[10] Extending his analysis of mobility seen earlier in Selection 12, Duncan demonstrates that racial factors are considerably more critical than those of social class. His conclusion is forceful: "In general, the supposition that the 'poor are poor because they are poor' is not only an intellectual obfuscation, but also a feeble guide to policy in what is obviously the most desperate and refractory sector of the 'poverty problem,' that is, the 'race problem.' "[11]

Selection 16 outlines the processes by which racial discrimination is translated into low income and how these processes might be reversed. Special antidiscrimination programs, Lester Thurow argues, are clearly indicated. First, he notes that programs to eliminate white poverty would only partially eliminate black poverty. Second, he points out that economic policies to reduce the national unemployment rate to 3 percent are necessary but not in themselves sufficient remedies. Third, he emphasizes the black need for on-the-job training, a task that the private sector must largely shoulder. He also stresses the importance of better labor market information, incentives for mobility, and the eradication of discrimination at all levels of government. Finally, Thurow urges a coordinated approach of productivity programs, guaranteed jobs, and direct income transfers. Examples of such programs are described later in Selections 24 and 26.

Part III closes with a summary article by Reynolds Farley and Albert Hermalin on the racial changes of the 1960s. Particular attention in Selection 17 is focused upon income trends and their intimate relation to education. Farley and Hermalin find that black gains tend to have been faster than those of whites during the decade but not so fast as to have substantially closed the racial discrepancies.

Housing Segregation and Racial Inequality in Southern Cities*

W. CLARK ROOF

While the demographic aspects of residential segregation are generally understood, less is known about the consequences of this phenomenon for minority-group relations. In research on minority assimilation, Lieberson (1961) has called attention to the important results which follow for a minority, depending on whether the group is residentially segregated or dispersed . . .

Apart from Lieberson's research, few attempts have been made to examine the importance of the residential segregation factor and to assess its significance for race relations theory. This paper reports an exploratory investigation of how residential segregation may be conceptualized as a variable phenomenon and incorporated into an economic competition theory of minority-group relations. The proposed model applies to the American South, although with some slight modification it should be relevant for other societal settings. The objective is two-fold: (1) to show that residential segregation indices are related to measures of educational, occupational, and income inequality; and (2) to suggest how the residential segregation factor may be in-

---

* Abridged from W. C. Roof, "Residential Segregation of Blacks and Racial Inequality in Southern Cities: Toward a Causal Model," *Social Problems*, 1972, *19*, 393–407. Reprinted with permission of the author, *Social Problems*, and the Society for the Study of Social Problems.

corporated into an empirically testable theory of minority-group relations . . .

The causal connections are not always stated explicitly, but there are two fundamental ways in which residential segregation is conceptualized in the literature as important theoretically: (a) as a structural basis for institutional and organizational separation, and (b) as heightening the visibility of racial group differences.

Residential segregation, first of all, enables a group to evolve and to maintain separate institutional structures which, in turn, may serve as a means for institutionalizing inequalities. Myrdal (1944:618) underscored this consequence of spatial separation when he described residential segregation as "basic in a mechanical sense" to other forms of discrimination . . . Theorists of the persuasion single out the structural consequences of residential segregation and the importance of these for preserving inequalities . . .

A second way in which residential segregation functions is to increase minority visibility. The importance of minority visibility lies in its capacity to evoke social psychological reactions on the part of the dominant group. Kephart's (1954) finding that the greater the number of Negroes arrested in a district in Philadelphia, the greater the over-estimation by policemen of the Negro rate, suggests that visibility increases at a more rapid rate than sheer number. Minority visibility is acknowledged as important also in theories of race relations which focus upon competition. Blalock, for example, observes that minority visibility accents *perceived* minority competition (1967). According to his theoretical model, the dominant group's motivation to discriminate is a function of both the *actual* and *perceived* economic threats and/or political power of the minority . . . Residential segregation by color, by virtue of its massiveness, is one of the most significant mechanisms underlying minority visibility. The greater the residential concentration, the greater the chances that a racial minority is perceived as a visible threat.

In the preceding discussion, two functions of residential

segregation were described. Both of these rest upon the assumption of a competitive racial order. Further elaboration of how residential segregation is linked to economic competition is possible if we examine van den Berghe's (1967) formulation of how race relations in modern industrial society have tended to shift their form from "paternalistic" to "competitive." The American South provides the setting in which to examine this transition.

In the agrarian South, race relations typically followed the master-servant model, where the division of labor was rigidly ascribed. Racial roles were generally well-defined, with the social expectations generally solidified around paternalistic norms of subservience and respect. In the agrarian order, van den Berghe notes that physical proximity is not problematic since status inequality is not threatened by close residential contact (1967). The "back-yard" pattern of scattered black residences, so frequently observed among the older southern cities (Myrdal, 1944), is reflective of this era in southern history. Older southern cities even today continue to show evidence of the ante bellum housing patterns and are much less segregated residentially than the newer cities in the region (Schnore and Evenson, 1966).

The newer southern cities, particularly those that grew up after the Civil War, emerged under industrializing economic conditions. Paternalistic patterns of residential intimacy were never established in these cities as they had been in the preceding era. These younger cities are characterized today by much larger black ghettos and, according to Taeuber and Taeuber (1965), by the highest rates of increase in residential segregation of any in the United States as of 1960 (1965). If human ecologists are correct in their assertion that spatial pattern is a suggestive index of social relationships, then the evidence in these younger southern cities points toward a distinctly new and different form of black-white relations. These cities reflect a "competitive" form of race relations, characterized by fewer intimate inter-racial contacts, greater ghetto segmentation, and more intense economic competition between racial groups. Van den Berghe (1967), in discussing these correlates of industrialization, singles out the importance of residential segregation in the process:

> To the extent that social distance diminishes physical segregation is introduced as a second line of defense for the preservation of the dominant group's position. The amount of contact between castes declines as the society becomes increasingly compartmentalized into racially homogeneous ghettoes with their nearly self-sufficient institutional structures.

"Physical" distance replaces "social" distance as a decisive regulatory mechanism in the transition from paternalistic to competitive race relations. Spatial concentration, by ensuring greater institutional separation and minority visibility, imposes barriers to effective economic competition and thereby aids in preserving dominant-group privileges.

Van den Berghe's formulation of competitive race relations draws attention to two features of the southern scene which have not always been made clear: (a) the variable and provocative nature of prejudice and (b) the significance of residential ghettoes for sustaining . . . a "sense of group position."

With respect to the first, it should be noted that theorists have often assumed a homogeneity in southern racial practices that was in fact not the case. Despite the cultural heritage of racism, southern discrimination in the post-Civil War years can also be described as increasingly provocative. C. Vann Woodward (1955) reminds us that much of the "Jim Crow" legislation—so important symbolically to lower-status whites—took place around the turn of the century when poor whites were gaining political leverage but yet were little better off economically than blacks. Blalock's (1957) research indicates that black-white differences in education, occupation, and income vary with percent non-white in 245 southern counties . . . Viewed in this manner, minority visibility may be far more important as a precipitating factor in race relations in the industrializing South than is often thought to be the case.

Van den Berghe also links the persistence of racial cleavages in contemporary, industrial societies to the enduring phenomenon of the racial ghetto. This formulation departs from much of earlier theorizing on southern race relations which tended to assume that industrialization and urbanization in the region would result in the decline of racial prejudice and the eventual assimilation of the black community . . . Blalock (1959), in his analysis of southern census data, finds little support for believing that urbanization prompts significant decreases in status inequalities. Matthews and Prothro (1963), likewise, find little evidence that either urbanization or industrialization is significantly associated with southern black voter registration and political participation.

Much of the literature on assimilation tends to minimize the significance of structural pluralism in race and ethnic relations, and the importance of residential patterns undergirding such pluralism. The residential base of a minority, in fact, takes on added significance in a modern competitive society, both as a locus of racial-ethnic identity and as a structural basis for sustaining inter-group images in the broader society . . . Since prejudice is to a large extent a product of the processes in which racial groups form images of themselves and others, residential segregation undergirds these collective processes, for it facilitates both group separation and perceived minority threat. In the absence of clearly-defined racial norms, residential structures foster competitive relations by ensuring a collective sense of group position, i.e., blacks relative to whites.

HYPOTHESES AND CAUSAL MODEL

The major exploratory hypothesis is:
   (1) Residential segregation indices of blacks in southern cities are positively related to black-white inequalities in education, occupation, and income.
Drawing from the theoretical statements of van den Berghe, Blalock, and others, we can formalize two additional propositions.

(2) Percent non-white is positively related to educational, occupational, and income inequalities.

(3) Age of southern city is inversely related to educational, occupational, and income inequalities.

Proposition 2 is supported by previous research (Blalock, 1957). The third proposition logically follows from (a) Schnore and Evenson's (1966) finding of a negative association between age of southern city and degree of residential segregation, and (b) Proposition 1 stated above. Age of city, also, is an indirect measure of paternalistic heritage, in van den Berghe's meaning of the term.

Examining the three "independent" variables—residential segregation, percent non-white, and age of city—in relation to status inequalities is facilitated through the use of postulated causal models (see Simon, 1954; Blalock, 1964). The advantages of this procedure, primarily, are that assumptions about the causal ordering of variables are made explicit; and the inferences made are subject to critical examination within the logic of those assumptions.

Based on the above reasoning, the simple chain model is proposed in Figure 1.

Given certain simplifying assumptions,[1] it is possible to formulate a set of prediction equations based upon the postulated model.[2]

SAMPLE AND MEASURES

A sample of 100 cities was randomly selected from a universe of all incorporated places of 50,000 or more inhabitants in the United States, having at least 1,000 non-white housing units for which block data were collected in the 1960 Census of Housing. Thirty-nine cities were southern by definition of the U.S. Census Bureau, and it is these city units on which the present analysis is carried out.

The major independent variable is the degree of black residential segregation in 1960. Taeuber and Taeuber's "index of residential segregation" (IRS), which is based upon block-

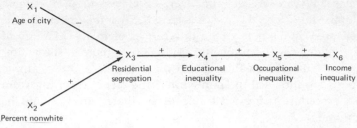

FIGURE 1.   *Model I*

specific data, was used in the operational procedure; index scores for each city were taken directly from their computations (1965, pp. 39–41). This index is computed as follows:

$$D = \frac{\Sigma |X - Y|}{2}$$

where D is the index of dissimilarity, X is the percentage of one population in a given subclass, and Y is the percentage of the other population in the same subclass. D for an urban area is computed by summing the absolute differences between X and Y for all city blocks and dividing the sum by two. The index may assume values between 0 and 100. The higher the value, the higher the degree of residential segregation.

Percent non-white was taken directly from the U.S. Census. Age of southern city was not as simple to construct. Following other researchers (Schnore, 1965), the number of decades since the city reached 10,000 inhabitants is used as a measure of a city's age.

With the three status inequality measures, inequality in each instance was indexed as the difference between whites and non-whites for a given city unit. Educational inequality is defined as the percentage differences between whites and non-whites of males 25 and over with more than six years of education. Occupational inequality is measured similarly by taking the percentage difference between the two groups of males 14 years of age and over, employed in professional, managerial, clerical, and sales jobs. Income inequality is measured by the percentage differences of males 14 years of age and over with an income of $1,500 or more. "Non-white" is used interchangeably with "black." While other ethnic groups are included in "non-white," the errors resulting from this procedure using a sample of southern cities should be minimal.

FINDINGS

Table 1 presents the zero-order associations among all pairs of variables. While few of the correlation coefficients can be considered strong, the table shows that the expected patterns do emerge. These patterns require specific examination.

TABLE 1.   *Zero-order Correlation Coefficients for 39 Southern Cities*

VARIABLE	1	2	3	4	5	6	7
(1) Age of City		.061	.566*	−.231	−.542*	−.205	−.344*
(2) Percent Non-white			−.079	.279	.174	.146	.178
(3) City Size				−.186	−.581*	−.272	−.462*
(4) IRS					.367*	.415*	.293*
(5) Educational Inequality						.504*	.637*
(6) Occupational Inequality							.370*
(7) Income Inequality							

* Statistically significant at .05 level.

Residential Segregation and Inequality

The first hypothesis examined is: the index of residential segregation (IRS) should vary positively with the status inequality measures. Using all three measures of status inequalities—educational, occupational, and income—the data support this conclusion. All three relationships are positive and are statistically significant at the .05 level. In order to minimize the possibility of making a spurious inference, partial correlation analysis was used as a means of statistically controlling for other, possibly confounding, variables. Table 2 shows the relationships of IRS and the three inequality measures while controlling for the effects due to percent non-white, city size, and age of city. As customary, the partials are somewhat weaker than the zero-order coefficients. Controlling for these additional variables produces noticeable effects in the case of income inequality. The relationship between IRS and income inequality weakens, with

TABLE 2. *Correlation Coefficients for IRS by Educational, Occupational, and Income Inequality Controlling for Percent Non-White, City Size, and Age of City*
(N = 39)

| | | PARTIAL CORRELATIONS | | | |
IRS by	Total	Percent Non-White Controlled	City Size Controlled	Age of City Controlled	Percent Non-White City Size and Age of City Controlled
Educational Inequality	.367*	.336*	.341*	.300*	.282*
Occupational Inequality	.415*	.404*	.389*	.392*	.379*
Income Inequality	.293*	.261	.254	.248	.236

NOTE: Dependent Variable is IRS (Index of Residential Segregation).

* Statistical significance at .05 level.

the controls introduced singularly or jointly, to a point below the .05 level of statistical significance. This result is not too surprising, however, given the ordering of the variables. Income inequality is farthest removed in the sequence of variables from IRS and would, most likely, be less related to it than the other two inequality measures. Judged on the basis of what happens to the relationships between IRS and both educational and occupational inequalities, our conclusion is that the hypothesized relationship is not substantially altered by controlling for percent non-white, city size, or age of city.

Percent Non-White, Age of City, and Residential Segregation

Percent non-white is shown to be positively related with IRS as well as with the educational, occupational, and income inequality measures. These relationships are generally weak, however, the strongest association being with IRS.

Age of city, as expected, is inversely associated with IRS and the inequality measures. The older the southern city, the *less* the residential segregation by color and the black-white status differentials. Though the association between age of city and residential segregation falls below the .05 level of statistical significance, yet two of the correlations between age of city and the inequality measures are moderately strong.

Since age of city as used here is at best only an indirect measure of paternalistic heritage, the possibility that its relationship to IRS is spurious deserves further examination. Quite clearly, age of city is bound up with city size ($r = .566$); and from a theoretical point of view it may seem somewhat more "sociological" to utilize the latter as the explanatory variable. Findings reported in Table 3 raise some question about such procedure however. Partial correlations are shown which indicate the association between IRS and each of the three independent variables—percent non-white, city size, and age of city—while controlling simultaneously for the other two. When age of city and percent non-white are controlled, the partial between city size and residential segregation is reduced from $-.186$ to a modest $-.091$. By contrast, the

TABLE 3. *Summary of Partial Correlation Analysis: IRS, City Size, Percent Non-White, and Age of City for 39 Southern Cities*

INDEPENDENT VARIABLE	CONTROLLED VARIABLES	PARTIAL CORRELATION
City Size	Percent Non-White and Age	.091
Percent Non-White	City Size and Age	.315*
Age	Percent Non-White and City Size	—.345*

NOTE: Dependent Variable is IRS (Index of Residential Segregation).
* Statistical significance at .05 level.

second-order partials involving percent non-white and age of city as independent variables are substantially increased from .279 to .315 and from —.231 to —.345, respectively. These findings indicate, at the very least, that variation in IRS attributable to age of city is *not* accounted for by city size. Moreover, the data suggest that the age of a city is a rather potent factor in affecting its current (1960) level of residential segregation regardless of size or non-white percentage. . . . Given this initial support for the hypotheses, next we examine the prediction equations . . . About half of the predictions made either do not hold or are quite poor. Such results are not too surprising given the fact that Model I was purposely simple as a first-approximation of the data patterns . . .

DISCUSSION AND RE-FORMULATION OF MODEL

As shown above, the data provide some support for the causal model. While the findings are by no means conclusive, there is enough support to suggest that the residential segregation hypothesis is plausible. At the very least, it seems worthy of further examination.

Following the logic of causal model construction, one approach in examining such a hypothesis is to modify the model in ways that are theoretically meaningful and will yield somewhat better empirical predictions. In doing so, it makes sense to introduce modifications where the largest discrepancies occur between actual and predicted values and, where possible, among variables operating near the beginning of the causal sequence (see Blalock, 1964: p. 80). Both criteria point to the need for modifying the model with respect to the relationship between a southern city's age and educational inequality . . . The data suggest adding an arrow between X_1 and X_4, i.e., the influence attributable to a city's age upon educational inequality being both direct and indirect (through the intervening variable of residential segregation). From a theoretical point of view, this possibility is quite consistent with the argument advanced in this paper. Among the younger, more industrialized cities of the South where competitive race relations are more keenly felt, educational institutions play a critical role in preparing whites to take advantage of competitive opportunities. By 1960, certainly, anything like comparable educational opportunity for blacks did not exist.

A second major discrepancy in Model I concerns the chain linkages among the inequality measures. On the basis of the empirical results, it appears that an arrow is needed directly linking residential segregation and occupational inequality, i.e., between X_3 and X_5. Segregated ghetto life results very likely in motivational and, perhaps, discriminatory consequences apart from those directly affecting educational opportunities. Stunted incentives and aspirations, isolation from dominant group opportunities for achievement, the evolution of distinctive subcultural and counter-cultural norms—all are examples of how occupational values may be aggravated by ghetto life. Moreover, perceived minority threat due to residential concentration may be a factor evoking dominant group members to intensify occupational discrimination, thereby restricting even those blacks with competitive skills to inferior positions. One final point should be made about how educational inequality is measured: using "years" of schooling ignores the serious issue of equality of education. These considerations point to the inescapable fact that southern blacks with educational levels comparable to whites are not as prepared to take full competitive advantage of their education.

In constructing a more satisfactory model the following modifications are introduced: (a) an arrow drawn between X_1 and X_4; (b) an arrow drawn between X_3 and X_5; and (c) an arrow drawn between X_4 and X_6, involving a direct linkage between educational inequality and income inequality . . . These modifications are shown in Model II as dotted lines . . . Model II predictions as a whole are a reasonably good fit, especially if allowances are made for the distortive effects of measurement error and sampling variation.

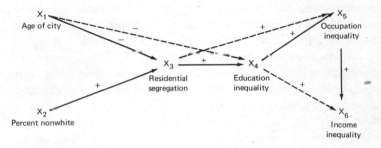

FIGURE 2.   *Model II*

CONCLUSION

The purpose of this paper was to examine how residential segregation as a variable may be incorporated into an economic competitive model of race relations in the American South. Age of southern city and percent non-white were suggested as determinants of level of residential segregation, which, together with the status inequality measures, provided the variables for testing a causal ordering of their interrelationships.

While the data do not support the simple chain model, considerable support was found for the modified, more complex, system of relationships. It appears that level of residential segregation is important not only for its direct effects on educational inequality but because of its direct and indirect effects upon occupational inequality as well. Moreover, as the fit of the causal predictions suggests, there is support for conceptualizing residential segregation as an intervening variable, between percent non-white and age of city on the one hand, and the three status inequality measures on the other.

Specifically, these findings raise the question as to whether it is the minority percentage itself or the *dispersion* of the minority population that is salient insofar as motivations to discriminate are concerned. Aside from implications for public policy, the inferences pertaining to residential segregation, if valid, are pertinent to race relations theory. If indeed the dispersion factor is pre-eminent, then greater attention to a minority's visibility is called for in competition theories of race relations . . .

Also, the findings demonstrate the crucial importance of the residential ghetto, with respect both to its structural and perceptual consequences. Whatever conclusions are reached in subsequent research on the motivational factors underlying discrimination, the implications of ghetto segmentation and its functions in a modern, industrial society have only begun to be examined. Van den Berghe's assertion that racial cleavages evolving out of ghetto segmentation "constitute one of the major sources of strain and disequilibrium in such systems" (1967) is likely to be borne out, and promises to be a theoretically significant point of departure for subsequent research. Further analyses of residential segregation will likely uncover the need for more complex models of causal influence . . .

Whatever refinements may come, methodologically and theoretically, the fact that residential segregation scores, age of city, and percent non-white are related as they are to status inequalities suggests that sociologists should proceed with caution in inferring that modernization brings about vast improvements in race relations. Current efforts at implementing school desegregation through busing in the South may, if continued long enough, modify the effects of ghetto life in the direction of less inequality. However, the ghetto is an enduring phenomenon, its importance in contemporary race relations will not soon disappear. If the findings of this study are at all valid, it appears that ghetto structures are in fact firmly implicated in a system of competitive race relations, and that the latter warrants less optimism about the elimination of racism in American life than many are prone to expect.

BIBLIOGRAPHY

H. M. Blalock, "Per cent non-white and discrimination in the south," *American Sociological Review*, 1957, 22, 677–682.

H. M. Blalock, "Urbanization and discrimination," *Social Problems*, 1959, 7, 146–152.

H. M. Blalock, *Causal Inferences in Nonexperimental Research.* Chapel Hill: University of North Carolina Press, 1964.

H. M. Blalock, *Toward a Theory of Minority-Group Relations.* New York: Wiley, 1967.

H. M. Blalock and A. B. Blalock, *Methodology in Social Research.* New York: McGraw-Hill, 1968.

W. M. Kephart, "Negro visibility," *American Sociological Review*, 1954, 19, 462–467.

S. Lieberson, "The impact of residential segregation on ethnic assimilation." *Social Forces*, 1961, 40, 52–57.

D. R. Matthews and J. W. Prothro, "Social and economic factors and Negro voter registration in the south." *American Political Science Review*, 1963, 57, 24–44.

G. Myrdal, *An American Dilemma.* New York: Harper & Row, 1944.

L. P. Schnore, *The Urban Scene: Human Ecology and Demography.* New York: Free Press, 1965.

L. F. Schnore and P. C. Evenson, "Segregation in southern cities," *American Journal of Sociology*, 1966, 72, 58–67.

H. A. Simon, "Spurious correlation: A causal interpretation," *Journal of the American Statistical Association*, 1954, 49, 467–479.

K. E. Taeuber and A. F. Taeuber, *Negroes in Cities.* Chicago: Aldine, 1965.

P. van den Berghe, *Race and Racism: A Comparative Perspective.* New York: Wiley, 1967.

C. V. Woodward, *The Strange Career of Jim Crow.* New York: Oxford University Press, 1955.

❪ 10 ❫

Black Unemployment
in the Ghetto*

*NATIONAL COMMITTEE AGAINST
DISCRIMINATION IN HOUSING*

The persistence of widespread poverty stemming from un-employment and under-employment among the nation's minorities, particularly among nonwhites, is a most critical domestic problem in the United States today.

Although Negroes live in all sections of the country, they are heavily concentrated in the core cities of metropolitan areas. Let us examine the unemployment and under-employment rates among nonwhites for the nation as a whole and for those who remain confined in central city ghettos . . .

For 20 years, nonwhite unemployment rates have fluctuated between 1½ and 2½ times those for whites, depending upon the state of the national economy. The lowest unemployment rate yet achieved by Negroes in the post-World War II period occurred during the Korean War when nonwhite unemployment fell from 9 per cent in 1950 to 4.5 per cent in 1953. With the end of the Korean War, nonwhite unemployment jumped 100 per cent and remained at a very high level throughout the remaining years of the 1950's and the early 1960's. In the recession years 1958 and 1961, nonwhite unemployment rose above 12 per cent . . .

* Abridged from National Committee Against Discrimination in Housing, *The Impact of Housing Patterns on Job Opportunities*. New York: NCADH, 1968; pp. 14–20. Reprinted with permission of the publisher.

The 1965 Special Census for South and East Los Angeles, taken following the Watts riot, showed that unemployment in racially-isolated areas of that city fell by only 10 per cent in the 1960's as compared with a decline of 50 per cent for the white unemployment rate. This disparity occurred despite notable increases in recent years in blue-collar employment— in construction, in manufacturing, and in service work of all types.

Of even greater significance is the fact that for the nation as a whole, nonwhite unemployment is increasing relative to white unemployment despite military activity in Vietnam and the over-representation of Negroes in the armed forces, which has undoubtedly removed many potentially unemployed persons from the unemployment rolls. Between 1965 and 1966, for example, while Vietnam spending more than doubled, the unemployment rate for whites fell almost 20 per cent while the unemployment rate for Negroes fell only 9.9 per cent: from 4.1 per cent to 3.3 per cent for whites, and from 8.1 per cent to 7.3 per cent for Negroes. Not only did Negroes bear a disproportionate share of the fighting in Vietnam, but here at home they did not participate in the economic boom that resulted from the national investment for military purposes . . .

National unemployment rates do not reveal the extent of job-related problems confronting the masses of Negroes who are concentrated in the nation's urban ghettos. Let us look now at unemployment rates for metropolitan areas and compare them with central city and suburban figures.

In poverty areas in 1966, the unemployment rate for nonwhites was 9.4 per cent, compared to 6 per cent for whites. An explanation is required in the case of this last figure, for the use of the designation "whites" in poverty areas includes, by definition, millions of Mexican-Americans and Puerto Ricans whose unemployment problems are similar to those of Negroes. For this reason, the "white"/"nonwhite" designations do not accurately describe majority/minority employment disparity. Thus, 9.4 understates and 6 per cent overstates minority/majority unemployment in poverty areas. In non-poverty areas, white unemployment was 3.6 per cent; non-white, 7.2 (Table 1).

More importantly, within poverty areas the *number* of nonwhites who were unemployed exceeds the *number* of whites who were unemployed, whereas the reverse is true for non-poverty areas. The bulk of the poor and unemployed in the largest SMSA's are Negroes, Mexican-Americans or Puerto Ricans. Negroes comprise from 81 to 96 per cent of the residents of poverty neighborhoods in Cleveland; 60 per cent of the poverty area residents of Oakland; 70 per cent in Boston; 81 per cent in Los Angeles; 65 per cent in San Francisco; 93 per cent in St. Louis . . .

If unemployment rates for areas of minority concentration within a metropolitan area are compared with unemployment rates for the metropolitan area as a whole (including the poverty districts), considerable insight is gained into the disparity between white and nonwhite unemployment problems. As shown in Table 2, this study has tabulated the unemployment rates for ghetto areas in Boston, Cleveland, Detroit, Los Angeles, New York, Philadelphia, St. Louis, San Francisco, Phoenix and San Antonio, and has compared these with unemployment rates for the respective metropolitan areas.

With the exception of San Antonio, each of these slum ghettos erupted in violence between 1965 and 1967. It is not difficult to see why.

TABLE 1.   *Unemployment in All Standard Metropolitan Statistical Areas**

| | POVERTY SECTIONS | | | | NON-POVERTY SECTIONS | | | |
| | *Nonwhite* | | *White* | | *Nonwhite* | | *White* | |
	Number	Rate	Number	Rate	Number	Rate	Number	Rate
Total	280,000	9.4	220,000	6.0	186,000	7.2	1,197,000	3.6
Men	182,000	10.2	148,000	6.3	100,000	6.9	731,000	3.4
Women	98,000	8.1	72,000	5.4	86,000	7.6	466,000	3.9

* March, 1966.
SOURCE: Bureau of Labor Statistics Report—*Monthly Labor Review*, Oct., 1966; page 1108, volume 89:10.

TABLE 2. *Unemployment Rates: Ghetto Areas and Surrounding Metropolitan Areas*

| | | UNEMPLOYMENT RATE | |
SMSA	Ghetto area	Ghetto*	SMSA†
Boston	Roxbury	6.9	3.7
Cleveland	Hough and surrounding neighborhood	15.6	3.5
Detroit	Central Woodward	10.1	4.3
Los Angeles	South Los Angeles	12.0	6.0
New York	Harlem	8.1	4.6
	East Harlem	9.0	
	Bedford-Stuyvesant	6.2	
Philadelphia	North Philadelphia	11.0	4.3
Phoenix	Salt River Bed	13.2	—
St. Louis	North Side	12.9	4.5
San Antonio	East and West Sides	8.1	—
San Francisco-Oakland	Mission-Fillmore	11.1	5.2
	Bayside	13.0	

* as of November 1966.
† average for year ending August 1966.
SOURCE: *1967 Manpower Report of the President*, page 75; metropolitan area data are based on special tabulation of data from the *Current Population Survey*.

In the Hough and other slum sections of Cleveland, for example, the unemployment rate was 15.6 per cent, compared with an average for the Greater Cleveland area of 3.5 per cent. In North St. Louis, where 80 per cent of all Negroes in St. Louis City reside, the unemployment rate was 12.9 per cent versus 4.5 per cent for the St. Louis metropolitan area. In Oakland (San Francisco), the comparable figures are 13 per cent and 5.2 per cent. Indeed, the severe unemployment which the Negro experienced in the 1960s is comparable to that experienced by the American public-at-large only in the depth of the Great Depression.

Even these figures do not tell the complete story, for unemployment data constitute an inadequate index to the job-location problem of many central city residents, especially Negroes. Conventional unemployment data measure only

insured unemployment, which presumes a previous and continuing work history. These data do not reckon with the ex-
traordinarily high non-labor force participation rates among
Negro males, nor with the extent of involuntary part-time
work within the Negro community, nor with the full-time
worker who earns less than minimum subsistence need, nor
finally, with the undercount of adult Negro males in the
census of 1960. This undercount has been variously estimated
to be between 10 and 15 per cent.

To understand these problems more fully, the U.S. Department of Labor undertook a special survey of joblessness and
poverty in 14 of the worst ghetto areas of the United States
(the Department called them slums). The survey was conducted, in cooperation with state agencies, during November
1966, and the results have recently been made public. It was
found, first, that Negroes constituted 3 of every 4 unemployed
in the areas studied and that their conventional unemployment rate was nearly 10 per cent. Among teenagers, 16 to 19
years old, the average unemployment rate was 28 per cent;
the unemployment rate for nonwhite boys in the age group
from 14 to 19 was 31 per cent, and for nonwhite girls, 46
per cent.

Secondly, nearly 7 per cent of the residents of the slum
ghettos were employed only part time although they would
have worked full time if the opportunity to do so was available. (For the nation as a whole the comparable figure was
then 2.3 per cent.) One out of every five working full time in
these areas *earned less than the basic minimum needs for a
family of four*, or $60 per week. Nearly 40 per cent of the
families studied reported incomes *under* $3,000 as compared
with one-quarter for the country as a whole. Moreover, if these
1966 figures are compared with modest but adequate income
requirements in areas where Negroes are concentrated—
$7,281 for a family of four in New York City, for example—it
is clear that a far greater percentage of these ghetto families
were unable to escape a life marked by poverty.

Two other survey findings are useful here. An inordinately
large number of ghetto residents of working age were not

counted in the labor force of these metropolitan areas. Some of these individuals doubtless did not want work, but most have probably given up hope of ever securing a well-paying job. Second, more than 20 per cent of adult men who were likely to be part of the population of these 14 slum areas—given normal distributions of male and female of the population as a whole—were not located by the Department's surveys. When all of these negative factors are taken into account, the unemployment problems of Negroes and of the areas in which they are resident take on even more shocking dimensions.

As a result of these surveys, the Labor Department developed a new technique for measuring unemployment. This new technique is called the sub-employment index, and it covers an entire employment-hardship area. The sub-employment index measures, first, those unemployed workers who are "actively looking for work and unable to find it"; second, those working part-time but seeking full-time jobs; third, heads of households earning less than $60 per week and individuals under 65 earning less than $56 a week in a full-time job; fourth, half the number of non-participants in the male age group 20–64 who are not in the labor force; fifth, a "conservative and carefully considered estimate of the male 'undercount' group." Sub-employment rates for the areas covered by the November 1966 survey are listed in Figure 1.

Average sub-employment for all of these cities was an incredible 34.6 per cent. This means that one out of every three residents of these racially- and ethnically-isolated communities who is already a worker or who could become a worker was unemployed, under-employed, or employed at poverty-level wages. [There are excellent indications that this crisis situation, if anything, had become even more severe by the middle 1970s.—Ed.]

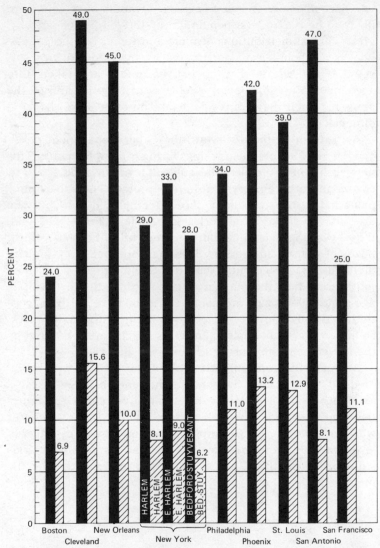

FIGURE 1. *Subemployment Index (Black Bars) and Standard Unemployment Index (Light Bars) in Ghetto Areas (Nov. 1966)*

⟦ 11 ⟧

Employment Discrimination on
the Government Job*

U.S. COMMISSION ON CIVIL RIGHTS

Recruitment programs which are well planned and executed and job requirements which have been stripped of irrelevant and nonessential elements cannot, by themselves, assure that greater numbers of minority workers will enter public service. The decisive factor is the minority worker's attitude toward the government as an employer. This attitude is most often influenced by the experience of other minority workers on the job.

PROMOTION

Promotional opportunities for minority employees are critical factors in the achievement of equal employment opportunity. Minority persons interviewed in all governments studied repeatedly criticized their limited access to higher level jobs and to supervisory positions. The survey data provide some support for these charges in that minorities are underrepresented in the official and managerial occupations . . .

Promotion is a process of selection from inside the system.

* Abridged from U.S. Commission on Civil Rights, *For All the People . . . By All the People: A Report on Equal Opportunity in State and Local Government Employment.* Washington, D.C.: GPO, 1969; pp. 57–62.

Consequently, many of the problems encountered in entry selection reappear. Promotions are generally based on one or more of the following factors: education and experience, length of service, performance, written and oral test results, and such character traits as leadership, personality, and cooperation. Stahl found that none of these factors alone is adequate as a measure of qualification for promotion and that appropriate combinations must be devised for each instance.[1]

Of the several factors considered in measuring promotion potential, those not present in entry selection are performance, supervisory evaluation, and length of service. In non-civil-service governments, promotions may be based entirely upon supervisory evaluation. This method, for example, was found to be in use in Shelby County, Tennessee. In Michigan, supervisory evaluations accounted for one-quarter of the final score. The problems presented here stem from the extent to which the evaluation is subjective and to the possibility of discrimination. Two Philadelphia respondents charged that supervisors' evaluations frequently are used against minority group employees who become eligible for promotion. This, they stated, is accomplished by systematically lowering efficiency ratings from "outstanding" to "satisfactory." An official of the Michigan State Civil Rights Commission said that it is quite common in Detroit for a Negro employee to get high efficiency ratings until he has accumulated enough seniority for promotion at which point his ratings begin to decrease. A Memphis respondent noted that "ratings include ability for leadership but Negroes are never given the opportunity to lead so how can they be rated on leadership?" . . .

Seniority or length of service is another factor which is often said to limit promotional opportunities for minorities. In many areas, since minorities have been systematically excluded from employment in the past, they are not on equal footing with majority group employees. Seniority, however, often is a test of endurance rather than of ability. One public personnel expert says that:

. . . some highly inbred government organizations take satisfaction in a tightly knit promotion-from-within-policy. Yet they are far from the best-run agencies in their respective jurisdictions. Too often there has been an over-emphasis on seniority. . . . Over-emphasis on "years of experience" still plagues many agencies in their effort to achieve objectivity in selection for promotion. Quite often the highly touted "20 years of experience" is merely one year of experience 20 times.[2]

Stahl found, however, that while some public units give seniority an arbitrary weight on promotion examinations, the great majority merely provide that seniority shall be given consideration.[3]

Seniority carried varied weight in several of the jurisdictions studied in considering individuals for promotion. In Oakland, California, it accounted for 10 percent of the final score. In Fulton County, Georgia, up to 10 extra points were given for seniority. One respondent emphasized the need to recruit Negroes into the Oakland government, especially as policemen and firemen, to insure favorable promotion opportunities in the future. He said it was especially crucial since a large number of employees hired immediately after World War II will be retiring in a few years.

The Commission's study found several examples in which emphasis on seniority was a barrier to minority promotion. An Atlanta personnel official confirmed that black employees were not promoted at the same rate as whites because "seniority is involved" and "Negroes have not filled many jobs until recently." In Detroit, all promotions in the fire department are made solely on the basis of seniority . . .

Except where seniority is the sole or primary factor, the promotion system is frequently more flexible than the entry process. There are a number of ways in which an advanced level position can be filled: (1) by open competitive examination where anyone who meets the prerequisities can compete; (2) by closed competitive examination for which only specific incumbent employees are eligible; (3) by a noncompetitive examination in which the individual merely obtains a passing score; (4) by a combination of other factors such as recommendation or seniority. It also is possible for an individual to be promoted or advanced at the discretion of his agency. For example, in Louisiana, a civil service official reported that employees earning less than $400 per month can be promoted as long as they meet the basic job requirements. In Detroit, a department may approve an in-service promotion without clearing it through the civil service commission if the employee has been in-grade for 1 year and is not being promoted more than two classes.

Flexibility, however, inevitably leads to manipulation. The chairman of the board of supervisors for Wayne County has said that there is a "subtle agreement" between department heads and the civil service commission. Through this arrangement, he said, some county department heads reject Negroes who are at the top of civil service job eligibility lists and fill vacant positions with white persons who are transferred from existing county jobs. He said: "Department heads always have some sort of reason for rejecting the Negro applicant, but the whole process is repeated too many times to be unintentional." . . .

General charges of discrimination in promoting minorities were found in several jurisdictions. At a 1966 open meeting held by the Tennessee State Advisory Committee to the U.S. Commission on Civil Rights, the executive secretary of the Memphis Branch of the National Association for the Advancement of Colored People charged the Shelby County government with discrimination and said:

In the Engineers Department there is one air conditioner maintenance man. He receives the pay of a porter. However, he trains whites in air conditioner maintenance, but he doesn't receive pay in this category. . . .

In the Record Room Department there is one Negro, who in some instances does work out of her category, but she is classified as a maid. There is one Negro with a higher classification in this department.

At the same meeting a county commissioner presented an outline of an affirmative action program designed to upgrade black employees. Among the steps taken he cited on-the-job training programs and a special screening of all black employees to determine who might be qualified for upgrading. As a result eight black employees were upgraded. These promotions evidently were of a minor nature for the data collected in this survey indicate only one black employee classified in the official and managerial category and two black supervisors in the corrections department.

Personnel officials in Memphis stated that Negroes were a small minority among supervisors and that no black employees supervised white employees. The reluctance to allow Negroes to supervise whites may account for the extremely small number of black employees in supervisory positions in the South as well as in some northern agencies. In the Memphis Public Works Department, most of the laborers are black and most of their supervisors are white. This situation contradicts statements of department officials that they prefer to promote from within before seeking new personnel. One official stated that labor foremen are hired or promoted on the basis of a written examination and black laborers do not qualify. "In fact," he said, "many of the laborers are plain darn lazy and satisfied with a laborer's salary."

In 1965 the San Francisco Human Rights Commission collected data on city employees by race, occupation, and whether the job was an initial entrance, promotion, or executive appointment position. Although the data do not indicate length of service, they do provide some insights into where minorities stand with respect to promotions. An official responsible for collecting the data indicated that length of service may not be a crucial factor. Based on his experience with the San Francisco Civil Service Commission and the Human Rights Commission, he stated that Negroes tended to have more experience than whites in service, institutional, and transport occupations, yet the proportion of Negroes in promotion level jobs was smaller than the proportion of whites.

The data showed that the proportion of employees in promotive as opposed to entrance or appointive positions was about equal for the majority group and Oriental Americans (31.3 percent and 33.0 percent, respectively), but was considerably lower for Spanish Americans and lowest for black employees (13.7 and 10.7 percent, respectively.) The representation of Negroes in promotive positions is exceptionally weak in the white-collar occupational groups. Only 3.5 percent of black employees in semiprofessional and technical positions are in promotive positions compared to 31.0 percent of the majority group, 38.5 percent of Oriental Americans, and 25.0 percent of Spanish Americans. Black representation in promotive positions is more variable in the blue-collar and service worker occupational groups.

The San Francisco data, then, suggest that the promotion rate for Negroes and Spanish Americans is lower than that for other employees . . .

PREJUDICED ATTITUDES AND BIASED TREATMENT

Blatant examples of discriminatory treatment of minority employees were reported to, or observed by, Commission staff in several governments. Segregated facilities, segregated work assignments, social ostracism, and lack of courtesy were all reported to exist. One San Francisco department head reportedly refers to Negroes as "boys" and Orientals as "Chinamen." In the South, Negroes are often called "boy" or other inappropriate names. In Shelby County, it was reported that instead of saying "Mr." or "Mrs." some white employees used the terms "reverend" or "doctor." In the same county a recently upgraded Negro is not welcome at the lunch table with his white colleagues. The public works department in Detroit was alleged to assign workmen to crews on a segregated basis. The park commission in Memphis used integrated staffs on "integrated" playgrounds but no black workers are assigned to white area playgrounds.

In Louisiana, the building housing the department of highways has maintained segregated washroom facilities in spite of the fact that the Governor ordered that all signs designating segregated facilities be removed from State buildings. When questioned about the signs, a top official of the department stated that this policy would not change because "I don't think it [desegregated washrooms] is healthy for the employees of this department." Drinking fountains are not segregated, but he felt this was not inconsistent with his views on washrooms because, he said: "There's no way they can get their mouth [sic] down on a drinking fountain."

Such an example of blatant racism openly admitted by a public official is atypical. Other public officials, however, revealed obviously prejudiced attitudes to Commission staff. A Houston official stated bluntly: "I will admit that there is prejudice here. I am prejudiced myself. I am a Texan." A high level staff member of the Pennsylvania Civil Service Commission said that if given three secretarial candidates of whom one was black, he "would naturally select one of the two white secretaries." He explained that he felt that "A boss must be able to identify with his secretary and a sense of closeness must prevail." He stated that: "It would be normal to assume that a boss would enjoy a close relationship with a secretary of his own race." A district personnel officer of the California Department of Public Works emphatically stated that 99 percent of disciplinary actions in the maintenance department were against nonwhites. When he checked his files, he found that 99 percent of disciplinary actions were against white, not black employees.

In Baton Rouge, the director of finance was asked if he would hire a Negro. He responded by asking the interviewer if he would steal a million dollars. The personnel director of the Georgia State Highway Department, explaining why there was no black secretarial help in the department, said:

There are no Negroes at all there. It will be a while before we do hire them. The people in the office don't want them. We are not required to hire them by the Civil Rights Act of 1964. . . . States and municipalities are excluded by the Civil Rights Act from hiring Negroes. . . . But I am sympathetic to them. I'm not opposed to hiring a nigger.

Far more common than these direct expressions of racial prejudice were the expressions of indifference to the subject of equal employment opportunity. Many officials showed no concern about current issues in the field of equal opportunity. Again and again personnel people conveyed the belief that their responsibility in equal opportunity hiring stopped after

they had selected eligible applicants from lists on a nondis-
criminatory basis. They assured Commission staff that they
followed this rule to the letter. But concern with some of the
less obvious inequalities discussed in the preceding sections,
such as excessively high qualifications or testing devices
which do not fairly evaluate potential job performance, was
not seen as part of the job. The Oakland Department of
Streets and Engineering illustrates this point. An official
stated that he believed that minorities in his agency were
probably promoted as fast as whites. While he agreed that "it
would be useful" to collect promotion statistics since "you
can't tell now that promotions are equal," he was more concerned about the paperwork involved although he "would not
object" in principle to collecting promotion data . . .

Still other officials refused to recognize overt discrimination
as a problem but instead placed the blame on minority members. One southern official said: "I don't think they [Negroes]
are educating themselves well enough to take advantage of
the opportunity of employment." The director of a northern
county civil service commission expressed the opinion that,
as a whole, black employees in his county have a bad attitude
toward employment and responsibilities.

A general lack of sensitivity to the reluctance of minorities
to apply for jobs in governments and agencies with reputa-
tions for discrimination was evident in the South. A Louisiana
administrator in the department of highways assured Commission staff that all jobs are open to Negroes and dismissed
the need to communicate this to the black community. This
department (the same one with segregated washroom facilities) has six black employees out of a total of 1,499. The
sentiments of the black community were expressed by a local
civil rights leader:

Black people know that people at the Capitol are white. We know
our place. We know we're not supposed to be there. . . . It's not
a question of what's on the books—it doesn't need to be. We can
get the picture in a lot of ways. . . . This fear of working in white
men's jobs just permeates the State. Most Negroes are afraid of
white people, afraid of working with them, and think they are
inferior to them.

A white official in Atlanta recognized this problem when he said: "When you walk into City Hall, you will see that it is a white man's world." This general feeling was expressed in other governments. When visible government—those working in city halls, county courthouses, and State capitols—tends to be all-white, the sincerity of a government's commitment to equal opportunity is seriously questioned by the minority community.

(12)

Patterns of Occupational Mobility Among Negro Men[*]

OTIS DUDLEY DUNCAN

The first reasonably adequate data on occupational mobility of American men became available only in 1964.[1] The initial tabulations did not include a breakdown by race, but this information is now at hand. Previous reports on patterns of mobility in the total male population[2] may be supplemented by a comparison of the patterns observed among Negro and non-Negro men.[3]

NET SHIFTS

Respondents to the questionnaire on "Occupational Changes in a Generation," administered as a supplement to the March, 1962 Current Population Survey, were classified

[*] Abridged from O. D. Duncan, "Patterns of Occupational Mobility Among Negro Men," *Demography*, 1968, 5, 11–22. Reprinted with permission of the publisher and author.

by occupation at three stages in the life cycle: the occupation of the father (or other family head) as of the respondent's sixteenth year; the respondent's first full-time civilian job; and the respondent's current occupation in March, 1962. (This pertained to the job held during the survey week for the employed, and to the last job held for the experienced unemployed.) The occupation classification is the conventional census major occupation grouping, extended by subclassifications according to industry or class of worker, or condensed by combining major groups into broader categories. There are three mobility tables, representing the transition from father's occupation to first job, from first job to 1962 occupation, and from father's occupation to 1962 occupation. Marginal distributions of these tables, using the extended classification, are shown for Negro and non-Negro men in Table 1.

TABLE 1. *Percentage Distribution by Occupational Origins and Destinations (Extended Classification), by Race, for Civilian Men Aged 25–64 Years, for the United States, March, 1962*

	FATHER'S OCCUPATION		FIRST JOB		1962 OCCUPATION	
OCCUPATION	Negro	Non-Negro	Negro	Non-Negro	Negro	Non-Negro
Professional, technical, and kindred workers						
1. Self-employed	0.4	1.3	0.3	0.7	0.2	1.6
2. Salaried	2.2	3.1	1.5	7.8	2.5	10.9
Managers, officials, and proprietors, except farm						
3. Salaried	0.4	3.8	0.2	1.3	1.1	8.6
4. Self-employed	0.9	7.7	0.1	0.6	1.4	7.5
Sales						
5. Other	0.1	2.1	0.2	1.5	0.1	3.4
6. Retail	0.5	1.8	1.2	5.1	0.5	1.6
7. Clerical	1.0	3.3	3.6	11.3	4.8	6.3

TABLE 1. *(Continued)*

OCCUPATION	FATHER'S OCCUPATION		FIRST JOB		1962 OCCUPATION	
	Negro	Non-Negro	Negro	Non-Negro	Negro	Non-Negro
Craftsmen, foremen, and kindred workers						
8. Manufacturing	1.6	6.1	1.1	3.4	3.1	7.6
9. Construction	3.2	5.0	1.1	2.3	2.9	5.1
10. Other	2.3	6.8	1.7	4.0	3.5	7.5
Operatives and kindred workers						
11. Manufacturing	4.7	7.9	12.0	15.2	11.6	9.8
12. Other	4.3	6.8	11.2	11.0	11.4	7.2
13. Service	5.5	4.2	10.4	3.2	15.2	4.5
Laborers						
14. Manufacturing	4.0	1.5	7.8	4.8	6.4	1.7
15. Others	9.2	3.7	14.4	7.4	17.6	3.0
16. Farmers	34.5	25.0	3.2	3.1	3.1	5.4
17. Farm laborers	5.0	2.4	21.2	13.6	4.6	1.4
18. Not reported[a]	20.3	7.3	8.9	3.7	10.0	6.9
Total	100.0	100.0	100.0	100.0	100.0	100.0
Number (000)	3,514	36,455	3,514	36,455	3,514	36,455

[a] Father's occupation or first job was not reported, or the respondent was not experienced in the civilian labor force (1962).

SOURCE: March 1962 Current Population Survey and supplementary questionnaire, "Occupational Changes in a Generation" (unpublished tables). See "Lifetime Occupational Mobility of Adult Males: March 1962," *Current Population Reports*, P-23, No. 11, May 12, 1964, for definitions and explanations.

A significant shift is observed between the distributions at the first and second stages of the life cycle, and again between the second and third. When classified by father's occupation, Negro men are "over-represented" at the level of service occupations and all lower categories and "under-

represented" among all higher categories.[4] When the classification is by first job, the same pattern prevails, except that
there is overrepresentation in one additional category—nonmanufacturing operatives. In terms of 1962 occupations,
there are two further variations: underrepresentation among
farmers and overrepresentation among both categories of
operatives.

There is considerable resemblance between the patterns of
net shifts between career stages for Negroes and non-Negroes,
but some major dissimilarities warrant notice. From father's
occupation to first job, there is a net shift into service jobs
and sales work (other than retail) for Negroes, but not for
non-Negroes. Non-Negroes experienced net shifts into salaried
professional employment, while the Negroes did not. From
first job to 1962, net shifts occurred for Negroes, but not for
non-Negroes, into nonmanufacturing laborer and operative
pursuits and into clerical occupations. Non-Negroes, unlike
Negroes, underwent net shifts into farming (owners and
tenants), non-retail sales jobs, and professional self-employ-
ment. Among the seventeen occupations, there were six for
which the composite pattern of net shifts, father's to first occupation and first to 1962 occupation, showed disparity by
race. Negroes failed to match the non-Negro pattern of net
shifts into self-employed professional jobs in 1962, into
salaried professional first jobs, and into farming in 1962,
and failed to match the net shifts out of clerical first jobs, out
of first jobs as manufacturing operatives, and away from
father's occupation in nonmanufacturing operative pursuits.
Although only net shifts have been discussed thus far, it is
clear that the occupational history of Negroes differs in many
particulars from that of whites.

The Negro sample is too small to permit analysis of gross
mobility in the 18×18 mobility tables. Nevertheless, some
striking results at this level of occupational detail can be obtained by an indirect method. For the total male sample, it is
possible to compute the transition matrix from each of the mobility tables, showing the probability that a man originating in
occupation group i finds his destination in occupation group j,

for each of the 324 (i,j) pairs. The "expected" destination distribution for either Negroes or non-Negroes is obtained by multiplying the origin distribution of that racial category by the transition matrix for all men. The assumption, in other words, is that the pattern of gross mobility is the same for Negroes and non-Negroes. The "expected" distributions so derived appear in Table 2. Differences between the "expected" destination distributions of Negroes and non-Negroes are solely a function of the differences in origin distributions. These differences may be taken to measure the impact of differentials in origin status, apart from differentials in subsequent mobility experience.

It is apparent from the strong patterning of the differences in Table 2 that the differences in origins are consequential. Even with the same probabilities of mobility, but given the difference in father's occupation, Negro first jobs manifest overrepresentation among service workers and all lower categories and underrepresentation in all higher categories. Similarly, when mobility from first job to 1962 occupation is (hypothetically) the same for Negroes and non-Negroes, the former are overrepresented in the last nine categories and underrepresented in the first nine. Using the same kind of hypothesis for mobility over the total span from father's occupation to 1962, we find Negro overrepresentation in all farm and manual occupations, except manufacturing craftsmen (where there is near parity), and underrepresentation at all white-collar levels.

Despite the evident importance of origins in producing occupational differentials at the time of working-force entry or as of 1962, the same analysis shows that this source of disparity is much less important than are differentials in mobility patterns. This conclusion is reached by summarizing the differences between Negroes and non-Negroes in both actual and "expected" destination distributions, as well as in origin distributions, by means of the index of dissimilarity (the sum of the positive percentage-point differences between corresponding entries in the respective Negro and non-Negro distributions). Index values are shown in Table 3.

TABLE 2. *Percentage Distribution by Occupational Origins and Destinations (Extended Classification), by Race, for Civilian Men Aged 25–64 Years, for the United States, March, 1962*

OCCUPATION	FIRST JOB FROM FATHER'S OCCUPATION		1962 OCCUPATION, FROM FIRST JOB		1962 OCCUPATION, FROM FATHER'S OCCUPATION	
	Negro	Non-Negro	Negro	Non-Negro	Negro	Non-Negro
Professional, technical, and kindred workers						
1. Self-employed	0.4	0.7	0.7	1.5	0.9	1.5
2. Salaried	4.8	7.5	6.1	10.6	7.1	10.5
Managers, officials, and proprietors, except farm						
3. Salaried	0.7	1.3	5.5	8.2	5.7	8.2
4. Self-employed	0.3	0.6	6.1	7.1	6.0	7.1
Sales						
5. Other	0.7	1.4	2.1	3.2	2.0	3.2
6. Retail	3.7	4.8	1.4	1.6	1.4	1.6
7. Clerical	8.4	10.8	4.8	6.3	5.9	6.2
Craftsmen, foremen, and kindred workers						
8. Manufacturing	2.6	3.3	6.9	7.2	7.0	7.2
9. Construction	2.0	2.2	5.4	4.8	5.2	4.9
10. Other	3.3	3.9	7.5	7.1	7.3	7.1
Operatives and kindred workers						
11. Manufacturing	14.2	15.0	11.3	9.8	11.3	9.8
12. Other	10.8	11.0	8.9	7.4	8.6	7.5
13. Service	4.1	3.8	7.4	5.3	6.7	5.3
Laborers						
14. Manufacturing	5.7	5.0	2.7	2.1	2.7	2.1
15. Others	9.3	7.9	5.7	4.1	5.8	4.1
16. Farmers	4.2	3.0	6.5	5.0	6.8	5.0
17. Farm laborers	19.8	13.7	2.3	1.6	2.4	1.6
18. Not reported[a]	5.1	4.1	8.7	7.0	7.4	7.2
Total	100.0	100.0	100.0	100.0	100.0	100.0

[a] Father's occupation or first job was not reported, or the respondent was not experienced in the civilian labor force (1962).

TABLE 3. *Indexes of Dissimilarity and Net Mobility, Summarizing Comparisons of Occupational Mobility (Extended Classification) of Negro and Non-Negro Men Aged 25–64 Years, for the United States, March, 1962*

COMPARISON	FATHER'S OCCUPATION TO FIRST JOB	FIRST JOB TO 1962 OCCUPATION	FATHER'S OCCUPATION TO 1962 OCCUPATION
Dissimilarity between Negro and Non-Negro, with respect to:			
Origins	34.4	30.4	34.4
Destinations	30.4	42.3	42.3
"Expected" destinations	10.7	12.1	9.5
Net Mobility, Origin to Destination			
Negro	47.6	19.3	42.6
Non-Negro	45.6	37.3	22.1

SOURCE: Tables 1 and 2.

Consider the transition from father's occupation to first job. In terms of origins (in this case, father's occupation) the dissimilarity between Negroes and non-Negroes amounts to 34.4 percent. Given this disparity, but assuming that Negroes and non-Negroes have the same probabilities of moving from a given origin to each destination, a dissimilarity of only 10.7 percent would be observed in terms of first jobs. This "expected" dissimilarity is only one-third as large as the actual dissimilarity of first jobs—30.4 percent.

Similarly, given a common matrix of transition probabilities to describe the movement from first jobs to 1962 occupations, the dissimilarity of 30.4 percent observed at the origin stage would shrink to 12.1 percent at the destination. The actual result, however, is a dissimilarity of 42.3 percent at the destination, or about three and one-half times the "expected" dissimilarity.

Looking finally at the whole period, father's occupation to 1962 occupation, we see that the initial dissimilarity of 34.4 percent is transformed into a dissimilarity of 42.3 percent at the destination, although the latter would have been only two-ninths as great (9.5 percent) had Negroes and non-Negroes been subject to the same probabilities of occupational mobility . . . Most of the difference in destinations is produced by differences in mobility patterns, and only the lesser part is due to the difference in origins. For those concerned with rectification of racial inequalities in occupational status, the conclusion may seem either encouraging or discouraging. On the one hand, if barriers to Negro mobility (call them "discrimination" if you like) could be removed, there would ensue a rapid convergence of Negro and non-Negro occupation distributions. On the other hand, raising the level of the Negro "input" to the mobility process, but leaving that process itself intact, results in only a modest gain for Negroes. This has been the disquieting conclusion of analyses of the role of education in Negro occupational advancement.[5]

It may be noted in passing that "removing the barriers to Negro mobility" does not merely mean engendering a large amount of mobility. In *net* terms, the mobility of Negroes from father's to 1962 occupation was 42.6 percent and that of whites was 22.1 percent (Table 3). In large part, however, this striking net change in the Negro distributions between the two stages of the life cycle merely represents a diminution of the heavy concentration in farming and its replacement by concentrations at the lower manual levels . . .

PATTERNS OF MOVEMENT

To study gross changes in occupational status between stages of the life cycle, it is necessary to collapse the occupational categories rather drastically. In the Occupational Change in a Generation sample, each respondent represents, on the average, about 2,170 members of the population, although the effective sampling ratio varies over strata. Hence the number of Negroes under study is of the order of 1,500. The five-fold occupational classification used in subsequent tables provides about the maximum amount of detail that can be presented even with an appreciable liberalization of the Census Bureau's criterion for minimum base populations. Unfortunately, the degree of aggregation thus imposed is such as to impair comparability between Negroes and non-Negroes, since their distributions by specific occupations within broad categories may be quite different. Conclusions must be appropriately qualified.

Table 4 shows the percentages of men with specified father's occupation who found first jobs at each of the five levels of the condensed occupational classification. At every level of origin, Negroes enjoyed less access to the higher levels of working force entry than did non-Negroes. Indeed, the modal experience of Negroes in all four categories of nonfarm origin was to find lower manual first jobs. If the figures can be trusted, it is especially noteworthy that higher white-collar origins were of little value to Negroes for setting the stage for entry into white-collar work. The greatest similarity between Negro and non-Negro entry patterns occurred for men with farm origins. Approximately one-half of both groups found their first regular employment on the farm (predominantly as farm laborers, as one can infer from Table 1). Yet among those who moved from the farm, Negroes were rather more likely than non-Negroes to go into lower manual jobs, while an appreciable fraction of non-Negroes found work at the higher manual or white-collar levels.

Not only was the lower manual job the typical level of working-force entry for Negroes, the bulk of the Negro men starting there remained there while the majority of non-Negro men were able to rise to a higher level in their subsequent careers, as Table 5 shows. No less than 70 percent of Negroes who entered this type of employment were still at this level in 1962, as compared with a proportion only one-half as large for non-Negroes. Broadly speaking, therefore, the first job represents only a temporary lowering of occupational status for many non-Negroes, but a permanent lowering of status for many Negroes. Even among the Negroes who managed to enter the work force at a higher level, moreover, the first job did not provide as auspicious a career

TABLE 4. *Transition Percentages, Father's Occupation to First Job (Condensed Classification), by Race, for Civilian Men Aged 25–64 Years, for the United States, March, 1962*

RACE AND FATHER'S OCCUPATION[a]	FIRST JOB[a]						TOTAL	
	Higher white collar (1–4)	Lower white collar (5–7)	Higher manual (8–10)	Lower manual (11–15)	Farm (16–17)	Not reported (18)	Percent	Number (000)
Negro								
Higher white collar (1–4)	2.9	5.9	14.7	71.3	0.0	5.1	100.0	136
Lower white collar (5–7)	13.0	29.6	0.0	53.7	3.7	0.0	100.0	54
Higher manual (8–10)	4.1	12.3	7.0	62.6	1.2	12.8	100.0	243
Lower manual (11–15)	3.1	4.6	3.8	74.7	6.7	7.2	100.0	976
Farm (16–17)	0.5	2.3	1.9	39.7	49.6	6.0	100.0	1,389
Not reported (18)[b]	1.7	6.2	4.8	56.3	13.9	17.2	100.0	714
Total percent	2.0	5.0	3.8	55.8	24.4	8.9	100.0	
Number (000)	70	175	134	1,961	858	314	......	3,515

Non-Negro

Higher white collar (1–4)	28.2	27.6	9.3	29.0	2.3	3.5	100.0	5,834
Lower white collar (5–7)	20.4	32.0	7.8	32.9	2.8	4.1	100.0	2,653
Higher manual (8–10)	7.3	20.2	17.2	48.0	4.6	2.8	100.0	6,520
Lower manual (11–15)	6.1	17.0	9.1	59.6	4.6	3.5	100.0	8,795
Farm (16–17)	4.5	7.1	6.2	30.9	48.7	2.7	100.0	9,991
Not reported (18)[b]	6.8	18.8	9.0	42.6	12.0	10.7	100.0	2,664
Total percent	10.5	17.8	9.7	41.6	16.7	3.7	100.0	
Number (000)	3,831	6,484	3,532	15,156	6,094	1,360	.....	36,457

[a] See Table 1 for code identifications of occupation groups combined.
[b] See Table 1, n. (a).
SOURCE: See Table 1.

177

TABLE 5. *Transition Percentages, First Job to 1962 Occupation (Condensed Classification), by Race, for Civilian Men Aged 25–64 Years, for the United States, March, 1962*

RACE AND FIRST JOB[a]	1962 OCCUPATION[a]						TOTAL	
	Higher white collar (1–4)	Lower white collar (5–7)	Higher manual (8–10)	Lower manual (11–15)	Farm (16–17)	Not reported (18)	Percent	Number (000)
Negro								
Higher white collar (1–4)	53.5	2.8	7.0	25.4	2.8	8.5	100.0	71
Lower white collar (5–7)	12.0	33.1	3.4	44.6	1.7	5.1	100.0	175
Higher manual (8–10)	4.4	11.8	36.8	31.6	1.5	14.0	100.0	136
Lower manual (11–15)	4.2	5.0	9.6	70.3	2.6	8.3	100.0	1,960
Farm (16–17)	1.4	1.3	6.5	56.2	23.3	11.2	100.0	857
Not reported (18)[b]	7.0	1.6	8.3	59.9	4.5	18.8	100.0	314
Total percent	5.2	5.4	9.4	62.3	7.7	10.0	100.0	.....
Number (000)	181	191	331	2,188	271	351	.....	3,513

Non-Negro

Higher white collar (1–4)	77.1	8.9	4.5	4.3	1.2	4.0	100.0	3,830
Lower white collar (5–7)	39.4	26.1	11.4	16.6	1.2	5.4	100.0	6,484
Higher manual (8–10)	26.9	7.5	38.7	18.6	2.3	6.1	100.0	3,530
Lower manual (11–15)	20.1	9.3	24.8	36.5	2.7	6.6	100.0	15,157
Farm (16–17)	10.1	5.3	18.3	29.5	29.7	7.1	100.0	6,095
Not reported (18) [b]	22.1	7.1	15.9	23.8	3.6	27.5	100.0	1,360
Total percent	28.6	11.3	20.2	26.2	6.8	6.9	100.0	
Number (000)	10,415	4,129	7,362	9,556	2,476	2,518		36,456

[a] See Table 1 for code identifications of occupation groups combined.
[b] See Table 1, n. (a).
SOURCE: See Table 1.

beginning as for whites. Downward mobility from first job to 1962 among men who began at the white-collar or higher manual levels was much more frequent for Negroes than for non-Negroes.

Presenting mobility over the whole life cycle to the date of the survey, Table 6 demonstrates that the "holding power" of higher levels of origin is considerably less for Negroes than for non-Negroes, while the holding power of lower manual origins is much greater. Negroes left the farm in greater proportions than did whites, but the bulk of them were in lower manual pursuits in 1962, whereas about three in seven non-Negro men who originated on farms had achieved a white-collar or higher manual status.

To reduce the comparison between Negroes and non-Negroes in Table 6 to a pair of summary measures, we may compute Pearson's coefficient of mean square contingency between father's occupation and 1962 occupation: for Negroes it is 0.30; for non-Negroes, 0.42. It makes more difference what your father did if you were not a Negro than if you were. From one point of view, the occupational mobility data suggest that the Negro family has a lesser impact on its son's occupational chances than does the non-Negro family. Or, to put it another way, the intergenerational transmission of a strictly occupational advantage or handicap is greater for non-Negroes than for Negroes. In this respect, the Negro occupational mobility pattern is a more "open" or "equalitarian" one, but it is an equality that consists in the sharing by all members of the race in a lack of access to skilled or prestigious occupations.

Some of the details of the processes that produce this contrast are coming to light in analyses whose conclusions may be summarily stated here. Family background of Negroes—in the sense of the level of socioeconomic status, stability, and structural integrity of the family—is less favorable than that of non-Negroes. This initial handicap is translated into a lower level of educational attainment on the part of Negro youth. Yet, the disparity in educational attainment is too great to be attributed solely to measurable background handicaps. There is a residual difference that appears as a coefficient for "race" in a statistical model and that may be tentatively interpreted as an estimate of "racial discrimination" in educational opportunity.[6] The handicap of educational disadvantage is naturally translated into inferior occupational achievement on the part of Negroes. But again, the occupational differential cannot be fully accounted for by educational disadvantage, nor even by the combination of educational disadvantage and handicaps of family background. A specifically racial differential remains.[7] Finally, although it is not yet possible to assemble all the components into a single quantitative representation of the stratification process, it is virtually certain that the entire configuration of family background factors, educational levels, and occupational achievement is insufficient to account for differences between Negroes and non-Negroes in earnings and family income. There is a residual effect for "race," whether it can legitimately be taken to be a measure of "discrimination" in some strict sense of the term or not.

OUTCOMES OF MOBILITY

Returning to the materials at hand, which concern occupational mobility per se abstracted from the complex of socioeconomic factors involved in the process of mobility, we may indicate two other ways to summarize the data in order to bring out some consequences of racial differences in mobility patterns.

First, the array of inflow percentages (Table 7), although derived from data already reviewed, puts a somewhat different perspective on the relative prevalence of upward and downward mobility among Negro and non-Negro men. Whereas we have seen that the probability of movement into the higher white-collar level is small for Negroes, irrespective of origin, Table 7 shows that of the men who do achieve this level, a much higher proportion of Negroes than of non-Negroes have moved up from humble origins. Over two-

TABLE 6. Transition Percentages, Father's Occupation to 1962 Occupation (Condensed Classification), by Race, for Civilian Men Aged 25–64 Years, for the United States, March, 1962

RACE AND FATHER'S OCCUPATION[a]	1962 OCCUPATION[a]						TOTAL	
	Higher white collar (1–4)	Lower white collar (5–7)	Higher manual (8–10)	Lower manual (11–15)	Farm (16–17)	Not reported (18)	Percent	Number (000)
Negro								
Higher white collar (1–4)	10.4	9.7	19.4	53.0	0.0	7.5	100.0	134
Lower white collar (5–7)	14.5	9.1	0.0	69.1	0.0	7.3	100.0	55
Higher manual (8–10)	8.8	6.8	11.2	64.1	2.8	6.4	100.0	251
Lower manual (11–15)	8.0	7.0	11.5	63.2	1.8	8.4	100.0	973
Farm (16–17)	3.1	3.0	6.4	59.8	16.2	11.6	100.0	1,389
Not reported (18)[b]	2.4	6.5	11.1	65.9	3.1	11.1	100.0	712
Total percent	5.2	5.4	9.5	62.2	7.7	10.0	100.0	
Number (000)	182	190	334	2,184	272	352		3,514

Non-Negro

Higher white collar (1–4)	54.3	15.3	11.5	11.9	1.3	5.6	100.0	5,836
Lower white collar (5–7)	45.1	18.3	13.5	14.6	1.5	7.1	100.0	2,652
Higher manual (8–10)	28.1	11.8	27.9	24.0	1.0	7.3	100.0	6,512
Lower manual (11–15)	21.3	11.5	22.5	36.0	1.7	6.9	100.0	8,798
Farm (16–17)	16.5	7.0	19.8	28.8	20.4	7.5	100.0	9,991
Not reported (18)[b]	26.0	10.3	21.0	32.5	3.9	6.4	100.0	2,666
Total percent	28.6	11.3	20.2	26.2	6.8	6.9	100.0	
Number (000)	10,414	4,130	7,359	9,560	2,475	2,517		36,455

[a] See Table 1 for code identifications of occupation groups combined.
[b] See Table 1, n. (a).
SOURCE: See Table 1.

TABLE 7. Inflow Percentages, 1962 Occupation by Father's Occupation (Condensed Classification), by Race, for Civilian Men Aged 25–64 Years, for the United States, March, 1962

RACE AND FATHER'S OCCUPATION[a]	1962 OCCUPATION[a]						
	Higher white collar (1–4)	Lower white collar (5–7)	Higher manual (8–10)	Lower manual (11–15)	Farm (16–17)	Not reported (18)	Total
Negro							
Higher white collar (1–4)	7.7	6.8	7.8	3.2	0.0	2.9	3.8
Lower white collar (5–7)	4.4	2.6	0.0	1.7	0.0	1.1	1.6
Higher manual (8–10)	12.1	8.9	8.4	7.4	2.6	4.5	7.1
Lower manual (11–15)	42.9	35.8	33.5	28.2	6.6	23.3	27.7
Farm (16–17)	23.6	21.6	26.6	38.0	82.7	45.7	39.5
Not reported (18)[b]	9.3	24.2	23.7	21.5	8.1	22.5	20.3
Total	100.0	100.0	100.0	100.0	100.0	100.0	100.0
Non-Negro							
Higher white collar (1–4)	30.4	21.6	9.1	7.3	3.1	12.9	16.0
Lower white collar (5–7)	11.5	11.7	4.8	4.0	1.6	7.4	7.3
Higher manual (8–10)	17.6	18.6	24.7	16.3	2.7	18.8	17.9
Lower manual (11–15)	18.0	24.6	26.9	33.1	6.2	24.3	24.1
Farm (16–17)	15.9	16.9	26.9	30.1	82.2	29.8	27.4
Not reported (18)[b]	6.6	6.6	7.6	9.1	4.2	6.8	7.3
Total	100.0	100.0	100.0	100.0	100.0	100.0	100.0

(a) See Table 1 for code identifications of occupation groups combined; see Table 6 for marginal totals.
(b) See Table 1, n. (a).

184

fifths of the Negroes, but less than one-fifth of non-Negroes, who were in higher white-collar occupations in 1962 had fathers whose occupations were classified as lower manual. A similar though smaller differential is noted for inflow into lower white-collar occupations. In sociological jargon, then, an overwhelming preponderance of the small Negro "middle class" is composed of men new to that status, while a very substantial minority of the non-Negro "middle class" consists of men who originated there.

Second, Table 8 makes explicit the racial composition of the several sets of men defined by contrasting mobility experience. Since Negroes are underrepresented at the upper occupational levels, both in terms of origins and in terms of destinations, it is not surprising that they are extremely underrepresented among men who originated at a high level and who remained there. Less than one-half of one percent of men who "inherited" higher white-collar status are Negroes. Correlatively, there is marked overrepresentation of Negroes among men who "inherited" lower manual status or who achieved this status via mobility from a farm origin . . . When we speak of people "inheriting poverty"—as distinguished from those who find themselves in poverty despite a more favorable start in life—we are referring to a group that is quite disproportionately made up of Negroes. At least, that is the inference if we assume that patterns of mobility among income groups are somewhat like those among occupations.

COMMENT

There is little basis except conjecture for an estimate of how different the current pattern of racial differentials in occupational mobility may be from those prevailing in the past. It is virtually certain, however, that this pattern cannot prevail indefinitely in the future. For both Negro and non-Negro men aged 25–64 years in 1962, but especially for the former, the experience recorded in the intergenerational table is, in large measure, the story of a massive movement out of the

TABLE 8. *Percentage Negro for Each Combination of Father's Occupation and 1962 Occupation, for Civilian Men Aged 25–64 Years, for the United States, March, 1962*

	1962 OCCUPATION[a]						
FATHER'S OCCUPATION[a]	Higher white collar (1–4)	Lower white collar (5–7)	Higher manual (8–10)	Lower manual (11–15)	Farm (16–17)	Not reported (18)	Total
Higher white collar (1–4)	0.4	1.4	3.7	9.2	0.0	3.0	2.2
Lower white collar (5–7)	0.7	1.0	0.0	8.9	0.0	2.1	2.0
Higher manual (8–10)	1.2	2.2	1.5	9.3	9.6	3.3	3.7
Lower manual (11–15)	4.0	6.3	5.4	16.3	10.5	11.8	10.0
Farm (16–17)	2.5	5.6	4.3	22.4	10.0	17.7	12.2
Not reported (18)[b]	2.4	14.4	12.4	35.1	17.6	31.6	21.1
Total	1.7	4.4	4.3	18.6	9.9	12.3	8.8

(a) See Table 1 for code identifications of occupation groups combined; see Table 6 for marginal totals.
(b) See Table 1, n. (a).
SOURCE: See Table 1.

farm sector. Such a movement cannot recur for future cohorts for the simple reason that much smaller proportions will have farm origins. It may prove to be true that the historical movement of Negroes from the farm into lower manual occupations is a prelude to their achieving a more nearly representative distribution in the entire occupation structure in the future. But, for this to happen, Negroes must have much greater access to higher occupational positions than in the past.

⟦ 13 ⟧

Negro-White Occupational Differences in the Absence of Discrimination*

STANLEY LIEBERSON AND
GLENN V. FUGUITT

The disadvantages faced by racial and ethnic groups are one of the central concerns in the study of intergroup relations, but insufficient attention has been paid to the two basic types of handicaps. First, there is the disadvantage that occurs when members of a group are rejected or discriminated against solely because of their race or ethnic origin. The difficulties faced by Negroes with sufficient funds in the

* Abridged slightly from S. Lieberson and G. V. Fuguitt, "Negro-White Occupational Differences in the Absence of Discrimination," *American Journal of Sociology*, 1967, 73, 188–200. Reprinted with permission of the authors and the University of Chicago Press.

housing market are an obvious instance of discrimination based on racial or ethnic membership. A second basic disadvantage faced by a group is not the product of immediate discrimination, although it may reflect earlier discriminatory acts. This situation occurs when members of a group occupy a position in the social structure which puts them at a disadvantage by lowering their opportunities even under the operation of non-racial or universalistic criteria. For example, if discrimination against Negroes on the job market were to disappear, they would still hold jobs inferior to whites because of lower education, poorer training, and the like. Suppose an employer wishes to hire only applicants with a high school education. Assuming that he indiscriminately chooses whites and Negroes at random, fewer Negroes will be hired on a proportional basis simply because the segment of the Negro labor force with a high school education is smaller than that for whites. Thus the net effect of racially neutral employment practices may still favor one group over another.

The analytical distinction between the disadvantages derived from discrimination and those based on universalistic social processes is applied in this paper to the occupations held by Negro men. Even if the present disadvantaged status of Negroes in the United States is entirely a consequence of discrimination, a complete end to discrimination would not mean an immediate end to their social and economic liabilities. The difficulties faced because of job training and education requirements, work experience, and similar factors suggest taking an intergenerational approach, since it is across generations that most major shifts in occupation may take place.[1] By means of a simple mathematical model, the Markov chain, the possible consequences an end to discrimination would have on Negro-white occupational differences are traced in terms of intergenerational occupational mobility. The results generated by the Markov model are used to describe the implications of current non-discriminatory disadvantages faced by Negroes rather than as a means of prediction, for we are aware that our assumptions do not fully describe what will realistically be expected to occur.

METHODS

The Markov model has had a variety of applications in the social sciences in recent years, particularly in the study of social mobility. It assumes a set of observations that may be classified into a finite number of different states. A given observation may move from one state to another over a time period t, and there is a sequence of such time periods. The probability that an observation will move from state i to state j between t and $t + 1$ is given by P_{ij}. The basic assumption of the model is that the probability of moving from i to j depends only on the state at time t and that this probability is constant over the sequence of time intervals.

Consideration of the Markov-chain process can be greatly simplified by matrix algebra . . .

An intergenerational-mobility table may be transformed into a matrix of transition probabilities necessary for the Markov model. The proportional distribution of the sons' occupations tabulated by the occupations of their fathers can be treated as rows of p_{ij} values, with each row adding to 1.000. In Table 1, which provides the basic set of p_{ij} values, we see, for example, that the probability of becoming a professional for the son of a professional is .410, whereas p_{ij} for the son of a craftsman becoming a professional is .130.

In this paper we have operationalized an end to discrimination by assuming that an intergenerational-mobility table for all men applies to Negroes as well as whites. This table is used because data were not available for whites alone. However, the matrix is heavily weighted by the white rates, since Negroes are a relatively small proportion of the total labor force. The matrix of transition probabilities obtained from this mobility table is successively multiplied by the appropriate occupational-distribution vector for Negro men as well as by the corresponding white vector, yielding expected occupational distributions for the two races under the Markov assumption. If this P is a regular stochastic matrix (and it is), we know that both Negro and white occupational dis-

TABLE 1. *Son's Occupation by Father's Occupation, 1962*

FATHER'S OCCUPATION	SON'S OCCUPATION (SEE STUB)										All Sons
	1	2	3	4	5	6	7	8	9	10	
1. Professional, technical, and kindred	.410	.175	.090	.069	.087	.103	.031	.019	.012	.004	1.000
2. Managers, officials, and proprietors, except farm	.216	.341	.091	.071	.139	.085	.025	.019	.010	.003	1.000
3. Sales workers	.195	.300	.150	.062	.119	.104	.032	.020	.017	.001	1.000
4. Clerical and kindred	.281	.178	.078	.097	.169	.092	.061	.030	.014	.000	1.000
5. Craftsmen, foremen, and kindred	.130	.165	.047	.078	.294	.175	.051	.048	.008	.004	1.000
6. Operatives and kindred	.117	.122	.044	.066	.239	.259	.059	.076	.009	.009	1.000
7. Service workers, including private household	.101	.142	.057	.095	.210	.209	.111	.063	.010	.002	1.000
8. Laborers, except farm and mine	.059	.080	.036	.080	.226	.263	.091	.142	.012	.011	1.000
9. Farmers and farm managers	.053	.115	.025	.047	.197	.205	.052	.085	.178	.043	1.000
10. Farm laborers and foremen	.023	.075	.020	.038	.205	.260	.081	.134	.062	.102	1.000

NOTE: Persons not reporting their fathers' occupations are excluded.

tributions will approach convergence at equilibrium, which is determined by the values of P alone. What is of interest here is the changing pattern of Negro-white differences over time until they become negligible, which depends both upon the P matrix and the two initial vectors used. This process tells us about the joint effect of intergenerational mobility and racial differences within the social structure.

An alternate analysis was carried out using an educational-mobility table. Assuming that an end to discrimination would result in common intergenerational-educational-mobility patterns for Negroes and whites, expected educational distributions for the two races are projected across generations to convergence. These are then converted into another set of occupational distributions by means of a cross-tabulation of education and occupation.

An end to discrimination is operationalized here by positing common intergenerational-mobility patterns for Negroes and whites. Factors other than discrimination, however, such as family structure and possible differences in level of aspiration, may make for differences between the mobility of Negroes and whites having the same occupational or educational background.[2] Thus this procedure may overstate the rate of upward mobility for Negroes under the assumption that racial differences not explained by structural characteristics are a function of discrimination.[3]

There are a number of aspects of the model which are unrealistic, in addition to the obvious one of an immediate end to discrimination. By applying occupational- or educational-mobility rates under Markov assumptions, we assume that the mobility pattern is unchanged over a series of generations. In point of fact, mobility matrixes have changed through the years in the United States.[4]

Fertility, mortality, and the length of generations differ between the races as well as across educational and occupational groups, but these facts are ignored since the data necessary for making such adjustments are not available. While these demographic forces are significant for explaining the patterns of social mobility in the United States or for policy decisions, it is convenient to assume the constancy of these vital processes for the problem tackled here. In effect, it is assumed that each father will have one son who will survive to take an occupation according to the mobility table and to have one male forebear, etc.

The unit of analysis here is the occupational (or educational) distribution of white or Negro males thirty-five to forty-four years of age. In the *Current Population Survey* from which the occupational-mobility table was obtained, respondents were asked their fathers' occupations when the former were sixteen. Since the mobility rates are applied over successive hypothetical generations, this age range was chosen because these men are the ones most likely to have sixteen-year-old sons.

We repeat that our objective is not to make predictions about what will happen or to compare data generated by our model with empirical data obtained now or in the future. Rather, the importance of universalistic disadvantages suffered by Negroes because of their structural position is demonstrated by projecting current patterns of intergenerational mobility under the hypothetical case where no future racial discrimination exists in employment.

FATHER'S OCCUPATION

Our basic source of intergenerational occupational mobility is a table cross-tabulating the current occupations of male respondents twenty-five to sixty-four years of age by their fathers' occupations when the respondents were sixteen (Table 1). These data were obtained by the U.S. Bureau of the Census in a 1962 *Current Population Survey*.[5] The table mixes together a wide variety of cohorts among both generations. A sixty-four-year-old respondent who was born when his father was forty would report his father's occupation for a year actually preceding the birth of some twenty-five-year-old respondent's father. It was necessary to substitute this for the appropriate table based on males thirty-five to forty-four since the latter was not published in full. The two marginal distributions and the principal diagonal were given, however, and show low deviations from corresponding values in the complete table we used . . .

Negro-white differences in occupational composition in 1960 are shown under the first-generation heading in Table 2. The index of dissimilarity between the races is 40. In other words, 40 per cent of one or the other race would have to change occupational categories if the two races were to have identical occupational distributions. Markov-chain analysis enables us to compare the occupations of each race in the thirty-five to forty-four age group with those that would eventually occur in each generation and at final equilibrium, under the assumption that current rates of intergenerational mobility persist indefinitely. This final equilibrium is much closer to first-generation whites than Negroes; the indexes for the two groups from the equilibrium stage are 16 and 48, respectively. (The equilibrium stage is defined in this paper as the point at which P, on being raised to successive powers, is equal to a matrix having rows identical to each other at two decimal places. At this point in the process both whites and Negroes have distributions equal to these rows and hence identical to each other to two decimal places. Since the true equilibrium stage is approached but not reached by P raised to any power, the white and Negro distributions are never exactly identical but rather converge asymptotically.)

If discrimination had disappeared by 1960, then the next generation of Negro and white men would have had the occupational composition shown under the second-generation heading. If the current set of father-son patterns continue, Negroes and whites will be considerably closer in occupational composition in the next generation (the index of dissimilarity is only 13). The gains for Negroes in one generation without race-specific discrimination are very great. In the first generation, 13 per cent of whites and 4 per cent of Negroes are professionals. By contrast the Negro percentage in professional occupations would increase in one generation to 12 per cent, while that of whites would increase to 18 per cent.

TABLE 2. *Negro-White Occupation Composition: Frequency Distributions and Indexes of Dissimilarity*

	PERCENTAGE DISTRIBUTIONS BY GENERATION AND RACE									
	First (1960)		Second		Third		Fourth		Seventh	
OCCUPATION	White	Negro	White	Negro	White	Negro	White	Negro	White	Negro
Professional, technical, and kindred	13	4	18	12	20	18	21	20	22	22
Managers, officials, and proprietors, except farm	14	2	18	13	19	18	20	19	20	20
Sales workers	7	1	7	5	7	6	7	7	7	7
Clerical and kindred	7	6	7	7	7	7	7	7	7	7
Craftsmen, foremen, and kindred	24	13	20	22	19	20	18	19	18	18
Operatives and kindred	20	30	17	22	16	18	15	16	15	15
Service workers, including private household	4	13	5	8	5	5	5	5	5	5
Laborers, except farm and mine	5	22	5	8	5	6	5	5	4	4
Farmers and farm managers	5	4	2	2	1	1	1	1	1	1
Farm laborers and foremen	1	5	1	1	1	1	1	1	1	1
Total	100	100	100	100	100	100	100	100	100	100
Indexes of dissimilarity:										
White-Negro	40		13		4		2		0	
White-equilibrium	16		6		3		1		0	
Negro-equilibrium	48		19		7		3		0	

The percentage of Negro professionals would triple in the course of a single generation without discrimination, although it would still be lower than that of whites. The percentage of Negroes employed as laborers (excluding farms and mines) would drop from 22 to 8 per cent in the same generation. It is evident that the second-generation occupational composition of both whites and Negroes is much closer than the first to the final or equilibrium occupational composition. There is a drop in the index from 16 to 6 for whites and from 48 to 19 for Negroes.

In the third and fourth generations the races would, of course, become increasingly alike in their job distributions. By the fourth generation, there would be virtually no difference in occupational composition between Negro and white men aged thirty-five to forty-four, although it would take seven generations for complete equality. In short, were racially based discrimination on the job market to have ended in 1960 in the United States, and if each twenty-year-old father had a son, then under the assumptions described earlier it would take about eighty years before racial occupational inequality would be virtually nil. However, very rapid progress would be made long before this, with a radical decline in racial differences in just one generation, resulting in differences of 6 percentage points or less for any one occupational group. After two generations, or about forty years, there would be differences of 2 percentage points or less.

EDUCATION

Based on a regression analysis of intergenerational occupational mobility in Chicago, Duncan and Hodge reported that the influence of education on a man's occupation is greater than that of his father's occupation. Moreover, they concluded that the latter factor "was influential in large part because of its association with education."[6] Nevertheless, ideally we would like to introduce both factors into a Markov process such as that presented by Carlsson for Sweden, in which he was able to consider the joint influence of father's occupation and son's education.[7] Unfortunately, we were unable to obtain such data for the United States. However, the October, 1960, *Current Population Survey* reports the educational status of men twenty to twenty-four years of age cross-tabulated by the education of their fathers.[8]

Table 3 shows the transition matrix that can be developed on the basis of these data. The table slightly misstates final educational attainment since some of the sons may yet complete their education. Such a bias should not be great, however, and therefore this is a reasonably appropriate matrix for the unit of this study, males thirty-five to forty-four. The table shows that father's education significantly influences his sons' education even in the current period of rising levels of attainment. For example, among fathers who failed to graduate from high school, nearly one-half of their sons likewise did not complete high school. This is far greater than the percentage failing to complete high school among the sons of more highly educated fathers . . .

The educational status of Negroes is lower than that of whites. About three-quarters of the non-white men thirty-five to forty-four years of age in the experienced civilian labor force had not completed high school in 1960 compared with

TABLE 3.   *Education of Sons Twenty to Twenty-four Years of Age by Father's Education, 1960*

	SON'S EDUCATION		
FATHER'S EDUCATION	Less than High School	High School	More than High School
Less than high school	.43	.34	.23
High school	.10	.36	.54
More than high school	.05	.15	.80

SOURCE: U.S. Bureau of the Census, *Current Population Reports, Population Characteristics*, Ser. P-20, No. 110, July, 1961: Table A.

slightly less than one-half of the white males. If the educational-mobility rates for the total population were to operate for both non-whites and whites, the educational status of the two groups would come together over future generations.

In 1960, the index of dissimilarity in education between white and non-white employed men was 29 (see Table 4). This would drop to 13 in the second generation, 6 in the third

TABLE 4. *Educational Composition by Race: Frequency Distributions and Indexes of Dissimilarity*

GENERATION AND RACE	PERCENTAGE DISTRIBUTIONS			Index of Dissimilarity
	Less than High School	High School	More than High School	
First:				
White	46	31	23	} 29
Non-white	75	16	9	
Second:				
White	24	30	46	} 13
Non-white	34	33	33	
Third:				
White	16	26	58	} 6
Non-white	20	28	52	
Fourth:				
White	12	23	64	} 4
Non-white	14	25	61	
Fifth:				
White	11	22	67	} 2
Non-white	11	23	66	
Sixth:				
White	10	22	68	} 1
Non-white	11	22	67	
Seventh:				
White	10	21	69	} 1
Non-white	10	22	68	
Eighth:				
White	10	21	69	} 0
Non-white	10	21	69	

generation, and would eventually reach 0 in the eighth generation. Thus, if the current relation between fathers' and sons' educations were to persist, educational equality would be fairly close after several generations, with white and non-white difference for each educational class within 3 percentage points at the end of about 60 years. Identical percentage distributions would not be attained, however, for about 140 years, allowing 20 years for each generation.

EDUCATION AND OCCUPATION

Examination of the occupational composition of the races in each generation, based solely on the cross-tabulation between occupation and education existing for white men thirty-five to forty-four years of age in 1960, allows us to convert the projected educational differences into a measure of the occupational differences that would result.

The relationships between fathers' education and sons' education, and then in turn between sons' education and occupations, are more complex than our data allow for. In particular, it is not possible to determine whether there is any statistical interaction between the variables. Rather, an additive model is assumed in which one can examine the influence of educational attainment on racial differences in occupational composition.

In 1960, as well as in earlier periods, whites and non-whites with the same level of education obtained different degrees of occupational success.[9] Table 5 shows the relationship between education and occupation for men thirty-five to forty-four years of age separately by race. There are differences which are clearly unfavorable to non-whites. For example, a quarter of all non-whites with less than a high school education are laborers (except farm and mine), whereas less than 10 per cent of whites with a similar level of education are so employed. These racial differences in occupational composition between men with the same educational achievement no doubt reflects discrimination against Negroes on the job

TABLE 5. *Occupational Percentage Distributions by Education and Race for Males in the Experienced Civilian Labor Force Ages Thirty-five to Forty-four, 1960*

OCCUPATION	LESS THAN HIGH SCHOOL		HIGH SCHOOL		MORE THAN HIGH SCHOOL	
	White	Non-white	White	Non-white	White	Non-white
Professional, technical, and kindred	2	1	7	3	41	36
Managers, officials, and proprietors, except farm	8	2	16	5	23	8
Sales workers	4	1	9	3	11	3
Clerical and kindred	4	2	10	14	7	15
Craftsmen, foremen, and kindred	29	13	28	18	9	10
Operatives and kindred	31	32	17	26	4	11
Service workers, including private household	5	12	4	15	2	10
Laborers, except farm and mine	8	26	3	13	1	5
Farmers and farm managers	6	4	5	2	2	1
Farm laborers and foremen	3	6	1	1	0	1
Total	100	100	100	100	100	100

SOURCE: U.S. Bureau of the Census, *U.S. Census of Population: 1960. Subject Reports. Educational Attainment.* (Final Report PC(2)-5B), Table 8.

market, lower-quality education for Negroes with the same
formal levels of attainment as whites, and the technical fact
that educational attainment has only been trichotomized.

Using the educational composition projected for future generations of whites and non-whites, we shall assume that there
is no longer any discrimination between the races in quality
of education under two different conditions: first, that there
is no discrimination between job applicants with the same
level of schooling and, second, that the influence of education
on occupation remains different for the races. Table 6's first
two columns for each generation show, respectively, the
occupational composition of whites and non-whites under the
first condition. If the influence of education on occupation
for non-white men in 1960 was the same as that found for
white men, then in 1960 the index of dissimilarity between
the races in occupations for men thirty-five to forty-four
years of age would have been 14 rather than 38.[10]

The indexes of dissimilarity indicate that a rapid decline
would occur in racial occupational differences if non-white
educational mobility were the same as for the total population and if Negroes and whites with the same educational
attainment were employed identically in the job market. In
the second generation the index would be only 8; in the third
generation it would be 4; and virtually complete identity
would be reached in the eighth generation, with an index of
0. The progress of occupational equality found earlier by
examining the influence of fathers' occupations on those of
sons' is rather similar to that obtained by means of this approach to occupations based on the influence of education.
The second-generation index of dissimilarity would be 13
under the first model and 8 under the second approach, but
they would be identical in the third generation, and both
reach exact equality one generation apart. In either case then,
a sharp decline in racial differences would occur in the course
of one generation if there were no longer discrimination in
the United States.

By contrast, observe what happens to white–non-white
occupational differences if it is assumed that the influence of

TABLE 6. *Influence of Education on Occupation by Generation and Race: Percentage Distributions and Indexes of Dissimilarity*

	PERCENTAGE DISTRIBUTIONS BY GENERATION AND RACE														
	First			Second			Third			Fourth			Eighth		
OCCUPATION	W	*WN	†WN	W	*WN	†WN	W	*WN	†WN	W	*WN	†WN	W	*WN	†WN
Professional, technical, and kindred	12	6	4	21	16	13	26	24	20	28	27	23	30	30	26
Managers, officials, and proprietors, except farm	14	10	3	17	15	5	19	18	6	19	19	6	20	20	6
Sales workers	7	5	1	9	8	2	9	9	3	10	10	3	10	10	3
Clerical and kindred	7	5	6	7	7	10	8	7	12	8	7	13	8	8	14
Craftsmen, foremen, and kindred	24	27	13	20	22	13	17	18	12	16	17	12	15	15	12
Operatives and kindred	21	27	29	15	18	23	12	13	20	10	11	18	9	9	16
Service workers, including private household	4	5	13	3	4	13	3	3	12	3	3	12	3	3	11
Laborers, except farm and mine	5	7	22	3	4	15	2	3	11	2	2	10	2	2	9
Farmers and farm managers	5	6	4	4	5	3	3	4	2	3	3	2	3	3	2
Farm laborers and foremen	1	2	5	1	1	3	1	1	2	1	1	1	0	0	1
Total	100	100	100	100	100	100	100	100	100	100	100	100	100	100	100
Index of dissimilarity between whites and non-whites		14	38		8	35		4	31		2	30		0	29

* Based on white relationship between education and occupation.
† Based on non-white relationship between education and occupation.

education on occupation for non-white men in 1960 applies to future generations of non-whites (shown in the third column under each generation). The index of dissimilarity is actually 38 between the races in 1960. We again observe that racial dissimilarities in occupation decline in each succeeding generation, but at a rather slow rate. The index is 35 in the second generation, 31 in the third, and eventually flattens out at 29 in the eighth and later generations. Non-whites are still occupationally disadvantaged, despite the equality in formal educational attainment, because they do not obtain the same jobs as whites with identical education.

The equilibrium stage under assumption 2 provides important implications about the future status of Negro-white employment if their levels of formal education were the same but the current non-white relationship between education and occupation remained unaltered. Non-whites would still be overrepresented in the lower job levels even after educational parity with whites was achieved. Inspection of the results for the eighth generation in Table 6 indicates that Negroes would be far more likely to be employed as laborers, service workers, and operatives. Although they would also be overrepresented in the clerical occupations, Negro men would be less likely to be employed as managers, officials, and proprietors, as well as sales workers. To a lesser degree they would remain underemployed as professionals and craftsmen.

Compare the actual occupations held by non-white men aged thirty-five to forty-four in 1960 with the occupational composition that would have occurred for non-white men in 1960 if their formal levels of education had yielded the same occupations as those of whites yielded (the second and third columns, respectively, under the first generation in Table 6). The index of dissimilarity in occupations between the races would have been 14 rather than 38. Thus the first index, which reflects only the lower formal education among Negroes, is little more than one-third the size of the actual difference in 1960.[11] The actual racial gap in 1960 reflects the additional influences of discrimination against non-whites of comparable achievement, inferior quality of education for Negroes, the possible masking of greater educational attainment of whites because of the broad categories used, and a wide array of other possible factors, such as access to opportunities.

These results indicate that if Negro formal educational attainment were to reach the same level as that of whites, the effect on Negro-white occupational equality would be limited if other factors remained unchanged. Moreover, if the educational matrixes were to continue to operate in the future, and if the current relationship between education and occupation for non-whites were to remain unaltered, the racial index of dissimilarity in occupations would decline from 38 to 29 after eight generations, but never get lower than that.

DISCUSSION

We have distinguished between two types of handicaps faced by Negroes. The first, discrimination, involves rejection of Negroes simply because they are Negroes; the second occurs because the group occupies an inferior aggregate position on variables which, although racially neutral, operate to their disadvantage. Using an intergenerational approach, by means of the Markov-chain model, we operationalized the end to discrimination by assuming both races follow mobility patterns found to prevail for the total population. Starting with observed Negro and white occupational distributions for 1960, we then traced the changes that would take place over several generations. An alternative approach started with educational mobility, and we then employed the relation between education and occupation to produce comparable occupational distributions.

Using both approaches, Negro and white distributions converged rapidly, at least in terms of a generational time scale, so that differences were negligible after about sixty or eighty years. Whether this convergence is "fast" or "slow" is of course beyond the purview of the sociologist. These data do underscore the position that an end to discrimination will not result in occupational equality immediately . . .

We wish to reiterate our cautions about the assumptions made, the crudeness of the data used, and the uncertainty about the long-run continuation of the transitional probabilities employed to project future occupational composition. Somewhat different conclusions could be obtained if different assumptions were made about the ongoing social processes. Based on changes in median education between 1940 and 1960, Broom and Glenn projected identical medians for men within forty-five years from 1960, a much shorter period than our approach indicates.[12] However, it appears unlikely, under any circumstances, that Negro-white occupational equality could be reached in a decade or two even if racial discrimination in the job market were completely eliminated.

But even if our data were more complete and included the entire range of working years, occupational structure and changes in structure could not be deduced from intergenerational occupational mobility. We have traced the consequences of certain artificial assumptions on an intergenerational succession of fathers and sons thirty-five to forty-four years old, and any possible implications are so limited.

Based on the gross influence of father's occupation on son's occupation, several generations would be required before racial parity in the labor force could be met, although we found that men thirty-five to forty-four years of age were much closer in occupational composition after one generation. In analyzing the education of men thirty-five to forty-four and its influence on both their occupations and the education of the next generation, it was not possible to consider the effect of occupation on the next generation's educational attainment. However, about a third of the racial difference in occupational composition in 1960 for the thirty-five- to forty-four-year-old generation could be attributed to differences in formal levels of educational attainment. Again, it would take several generations to overcome current educational disadvantages faced by non-whites even if all other factors, including the quality of Negro education and the relationship between education and occupation, were eliminated. Thus our simple projections into the future of current patterns indicate that disadvantages to a group can continue, although not indefinitely, even when the initial thrust of discrimination is eliminated.

An important implication of Markov's theory is that the length of time necessary for occupational parity between the races is a function of the transitional matrixes but is in general not influenced by the initial vector (in this case, the current occupational or educational composition of the races). As a consequence, the number of generations necessary for the attainment of racial equality in the absence of discrimination is not at all influenced by the initial occupational or educational handicaps but is purely a function of the fluidity between generations in the society. On the other hand, although the time necessary for equality is not affected, the initial occupational or educational differences between the races determine the magnitude of the racial differences in each generation and therefore the severity of the social problem.

Race and ethnic relations nearly always involve one group enjoying an edge over another in the economic and social spheres. In determining the sources of these advantages, it is necessary to consider both the structural, non-racial factors and the discriminatory factors. Granted that the inferior position occupied by a group may often be a product of current and past discriminations, the effect of this position then becomes independent of its causes. In this sense, we have seen that Negro-white occupational differences would not be eliminated immediately after the demise of discrimination. Indeed, if the United States were a castelike society where all children took up the occupations of their fathers, then the absence of discrimination would *never* lead to occupational equality between the races. On the other hand, if occupational mobility were so open that neither fathers' education nor occupations had any influence on the occupations pursued by their offspring, then discrimination would be the only means for maintaining occupational differences between the races, and the elimination of one would lead to disappearance of the other in one generation. Thus the differential positions occupied by racial and ethnic groups in society may be viewed as a function of the interaction between discriminatory practices and structural, non-racially based, social processes.

(14)

School Integration and Occupational Achievement of Negroes*

ROBERT L. CRAIN

Much has been written about Negro poverty and its roots in the Negro's lack of skills and in racial discrimination. But even if all Negroes had skills and there were no discrimination, the segregation of Negroes, residentially and socially, would lower their incomes, simply because Negroes would continue to be denied access to a valuable resource—information about employment opportunities. [See Selections 9 and 13.]

American Negroes live in a society which is largely segregated. In this society, there are whole occupations and industries which have very few Negro workers. Sometimes this is due to historical accident; the industry is located in a region which

* Abridged from R. L. Crain, "School Integration and Occupational Achievement of Negroes," *American Journal of Sociology*, January 1970, 75, 593–606. Reprinted with permission of the author and the University of Chicago Press. Copyright 1970 by the University of Chicago. All rights reserved.

has few Negroes, for example. In other instances their absence is due to discrimination, sometimes subtle and sometimes not, or it is simply because Negroes do not apply for these jobs. In many cases, they do not apply because they do not know when a job becomes open. It is a common observation that one of the most significant forms of unfair employment practice is the hiring of new employees from referrals made by the present staff; if the staff is all white, the persons who apply will be friends, relatives, and neighbors who are also white. The employer who advertises publicly for help must bear the costs of interviewing large numbers of applicants and must depend only upon the application blank in making a decision. If there is a demand for that type of employment, he is wasting money by advertising when he can staff his plant without doing so. The best jobs are, therefore, not advertised. Even if the employer does advertise publicly, . . . friends, neighbors, and relatives of present employees still have the inside track.

In a segregated community, Negroes must depend upon other Negroes for information about job opportunities. If Negroes are segregated into low-paying employment, they will, of course, have limited knowledge of better-paying opportunities. As Sheppard and Belitsky (1967) observe, for the poor to depend upon friends and relatives is rather like "the blind leading the blind." . . .

Thus we are arguing that occupational opportunities for Negroes will be limited until there is at least partial racial assimilation—until Negroes have sufficient contact with whites to learn about job opportunities and obtain referrals from white employees. There are numerous barriers to this kind of assimilation. The most obvious one is the amount of prejudice of whites toward Negroes and of Negroes toward whites. But even if there were no personal prejudice, the present patterns of racial segregation in social relations and in housing could persist through inertia, and continue to limit sharply the occupational achievement of Negroes for many years.

SCHOOL INTEGRATION

The public school is an important factor in the process of assimilation. Negroes who have attended integrated schools continue to have a large number of white friends as adults; they are more likely to live in integrated neighborhoods, to favor integrated schooling for their children, and to prefer belonging to integrated voluntary organizations (Crain, 1971). This means they will have greater opportunities to move into a biracial employment market rather than being restricted to the traditional ghetto employers. Hence, Negroes who attended integrated schools should have less-traditional patterns of employment and, as a consequence, higher occupational prestige and income. In order to substantiate this argument, we will present data showing that (a) Negroes from integrated schools are more likely to hold "nontraditional" jobs—jobs which have relatively few Negroes in them, (b) Negroes in nontraditional jobs will earn more money than those in traditional jobs, hence (c) Negroes from integrated schools will have higher incomes, and (d) Negroes with white friendships will have access to information about the labor market which they can use to obtain these nontraditional jobs, hence (e) Negroes from integrated schools will have more knowledge about jobs. We shall present the findings separately for each sex; the pattern is somewhat different for males and females.

Data to establish these five points are drawn from a 1966 survey of Negroes, aged twenty-one to forty-five, living in the metropolitan areas of the North. The sample was weighted to overrepresent Negroes in higher-income neighborhoods and in the smaller metropolitan areas; the tables are hence weighted to reflect the actual population. The true number of cases is approximately 40 percent of the weighted Ns shown in the tables. Interviewing was conducted by an all-Negro staff.

Block quota sampling was used: . . . The original sample was 1,624 cases and the weighted N is 4,153. We will focus largely upon that one-third of the sample which attended northern high schools and who report an occupation; this is 1,231 weighted cases.

INTEGRATION AND NONTRADITIONAL EMPLOYMENT

Table 1 records the percentage of Negroes for each of the eight major urban occupational groups in the 1960 census and the percentage of alumni of integrated high schools and of segregated high schools in each of these occupations. Negro men tend to be concentrated in the lower blue-collar occupations—operatives, service workers, laborers—and in the lowest of the white-collar occupations—clerical work. Conversely, Negro men tend not to be professionals, managers, salesworkers, or craftsmen, hence, we shall call these four major occupational groups nontraditional. Approximately one-third of the male Negro alumni of integrated high schools are in three nontraditional occupations: crafts, sales, and the professions, while only one-fifth of the Negroes who attended segregated schools are in these three groups. Male Negro managers, owners, and proprietors tend to come from segregated schools, but contact with whites is not necessary to enter these occupations, since almost all Negro managers are in businesses serving largely Negro clientele. (If the data were available, we would hypothesize that Negro businessmen serving white clientele would be more likely to have had integrated schooling.)

Contrary to popular belief, Negroes who attended integrated schools do not come from higher-status or more stable families, and therefore these results do not change when background variables are introduced as controls.

One reason Negro clerks are slightly more likely to be from segregated schools is that Negro clerical positions are available in the largest metropolitan areas where there also is the largest number of segregated schools. When city size is introduced as a control variable, the apparent predominance

Table 1. Occupations of Alumni of Segregated and Integrated Northern High Schools, by Sex, and Percentage of Negroes in Each Occupational Group

OCCUPATIONAL GROUP	MALES				FEMALES			
	High School Was			Negroes in Group (%)	High School Was			Negroes in Group (%)
	Integrated (%)	Segregated (%)	Difference		Integrated (%)	Segregated (%)	Difference	
Professional	11	8	+3	5.9*	14	4	+10	10.7*
Managers, owners, proprietors	3	6	−3	4.2*	1	0	+1	5.3*
Clerical	11	13	−2	11.3	22	32	−10	6.7*
Sales	3	0	+3	4.7*	2	3	−1	4.7*
Craftsmen	19	13	+6	7.5*	2	2	0	11.4
Operatives	31	40	−9	14.3	22	21	+1	13.2
Service	15	10	+5	29.1	36	38	−2	38.8
Labor	6	10	−4	27.4	0	0		32.7
Total	99	100			99	100		
N†	(498)	(227)			(372)	(134)		

Note.—Alumni of southern high schools excluded from this table.

* Indicates nontraditional occupation.

† Weighted; true N is approximately 0.4 times N shown for all tables.

of men from segregated schools in clerical work becomes smaller.

Negro women from integrated schools are much more likely to enter the professions. But otherwise, our thesis does not hold for women; Negro women from integrated schools are not more likely to have nontraditional jobs.

The eight major occupational groups are broad categories, and we can continue this investigation by looking at differences in the detailed occupational classifications within each major group. In Table 2, we look within each major occupational group and see that Negroes from integrated schools are more likely to hold those occupations whose work force is less than 3 percent Negro, which we shall define as nontraditional (U.S. Bureau of the Census 1960, Table 3, pp. 21–30). We also see in Table 2 that Negro women from integrated schools are more likely to hold nontraditional occupations in the professions, and in clerical and sales positions. There are no Negro female occupations in the general category of craftsmen, operatives, or service which are not more than 3 percent Negro . . .

These two tables yield convincing evidence (at least for males) of our general point that Negro alumni of integrated schools are in "integrated" jobs. In Table 3, we see that those respondents who hold these nontraditional occupations within each major census classification tend to have higher incomes. In the case of males, those in nontraditional occupations have noticeably higher incomes in all five test groups. However, the pattern for females is completely mixed, and apparently meaningless; for example, the very high correlation for Negro professional women is based almost entirely on the high income of Negro schoolteachers, a traditional occupation.

One might argue that the Negroes in these nontraditional occupations are better qualified, and to some extent this is true. In Table 4, we see that Negroes in nontraditional occupations tend to have higher educational attainment. However, observe that the association between education and nontraditionalism is weaker than the association between income and

TABLE 2. *Percentage of Respondents from Each Major Occupational Group in (Detailed) Occupations Which Are Less Than 3 Percent Negro, by Integration and Region of High School, and by Sex*

MAJOR OCCUPATIONAL GROUP	MALES High School Was			FEMALES High School Was		
	North, Integrated (%)	North, Segregated (%)	South, Segregated (%)	North, Integrated (%)	North, Segregated (%)	South, Segregated (%)
Professional	36 (56)	33 (18)	31 (35)	8 (49)	0 (6)	0 (45)
Clerical, sales	19 (67)	13 (30)	30 (49)	58 (89)	43 (47)	58 (36)
Craftsmen	56 (93)	41 (29)	15 (113)	...	...	...
Operatives	4 (155)	0 (91)	0 (179)	...	...	...
Service	8 (76)	0 (22)	0 (51)	...	...	...

Note.—Sign test, differences among northern-educated respondents significant $p < .01$ (one-tailed).

TABLE 3. *Association Between Percentage Negro (Detailed Occupational Categories) and Income, Within Major Occupational Categories, by Sex*

OCCUPATIONAL CATEGORIES	MALES γ	MALES Total N	FEMALES γ	FEMALES Total N
Professional	−.38	118	+ .42	108
Managers, owners, proprietors	*	50	+1.0	13
Clerical and sales	−.31	173	− .01	193
Craftsmen	−.21	303	+1.0	22
Operatives	−.03	623	+ .06	236
Service	−.65	209	+ .18	465
Laborers	*	195	*	3

* When the data are quartiled, there is no variance in male managerial occupations, which have few Negroes without exception, or in laboring occupations, all of which have many Negroes.

nontraditionalism; in Table 4, γ is generally lower than in Table 3. (Our measures of education and income are distributed through five categories with approximately the same marginals; therefore γ in both cases is comparable.)

In Table 4, we again see no pattern for females. Those who

TABLE 4. *Association Between Negro (Detailed Occupational Categories) and Education, Within Major Census Occupational Categories, by Sex*

MAJOR CATEGORY	MALES γ	MALES Total N	FEMALES γ	FEMALES Total N
Professional	−.15	118	+ .52	113
Managers, owners, proprietors	*	50	+1.00	13
Clerical and sales	−.41	177	− .12	204
Craftsmen	−.11	307	+ .07	28
Operatives	−.03	635	+ .01	251
Service	−.37	209	− .24	511
Labor	*	197	*	3

* When the data are quartiled, there is no variance in male managerial occupations, which have few Negroes without exception, or in laboring occupations, all of which have many Negroes.

have nontraditional occupations are not better educated. This is consistent with the idea that occupational discrimination and inequality is greater for Negro males than for Negro females.

It seems a reasonable assumption that discrimination against Negroes in employment and the higher salaries in occupations which have few Negroes is a result of competitive efforts on the part of white male employees to protect their economic situations (Hodge and Hodge, 1965). If this is the case, then it seems reasonable that white women, as a class more preoccupied with family and less with occupational roles, would be less likely to press for a similar occupational pattern of discrimination against Negro women.

Even so, Negro women still benefit occupationally from integrated schooling, according to these data. There are too few cases to make a truly firm statement, but Table 1 shows the overwhelming majority of Negro professional women have been educated in integrated schools.

Tables 5 and 6 show that Negroes who attend integrated high schools have higher occupational prestige and higher

TABLE 5.   *Occupational Status of Students from Integrated and Segregated High Schools*

OCCUPATIONAL STATUS	REGION AND INTEGRATION OF HIGH SCHOOL		
	North, Integrated	*North, Segregated*	*South, Segregated*
Mean occupation prestige, men	35.7	34.0	34.6
Standard deviation	12.3	12.6	13.8
Total N	(489)	(229)	(494)
Mean occupation prestige, women	36.1	31.3	31.6
Standard deviation	13.9	12.6	16.3
Total N	(372)	(136)	(384)

Note.—Effect of integration for northern males N.S.; effect for females, $p < .01$ (one-tailed); occupational prestige scores developed at NORC by Robert W. Hodge, Paul M. Siegel, and Peter H. Rossi.

TABLE 6. *Income of Alumni of Segregated and Integrated High Schools, for Males, with Background Variables Controlled*

ADDITIONAL VARIABLES INCLUDED	INCREASE IN ANNUAL INCOME (MEDIANS) DUE TO HIGH SCHOOL INTEGRATION FOR MALES (ROUNDED TO TEN-DOLLAR UNITS)
None	$ 340
Age	$ 220
Age, stability of family of origin	$ 390
Age, educational attainment	$— 40
Age, educational attainment, and stability of family of origin	$ 210

incomes. (Data on income for women is not presented; since so many women work part-time, the results are difficult to interpret.) The occupational prestige effect is considerably stronger for women than for men. The differences for men do not reach the .05 level of significance, but they are in the predicted direction and are not small. The difference between the median annual income of alumni of integrated and segregated high schools is $344 per year for males. Some of this can be attributed to age (with the increasing number of segregated schools, young Negroes do not have as much opportunity for integration) but more than $200 difference remains after an age control has been introduced in Table 6.

There are only 300 male graduates of northern high schools in the sample, so it is not possible to estimate accurately the real dollar return resulting from an integrated education. The young Negro men from broken homes in this sample are more likely to have gone to integrated schools, and men from stable homes earn approximately $600 more per year when educational attainment, age, and high school integration are controlled. When family stability is introduced as a control, the effect of integration rises sharply, to $390.

Much of the income difference is due to the higher education of alumni of integrated schools. The average high school graduate (including those with college) earns about $800 more per year than the average person who did not finish high school (again, controlling for integration, age, and family stability). Since 20 percent more students from integrated high schools graduate (Crain, 1971), we would expect the increased educational attainment to increase the income of alumni of integrated schools by about $200 per year. We have computed two estimates of the effect of integration independent of education in Table 6. With only age as an additional control, we remove all of the effect of integration; but when we use family stability also, we have $210 remaining independent of education. Clearly, a larger sample is needed to make this estimate; but until one appears we must assume that integration has a net effect on income, independent of other variables including the higher educational attainment which also results from integration, of about $200 per year—not a small difference over the forty- to fifty-year working life of an adult male. Lifetime income of alumni of integrated schools is increased about $10,000; we estimate that only two-thirds of this amount is due to differences in educational attainment. Note that higher educational attainment is not a very parsimonious explanation of the fact that Negroes from integrated schools are more likely to work in nontraditional occupations. In the remainder of this paper we will argue that alumni of integrated schools make more money because they are more likely to associate with whites; they have integrated jobs for the same reason they are more likely to live in integrated neighborhoods.

THE JOB-FINDING PROCESS

The findings of Tables 5 and 6—that alumni of integrated schools have better jobs and earn more money—is reasonable if one assumes that having informal contacts into the white job market is the crucial factor. Tables 7–11 provide some evidence for this point of view. Table 7 gives the responses to the question, "How did you find your present (or last)

Table 7. *Answers to Question on Source of Present Job*

SOURCE	NATIONAL SAMPLE (%)	NEGRO SAMPLE '(%)
Family	14	13
Friends	24	25
Union	1	3
Want ads	7	10
State employment	6	10
Private employment	4	7
Visiting prospects	24	18
Ask previous employer	2	2
High school	1	0
College	3	1
Other	16	10
Total	102	99
N	(566)*	(3,537)

* Unweighted N for national sample aged 21–45, who have worked within the past two years.

job?" and compares the responses of the Negroes in our northern metropolitan sample and those of a national sample. The similarities are more striking than the differences, and in general the results point up the importance of informal means of communication in the job hunt. On the whole, the findings are quite consistent with Sheppard and Belitsky's (1967) study on job seeking. Although only a little more than one-third of the respondents say that family or friends referred them to their present job, another one-quarter of the national sample and one-sixth of the Negro sample mentioned "visiting plants" as the way in which they found employment. This presumes that the respondent had some idea of what plants to visit; in a large city, this requires more than a casual knowledge of the labor market. The largest differences between the Negroes and the national sample are in this category. It may well be that Negroes anticipate discrimination and hence are less willing to make the grand tour of possible employers. Negroes use formal means of obtaining job referrals, such as the union, newspaper advertisements, and public or private employment services more than whites do and use family and friends as a referral method less often.

The next question is what kinds of persons are useful sources of information about jobs? In the absence of data, we will make two straightforward assumptions: first, we assume that better-educated persons are more valuable contacts, since they may have more general knowledge, more influence, or may know more precisely what management wants in the way of qualifications. Second, we assume that whites know more about higher-paying jobs than Negroes do. Negroes who attend integrated schools are more likely to associate with whites in later life, and have a double advantage in that their contacts with whites also bring them into contact with persons who are better educated. Respondents were asked whether they could go for advice to a relative or friend who was a college graduate. (They were not asked what race the relative or friend was.) Respondents who attended integrated schools are not more likely to have relatives who are college graduates, but they are considerably more likely to have college-educated friends, as shown in Table 8. In this table, there is essentially no difference among northern-educated respondents who had themselves attended college; in all cases, they were likely to have college-educated friends. Southern migrants are at a slight disadvantage here, possibly because they have migrated after completing their education and thus have left their college classmates behind. There is a slight tendency for females with some college education who attended segregated high schools to report more college-educated friends, but the number of such cases is tiny. When we turn to respondents who themselves did not attend college, we find that those who attended integrated high schools have very distinct advantages, while alumni of segregated northern high schools are no more likely to have a college-educated friend available than are migrants who attended southern high schools. Since alumni of integrated high schools have

TABLE 8. *Percentage of Respondents Who Say They Could Seek Advice from a Friend Who Is a College Graduate, by Integration of High School, Educational Attainment, and Sex*

| | TYPE OF HIGH SCHOOL | | |
SEX	Northern, Integrated (%)	Northern, Segregated (%)	Southern, Segregated (%)
Males:			
No college	62	44	45
	(354)	(212)	(427)
Some college or college graduate	82	85	75
	(164)	(48)	(120)
Females:			
No college	47	33	35
	(536)	(257)	(636)
Some college or college graduate	65	78	69
	(130)	(56)	(147)

more white contacts, it seems safe to assume that many of these college graduate friends are white.

From this point, the chain of argument is supported indirectly by the evidence. We hypothesize that better-educated friends are more likely to know of job opportunities. This is supported by Table 9, which shows that those respondents who do have college graduate contacts are considerably more likely to be able to name an employer who would hire them. Notice that the differences are greater for respondents who themselves have some high school or are high school graduates. This is consistent with the possibility that college graduate contacts and other persons that these respondents could use for referrals would be more familiar with occupations requiring at least minimal educational qualifications. Or it may be that respondents with less than eighth-grade educations have access to low-status jobs which are easier to learn about, and which require fewer personal referrals.

TABLE 9. *Knowledge of Another Job Opportunity, by Sex, Education, and Contact with a College Graduate (Percentage)*

SEX AND CONTACT WITH COLLEGE GRADUATE	PERCENTAGE KNOWING OF ANOTHER JOB, BY EDUCATION				
	Eighth Grade	Some High School	High School Graduate	Attended College	
Males:					
With college graduate contact	32	37	41	52	
	(217)	(414)	(365)	(332)	
Without college graduate contact	29	17	21	...	
	(184)	(185)	(122)	(30)	
Difference	+ 3	+20	+20	...	
Females:					
With college graduate contact	22	29	39	53	
	(148)	(459)	(437)	(297)	
Without college graduate contact	20	19	24	...	
	(177)	(372)	(212)	(58)	
Difference	+ 2	+10	+15	...	

Note.—Net effect of college graduate contact, among those with high school education or less: males, 15%; females, 10%.

Table 10 shows that respondents who have white friends know of more job opportunities than those with fewer white contacts. The results for males, however, are quite weak; the differences for females are considerably stronger. It is possible that Negroes with high levels of white contact are more gregarious in general, and the fact that their friends are white is irrelevant. Table 11 considers this argument by controlling on the response to, "How often do friends and relatives visit your home?" In general, contact with whites is a more important factor than total amount of home visiting.

Table 12 closes this part of the argument by showing that alumni of integrated schools are more likely to name a prospective employer. This is not the case for respondents under thirty; but the differences among older respondents are quite large for both sexes.

We have presented data showing that part of the effect of school integration on occupational achievement can be attrib-

TABLE 10. *Contacts with Whites and Knowledge of Another Job, by Sex and Education of Respondent (Percentage Knowing of Another Job)*

| SEX AND EDUCATION | CONTACT WITH WHITES | | | |
	Low (0)	*(1–2)*	*(3–4)*	*High (5)*
Men, high education	. . .	55	20	52
	(30)	(45)	(64)	(215)
Men, low education	24	25	32	29
	(261)	(332)	(359)	(541)
Women, high education	. . .	34	41	43
	(30)	(64)	(58)	(203)
Women, low education	12	20	29	30
	(444)	(487)	(386)	(488)

Note.—For men, net effect of contact with whites, independent of education = +4. For women, net effect of contact with whites, independent of education = +12.

TABLE 11.   *Percentage Knowing of Another Job by Present Contact with Whites, by Frequency of Friends' Visits, and by Sex (Percentage Naming Another Employer)*

FREQUENCY OF VISITS	PRESENT CONTACT WITH WHITES		
	Low	*Medium*	*High*
Males:			
Few days per week	34.9	33.8	38.3
	(189)	(281)	(399)
Once per week	19.6	14.2	24.1
	(112)	(134)	(170)
Less than once per week	33.0	30.5	39.6
	(179)	(190)	(182)
Females:			
Few days per week	20.3	32.6	35.8
	(301)	(276)	(338)
Once per week	13.8	27.1	28.6
	(160)	(207)	(154)
Less than once per week	12.0	20.5	32.2
	(249)	(273)	(208)

Note.—Net effects (first col. vs. third col.): For men, net effect of contact with whites, independent of visiting = +3%, net effect of visiting, independent of white contact = +1%. For women, net effect of contact with whites, independent of visiting = +17%, net effect of visiting, independent of white contact = +8%.

uted to the effect of high contact with whites on job-seeking behavior. There are other effects as well; alumni of integrated schools are more likely to have attended college and score higher on an efficacy scale, which itself is associated with more aggressive job seeking. (Efficacious persons are more likely to know of another job, controlling for sex and educational attainment.) . . .

CONCLUSIONS

There are so many possible ways in which interracial contacts might benefit the Negro job seeker that it is difficult to

TABLE 12. *High School Integration and Knowledge of Another*
Job by Age and Sex of Respondent
(Percentage Naming Another Employer)

| | HIGH SCHOOL INTEGRATION | | |
AGE AND SEX	North, Integrated	North, Segregated	South
Males:			
Under 30	38	38	38
	(212)	(169)	(202)
30–39	46	10	30
	(195)	(68)	(189)
40+	40	15	24
	(106)	(27)	(152)
Females:			
Under 30	35	34	21
	(306)	(174)	(248)
30–39	24	18	27
	(237)	(78)	(317)
40+	30	19	20
	(106)	(53)	(200)

say what part of the process is most important. Only one-quarter of our sample stated that they obtained their present job through friends, but this did not mean that the other three-quarters did not benefit from informal contact. Even the most casual information about employment can be valuable, and such information tends to filter through the social system in many ways. One irony is that if a single Negro is hired by a large plant, there are more white employees who know that the firm is integrated than there are Negroes; thus we arrive at the curious hypothesis that whites will have more information about jobs which are becoming "open" than will Negroes.

In general, the argument that has been advanced here does not hinge upon actual job discrimination. In the absence of all discrimination and prejudice, American Negroes would still suffer the consequences of racial segregation in housing, voluntary associations, and informal social relations. These consequences are not merely psychic or social in character;

they can be measured in crude monetary terms as well. The public school thus becomes a doubly important instrument of social mobility for Negroes; in addition to its obvious educational value, it provides an opportunity to begin building the interracial associations which permit an escape from the ghetto.

BIBLIOGRAPHY

Robert L. Crain, "School Desegregation and the Academic Achievement of Negroes." *The Sociology of Education*, 1971, 44, 1–26.

Robert W. Hodge and Patricia Hodge, "Occupational Assimilation as a Competitive Process." *American Journal of Sociology*, 1965, 71, 249–264.

H. L. Sheppard and A. H. Belitsky, *The Job Hunt*. Baltimore: Johns Hopkins University Press, 1967.

U.S. Bureau of the Census, 1960. *Census of the Population. Occupational Characteristics*. Washington, D.C.: GPO, 1960.

(15)

The Racial Integration
of the Schools*

THOMAS F. PETTIGREW

INTRODUCTION

William McCulloch, the former Republican from Ohio's Fourth Congressional District, served for many years as the ranking minority member of the Judiciary Committee of the

*Abridged from "The Case for the Racial Integration of the Schools," delivered June 29, 1973, at the Cubberley Conference, Stanford University.

U.S. House of Representatives. In 1972 the elderly Mr. Mc-Culloch had to endure listening to the testimony of dozens of angry "antibusing" witnesses who came before the committee. Gently the soft-spoken Ohioian would ask each of these witnesses the same question.

"Do you *really* want to change the basic rules of American society?" And without waiting for an answer, Mr. McCulloch would point out that black Americans had been told for 350 years by white Americans to play by the democratic rules, to eschew violence in favor of the ballot box and court action and the promise of this great nation would apply to them, too. So they did play by the rules right on through to the 1954 Supreme Court ruling outlawing *de jure* racial segregation of the public schools.

"Isn't that your problem?" prodded Mr. McCulloch of each antibusing witness. "Isn't it true that black Americans have played by the rules so well that they've won in the courts? And because they've won you now wish to change the rules on them, to tell them that it was all a lie what we white people have been telling black people all these years. Isn't that what you come before us today to advocate?"

Well, how do we answer the pointed query of the Honorable Mr. McCulloch? *Are* we going to change the basic constitutional rules of our democracy to avoid interracial schools? This question provides us with the historical backdrop upon which to consider the racial integration of the schools.

THE STATUS OF SCHOOL DESEGREGATION

The situation in school desegregation is complex. While President Nixon has repeatedly attacked "busing" for integration, the federal courts have grown impatient with "deliberate speed" and begun ordering sweeping school desegregation. These court orders have particularly affected such Southern cities as Richmond, Charlotte, and Memphis, though Denver, Minneapolis, Boston, and other Northern cities have recently received similar directives. Public school statistics reflect this trend. Black children in all-black schools declined from

40 percent in 1968 to 12 percent in 1971; and those in pre-dominantly white schools rose from 18 percent in 1968 to 44 percent by 1971. Indeed, the special pressure on the South means that by the fall of 1970 a greater percentage of black children in the South attended majority-white schools than in the North (38% to 28%).

But there is another, less positive side to current trends. Many areas without court orders continue to practice massive racial segregation in their public schools as if the racial changes over the past generation had never happened. Cin-cinnati, for example, in 1973 still had about three-fifths of its pupils attending schools that are over 90 percent of their own race. Moreover, a number of urban districts, such as Louis-ville and Washington, D.C., achieved considerable school desegregation within their boundaries in past years only to find themselves resegregating as white families continue to move out to the suburbs and black families remain con-strained to central city residence through a vast and effective system of racial discrimination in housing. Finally, the growth of interracial schools under court pressure has raised a third and critical issue: How do you go beyond mere desegregation to attain true integration?

In summary, then, three problems persist. First, some areas have yet to initiate the school desegregation process. Second, many central cities are becoming overwhelmingly black school districts due to demographic patterns and housing discrimina-tion. Third, those districts with stable desegregation must now achieve genuine racial integration.

There are four major causes of public school segregation in urban areas, the relative importance of which is not widely understood. The most immediately critical are (1) long-term trends in racial demography and (2) the antimetropolitan nature of school district organization. Contributing further to the problem are (3) the effects of private schools and (4) intentional segregation within districts.

The magnitude of the first two factors becomes apparent as soon as we check the relevant data. There are approximately 17,000 school districts in the United States, with most of the recent consolidation of districts limited to rural areas. Thus there are still over 75 school districts in the Boston metropolitan area and 96 in the Detroit metropolitan area. There is pitifully little cooperation between central city and suburban school systems, and often vast fiscal and social disparities between them. In addition the 1970 census reveals that 78 percent of all black Americans in metropolitan areas reside within central cities, while 59 percent of all white Americans in metropolitan areas reside in suburbs. This extensive racial separation at the suburban line was evident back in 1950 and 1960, too, but has increased in each of these decades. The educational implications of these demographic data are made more severe by the fact that younger white families with school-age children are even more likely to be living in the suburbs than metropolitan whites in general. And racial housing trends are not encouraging and offer no hope for extensive relief of school segregation by race in the next generation. Consequently, America would face an enormous problem of *interdistrict* segregation of public schools even if there were no patterns of *intradistrict* separation.

But, of course, the nation also faces the task of overcoming sharp racial segregation within such school districts as Cincinnati, Philadelpia, Chicago, New York, and Los Angeles. In cities with large Roman Catholic populations, this intradistrict segregation is unwittingly increased by the absorption of many white children in the parochial school system. Since only about 6 percent of black Americans are Roman Catholics, a large church school system necessarily limits the available pool of school-age white children for a central city public school system. Indeed, urban private schools of all descriptions act in this manner. The South has not had a tradition of private education. But white private school enrollment in the South rose from about 300,000 in 1968 to 500,000 in 1971, though this still represents only about 4 percent of the region's public school enrollment.

Finally, though fourth in signficance, blatantly racist local leadership cannot be ignored. The Hickses and Wallaces of

American political life have exacerbated the problem of intradistrict segregation by their open advocacy of separation and steadfast refusal to take even preliminary measures to ease the problem. But while the public resistance of these antiblack politicians captures the headlines, such structural factors as demographic trends, the antimetropolitan nature of school organization and private-school effects remain more critical.

From this analysis we can readily appreciate the positive significance of present efforts to achieve *metropolitan*-based educational desegregation and truly democratic, *integrated* classrooms. We can also appreciate the negative significance of present political attempts to perpetuate three basic myths of resistance—the myths of "*de facto* segregation," "the neighborhood school," and "the dangers of busing." Let us consider each of these myths briefly.

THE THREE MYTHS OF SEGREGATIONIST RESISTANCE

The Myth of "De Facto Segregation"

There has long been a sharp discrepancy between the legal and the social science views of American race relations. In particular, the legal distinction between *de jure* and *de facto* racial segregation received no empirical support whatsoever in research. This disconfirmation exists even when we recall the derivation of the legal distinction from "the state action" prohibition of the Constitution's Fourteenth Amendment. "State action" need not be an explicit law of a Southern state that requires racially separate schools; it may more often be school board decisions of attendance boundaries, new school placement, and the like, as well as city council zoning actions that act to increase residential segregation by race. For public school segregation to be accurately termed *de facto*, its origins must be completely untainted with such broadly defined "state action." It can be said with confidence that social science research on American race relations has yet to uncover such *de facto* segregation in any public realm anywhere in the nation. *De jure* racial segregation is the harsh fact of American society; so-called *de facto* segregation simply does not exist.

Increasingly the federal district courts in Northern cities are coming to accept this fact. Judges are ruling in Denver, Minneapolis, and other cities that *de jure* segregation exists in their public schools and must be ended under the *Brown v. Board of Education* doctrine just as in Southern cities. This trend is what gives the Supreme Court's affirmation in 1973 of the Denver desegregation decision such broad national significance. Ironically, just as the federal courts discard the conception of *de facto segregation*, President Nixon lent new life to the myth by making it the legal cornerstone of his approach to racial segregation.

The Myth of "the Neighborhood School"

The ex-President also legitimized the idea that racial and social class desegregation is appropriate only if it can occur in "neighborhood schools." Given the enormity of the housing segregation patterns by race and class, this argument is obviously an attempt to maintain homogeneous schools as long as the country possesses homogeneous residential areas.

Additional considerations contribute further evidence as to the speciousness of this contention. To begin with, there are relatively few "neighborhood schools" in urban areas today— "neighborhood," that is, in the true *Gemeinschaft* sense that the school draws its students from a small area where virtually all of the resident families know each other and constitute a genuine community. What "neighborhood school" apparently means to its advocates is "local and conveniently nearby." But then one wonders if it is being upheld as a sacred ideal less for its presumed educational value than as a parental convenience.

Nor can "neighborhood schools" validly be described as "traditionally American." True, the fabled log-cabin school of the frontier had by necessity to be within walking distance of its pupils. But the frontier school was the classic example of a "common school," bringing together American children from all walks of life. To compare the homogeneous local urban school as the historical outgrowth of the heterogeneous rural school is to ignore the powerful social class "desegregating" function of the common school. The concept of "the neighborhood school" has been in educational circles since the Chicago city planners' use of it in the 1890s; yet it did not win popular acclaim until the desegregation process gained momentum in recent years. Such timing is enough to make even a prudent person suspicious.

Furthermore, there is no evidence of the educational merit of the "neighborhood school." Indeed, if it has to be small it is probably an anachronism and highly inefficient like the corner grocery of bygone decades. But what about parental involvement? There can be doubts raised as to how much parental involvement urban "neighborhood schools" can boast of now. In any event there is no evidence that there exists a close and negative association between the size of the attendance area and parental involvement or that only a local school can generate such concern.

The Myth of "the Dangers of School Busing"

This third myth is the most virulent and has been given increased currency by numerous politicians including the ex-President. Proposed bills to end school busing for racial desegregation proliferate; and constitutional amendments to end the practice forever receive serious attention.

A curious historian looking back upon this racial era from the perspective of the next century will have to dig hard to explain this national mania. Complicating the task is an array of facts that make school busing a strange target. In 1972, nineteen million pupils (43.5% of the total enrollment of public schools) were being regularly transported to school at public expense, a massive effort that requires 256,000 buses traveling 2.2 billion miles at a cost of $1.7 billion annually.

Legally authorized in 48 states since 1919, fifteen states today even permit the transportation of students to private schools at public expense. Clearly, travel-conscious America has no objection whatsoever to the busing of school children per se.

The political issue arises only when the transportation is designed to further the racial desegregation of schools. Only 3 percent of all bused students are transported for desegregation, and more public funds are still expended for transportation to racially segregated schools than to desegregated schools. Likewise, the dangers of bus accidents have been stressed for this 3 percent while ignored for the remaining 97 percent who are transported for "acceptable" reasons. Fortunately the relevant data reveal that the school bus is by far the safest mode of transportation. In 1968, according to the National Safety Council, the occupant death rate per 100 million passenger miles was 0.06 for school buses as compared to 0.24 for regular buses and 2.40 for automobiles. And the Pennsylvania Commission on Human Relations recently announced that over a five-year period, the state's school children were over three times safer per mile being bused to school than walking to school.

So why the national excitement? The movement ostensibly against busing has been forming over the past seven years. It gained momentum when federal judges in a number of key cities ordered busing solutions to correct urban patterns of widespread school segregation by race in situations where other alternatives were not available.

Survey data show that once Nixon explicitly legitimized the movement, it rose in strength even among so-called "moderate" white Americans. While 41 percent of a national sample of adult Americans told Harris Survey interviewers in early 1971 that they were unwilling to see school children bused for integration in their communities, 69 percent were unwilling by March 1972. Opposition was, not surprisingly, most intense in the Deep South and among whites, for blacks *favored* busing for integration in 1972 by 54 to 34 percent. In sharp contrast, by an overwhelming margin of 83 to 15 percent, parents whose children are bused to school for largely nonracial reasons are satisfied with the arrangement. Despite insistent denials, then, a future historian is likely to conclude that "busing" became in our time the polite, culturally sanctioned way to oppose the racial desegregation of the public schools. It's not the distance, stated a white mother in Richmond, Virginia, candidly, "It's the niggers."

BUT DOES RACIAL INTEGRATION OF THE SCHOOLS "WORK"?

Recently a fourth myth has developed as a part of the movement to turn back the racial clock. Bluntly, this fourth myth asserts that "science shows busing doesn't work." It originates from a much-publicized article in the Summer 1972 issue of *The Public Interest*.[1] Authored by David Armor, a sociologist at the Rand Corporation, this article claimed to be a "scientific" appraisal of "the evidence on busing." The mass media, as yet unequipped to evaluate material that purports to be social science, soon spread its anti-integration contentions across the nation.[2] Nixon campaigners immediately began to exploit the article as "scientific proof" of their anti-busing position, and Armor himself began appearing before congressional committees and in courts throughout the country as an "expert witness" on behalf of maintaining the racial segregation of the public schools.

Soon, however, a critique of Armor's article appeared.[3] It was written by four of his former colleagues at Harvard (including the present author), and it asserted that the Armor article was neither "scientific" nor the complete evidence. From an assortment of "evidence" Armor concludes that "busing" fails on four out of five counts. It does not lead, he argues, to improved achievement, grades, aspirations, and racial attitudes for black children; yet, despite these failures, he admits that desegregated schools do seem somehow to lead more often to college enrollment for black students.

The picture is considerably more positive, as well as more complex. For example, when specified school conditions are attained, research has repeatedly indicated that desegregated, compared to segregated, schools improve the academic performance of black pupils. Other research has demonstrated that rigidly high and unrealistic aspirations actually deter learning. Thus a slight lowering of such aspirations by school desegregation can lead to better achievement and cannot be regarded as a failure of "busing." And "militancy" and "black consciousness and solidarity" are not negative characteristics, as the article asserts, and their alleged development in desegregated schools could well be regarded as a further success, not a failure, of "busing." Moreover, the evidence that desegregated education sharply expands the life opportunities of black children is more extensive than Armor indicated (see, for example, the previous selection by Crain in this volume).

Consequently Armor's sweeping policy decision against "mandatory busing" is neither substantiated nor warranted. His anti-integration argument was based on special case data selected to fit the thesis. Obscured in his response was the fact that actually he was begrudgingly in *agreement* with his critics on a number of important points concerning the effects of interracial schools.[4] Marshall Smith,[5] one of the original critics, has summarized three important points:

1. *Insofar as we can tell from existing research, racial desegregation (induced or voluntary—via busing or other transportation) does not negatively influence and may often benefit the achievement of white students* . . .

2. *Insofar as we can tell from the existing research, desegregation (induced or voluntary—via busing or other transportation) does not harm and may often benefit the achievement of black students.* Although this may appear to be a controversial statement, in no place does Armor find that black students in desegregated situations do less well on standardized tests than they did prior to desegregating, or than similar black students do in segregated situations . . .

3. *There are indications that desegregated education increases the chances of black students attending post-secondary educational institutions.* As shown by Crain, the implications are great . . . The consequences of increasing years of schooling for later income and occupational status are far greater than the consequences of increasing scores on achievement tests.

ACHIEVING INTEGRATION OUT OF DESEGREGATION

No responsible observer ever claimed that *all* interracial schools would be "good" schools. It takes little imagination to design desegregated schools that are living hells for both black and white pupils. The question, then, is not: Do *all* interracial schools work well? The key questions, neatly skirted by Armor and other political foes of biracial education, are: How do we make interracial schools effective? And what are the discernible differences now between effective interracial schools and ineffective ones?

The racial desegregation of schools is not a static but a complex, dynamic process. One must search for the critical conditions under which the process seems to be most beneficial for all students. For this purpose, it is important to distinguish between *desegregation* and *integration*. Desegregation is achieved by simply ending segregation and bringing blacks and whites together; it implies nothing about the quality of the interracial interaction. Integration involves positive intergroup contact with cross-racial acceptance and equal dignity and access to resources for both racial groups. Now that desegregation is reasonably widespread, an important question for education becomes: How do we achieve integration out of desegregation?

Unfortunately, competent research directed specifically upon this question is scarce. But eight conditions that appear to maximize the probability that integration can occur in a school can be tentatively advanced on the basis of laboratory and classroom research, social psychological theory, and observation.

There Must Be Equal Racial Access to the School's Resources

This critical condition means far more than just equal group access to the library and other physical facilities. More important, it refers to equal access to the school's sources of social status as well. It is a compelling fact that the two most frequently voiced complaints in desegregated schools revolve around membership in the cheerleading squad and the student government—both sources of student status. Blacks in the minority often note that they are welcome to participate in those activities with universalistic standards such as athletics but not as welcome in more particularistic activities such as cheerleading and student government leadership.

Classroom—Not Just School—Desegregation Is Essential If Integration Is to Develop

Many of our so-called "desegregated" schools today are essentially internally segregated. This internal segregation is achieved in many not-so-subtle ways, ability grouping and curriculum separation being prime examples. But sometimes the methods can be quite elaborate. For example, transported minority children in a Riverside, California, school arrive and leave an hour earlier than untransported white children so that they can have entirely separate reading classes.[6] However it is managed, segregation by classroom does not and cannot provide the benefits that generally attend integration.[7]

Strict Ability Grouping Should Be Avoided

The principal means of separating majority and minority pupils within schools is by rigid ability grouping across various subjects. Such grouping is typically based on achievement and IQ tests standardized only on majority samples. And ability grouping is increasing in American schools, even penetrating down into the elementary grades. Some grouping by subject matter is, of course, necessary; Algebra 2 must follow Algebra 1, chemistry requires certain basic skills in arithmetic. Rather it is the across-the-board classification of students into "dull," "average," and "bright" that not only segregates by race and social class but through labeling sets the aspirations of both teachers and students in concrete and produces self-fulfilling prophecies of achievement. Told they are dumb and treated as if dumb, all but the most rebellious and self-confident pupils become in fact dumb.

Thus school systems, such as those of Sacramento, California, and Goldsboro, North Carolina, that maintained classrooms of heterogeneous ability levels by resisting ability grouping with more open classrooms and team teaching have tended to demonstrate the most encouraging achievement effects of desegregation.[8] By contrast, systems such as Riverside, California, which increased its use of ability grouping with the onset of desegregation, have tended to show the most disappointing results.[9]

School Services and Remedial Training Must Be Maintained or Increased with the Onset of Desegregation

Typically there is no reduction in *local* funds but an overall decrease due to narrowly conceived federal guidelines for the use of Title I moneys under the 1965 Elementary and Secondary Education Act.[10] Actually the act does not expressly forbid Title I funds for children from low-income families from following the children on the bus to the desegregated school, for desegregation and so-called compensatory education are most effective when they are combined rather than treated as opposite alternatives.

Desegregation Should Be Initiated in the Early Grades

During the 1950s the White Citizens' Councils of the Deep South sternly opposed the racial desegregation of the public schools and particularly objected to beginning the process in the primary grades. "It's not fair," they argued. "The very young children simply wouldn't know any better than to become friends."

Relevant research supports the Citizens' Councils' observation, if not their conclusion. The Coleman Report data show higher achievement among black children who began their interracial schooling in the first five grades.[11] And specific studies in Hartford, Connecticut, Ann Arbor, Michigan, Newark-Verona, New Jersey, Bridgeport-Westport, Connecticut, and Riverside all show, too, the best achievement gains for those who begin desegregation in kindergarten and the first grade.[12] The Coleman data also indicate that the most positive attitudes toward having interracial classes and blacks as close friends are evinced by white children who begin their interracial schooling in the earliest grades.[13] Racial isolation is a cumulative process. Its effects over time on children of both races make subsequent integration increasingly more difficult. Separation leads them to grow apart in interests and values.

Recently, the nation witnessed dramatic evidence of this critical condition for obtaining integration. Following the assassination of Dr. Martin Luther King in April 1968, a series of interracial confrontations and conflicts erupted in many biracial schools. Some observers immediately interpreted this strife as evidence that desegregation "cannot work," that it "only leads to trouble." Yet a diametrically opposite explanation is more plausible. This interracial conflict was centered at the high school level and typically involved black and white students who in the earlier grades had attended largely uniracial schools. The hostile students, then, were unfortunately living what they had been taught; that is, their first eight years of schooling taught them that segregation was the legitimate American norm and did not prepare them for harmonious interracial contact in high school. It was not desegregation that "failed." Rather it was racial segregation in the formative years that had "succeeded," as it has throughout our nation's history, to develop distrust and conflict between Americans of different skin colors.

The Need for Interracial Staffs Is Critical

Another correlate of the high school strife following Dr. King's murder underlines the importance of black teachers and administrators in the public schools. One study has shown that high school "disruptions" during 1968–1970 occurred far less often when the black staff percentage was equal to or greater than the black student percentage.[14] To be sure, there are more positive reasons for the development of thoroughly interracial staffs than the prevention of conflict. Genuine integration among students may be impossible to achieve unless the staff furnishes an affirmative model of the process. Black students report a greater sense of inclusion and involvement when blacks as well as whites are in authority. And black and white teachers learn the subtleties of the process from each other under optimal intergroup contact conditions—interdependently working toward common goals as equals under authority sanction.[15]

There is growing evidence, too, that the role of the principal is decisive in generating an integrated climate within a school. This fact suggests that it is important not just to have an interracial mix of teachers but a mix of administrators as well.

Substantial, Rather than Token, Minority Percentages Are Necessary

Coleman's original analysis of his national data revealed that black children who were the only members of their race in a classroom tended to score either quite high or quite low on both mathematical and reading achievement tests.[16] Such tokenism is psychologically difficult for black children. Without the numbers to form a critical mass, black students can come to think of themselves as an unwanted appendage, and white students can overlook the black presence and even perceive it as a temporary situation. But once the minority percentage reaches about 20 to 25 percent, blacks become a significant part of the school to stay. They are now numerous enough to be filtered throughout the entire school structure, on the newspaper staff and in the honor society as well as in the glee club and on athletic teams. Substantial minority representation, of course, does not guarantee intergroup harmony, but it is clearly a prerequisite for integration. Little wonder that Jencks and Brown find in a reanalysis of Coleman data that schools with 25 to 50 percent black enrollment seem to teach their black pupils more than those with one to 25 percent black enrollment.[17] Tokenism, then, appears not only to exact a heavy psychological cost from black children but may hold fewer academic benefits for them in addition.

Finally, Race and Social Class Must Not Be Confounded in the Interracial School

When the white children of a biracial school are overwhelmingly from affluent, middle-class families and the black children are overwhelmingly from poor, working-class families, the opportunities to develop integration are severely limited. Such confounding of race and class heightens the probability for conflict. Much of this conflict may be generated by value differences between classes, but in race-conscious America such class conflict is typically seen as race conflict. To meet this eighth condition for the development of integration, the inclusion of working-class white children and middle-class black children is essential. The crucial group in shortest supply are the middle-class blacks, though their absolute numbers have expanded about 14 times since 1940. The middle-class black child, then, should be seen as an invaluable resource for lowering the correlation within biracial schools between race and class.

A FINAL WORD

The basic case for the racial integration of the public schools is founded not on social science evidence but on our nation's traditional view of justice as well as the American dream. It is a cumulative process with potential academic and attitudinal benefits for both black and white children, but it is not a paternalistic program conducted "for" blacks or "for" whites. Rather it should be viewed as one component of the massive racial changes required to make the United States viable as an interracial society.

(16)

Poverty and Discrimination:
A Brief Overview*

LESTER C. THUROW

INCOME

According to the official definition of poverty, the proportion of the population living in poverty has slowly but steadily declined in the period since the Second World War, at a rate that would require some four decades to eliminate it. If the easier poverty cases are removed first, an increasing proportion of hard-core cases will slow the rate and more than four decades will be necessary. However, if long-run relative income distribution definitions of poverty are used, such as 50 percent of median incomes, there has been no decline in the postwar period. The distribution of income in this period has not changed.

Nor has discrimination declined. The average Negro family income has consistently remained near 55 percent of the white income. For a given average income level the white and black distributions have similar shapes, but the Negro distribution lags approximately thirty years behind the white. On the basis of relative measures such as these, discrimination has neither declined nor increased. In absolute terms, however, between 1947 and 1970 the average income gap between white and

* From L. C. Thurow, *Poverty and Discrimination*. Washington, D.C.: The Brookings Institution, 1969; Chapter 9. Reprinted with permission of the publisher and author. Copyright © 1969 by the Brookings Institution, Washington, D.C. All rights reserved.

Negro families widened from $2,700 to $3,700 (in 1970 dollars).* Relative measures indicate a stable pattern of discrimination, absolute measures a more intense pattern.

POVERTY

Poverty can be eliminated without understanding its causes simply by transferring income to the poor. If this is not to be the sole instrument, however, and if society wants individuals to earn their incomes by producing goods and services, the structural causes of poverty must be identified. Programs to combat the factors that produce poverty cannot be designed without both qualitative and quantitative knowledge of the factors. The relative size of their impact is important in determining the priorities and magnitudes of different programs.

An econometric model was developed to isolate and quantify the causes of poverty and to explain variations in its incidence among states. The distributions of human capital, physical capital, and employment opportunities were shown to have important effects on both white and Negro poverty. Quantitatively their effects seem similar, but the factor of racial discrimination affects only Negro poverty and not white. Everything else being equal, poverty is greater for Negroes. Thus white and Negro poverty are not identical. Income redistribution goals . . . may be color blind, but policy instruments must be color conscious. The package of programs that will cure white poverty will not cure Negro poverty. Something extra is needed.

Discrimination further complicates the analysis of poverty, since it is not just another independent factor which can be added to the analysis. It may have some independent effects, but primarily it works through the other causes of poverty. If incomes are assumed to be a simple function of education levels, there are still three effects of discrimination on Negro

* Data updated by the editor.

incomes. Preventing Negroes from acquiring education reduces income—more of them are poor because they have less education. Negroes have lower marginal returns to education —the twelfth year of education may raise white incomes by $500 and those of blacks by only $250. The absolute incomes associated with varying educational levels differ—improving the level from two and one-half to six years of schooling increases white incomes from $1,900 to $3,200 and eliminates white poverty, but increases black incomes only from $1,600 to $2,400, leaving them still poor. As a result, education may be an efficient variable to raise white income levels, but inefficient where Negro income is concerned.

Thus programs which would eliminate all white poverty would only partially eliminate Negro poverty. Specific programs must be designed to eliminate discrimination, oriented to Negro poverty, not white.

ECONOMIC POLICIES

Increasing the utilization of economic resources would reduce both poverty and discrimination. Reducing unemployment by 1 percentage point would reduce the number of persons in poverty by 1.25 million; the long-run effects of higher resource utilization would be even greater. Unbalanced labor markets and severe shortages of labor would create strong incentives for making the changes necessary to reduce poverty and discrimination. Alterations in training programs, employment standards, and individual incentives would further reduce poverty and the inequities in the distribution of income. Improvements would be especially noticeable for the Negro. Tight labor markets would increase both white and Negro incomes, but the favorable effects would be larger for Negroes. Lowering the unemployment rate from 7 percent to 3 percent would increase Negro family incomes from 50 percent of white incomes to 60 percent.

Although unbalanced labor markets have sizable direct effects on incomes and important indirect effects on other sources of higher incomes, such as training programs, higher utilization rates cannot totally eliminate either poverty or discrimination. Other changes are needed, but these may require tight labor markets as necessary conditions. Analysis indicates that 3 percent unemployment should be a major target for the war on poverty and discrimination.

HUMAN CAPITAL

Individual skills and knowledge—human capital—are an important determinant of the distribution of income. For the poor and for Negroes, rational factors lead to systematic underinvestment in their own human capital. The result is a widening gap in the human capital between the rich and the poor, between whites and blacks.

By means of the human capital function income flows were examined and the returns to education and experience were isolated for whites and Negroes in the North and South. The marginal returns to education and experience are much lower for Negroes than for whites. Negroes, and especially those in the South, receive fewer benefits from job experience. Lower wages for the same work, less on-the-job training, and a lack of adequate physical capital with which to work offer a partial explanation.

More important than the marginal returns to either education or training are the complementarities among education, training, physical capital, and technical progress. The complementarities between education and training are so great that programs to increase them must be carefully coordinated if either type of program is to have the expected payoff in terms of increasing incomes. The complementarities vary among races, regions, and occupations, but the joint effects of having both education and training are four times as large as the sum of their separate effects.

No program to raise incomes through raising education will succeed unless other measures are also taken. Raising functional literacy standards to eighth or tenth grade standards may be an important ingredient in raising incomes, but the effects will not be apparent unless it is combined with training opportunities and job opportunities. Eliminating discrimination is necessary if Negro education is to have a significant effect. As long as there is discrimination, more education produces little payoff.

Job experience or on-the-job learning is a major source of the gap between Negro and white incomes. Thus a major proportion of the task of increasing Negro human capital must be achieved in the private sector of the economy. Governments can provide significant incentives for private actions, but government education programs will have small returns unless the private job market can be cracked at the same time.

PHYSICAL CAPITAL AND
TECHNICAL PROGRESS

The distribution of income is much wider than would be predicted from the distribution of human capital alone. Only a small part of the difference can be explained by the distribution of the ownership of physical wealth; much must be explained by imperfect labor markets. With imperfect labor mobility, individuals who work with little physical capital or in areas with little technical efficiency receive low incomes, while those in areas with high capital-labor ratios and high technical efficiency earn large incomes. Competitive pressures do not equalize incomes for individuals with the same human capital. To explain the difference between the actual distribution and the income distribution that would be predicted on the basis of human capital, market imperfections must be severe and the distributions of physical capital and technical progress quite uneven. The impact of market imperfections is particularly harsh on Negroes.

A major part of the effort to eliminate low incomes among both whites and Negroes must be directed toward narrowing the distributions of physical capital and technical progress or toward making them irrelevant. Improving the mobility of the labor force is of major importance. This can be achieved directly by better labor market information or by providing incentives for mobility, indirectly by encouraging industrial firms to move into Negro areas.

DISCRIMINATION

. . . [My] theory suggests that much discrimination is based on the monopoly powers of whites.* Without such powers racial prejudices would have less impact on Negro incomes. With monopoly powers, however, whites may gain financially and enforce discriminatory practices that substantially lower Negro incomes. Functionally, monopoly can be reduced without changing the attitudes of the whites who discriminate. Equality need not wait until man has goodwill toward all races or until the government is willing to bribe him to be nice to his neighbor.

Quantitatively, the monopoly powers of the white community vis-à-vis the black community are a major force leading to lower Negro incomes and higher individual white incomes. Negro losses and white gains from discrimination amount to approximately $15 billion per year. In addition, discrimination causes a large reduction in the potential level of output of the American economy. Negro economic resources are not fully utilized and white resources are inefficiently utilized as a result of discrimination. Efficiency losses amount to approximately $19 billion per year.

The institutions of government are an important link in implementing discrimination. Either directly through legal restrictions or indirectly through harassment and expenditure decisions, the coercive powers of the white community flow through local, state, and federal government institutions. Eliminating discrimination in all levels of government may

* For a full description of Thurow's fascinating theory on racial discrimination, see his book cited earlier.

be one of the most effective means of eliminating the effects of discrimination throughout the economy.

PERSONS OUTSIDE THE LABOR FORCE

Programs to raise the earnings of individual workers cannot aid many families which are either completely or partially outside the labor force. Guaranteed jobs or sheltered employment have been suggested as a solution, but many cannot benefit from employment of any kind. For them, direct income transfers are necessary. In the long run, the negative income tax appears to be the most promising solution.

Examination of the problems and opportunities presented by both guaranteed jobs and direct income transfers reveals the need for integrating productivity programs, guaranteed job programs, and direct income transfers. All are necessary, each can function more efficiently if the other programs are also present, and each can be damaged if the others are not well coordinated with it. (See Selections 24 and 26.)

STRATEGIES FOR ELIMINATING POVERTY

Coordinated programs for creating tight labor markets, improving the distribution of human capital, increasing labor mobility, ending discrimination, and providing for those outside the labor force are all necessary to eliminate poverty and discrimination. No one program can work by itself. Theoretically direct income transfers are an exception to this rule, but politically they seem to be unacceptable.

As the analysis has shown, reducing the income gap between rich and poor and closing the income gap between black and white are interrelated problems. To succeed in either project would automatically bring improvement in the other; but no set of programs, except direct income transfers, can achieve either of them without recognizing the interaction between poverty and discrimination. Programs to eliminate poverty will not work for Negroes unless they operate on racial discrimination. Programs to put an end to racial inequality will not work unless they act on the causes of poverty which afflict black and white alike.

⟨ 17 ⟩

The 1960s: A Decade of Progress for Blacks?*

REYNOLDS FARLEY AND ALBERT HERMALIN

I. INTRODUCTION

Thirty years ago Gunnar Myrdal argued that the most important changes for blacks in this country would be changes in the values and beliefs of whites. He contended that blacks would make progress if and only if whites accepted blacks as equals and treated them in accord with democratic ideals (Myrdal, 1944, Vol. 2, p. 998).

In the ensuing years, numerous surveys have generally indicated that whites are increasingly willing to treat blacks as equals on a number of fronts . . . The proportion of all whites favoring integrated schools rose from 30 percent in 1942 to 75 percent in 1970; for integrated neighborhoods the advance was from about 44 percent in 1963 to 50 percent in 1970 (Greeley and Sheatsley, 1971). The Harris and Gallup polls discovered that a majority of whites approved of the civil rights laws enacted during 1963 and 1964. Campbell

* Abridged from R. Farley and A. Hermalin, "The 1960s: A Decade of Progress for Blacks?" *Demography*, 1972, 9, 353–370. Reprinted with permission of the publisher and authors.

and Schuman (1968, Chapter 3) surveyed the attitudes of urban whites following the racial riots which broke out in many cities during 1967. They discovered that most whites perceived that blacks were adversely affected by discrimination. The majority of whites favored laws to ban discrimination in the job market, claimed to be willing to work for a black supervisor, and said they would vote for a black candidate if he were the better man. Over half the whites expressed a willingness to pay higher taxes for a federal program which would upgrade jobs, schools, and housing for blacks. The attitudes of whites varied with the issue; occupational integration was more widely approved by whites than neighborhood integration.

If the attitudes of whites have changed, we would anticipate reductions in racial differences on a number of dimensions. In this paper we examine in some detail racial differentiation in income, occupation, and education, focusing on trends during the 1960s . . . The analysis here is based on annual publications of the Bureau of the Census and decennial census material.[1]

II. INCOME TRENDS

Family Income

Income is a crucial determinant of one's life style and living arrangements so we look first at change in income. The 1960s were a prosperous period and most measures of income show gains during this period. For instance, median family income (before taxes) in the United States rose from $5,400 in 1959 to $9,400 in 1969. A portion of this increase represents inflation, and to eliminate this factor we express income trends in terms of the purchasing power of the dollar in 1969. Controlling for inflation, we still find that median family income rose between 1959 and 1969, from $6,800 to $9,400 (U.S. Bureau of the Census, 1970a, Tables 7 and 8). This represents a real increase in purchasing power and means that families are able to buy more goods and services than they were a decade ago.

Rises in family income were greater among blacks than among whites. Median family income among whites rose about 25 percent while that of blacks went up 40 percent, and as an outcome, the ratio of nonwhite to white income rose. These trends are illustrated in Table 1, which shows the median income of families by color, the ratio of median incomes, and two other measures of the similarity or equality of income distributions, delta and the Gini index. The ratio of median incomes is shown as dollars of Negro or nonwhite income per $100 of white income. Delta, or the index of dissimilarity, is useful for comparing two groups which are distributed among categories such as income levels (Duncan and Duncan, 1955) . . .

The Gini index is a Lorenz curve measure which has been widely used to assess inequalities in the distribution of income. Its range is from -1.0 through 0.0 to $+1.0$ or, as used here, from -100 to $+100$. A Gini index of $+100$ indicates that there is no overlap of the income distributions of the

TABLE 1. *Income of White and Nonwhite Families, in 1969 Dollars, and Measures of Income Equality*

| | MEDIAN INCOME | | | MEASURES OF INCOME EQUALITY | |
YEAR	White Families	Nonwhite Families	Ratio of Nonwhite to White	Delta[a]	Gini[a]
1947	$5194	$2660	51	36	45
1959	7106	3661	52	35	45
1961	7361	3913	53	33	41
1963	7841	4165	53	33	42
1965	8424	4666	55	33	40
1967	9086	5641	62	28	35
1969	9794	6191	63	27	34

[a] Delta and Gini indices computed from current dollar distributions using ten categories.
SOURCE: U.S. Bureau of the Census, Current Population Reports, Series P–60, No. 75 (12–14–70), Table 8.

two races and that *all whites* have higher incomes than *any blacks*. A value of 0 indicates complete overlap and no racial differentiation in income, while a value of −100 means there is no overlap and *all blacks* are at higher income levels than *any whites* (Miller, 1966, pp. 220–221).

Turning once again to Table 1, gain in black income relative to that of whites appears quite dramatic during the 1960s compared to the earlier period, as measured by the delta or Gini indices or the ratio of nonwhite to white income. For each of these measures, the gain in the four-year period from 1965 to 1969 was greater than that for the eighteen-year span from 1947 to 1965. (Comparable data are not available prior to 1947, so longer trends on these measures cannot be computed.) At the same time, it must be noted that black income in 1969 was lower than that of whites ten years earlier, and that the absolute dollar gap between the two races has been quite constant at about $3,500 throughout the 1960s.

Family income varies systematically depending upon who heads the family and his or her age. To further analyze recent trends, we show—in Table 2—changes in family income by type of family and age of head. Husband–wife families, of course, include a married couple both of whom may be working. The woman in families with a female head has been widowed or divorced, lives apart from her spouse, or, in a few cases, has never been married (U.S. Bureau of the Census, 1970b, Table 13).

There were increases in real purchasing power among both types of families and for every age group of heads. The measures of racial differentiation imply that the income distributions of white and black families have become more alike. If we look at tabulations by age of head, we see that the most dramatic relative gains were made by black families with heads in the younger age categories. By 1970, black husband –wife families with heads under 35 had median incomes 82 percent as great as similar white families. Black families headed by a woman under 35 had incomes 90 percent as great as similar white families. Among families with older

TABLE 2. Income of White and Negro Families, in 1969 Dollars, by Type of Family and Age of Head

| FAMILY TYPE & AGE OF HEAD | INCOME IN 1959 | | | | | INCOME IN 1969 | | | | |
| | Median Income | | | Measures of Income Equality | | Median Income | | | Measures of Income Equality | |
	White Families	Non-white Families	Ratio of Non-white to White	Delta[a]	Gini[a]	White Families	Negro Families	Ratio of Negro to White	Delta[a]	Gini[a]
Husband–wife families										
Head < 35	$7150	$4564	64	33	42	$8677	$7100	82	14	18
35–44	8657	5411	63	36	45	11691	8785	75	25	33
45–64	8435	4659	55	34	45	11515	7356	64	31	38
65+	4011	2317	58	25	32	4827	3154	65	21	31
Total	7672	4577	60	33	41	10241	7329	72	23	29
Families with female heads										
Head < 35	2599	1838	71	18	18	3171	2842	90	13	13
35–44	4116	2376	58	26	29	5450	3951	72	25	20
45–64	5415	2477	46	32	40	6748	3597	53	31	41
65+	4638	2052	44	32	40	5699	2511	44	31	39
Total	4457	2184	49	30	37	5500	3341	61	25	31

[a] Delta and Gini indices computed from current dollar distributions using ten categories.

SOURCE: U.S. Bureau of the Census, Census of Population: 1930, PC(1)–1D, Table 224; Current Population Reports Series P-60, No. 75 (December 14, 1970), Table 17.

heads, there was some diminution of the racial difference, although it was quite small. As a result, black families of each type were more differentiated by age in the extent to which they approached white family income in 1969 than in 1959.

Problems of deprivation must be particularly acute in black families headed by women. These families had a median income in 1969 of $3,300 and about one-third of them received less than $2,500. They included an average of two children under 18, while white female-headed families included an average of one child (U.S. Bureau of the Census, 1970b, Table 1). Since 1960, the number of Negro families headed by a woman has grown more rapidly than the number of husband–wife families; and by 1970, female-headed families accounted for 28 percent of all black families (U.S. Bureau of the Census, 1971a, Table 2).

The regional data in Table 3 show that the ratio of black to white family income increased most rapidly in the South from 1959 to 1969, although it was lower there than in the other sections of the country. This regional pattern of change in family income differs somewhat from that found in examin-

TABLE 3. *Ratio of Negro to White Family Median Income by Region, 1959 and 1969 and Proportion of Female Headed Families, by Race and Region, 1960 and 1970*

| REGION | RATIO OF NEGRO FAMILY MEDIAN INCOME TO THAT OF WHITES | | PROPORTION OF FAMILIES HEADED BY FEMALES | | | |
| | | | Negro | | Whites | |
	1959	1969	1960	1970	1960	1970
Northeast	69	67	24%	32%	9%	10%
North Central	72	76	21	27	7	8
South	46	57	22	27	8	9
West	70	75	20	27	8	9

SOURCE: U.S. Bureau of the Census, Census of Population: 1960, PC(1)–1D, Tables 247, 266; PC(2)–1C, Table 14; Census of Population: 1970, PC(1)–B1, Table 58; Current Population Reports, Series P–60, No. 75, Table 37.

ing the regional trend in personal income of males and females shown in Tables 4 and 6. A number of factors are operating to account for these differences. First, the income of black men relative to that of whites increased more in the South than in the other regions, as shown in Table 4. Since male income is the predominant factor in family income, the regional pattern in Table 3 more closely resembles the racial pattern of male income than of female. A second change worth noting is the differential rate of growth by region of female-headed families. The proportion of black families headed by women increased in every region, a factor which limited gains in average family income since female-headed families report smaller incomes than families headed by a man (see Table 2). The increase in the proportion of black female-headed families was lowest in the South, as shown in Table 3, and this also contributes to the more rapid improvement in average Negro family income in that region.

Income of Persons: Men

In this section the focus is on racial differences in personal—not family—incomes in 1959 and 1969. Table 4 presents the median income for men of each race and measures of income equality and similarity for a number of characteristics—age, region of residence, occupation, and education—known to be associated with income differentials.

Between 1959 and 1969, the median income of each group of men rose, and with few exceptions the increases were greater for blacks than for whites. We can be certain that it was not just young blacks, blacks outside the South, those with college educations, or those with professional jobs who improved their economic position. Rather, purchasing power rose and racial differentiation in income declined among almost all groups.

There are differences in the relative rates of improvements. If we look at age data, we observe that the largest reductions in racial differentials occurred among the youngest groups. Black men 20 to 24 in 1970 had median incomes 91 percent

TABLE 4. Income of White and Negro Males, in 1969 Dollars, by Age, Region, Education, and Occupation, 1959 and 1969[a]

	INCOME IN 1959					INCOME IN 1969				
	Median Income		Ratio of Non-white to White	Measures of Income Equality		Median Income		Ratio of Negro to White	Measures of Income Equality	
SELECTED CHARACTERISTICS	White Men	Non-white Men		Delta[d]	Gini[d]	White Men	Negro Men		Delta[d]	Gini[d]
AGE										
20–24	$3408	$2183	64	23	29	$3822	$3466	91	8	7
25–34	6349	3667	58	38	49	8311	5558	67	34	44
35–44	7156	4050	57	41	53	9399	5810	62	36	49
45–54	6708	3543	53	39	51	9001	5117	57	40	52
55–64	5797	2833	49	35	46	7576	4263	56	34	41
65+	2307	1213	53	26	34	2941	1491	51	32	42
Total[b]	5464	2919	53	30	38	6765	3935	58	26	32
REGION[c] (for men 14 and over)										
Northeast	5824	4190	72	27	30	7055	5339	76	19	22
North Central	5701	4369	77	21	23	7133	5907	83	20	17
South	4440	2070	47	35	42	5841	3133	54	32	37
West	6013	4277	71	24	26	7255	5312	73	19	20

EDUCATION (for men 25 and over)

Elementary										
< 8	3422	2300	67	18	24	3613	2973	82	14	16
8	5031	3667	73	20	24	5460	4293	79	17	18
High school										
1–3	6313	4120	65	31	41	7309	5222	71	25	31
4	6972	4713	68	34	43	8631	6144	71	30	39
College 1–3	7682	5089	66	33	44	9575	7051	74	30	35
4	9791	6150	63	35	43	12437	8567	69	30	35

OCCUPATION (for year-round full-time workers only)

Professionals	8952	5254	59			11860	8606	73		
Managers	8842	4725	53			11157	6598	59		
Clerical	5602	5380	96	n.a.		8032	7263	90	n.a.	
Craftsmen	6660	4498	68			8905	6488	73		
Operatives	6262	4485	72			7525	5824	77		
Service	5401	3515	65			6671	4865	73		
Laborers	5448	3893	71			6278	5328	85		

a Data refer to men reporting income in 1959 or 1969. Median income figures shown in 1969 dollars.
b Includes some men under 20 who report income.
c Data for regions in 1960 refer to Negroes.
d Delta and Gini indices computed from current dollar distributions using ten categories.
SOURCE: U.S. Bureau of the Census, Census of Population: 1960, PC(1)–1D, Tables 219 and 262; PC(2)–5B, Table 7; 1960 Census of Population and Housing, One in One Thousand Sample of the Population; Current Population Reports, Series P–60, No. 75, Tables 45, 47, 50 and 59.

as large as white men in the same age span. At the other end
of the distribution, there is no evidence that the racial gap
diminished among men 65 and over.

We can make an abbreviated cohort analysis from data in
Table 4. Men 25 to 34 in 1960—when the information concerning 1959 income was obtained—were 35 to 44 in 1970.
Similarly, we have two readings on the cohorts of men who
were 35 to 44 and 45 to 54 in 1960. When we compare the
same cohorts with regard to income in 1959 and 1969, we
observe very small relative improvements for blacks. In most
cases black and white men had similar percentage increases
in income and the measures of income distribution declined
very little.

This analysis suggests that a primary reason why black
men improved their income in the 1960s was that young men
entering the labor market obtained incomes more nearly
equal those of young white men. Apparently, even during
the prosperous 1960s, there was not much relative improvement in income for black men who were 25 and over in 1960.

We wondered if the relative improvements in income experienced by black men during the 1960s were similar to improvements experienced by black men during the 1950s. To
explore this matter, we calculated ratios of median incomes
for the youthful age groups for the three most recent census
years, as shown in Table 5. (The income figures used are for
the year preceding the date shown.)

These ratios indicate that during the 1950s, young black
males did not gain on young whites. However, between 1960
and 1970, the ratio of nonwhite to white income rose, and
this implies that the 1960s differed from the previous decade
in terms of the progress made by blacks who were entering
the labor force.

During the 1960s racial differences in the income of men
decreased in all regions. The South remains distinctive because of its low income level and the very large racial differences in income. Incomes went up at all educational attainment levels and racial differences diminished. In both years,
the racial differentiation in income was greater among men

TABLE 5. *Ratio of Median Income of Nonwhite Men to White Men, for Selected Ages, 1950, 1960, and 1970*[a]

| | RATIO OF NONWHITE MALE INCOME PER $100 WHITE MALE INCOME | | |
YEAR	Total Males	Males 20–24	Males 25–34
1950	52	65	56
1960	53	64	58
1970	58	91	67

[a] Data for 1970 refer to blacks.

SOURCE: U.S. Bureau of the Census, Census of Population: 1950, P–C1, Table 139; Census of Population, 1960, PC(1)–1D, Table 218; Current Population Reports, Series P–60, No. 75, Table 45.

with extensive educations than among men who had only grammar school educations. This trend has accentuated from 1959 to 1969, as measured by the ratio of black to white income.

Despite the improvements in income, racial differences remain and black incomes lag far behind those of white men. The figures in Table 4 present income statistics for twenty-three different groupings of men. In twenty of the twenty-three groups, the median income of blacks in 1969 was less than the median income of whites a decade earlier.

Income of Persons: Women

Table 6 presents income information for women classified by their age, educational attainment, and region of residence. Among women, as among men, incomes rose during the 1960s and racial differences diminished. These trends were operative for all age groups, at all educational attainment levels, and in each region.

There are several important sexual differences in income trends. First, the gains in income by black women, relative to white women, seem more pervasive and extensive than those of black men. Median incomes rose 60 percent for black

TABLE 6. *Income of White and Negro Females, in 1969 Dollars, by Age, Region, and Educational Attainment, 1959 and 1969*[a]

| SELECTED CHARACTER-ISTICS | INCOME IN 1959 | | | | | INCOME IN 1969 | | | | |
| | Median Income | | Ratio of Non-white to White | Measures of Income Equality | | Median Income | | Ratio of Negro to White | Measures of Income Equality | |
	White Females	Non-white Females		Delta[d]	Gini[d]	White Females	Negro Females		Delta[d]	Gini[d]
AGE										
20–24	$2286	$1136	50	24	29	$2629	$2031	77	12	14
25–34	2522	1631	65	17	19	2985	3024	101	15	– 1
35–44	2765	1646	60	20	24	3303	2862	87	13	5
45–54	2986	1273	43	30	36	3740	2256	60	21	24
55–64	2201	1042	47	27	33	2990	1493	50	23	28
65+	1009	783	78	18	19	1432	1050	73	22	28
Total[b]	1902	1159	61	17	20	2182	1840	84	9	9

REGION[c] (for women 14 and over)										
Northeast	2202	2172	99	13	4	2422	2993	124	13	− 6
North Central	1755	1707	97	10	4	1969	2322	118	9	− 4
South	1659	922	56	25	29	2147	1327	62	18	20
West	2031	1944	96	11	5	2215	2481	112	10	− 6
EDUCATION (for women 25 and over)										
Elementary										
<8	1081	914	85	11	13	1303	1195	92	5	7
8	1435	1222	85	9	9	1688	1320	78	12	13
High school										
1–3	2131	1506	71	16	18	2355	2268	96	10	5
4	2809	2182	78	12	13	3234	3257	101	12	−2
College 1–3	3060	2729	89	9	6	3427	4247	124	12	−10
4	4745	4625	97	19	1	5707	6747	118	23	−16

[a] Data refer to persons who reported income in 1959 or 1969. Median income figures shown in 1969 dollars.
[b] Includes some income recipients under age 20.
[c] Data for regions in 1960 refer to Negroes.
[d] Delta and Gini indices computed from current dollar distributions using ten categories.
SOURCE: See Table 4.

women, only 35 percent for black men. If we perform a cohort analysis, we find that black women who were 25 and over in 1960 gained on their white peers, but this was generally not the case among black men.

Second, we find that by 1970 the median income of several groups of black women exceeded that of comparable white women, and the Gini indices demonstrate that black women were concentrated at higher income levels. In all regions except the South, the median incomes were higher for black than for white women. This was also the case among women who had completed secondary school. For instance, among college educated women, the median income of blacks was 20 percent greater than that of whites in 1969.

One might speculate that this occurs because black women work more hours per week or weeks per year. We do not have data which would permit an adequate test of this hypothesis. Nevertheless, at the aggregate level, there seem to be only small racial differences in the time women spend at work. In 1969, for example, 39 percent of the nonwhite and 41 percent of the white women in the labor force worked full-time for at least fifty weeks (U.S. Bureau of Labor Statistics, 1971, Table A-8). In 1959, there was a similarly small difference in the number of hours or weeks worked (U.S. Bureau of the Census, 1963a, Tables 194, 197, and 199).

Two factors may account for the higher incomes of black women. Labor force participation rates imply that black women work for a greater proportion of their lives than white women (Bowen and Finegan, 1969, pp. 252–254; Bancroft, 1958, Chapter 3; U.S. Bureau of the Census, 1963b, Tables 5–9). It is possible that black women often have greater seniority and experience than white women of a similar age. Second, since their husbands earn relatively little, black women may seek the most lucrative jobs available. White women may feel less need for income and when they seek jobs they may consider factors such as the place of employment or timing of the working day.

Income and Education

Many discussions of contemporary racial inequalities point out that blacks with a given education or holding a specific job receive lower incomes than whites with similar occupations or educations (Duncan, 1969; Price, 1969, Table VI-9). The nature of this inequality can be gauged, in part, from the data already presented in Table 4. In 1960, black men with a college education had a median income lower than that of white males with one to three years of high school. Even after the progress of the 1960s, a college educated black man had a lower median income than a white secondary school graduate in 1969. These differences do not exist between black and white females, since their incomes for the identical educational level are much more nearly equal, as reported in Table 6.

III. OCCUPATIONS AND EMPLOYMENT

Occupations of Employed Workers

Discussions of the manner in which people earn their livelihood can be focused around, first, the occupations pursued by workers and, second, the labor force status of adults. In this paper we will analyze occupational trends. Table 7 shows the distribution of employed men and women at dates between 1950 and 1970. Cautious interpretations of these data are appropriate since they are drawn from two different sources. The 1950 and 1960 data were gathered by decennial censuses while the more recent figures come from the Census Bureau's Current Population Survey, a monthly sample of 50,000 households.

Considering males first, the delta index comparing the occupational distributions of whites and nonwhites shows that there were decreasing racial differences in the 1960–1970 decade as contrasted with practically no change in the previous decade. More specifically, the relative gains for

TABLE 7. *Occupation of Employed Persons by Race and Sex, 1950–1970*[a]

OCCUPATION	NONWHITES					WHITES				
	1950	1960	1966	1968	1970	1950	1960	1966	1968	1970
Males										
Total percent	100	100	100	100	100	100	100	100	100	100
Prof., managerial	4	5	9	10	13	20	23	28	29	30
Clerical, sales	4	7	8	9	9	14	15	13	13	13
Craftsmen	8	11	11	13	14	20	22	20	21	21
Operatives, service	36	43	44	43	41	25	26	26	25	25
Laborers	24	22	20	18	17	7	6	6	6	6
Farmers, farm labor	24	12	8	7	6	14	8	7	6	5
Delta comparing occupations of whites and nonwhites[b]	37	38	36	33	31					

Females

Total percent	100	100	100	100	100	100	100	100	100	100
Prof., managerial	7	9	10	12	13	18	19	20	20	20
Clerical, sales	5	10	16	19	22	40	44	44	44	44
Craftsmen	1	1	1	1	1	2	1	1	1	1
Operatives, service	34	36	41	41	44	32	30	29	29	29
Pvt. household workers	42	39	28	24	18	4	4	4	4	4
Laborers	2	1	1	1	1	1	1	1	1	1
Farmers, farm labor	9	4	3	2	1	3	2	2	2	2
Delta comparing occupations of whites and nonwhites[b]	53	47	38	33	30					

[a] Figures for 1950 and 1960 refer to the week preceding the census enumeration. Data for other years refer to April of each year.

[b] These indices are computed from a detailed distribution of eleven occupational categories.

SOURCE: Daniel O. Price, *Characteristics of the Negro Population* (Washington: Government Printing Office, 1969) Table IV-3; U.S. Bureau of Labor Statistics, *Employment and Earnings*, Vol. 13, No. 11 (May 1967), Table A-17; Vol. 14, No. 11 (May 1968), Table A-17; Vol. 16, No. 11 (May 1970), Table A-19; U.S. Bureau of the Census, *Census of Population: 1960*, PC(1)–1C; Table 88.

blacks appear to have occurred since 1966 and the change since then far exceeds that of the prior sixteen years. From 1966 to 1970, the white occupational distribution has remained almost constant, while among blacks a gradual upgrading is in evidence. Before 1966, a trend toward higher status occupations was in evidence for whites and blacks with little consequent change in the degree of racial differentiation.

A look at recent changes in the *number* of men employed at white-collar jobs or as craftsmen (data not shown in this paper) reveals much greater percentage increases for nonwhites than for whites. At several of the higher occupational levels, black males were employed in large numbers for the first time during the 1960s. Despite this progress, large racial differences in occupational structure remain. Only 13 percent of the black men are professional or managerial workers compared to 30 percent among whites; 17 percent of blacks, in contrast to six percent of whites, work as laborers.

Substantial changes have occurred in the occupational distribution of nonwhite women in the last twenty years. In 1950, over one-half the employed nonwhite females worked as domestic help or on farms. This proportion declined and presently fewer than 20 percent of the nonwhite women hold such jobs. There have been sharp rises, during the 1960s, in the proportion of nonwhite women working at professional, clerical, and service jobs.

In an effort to understand what happened during the 1960s, we compared the 1960 and 1970 occupational distributions of women. We found that there was very little change in the distribution of whites, but among nonwhites there was a substantial shift during the decade. The fastest growing occupations were the more prestigious ones and, as a result, the racial difference in occupations of women decreased. The delta index, comparing black and white women on occupational distributions, shows that, unlike the male situation, growing similarity between the races was not confined to the 1966–1970 period. Some diminution of racial differences is evident from 1950 to 1960; the change became more rapid during the 1960s and roughly proportional across the decade.

IV. EDUCATIONAL ATTAINMENT

During the 1960s, the educational attainment of the adult population increased. Among black men, for example, the rise in median school years completed was from 7.9 to 9.8, while among whites, the change was from 10.6 to 12.2 years. Similar increases are evident for the female population. This occurred primarily because young people are remaining in school longer, reflecting the secular trend toward more education. In this section we report on the number of school years completed. We note at the outset that this may not be a satisfactory indicator of intellectual achievement . . .

Table 8 shows the median educational attainment in 1960 and 1970 for different age groups and two measures of educational equality—Gini and delta. For most of the age groups, attainment was greater in 1970 than in 1960; and the values of the delta and Gini indices declined, meaning that the white and black educational distributions became more similar.

Perhaps more interesting are the cohort changes which can be discerned by looking at different age groups. For instance, no more than 15 to 20 percent of the black men who were teenagers in the 1920s completed secondary school and their median attainment was about eight years. They lagged very far behind their white age peers in attainment. Among black males who were teenagers in the 1960s, over 60 percent completed secondary school and their median attainment exceeded twelve years.

Reading down the columns of delta or Gini indices in Table 8, one generally finds progressively larger values. Over time then the increases in attainment have been greater among blacks than among whites; and, as a result, racial differences in educational attainment are smaller among the young than among the old. This indicates that the 1960s were not unique; rather there has been a long-run trend toward smaller racial differentiation in attainment.

Traditionally, black women have completed more years of schooling than black men, while among whites, the sexual

TABLE 8. Indicators of Educational Attainment and Measures of Educational Equality by Age, Sex, and Color, 1960 and 1970

SEX AND AGE	1960						1970					
	Percent HS Graduate		Median Years Completed		Measures of Educ. Equality		Percent HS Graduate		Median Years Completed		Measures of Educ. Equality	
	White	Non-white	White	Non-white	Delta[b]	Gini[b]	White	Non-white	White	Non-white	Delta[b]	Gini[b]
MALES												
20–24	65	39	12.4	10.9	25	32	83	62	12.8	12.3	22	30
25–29	63	36	12.4	10.5	26	33	79	54	12.7	12.1	25	34
30–34	56	30	12.2	9.7	25	35	74	43	12.6	11.4	33	38
35–44	53	24	12.1	8.6	29	41	66	39	12.5	10.7	27	34
45–54	38	14	10.3	7.1	38	47	60	29	12.3	9.1	31	40
55–64	26	9	8.7	5.8	39	47	44	18	10.9	7.6	36	42
65+	17	7	8.2	4.4	37	43	27	8	8.5	4.0	45	52
Total[a]	41	20	10.6	7.9	30	36	57	32	12.2	9.8	28	33
FEMALES												
20–24	68	45	12.7	11.5	24	26	83	67	12.7	12.3	15	21
25–29	65	41	12.3	11.1	24	27	76	58	12.5	12.2	19	20
30–34	61	35	12.3	10.5	26	30	74	56	12.5	12.1	18	22
35–44	56	27	12.2	9.2	30	37	67	44	12.4	11.4	24	26
45–54	53	16	10.8	8.0	34	43	63	29	12.3	9.4	34	39
55–64	31	11	9.0	6.7	37	43	48	16	11.6	8.1	35	46
65+	22	7	8.5	5.1	39	45	32	10	8.8	6.0	40	44
Total[a]	44	23	11.0	8.5	26	32	58	34	12.2	10.3	22	27

[a] Total refers to population age 25 and over.
[b] Delta and Gini indices calculated from distributions showing seven educational attainment categories.
SOURCE: U.S. Bureau of the Census, Census of Population: 1960, PC(1)–1D, Table 173; Current Population Reports, Series P-20, No. 207 (November 30, 1970), Table 1.

difference in education has been much smaller. Some changes appear to be occurring and the median education of black males and females has become approximately equal. However, the proportion who are high school or college graduates remains higher among young black women than among men.

Even though racial differences in attainment are smaller now than they used to be, it is not obvious that they will disappear in the near future. On the one hand, if racial differences in attainment among young people continue to be small, the overall racial difference will diminish, because young people will be replacing older cohorts in which the racial differences were much greater. On the other hand, there are still substantial racial differences in enrollment rates and, hence, in the attainment of young persons. Table 8 shows that among people 20 to 24 in 1970, the proportion who graduated from high school was 15 or 20 percentage points greater for whites than for Negroes.

When enrollment rates are scrutinized more carefully, we observe sharp increases, from 1960 to 1970, in the proportion of blacks 18 to 21 attending school. By 1970 about one-quarter of the blacks of college age were enrolled in colleges or universities (U.S. Bureau of the Census, 1970c, Table 1; 1963a, Table 169). This is approximately the proportion of the same age range of whites who were enrolled in colleges in 1960.

Among whites, increases in enrollment at ages 18 to 21 were as great as among blacks, while at ages 22 and over, the increases were sharper among whites. These changes in enrollment suggest that racial differences through the completion of high school are being reduced but are not yet eliminated. However, at college ages racial differences in enrollment seem to be growing because of the recent jump in the enrollment rate of whites. There will continue to be racial differences in attainment and the proportion having a college education is likely to be much greater among whites than blacks.

V. CONCLUSION

. . . We structure this summary and conclusion in terms of a number of questions and answers, starting with those which can be answered quite directly and proceeding to others which, we feel, can be discussed only speculatively and generally.

1. *Have blacks made social and economic progress during the 1960s?*

The answer here, on the basis of our data, is unambiguously yes. Poverty was substantially reduced among blacks between 1959 and 1969, and on a number of key socioeconomic characteristics, such as income, occupation, and education there was a significant upward shift of blacks (U.S. Bureau of the Census, 1970d). In each case, differentials between whites and blacks narrowed. A diminution of racial differences was evident in most demographic groups, but . . . gains for black females appeared more substantial than for black males; young blacks gained more rapidly than the old.

2. *Has progress during the 1960s been more rapid than previously?*

With some qualification, the answer would seem to be yes. In a number of instances we have noted that gains from 1960 to 1970 far exceeded those of the previous decade. Information over longer time periods is not readily available so we cannot determine whether the 1960s represent a significant shift to a level of more rapid progress. Also, rates of progress will depend on the precise time periods chosen; it is likely that in certain past time periods, probably during World War II, progress among blacks was as rapid as that we have noted for the 1960s (Miller, 1964, pp. 40–43, 84–104; Price, 1969, pp. 130–131). With these reservations in mind, however, it does appear that certain important racial differences narrowed notably during the past decade.

3. *Does the progress of the 1960s signify an end to racial socioeconomic differentiation in the near future?*

Though the progress of the '60s appears rapid in a number

of respects, it does not, in our opinion, presage a short-run end to racial differences in income, occupation, or education. Overall differences between blacks and whites, particularly among males, in 1970 were still substantial, and, on a number of measures, blacks in 1970 were still behind the status that whites reached ten years earlier.

The progress among the young is noteworthy in a number of respects: progress here appeared rapid in comparison to previous decades, and differentials between races were relatively small for this age group. As this cohort ages, one may expect differentials at the older ages to diminish from those we now observe; furthermore, the children of these younger blacks can be expected to increasingly show higher status distributions on income, education, and occupation, on the basis of what we know about the influence of parental education and occupation (Blau and Duncan, 1967). But it must be noted that these developments, however encouraging they may be, are implicitly rather long range—of a generation or two in length. Furthermore, the differentials in higher education enrollment and attainment among the young further lengthen the time horizon for achieving racial equality.

4. *Do the trends of the 1960s imply that our society is becoming racially integrated?*

Improvements in the social and economic status of Negroes do not necessarily mean that racial integration is occurring. It is possible for black incomes to rise, occupations to be upgraded, and educational attainment to advance without there being any racial integration of workshops or offices, in the neighborhood or in schools. In brief, economic improvements and racial integration are different dimensions of race relations . . .

Several investigations of racial integration in neighborhoods indicate that there was no decline in segregation during the early 1960s (U.S. Bureau of the Census, 1967, p. 12; Clemence, 1967; Farley and Taeuber, 1968). Another study discovered that the public schools of this nation's largest cities in 1967 were highly segregated, the segregation level being similar to that of residential areas (Farley and Taeuber,

1971). Preliminary results from the census of 1970 indicate a continued outmigration of whites from numerous central cities while their suburban rings contain relatively few blacks (U.S. Bureau of the Census, 1971b, Table 1).

Our tables indicating racial differences in income and occupation suggest that blacks made particularly great advances after 1966. For this reason, it is possible that a detailed study of residential segregation carried out at present would show some increase in integration as compared to the early 1960s. On the other hand, it may be that the conditions for such a change are only now taking place, as growing numbers of whites are coming into contact with fellow employees who are black . . .

5. *What implications do these trends have for governmental policy?*

To answer this question there must be an accurate measurement of exactly what role governmental policies played in the changes we have described. Unfortunately, we cannot provide this analysis. We can identify three different views of the impact of federal policies during the 1960s.

One can point to a cluster of governmental actions that may have contributed to black socioeconomic gains in the 1960s, among them civil rights legislation; governmental prodding of employers, especially those under contract for goods and services; and federal, state, and local employment of blacks. With regard to the latter factor, Price (1969, p. 183) reports that increasing governmental employment was one of the major reasons why the occupational distribution of blacks was upgraded prior to 1960, and this trend may have continued in the past decade. Insofar as one gives salience to such factors, governmental policy would be viewed as a direct contributor to black socioeconomic advance.

An opposing view would contend that federal activities, including the civil rights legislation, merely reflect changing attitudes . . . Myrdal detected a growing awareness, on the part of whites, that blacks were not treated in consistency with our fundamental principles. Such an awareness may have increased in the 1960s and may explain some of the progress which we have described.

A third view would be that federal economic policies rather than civil rights actions are the key variable. We have alluded to several investigations which demonstrate that blacks began to "catch up" with whites during World War II. Studies of labor force trends indicate that during the Korean War, black workers were employed at rates approaching those of whites; but during the recession of the late 1950s and early 1960s, the racial difference grew wider (U.S. Bureau of Labor Statistics, 1970, Table 71). The late 1960s were a booming period with rapid expansion of employment, sharp increases in the revenues received by local governments, and a high rate of new constructions of both homes and buildings. During this period, young people—both black and white—found growing educational and social service facilities and a very favorable job market. In brief, the government's decision to simultaneously maintain a burgeoning domestic economy and dramatically expand military activities in Southeast Asia may account for the progress made by Negroes.

A further assessment of federal policies is needed to establish their role in effecting the changes of the 1960s and for developing future programs. With regard to future policy, it is our opinion that such programs should reflect recent progress as well as existing needs; mere continuation of older programs may not be in order. For example, the socioeconomic gains described suggest that many blacks are able to afford housing in middle class suburbs. Recent presidential statements on suburban and school integration seem to overlook these developments and may hinder integration at levels commensurate with socioeconomic gains. Though specification of governmental actions must be carefully worked out, we do feel that current opportunities and needs require more than a policy of "benign neglect."

6. *What is the consequence of this progress for the attitudes of blacks and whites?*

Our answer to this must also be speculative. Turning to blacks, we do not know what attitudes will become popular but we can isolate three possible outcomes. First, Franklin Frazier argued that Negroes were rapidly accepting the norms and values of white society (Frazier, 1939, Chapters 20 and

21; 1968, Chapter 16). He, along with DuBois and numerous other commentators, described the large size of the middle class black population and foresaw growth of this group (DuBois, 1970, Sections 23 and 28; Drake and Cayton, 1945, Vol. 2, Part 3). If there is a continuation of economic gains by blacks, this may lead to a fairly conservative black population, one which accepts the traditional ideals of American society. Racial accommodation may be the end result.

Second, a very different trend may emerge. We have noted that while blacks made gains they are still far behind whites. The racial gap in the purchasing power of families was as great in 1969 as a score of years earlier. Racial differences with regard to income are greatest among those at the higher educational levels. It may be that as blacks make progress, they will become increasingly aware of the gaps which separate them from whites. Blacks may become more insistent in demanding equality, and if it is not forthcoming, they may increasingly favor militancy or turn to violence (Pettigrew, 1971, Chapter 7).

Third, it may be that Negroes will pursue a separatist course. Apparently, we still have many ethnic residential enclaves and numerous churches, schools, and social organizations which cater to an exclusive ethnic group. We can imagine the development of similar institutions for the black population, and economic gains will place blacks in a stronger position to establish and maintain these organizations.

The black population of the United States is large. Its twenty-five million make it as numerous as some of the major nations of the world. Blacks are heterogeneous with regard to social background, region, religion, and political affiliation. There is no reason to expect that one set of attitudes will become predominant among Negroes. Surveys indicate a wide differentiation in the attitudes of blacks; and it appears to us that each of these three positions will be espoused by large numbers of blacks.

Finally, we turn to possible changes in the attitudes of whites. Two trends may produce more accommodating attitudes on the part of whites. First, educational attainment continues to increase, and since attainment is generally associated with more egalitarian views of racial issues, this argues for a diminution of prejudice. Second, we have speculated that there is a growing frequency of interracial contacts on the job and perhaps in schools. This also may reduce prejudicial attitudes held by either whites or blacks.

On the other hand, we do not know the extent to which the attitudes of whites depend upon general economic conditions. A fairly large proportion of whites, in the late 1960s, favored equal treatment for blacks on the job and supported better schools and welfare services for Negroes. In a time of affluence, it may cost whites very little to aver these views. At a different time, when jobs are scarce, tax revenues in short supply, and better homes unavailable, whites may be distinctly less amenable to the advances of Negroes.

BIBLIOGRAPHY

Gertrude Bancroft, *The American Labor Force*. New York: Wiley, 1958.

Peter M. Blau and Otis Dudley Duncan, *The American Occupational Structure*. New York: Wiley, 1967.

William G. Bowen and T. Aldrich Finegan, *The Economics of Labor Force Participation*. Princeton, N.J.: Princeton University Press, 1969.

Angus Campbell and Howard Schuman, *Racial Attitudes in Fifteen American Cities*. Ann Arbor: Survey Research Center, University of Michigan, 1968.

Theodore G. Clemence, "Residential segregation in the mid-sixties," *Demography*, 1967, 4, 562–568.

St. Clair Drake and Horace R. Cayton, *Black Metropolis*. New York: Harper & Row, 1945.

W. E. B. DuBois, *The Negro American Family*. Cambridge, Mass.: MIT Press, 1970 (Reprint ed.; original ed., 1909).

Otis Dudley Duncan, "Inheritance of poverty or inheritance of race?" In Daniel P. Moynihan (ed.), *On Understanding Poverty: Perspectives from the Social Sciences*. New York: Basic Books, 1969.

Otis Dudley Duncan and Beverly Duncan, "A methodological analysis of segregation indexes," *American Sociological Review*, 1955, *20*, 210–217.

Reynolds Farley and Alma F. Taeuber, "Racial segregation in the public schools." Unpublished manuscript, 1971.

Reynolds Farley and Karl E. Taeuber, "Population trends and residential segregation since 1960," *Science*, 1968, *159*, 953–956.

E. Franklin Frazier, *The Negro Family in the United States*. Chicago: University of Chicago Press, 1939.

E. Franklin Frazier, *On Race Relations* (ed. by S. Franklin Edwards). Chicago: University of Chicago Press, 1968.

Andrew M. Greeley and Paul B. Sheatsley, "Attitudes toward racial integration," *Scientific American*, 1971, *225*, 13–19.

Herman P. Miller, *Rich Man, Poor Man*. New York: Crowell, 1964.

Herman P. Miller, *Income Distribution in the United States*. Washington, D.C.: GPO, 1966.

Gunnar Myrdal, *An American Dilemma*. New York: Harper & Row, 1944.

Thomas F. Pettigrew, *Racially Separate or Together?* New York: McGraw-Hill, 1971.

Daniel O. Price, *Changing Characteristics of the Negro Population*. Washington, D.C.: GPO, 1969.

U.S. Bureau of the Census, *U.S. Census of Population: 1960*. PC (1)-1B, 1961.

U.S. Bureau of the Census, *U.S. Census of Population: 1960*. PC (1)-ID, 1963a.

U.S. Bureau of the Census, *U.S. Census of Population: 1960*. PC (2)-6A, 1963b.

U.S. Bureau of the Census, *Social and Economic Conditions of Negroes in the United States*. Current Population Reports, Series P-23, No. 24, 1967.

U.S. Bureau of the Census, *Income in 1969 of Families and Persons in the United States*. Current Population Reports, Series P-60, No. 75, December 14, 1970a.

U.S. Bureau of the Census, *Household and Family Characteristics: March, 1969*. Current Population Reports, Series P-20, No. 200, May 8, 1970b.

U.S. Bureau of the Census, *School Enrollment: October, 1969*. Current Population Reports, Series P-20, No. 206, October 5, 1970c.

U.S. Bureau of the Census, *Twenty-four Million Americans, Poverty in the United States: 1969*. Current Population Reports, Series P-60, No. 76, December 16, 1970d.

U.S. Bureau of the Census, *Marital Status and Family Status: March 1970.* Current Population Reports, Series P-20, No. 212, February 1, 1971a.

U.S. Bureau of the Census, *U.S. Census of Population: 1970.* PHC(2), 1971b.

U.S. Bureau of Labor Statistics. *Handbook of Labor Statistics: 1970.*, 1970.

U.S. Bureau of Labor Statistics, *Work Experience of the Population: 1969.* Special Labor Force Report 127, 1971.

PART IV

DISCRIMINATION IN CRIME, POLITICS, AND OTHER AREAS

THERE *are many realms in which racial discrimination operates in addition to housing, employment, education, and income. Indeed, there are too many such realms to be covered in a volume of this size and scope. Part IV, then, looks at two areas of special interest—the justice and political systems—and briefly notes data from a number of others.*

Table 1 provides some comparative data over time on a variety of indicators. Note for the first three health variables the familiar pattern: Both nonwhite and white rates consistently improve over the past generation, but the relationship between the racial rates changes only slightly.

TABLE 1. *Time Series of Social Data for Whites (W) and Non-Whites (N-W)**

VARIABLE		TIME PERIOD										
		1948–1950	1950	1951–1953	1954–1956	1957–1959	1960	1960–1962	1963–1965	1966–1968	1969	1971
1. Infant deaths per 1,000 live births	N-W	46.1	44.5	45.5	42.6	44.4	43.2	41.8	41.3[a]	—	31.6	30.2
	W	28.5	26.8	25.4	23.6	23.4	22.9	22.5	21.9[a]	—	18.4	16.8
2. Maternal deaths per 1,000 live births	N-W	—	2.2	—	—	—	1.0	—	.8[b]	.7	—	—
	W	—	.6	—	—	—	0.3	—	.2[b]	.2	—	—
3. Deaths from tuberculosis per 1,000 population	N-W	71.5	—	42.2	21.9	16.2	—	12.3	10.4[a]	—	8.0	—
	W	21.0	—	13.0	7.7	6.0	—	4.6	3.8[a]	—	1.7	—
4. Age-adjusted deaths from homicide per 100,000 population	N-W	29.1	—	26.1	23.6	22.0	—	21.5	22.4	—	41.3	—
	W	2.8	—	2.5	2.3	2.4	—	2.6	2.7	—	4.3	—
5. Age-adjusted deaths	N-W	4.2	—	3.9	3.9	4.3	—	4.6	4.8	—	6.5	—

		12.2	—	10.9	10.9	11.1	—	11.4	11.8	—	11.9	—
from suicide per 100,000 population	W											
6. Prisoners executed under civil authority, annual number	N-W	65	—	42	40	31	—	25	5	—	—	—
	W	42	—	41	34	23	—	23	9	—	—	—
7. Percent of families with female heads	N-W	—	17.6	—	20.7[b]	—	22.4	—	23.7[b]	23.2	27.3	28.9
	W	—	8.5	—	9.0[b]	—	8.7	—	9.0[b]	9.0	8.9	9.4
8. Percent of children living with both parents	N-W	—	—	—	—	—	75	75	71	71	69	64
	N-W	—	—	—	—	—	92	92	92	92	92	90

[a] Based on data for two years only.
[b] Based on data for one year only.

* SOURCES: Otis Dudley Duncan, "Discrimination against Negroes," *The Annals of the American Academy of Political and Social Science*, May 1967, 371, 91; and the U.S. Bureau of the Census, *Current Population Reports*, Series P-23, Nos. 42 and 46 (*The Social and Economic Status of Negroes in the United States*, 1971, 1972). Washington, D.C.: U.S. Government Printing Office, 1972 and 1973.

Thus nonwhite infant mortality was almost twice that of whites in the late 1940s, and despite reductions remained almost twice that of whites in 1971. Similarly maternal mortality declined by two-thirds between 1950 and 1969, yet the rate remained about three and a half times greater for nonwhites. And even more dramatic advances in preventing death from tuberculosis over these years also failed to end the fact that nonwhite rates stay between three and four times those of whites. The editor and his physician wife provide elsewhere a full discussion of health differentials by race and their relationships to discrimination.[1]

Variables 4 and 5 indicate substantial racial differences in death rates by homicide and suicide. Since over 90 percent of homicides involve the same race as murderer and victim, these victim data also shed light on crime as well as death. Both racial rates have gone up over this last turbulent generation. The much higher nonwhite rate relates at least in part to the far greater likelihood of blacks being Southern, young, and poor—all nonracial correlates of high homicide.[2] By contrast, suicide—more often found among higher-income persons—has higher rates among whites. Observe, however, that the white rates have remained relatively stable while the black rates rose during the 1960s. This increase may well relate to the growth of the black middle class documented in Part III.

Racial discrimination is more directly indicated in variable 6. Although only an eighth of the nation and considerably less than half of all convicted felons, black Americans have typically been the majority of those prisoners executed.[3] Thus the Supreme Court ruling against many forms of criminal executions is of particular importance to blacks.

The final two variables of Table 1 relate to family life. Though there has been considerable debate as to its meaning and causes, there is no argument that since 1950 a substantial increase in female-headed households has occurred in the black community. Similarly there has been a decline in the percentage of black children living with both parents. White rates have remained relatively stable. Much of this racial difference is a social class effect, yet these shifts have occurred at a time of rising black prosperity and the development of a large middle class. Thus the phenomenon's causes are poorly understood, though the form and failure of the nation's welfare programs are undoubtedly involved.

One less conspicuous type of racial discrimination is the degree of black invisibility in the nation's mass media. While some improvement—especially in television—has been made in recent years, a study by Johnson, Sears, and McConahay indicates that the problem remains.[4] *These investigators measured the amount and kind of attention paid to black people since 1892 by the two leading newspapers of Los Angeles. Both the* Los Angeles Times *and the* Herald Examiner *virtually ignored blacks throughout the twentieth century until just before the city's major riot in 1965. Indeed, coverage relative to the black proportion of the population actually diminished over the years. The riot occasioned a great increase in press coverage, but preriot levels soon returned. This type of coverage did shift, however, over this three-quarters of a century from largely stereotyped content to an emphasis upon interracial conflict—neither hardly a contribution to better race relations.*

Selections 18, 19, and 20 consider further examples of discrimination. First, Marvin Wolfgang and Bernard Cohen present a lucid discussion of racial factors in the country's administration of justice. They show how black people are more likely to be the victims of crime, with lower-income blacks more apt to be victims of crimes against persons and higher-income blacks of crimes against property. Next, they demonstrate how racial discrimination mars the American administration of justice. From abrasive contacts with the police to arrests and sentencing, blacks often receive discriminatory treatment. Sociological research has uncovered the not-so-subtle

structural ways discrimination operates in this realm. For
example, George Lowe and Eugene Hodges explored why
black alcoholics were so underrepresented in Georgia's
rehabilitation facility despite black rates of deaths related
to alcohol twice that of whites.[5] They found their answer
in the differential manner local communities deal with
deviant drinkers: Whites are disproportionately chan-
neled toward treatment, blacks to prison.

The power of local communities in Georgia to discriminate so blatantly raises the vital issue of power. A
convincing case can be made that virtually all of the racial
discriminatory patterns described in this volume can be
traced to the relative powerlessness of black people in the
American political system. Whole volumes can be usefully
devoted to this thesis, but we have space here only to
sketch out the depth of the problem. Out of 520,000
elected positions in the United States, black Americans
occupied in April 1973 only 2,621.[6] This figure means
only 0.5 percent, instead of the black population percentage of about 12 percent. Yet even this one-in-twenty-
four underrepresentation marks a major increase in black
elected officials in recent years. In 1969 there were only
1,185; thus, the 1973 figure of 2,621 constituted a
121 percent increase in four years. The most conspicuous
black gains have been in the U.S. House of Representatives and as mayors of such major cities as Gary, Indiana,
Newark, New Jersey, Los Angeles, California, Raleigh,
North Carolina, Atlanta, Georgia, and Detroit, Michigan.

But the exclusion of blacks from political decision
making involves both informal as well as formal positions.
And the enormity of this exclusion even in Northern cities
is difficult to grasp without a review of the relevant data.
Selection 19 provides this information for Milwaukee,
Wisconsin.

Selection 20 presents another summary of general
trends toward racial equality. The authors, Erdman Palmore and Frank Whittington, employ an "equality index"
that the careful reader will recognize is simply the op-

posite of the "index of dissimilarity" used by Lieberson and Fuguitt in Selection 13 and in other selections in this volume. The equality index is most easily thought of as the similarity between the two races; or, more precisely, the proportion of the white and "nonwhite" percentage distributions that overlap each other.

When this index is utilized for changes since 1940 in the income, education, and occupation distributions, we find what we noted earlier—significant relative black advances with substantial racial differentials remaining. Housing gains since 1950 are also apparent when quality and not racial desegregation is the focus. Similar to our conclusions based on the time series data of Table 1, the equality index reflects little or no improvement of blacks relative to whites in both mortality and marital status. The equality index, then, serves as a useful summary indicator of much of the material discussed in this volume.

⟦ 18 ⟧

Crime and Race*

*MARVIN E. WOLFGANG AND
BERNARD COHEN.*

THE VICTIMS OF CRIME

[T]here are several questions on which research casts some light: (1) Who are the victims of crime or who suffer most from criminality? (2) Is the oft-expressed fear among whites of being victimized by non-white criminals justifiable?

Until recently, there was virtually no information on the victims of crime in the United States, except for some useful and consistent local data on homicide and forcible rape. For the past few years, however, the UCR has been publishing data on homicides for the entire nation. The President's Crime Commission also presented the results of several studies based upon national samples of victims of property and violent crimes.

The UCR reveals that throughout the nation during 1967 Negroes were the most likely victims of homicide. Even in absolute numbers more blacks than whites were slain—5,990 blacks compared with 5,011 whites. Thus, while blacks comprise approximately 10 percent of the population, they constituted 54 per cent of the homicide victims. Most of these victims were males between 15 and 44; few were women, children or elderly people.[1]

Information about the victims of a wider range of offenses

---

* Abridged from M. E. Wolfgang and B. Cohen, *Crime and Race.* New York: The American Jewish Committee, 1970; pp. 40–43, 66–74, 77–86. Reprinted with permission of the publisher and authors.

was obtained through the special survey conducted by the National Opinion Research Center (NORC) for the President's Crime Commission,[2] covering a probability sample of 10,000 households and providing intensive interviews with each victim of a crime. The information sought included the type of crime, its location, the extent of injury, theft or damage, whether police were notified, and if not, the reasons for failing to report the incident.

The NORC data provide a great deal of new information on a national scale for index crimes other than homicide. A major finding is that non-whites are victimized more often than whites, not only by homicide, but also by robbery, rape, aggravated assault, burglary and auto theft. Only in crimes involving larceny $50 and over are whites more often the victims, most likely because fewer blacks possess large sums of money and expensive items. Black victim rates also are relatively low for such minor crimes as simple assault, malicious mischief and fraud.

Although blacks are consistently more often victimized than whites, the NORC findings show, there are differences according to economic levels (Table 1). In serious crimes against persons, blacks with incomes below $6,000 are almost twice as likely to be victims as whites in the same income

TABLE 1. *Victims of Serious Personal and Property Crimes per 100,000 Population, by Race and Income Level (1966)*

TYPE OF CRIME	INCOMES UNDER $6,000		INCOMES $6,000 OR MORE	
	Whites	*Negroes*	*Whites*	*Negroes*
Against person	402	748	244	262
Against property	1,829	1,927	1,765	3,024
(Number of interviews)	(10,008)	(3,462)	(15,452)	(1,827)

SOURCE: *Field Surveys II, Criminal Victimization in the United States: A Report of a National Survey,* by P. H. Ennis. The President's Commission on Law Enforcement and Administration of Justice, 1967, p. 32.

group; in the income category above $6,000 the discrepancy is much smaller. With respect to property crimes the opposite pattern prevails.

Blacks with incomes below $6,000 are only slightly more likely to be victims than are their white counterparts, but more affluent blacks are a great deal more likely to be victimized than are more affluent whites. Presumably, residential segregation increases the more affluent Negro's risk of being burglarized, because he lacks the protection provided in sheltered middle-class neighborhoods.

Another special field survey conducted for the President's Crime Commission examined victim data secured from the Chicago Police Department for the period September 1965 to March 1966.[3] When the race and sex of offenders and their victims in cases of rape, robbery and assault were analyzed, the patterns that emerged were similar to those of the NORC study. For all major offenses against the person, black males were most often the victims. As many as four out of 100 Negro men are victims of a robbery or assault and battery each year, and black women run the second highest risk of suffering such offenses. Thus, three out of every 100 Negro women are the victims of rape, robbery or assault and battery in Chicago each year.

White men and women have much less reason to fear attack than blacks. Fewer than one out of 100 white men is likely to be attacked in any given year; the probability rate for white women is much lower (35 out of 100,000).

The fear of being raped or assaulted is most real for Negro women. According to available statistics, Negro women are 18 times more likely to be victims of rape than are white women; and black women, like black men, stand a much greater chance of suffering armed or strong-armed robbery.

The data on assault with a dangerous weapon revealed that black males run the greatest risk of being shot, cut or stabbed (20 times greater than for white males), and black females run the next highest risk. The risks are lowest for white men and white women in that order. A Negro woman is four times more likely to be shot than a white man, and eight times more likely to be stabbed.

In summary, the Chicago study showed that the danger of being a victim of rape, robbery or assault and battery is six times greater for Negro men than for white men. The likelihood of a Negro woman being victimized is about eight times greater than that of a white woman and even four times higher than that of a white man. Regardless of sex, blacks are much more likely than whites to be victims of serious crimes against the person. These statistics suggest that blacks have an equal if not greater stake in reducing crime than do whites . . .

CRIMINAL JUSTICE AND THE POLICE

In the annals of the administration of justice are many cases of improper treatment of Negroes, Puerto Ricans, Spanish-Americans and other minority groups. There is widespread belief that blacks, particularly, are frequently subjected to illegal arrest, arrest on weak suspicion, illegal detention and corporal handling by the police. Compared to whites, they are jailed more than bailed. It is commonly believed that, beyond white proportions, they are convicted with little evidence and sentenced to more severe punishments of long duration. Instances of violence by police and the arrest of Negroes with less evidence than is required to arrest whites have been sufficiently numerous to cause alarm among private agencies and government bodies whose functions are to keep watch over the rights of our citizens.

That brutality and illegal arrests are not the pattern but only the exception; that some whites have grievances similar to those of Negroes; that the poor of any ethnic group suffer disadvantage and are less able to engage counsel, provide bail or pay fines, do not mitigate the situation. On the contrary; for the percentage of poor and uneducated within the white majority is tripled within the black minority. Thus, even if there were no race bias in the administration of justice, the social and economic class system would itself carry a burden of blame for the lack of equal protection and uniformity of treatment. Fortunately the U.S. Supreme Court in the *Gideon* case recognized one kind of disparity and initiated corrective measures by requiring that defendants who cannot afford lawyers must nonetheless be represented by counsel.

The police and the judiciary, keenly sensitive to criticism, have rarely been methodically examined by social scientists armed with hypotheses of discrimination. Moreover, there are presently no national judicial statistics available as basic documents for research on regional and other variations in conviction and sentencing practices. The data at hand come mostly from the President's Crime Commission, and from selective experience and local studies, some of which are especially useful for specific details or statistical analyses.[4-16]

The references cited here are only by way of illustration. Some are old, some new; but the story has remained essentially unchanged since Gunnar Myrdal, in his classic study in 1944, reported that, for the period 1920–1932, out of 479 Negroes killed by white persons in the South, 54 per cent were slain by white police officers.[17] The figures reached proportions that justify suspicion of unnecessary and unwarranted use of violence.

The President's Crime Commission has stated that permissive law enforcement and police brutality are the two basic reasons for minority-group resentment of the police.[18] Police are charged with failure to promote adequate protection and services in black neighborhoods, and with abuse of authority and physical or verbal misconduct in relation to blacks, Mexican-Americans, Puerto Ricans, and other minority groups. When Commission investigators asked blacks representing New York City's Bedford-Stuyvesant community to list areas of conflict and antagonism between local residents and the police, eight factors were mentioned: the abrasive relationship between the police and black juveniles; police toleration of narcotics traffic in the ghetto; the small number of black patrolmen stationed in the black neighborhoods; inefficient handling of emergencies by local precincts; lack of respect towards black citizens; low police morale; not enough foot patrolmen; inadequate patrol of black neighborhoods.[19]

Recent attitude surveys reveal that Negroes are significantly more dissatisfied than whites with the effectiveness of police law enforcement. Asked to rate police protection of citizens, blacks said it was "very good" only half as often as whites, while a rating of "not so good" was given twice as often.[20-21]

In Washington, D.C., 40 per cent of all black men queried, compared to 18 per cent of the white men, agreed with the statement that, "You would have to replace at least half of the police force to get a really good police force."[22] Polls in other cities show similar results. In Detroit, in 1965, two years before the riots, 58 per cent of the Negroes queried did not believe that law enforcement was fair.[23]

Other surveys probing the attitudes of people with regard to police discourtesy and misconduct report even greater differences between the races. A NORC national survey in 1966 found that more Negroes than whites feel police are disrespectful.[24] Among black males with incomes of less than $3,000, 22 per cent felt police did not show them respect compared to only 4 per cent for whites in the same income category. A 1965 Gallup poll indicated that 35 per cent of the black males interviewed, compared to only 7 per cent of the white males, believed there was police brutality in their areas.[25]

Findings of other surveys[26] show that more blacks than whites think police enjoy giving people a hard time, have seen unjustified police use of violence, believe the police treat Negroes worse than they do whites, and feel police are dishonest and corrupt. An intensive interview with 50 youths from the slums of Washington disclosed that the police were viewed as "the enemy" because of real or perceived abuse of authority, humiliation, and other police practices.[27] One resident of Watts said to an interviewer: "Two white policemen were beating a pregnant colored lady like a damn dog. They need their heads knocked off. I agree 100 per cent with the Negroes going crazy. They should have killed those freaks."[28]

Although the national surveys do not differentiate between attitudes towards white and black police officers, an intensive survey of blacks in Philadelphia revealed that the black officer does not fare any better. In fact, Negro policemen are often the object of greater criticism.[29] "Negro officers are not accepted by their own people primarily because the policeman's role is that of one who has a reputation for maintaining society's *status quo.*"

What do we know about the way policemen feel about blacks? One of the few studies in this area is a President's Crime Commission Survey conducted by Albert J. Reiss.[30] The data were obtained through direct observation of police-citizen encounters in Boston, Chicago and Washington during a seven-week period in the summer of 1966. Officer attitudes were classified in four broad categories ranging from "highly prejudiced or extremely anti-Negro" to "pro-Negro."

The survey revealed that the majority of white officers hold anti-Negro attitudes. "In the predominantly Negro precincts, over three-fourths of the white policemen expressed prejudiced or highly prejudiced sentiments toward members of the Negro race," Reiss reported. "Only 1 per cent expressed attitudes sympathetic toward Negroes. A larger proportion of officers verbalized 'highly prejudiced' attitudes in the heavily Negro precincts than did officers in either of the other two kinds of racially populated areas."[31] It is interesting to note that one out of 10 Negro officers in predominantly Negro precincts was also extremely anti-Negro in attitude.

The fact that many policemen are anti-Negro in *attitude* does not necessarily mean that they *behave* in a discriminatory way in encounters with Negroes. Verbally expressed attitudes may or may not reflect actual conduct. Indeed, Crime Commission studies indicate that in the vast majority of encounters officers handle themselves with courage and restraint.[32] Another study, conducted in a midwestern city in 1951, disclosed that police officers believed the only way to handle certain groups of people—such as Negroes and the poor—was to treat them roughly. The same study concluded, however, that brute force was not used as frequently as the officers' verbal responses would suggest.[33]

Yet, while there are no consistent data about the extent of police brutality, studies conducted by the Crime Commission leave no doubt that such brutality exists,[34] not only in the South, where blacks have long been subjected to excessive police force, but in Northern cities as well. Commission observers who systematically accompanied police on field patrol, and witnessed 5,399 police-citizen encounters during 850 eight-hour patrols, reported 20 instances in which officers used force that was clearly not required.[35]

However limited the documentation of police abuse may be, there is no doubt that most minority-group members believe it exists, particularly in the handling of black youth. "They slap you, kick you, strong-arm you, spit on you, everything,"[36] one juvenile explained. Such charges are heard repeatedly in black communities.

Field interrogation—the practice of stopping people in the street for questioning "on suspicion," without evidence that they have broken the law—has been cited as a major source of friction between police and minority groups. Data on police handling of "suspects" and offenders from initial contact to the time they are charged with a specific offense reveal that blacks are subjected to more field interrogation and searches than whites, and more frequently picked up on suspicion, arrested, booked and charged.

Negro leaders charge "that field interrogations are predominantly conducted in slum communities, that they are used indiscriminately and that they are conducted in an abusive and unfriendly manner."[37] They believe field interrogations are applied selectively and serve to degrade and deprecate the citizen. "Race has an undue influence on who is stopped," one black spokesman told a Crime Commission interviewer.[38] A study of juvenile offenses in a western city bears out these charges. Negro youngsters were stopped more often than whites, in many cases without any evidence that an offense had been committed.[39]

Police argue that field interrogations and "aggressive patrol" are necessary to deter and prevent crime. Stopping people who are behaving in a suspicious or unusual manner, they maintain, leads to many arrests.[40] But blacks insist that the police encounter very few crimes actually in progress and that usually, by the time the officers arrive at the scene, the perpetrator is no longer in sight. Thus, they tend to view field interrogation and similar tactics as deliberate harassment. "The police do not respect Negro juveniles as human beings; he is picked up if he has a beard, picked up if he has the wrong clothing on, picked up if he's a 'beatnick' and picked up if he's out after curfew hours without a chance to explain or give a reason; if he has a motorcycle, he is likely to be stopped. . . . they are not treated as human beings."[41]

After being stopped, many more Negroes than whites are searched by the police. A University of Michigan study found this to be true whether police are dispatched to the scene by radio, or they personally observe and respond to an incident.[42] Negroes object to the search less often than whites, the study reported, and they are more likely to carry dangerous weapons.[43]

In comparing arrest statistics for blacks and whites, it is important to remember, then, that one reason for the high arrest rates among blacks is that they are more likely to be stopped, picked up on suspicion and subsequently arrested. A recent study of police interaction with gang members disclosed that a major reason the criminal records of gang members have so many charges of "suspicion of robbery" and "suspicion of rape" is that the police officer, after detaining the youth, often will arrest and charge him, with little or no evidence, to avoid loss of face.[44]

Some comment should be made about police discretion in the handling of juvenile cases that may partly explain what at first appears to be discriminatory treatment. In most large cities, juvenile-aid division officers are empowered to decide, upon taking a juvenile into custody, whether to release him to his own parents as an "unofficial," "remedial" disposition of the case, or to turn him over to the juvenile court under an "official" or "arrest" disposition. We have already pointed out that some studies have shown that juveniles from minority groups are more often arrested than given remedial action.[45]

The contention by police and some social agencies is that the home of the juvenile is often an undesirable environment; by means of an official arrest, they can put him in the hands of persons who will interview, diagnose and help treat his problems. This rationale may be logical within a limited setting and policy of social action. But we cannot overlook what the official label of delinquency may do to a boy's image of himself and to his image in the eyes of the community. Nor can we overlook the underlying fact of the minority boy's less desirable home and neighborhood environment, and the social and cultural deprivations that caused them to be so.

In several cities, civilian complaint review boards have been created in response to allegations of police misconduct and brutality. Two striking facts emerge from the few studies and reports of civilian review boards: (1) many more blacks than whites report instances of police misconduct to the boards; (2) few of the cases reported result in sanctions against the police.

In a survey of complainants to the Philadelphia Police Advisory Board from 1958 to 1966, the data indicated that nearly 64 per cent were non-white and less than 33 per cent white (the race of the remaining 3.7 per cent was not ascertained). Non-whites comprise a little over 25 percent of the city's total population.[46] In New York City, where approximately 20 per cent of the population is black, blacks are also overrepresented as complainants. Of the 1,281 complainants served by New York's Civilian Complaint Review Board during 1967, 36 per cent were Negroes. Citizens of Hispanic origin, who constitute 11 per cent of the city's population, accounted for 14.4 per cent of the complaints.[47] Since, as was demonstrated earlier, minority-group members are more likely than whites to be stopped, interrogated, searched, arrested and charged, it is reasonable to assume they also tend to experience excessive police force and abuse of authority.

Much criticism has been leveled against existing review boards because so many of the cases brought before them are dismissed, and because, it is charged, disciplinary action even when taken is often not meaningful. In Detroit, for instance, the Michigan Civil Rights Commission found "that disciplinary action taken by the Detroit Police Department in proven cases of brutality show a practice of differential treatment that will not deter future recurrence of such misconduct."[48] Only in two out of 32 cases of proven brutality did disciplinary action go beyond a written reprimand to the officer involved.[49]

Statistics from New York and Philadelphia tend to corroborate this pattern. Of the 1,027 cases considered by the board in New York during 1967, disciplinary action was recommended in only 39 or 4 per cent.[50] And in Philadelphia, where the Advisory Board has been entirely independent of the Police Department, only 18 out of a total of 131 non-white complaints (14 per cent) resulted in recommendations for discipline. In 12 cases the officer was suspended for periods ranging from one to 30 days; in six cases he was reprimanded. In no instance was the officer transferred, demoted, or dismissed.[51]

Police brutality, abuse of authority, ethnic slurs, or discourteous behavior, especially when they go unpunished, not only constitute a serious threat to community support of the police, but also undermine the citizens' respect for law enforcement agencies—and for the law itself. Adequate machinery for registering complaints about police treatment and stern disciplinary action in cases of proven misconduct are essential to improve police-community relations.[52]

CRIMINAL JUSTICE AND THE COURTS

Harold Garfinkel, who examined 821 homicides in 10 counties of North Carolina between 1930 and 1940, concluded that proportionately fewest indictments were made when whites killed Negroes; most were made (94 per cent) when Negroes killed whites.[53] Of those charged with first degree murder, 28 per cent of the whites who killed Negroes, but only 15 per cent of the Negroes who killed whites, were acquitted. Of those convicted, none of the whites who killed Negroes received life imprisonment, but 10 per cent of the Negroes who killed whites did; and none of the whites who killed a Negro was sentenced to death, contrasted with 37 per cent of the Negroes who killed whites. The general attitude of the courts was that the slaying of a white by a Negro was almost prima facie evidence of guilt; a white killing another white required objective administration of justice; a Negro killing another Negro was just a routine affair deserving only moderate attention; and the slaying of a Negro by a white probably involved some mitigating circumstance like provocation.

In an equally useful research, Guy B. Johnson studied 220 homicide cases in Richmond, Virginia, from 1930 to 1939, and 330 homicides in five counties of North Carolina from 1930 to 1940. There were five cases of whites killing Negroes, but not a single conviction, and 24 cases of Negroes killing whites, of which 22 resulted in conviction. Johnson also noted that of the 141 Negro-Negro homicides, not one resulted in the death penalty and only eight in life imprisonment; but of the 22 cases with Negro offenders and white victims, six concluded with a death sentence and seven with life imprisonment.[54]

The Civil Rights Act of 1875 clearly specified that no state could exclude anyone from jury service because of race, color or previous condition of servitude. Since then, there have been many court decisions affirming the illegality of anti-Negro discrimination in the makeup of grand and trial juries.

In *United States ex rel. Seals* v. *Wiman*, 304 F. 2d 53, 67 (5th Cir. 1962), a Federal Circuit Court of Appeals set aside a state conviction because evidence showed that Negroes constituted 31 per cent of those qualified for service but only 2 per cent of the jury rolls. The Court held this was a prima facie case of discrimination. Similarly in *Whitus* v. *Georgia*, 385 U.S. 545 (1967), the U.S. Supreme Court reversed a lower-court conviction because the disparity between the percentage of Negroes on the tax digest (21.1 per cent) and their percentage on the grand jury venire (9.1 per cent) and petit jury venire (7.8 per cent) "strongly points" to the conclusion that discrimination was practiced.

In *Jones* v. *Georgia*, 389 U.S. 24 (1967), the U.S. Supreme Court reversed the lower court's decision, holding that the disparity between the percentages of Negroes on the tax digest (20 per cent) and on the venires (5 per cent) constituted prima facie evidence of discrimination.[55]

The law also prescribes how to determine whether a fair

cross section of the community has been chosen. In *United States* v. *Flynn*, 216 F. 2d 354, 383 (2d Cir. 1954), the Federal Circuit Court of Appeals held that venire lists, from which juries are chosen, should be compared with lists "that would have resulted from random selection subjected to those proper methods of qualification." A few scholars have shown how statistical decision theory provides a method for making that comparison.[56]

Despite the protections stipulated in the law, however, there are many communities like Harris County, Texas, where, as W. S. Robinson pointed out, Negroes made up 20 per cent of the population and 10 per cent of those paying poll tax; yet, from 1931 to 1938, only 18 Negroes were summoned for grand jury duty, and only five Negroes were among the 384 persons who served.[57] There are places where no Negroes were ever called to jury duty. Doubtless a rare exception, even in the North, is Philadelphia, where the representation of Negroes on juries is about double their proportion of the population—a situation most likely due to their readiness, in contrast to the reluctance of whites, to accept jury service. In Los Angeles County, where many Mexicans and Mexican-Americans are processed through the courts, Edwin M. Lemert reported that, up to 1945, according to available data, there had never been a Mexican-American member of the grand jury.[58]

Current statistics for certain northern communities show that Negroes and Puerto Ricans still are generally excluded from jury duty. Michael O. Finkelstein analyzed the venire records of persons selected to the Grand Juries in Manhattan, the Bronx, and Westchester for the years 1965–1967.[59] The data revealed that Harlem districts, which are heavily populated with Negroes and Puerto Ricans, contributed less than 1 per cent of the Manhattan veniremen although they comprised 11 per cent of the voting population. If veniremen were chosen at random from the registered voters lists, disparities this large would virtually never occur. (The mathematical probability, computed for the Manhattan grand jury venires in 1967, was even smaller than the probability of being dealt

24 consecutive royal flushes in an honest game of five-card draw poker.[60])

In Westchester, the towns of Mount Vernon, New Rochelle and Yonkers—where large numbers of Negroes reside—were also grossly underrepresented on the jury rolls. For instance only five New Rochelle and Yonkers residents were on the venires from 1965 through 1967. By comparison, Scarsdale, New York, which has a very small Negro population, contributed 355 names.[61] Thus, it is evident that despite numerous court rulings and the explicit prohibition against discrimination in jury selection in the Civil Rights Act of 1957, there is a persistent pattern of discrimination in many jurisdictions.

We have seen that Negroes are less likely to serve on juries, but more likely to be convicted, especially in cases involving interracial offenses. Are they also likely to receive more severe sentences? Although not all studies agree, most research has found that Negroes and other minority-group members are treated more severely in the courts. The late Warden Lewis E. Lawes of Sing Sing Prison stated that "only the poor, the friendless and the foreign born" are sentenced to death and executed.[62] Today, blacks and other minority groups probably have replaced the foreign born in this respect. Hugo Bedau, student of capital punishment and author of *The Death Penalty in America*, declares that "racial discrimination in the United States makes the death penalty weigh more heavily, proportionately, on Negroes than on whites . . ."[63]

According to the previously cited works of Johnson and Garfinkel, blacks are more likely than whites to be sentenced to imprisonment or death in homicide cases. A more recent report, issued by the Ohio State Legislature Research Commission, found that, during 1950, blacks accounted for 37 per cent of all death sentences although they made up only 6.5 per cent of the state's population. Moreover, of those sentenced to death, whites more frequently than blacks had their sentences commuted to life imprisonment.[64]

Far more often than whites, blacks who are found guilty of rape receive death sentences and are executed. According to the Federal Bureau of Prisons, seven men convicted of rape were executed in the United States in 1958—all of them black.[65] In 1960, all eight persons executed for rape were also black.[66] Whites charged with rape generally receive more lenient treatment, detailed studies by states reveal. In Florida, sentences meted out for rape during the years 1940 to 1964 were examined by race of the offender and victim. Of the 125 white males who raped white females, six, or about 5 per cent, received death penalties (four of the latter involved attacks on children). Similarly, of the 68 black males who raped black females, three—or about 4 per cent—received death sentences (two of these involved attacks on juveniles). But of the 84 Negroes convicted of raping white women, 45, or 54 per cent, received the death penalty (only one involved an attack on a juvenile). Not one of the eight white offenders who raped a black victim was sentenced to death.[67]

The same patterns appear in the data for other Southern states where rape is a capital crime. One study, designed to determine the effect of racial factors on capital sentencing for rape in Arkansas, from January 1, 1945 through August 31, 1965, found that of 34 black defendants 29 per cent were sentenced to death; of 21 white defendants 19 per cent received the death sentence. In other words, a black defendant was one and one half times as likely to be sentenced to death for rape as a white.

When the race of the victim was taken into account in the Arkansas study, the data were even more startling. When the victim was white, the death penalty was imposed in virtually every case. Of the 14 cases resulting in death sentences, 13 involved white victims and only one a Negro victim. In nine of the 13 cases, a Negro male was the defendant; the other five death penalties were imposed in cases where offenders and victims were of the same race.[68]

Blacks convicted of raping white victims were most frequently sentenced to death. Of the 19 defendants in rape cases involving a black defendant and a white victim, nine—or 47 per cent—were sentenced to death. By contrast, of the 36 cases involving white offenders and white victims or black offenders and black victims, only five—or 14 per cent—received a death sentence.

Blacks usually receive longer prison terms than whites for most criminal offenses. In a study of persons convicted of burglary and auto theft in Los Angeles County, most of them first offenders and unskilled laborers, Edwin M. Lemert and Judy Rosberg found that more whites than Negroes were given short sentences. Forty-five per cent of the whites and 27 per cent of the Negroes were given four months' imprisonment or less, or probation; 42 per cent of the whites and 47 per cent of the Negroes received four to nine months; and 13 per cent of the whites and 27 per cent of the Negroes got 10 to 20 months.[69]

Another extensive study conducted by Henry Bullock examined the records of 3,644 black and white convicts who were serving sentences for burglary, rape and murder in the Texas State Prison in 1958. Bullock found that the relationship between race and length of sentence held firm, regardless of type of offense, type of plea, number of previous felonies, cultural region and degree of urbanization of the area where the offense was committed. The author found, however, that while blacks received longer prison terms than whites for burglary, they were given shorter sentences for murder. This seemingly contradictory pattern is most likely explained by the fact that murder is primarily an *intraracial* phenomenon, and burglary often *interracial*. Bullock speculates:

. . . these judicial responses possibly represent indulgent and non-indulgent patterns that characterize local attitudes concerning property and intraracial morals. Since the victims of most of the Negroes committed for . . . [murder] were also Negroes, local norms tolerate a less rigorous enforcement of the law; the disorder is mainly located within the Negro society. On the other hand, burglary is mainly an interracial offense. When a Negro is an offender, his attack is usually against the property of a white person. Local norms are less tolerant, for the motivation to protect white property and to protect "white" society against disorder is stronger than the motivation to protect "Negro" society.[70]

In some communities, the citizens as well as the police and judges have an attitude of "live and let live" as long as "they keep it among themselves." This attitude, when expressed by the assignment of fewer police officers to highly populated

Negro neighborhoods, may mean that considerably less crime by Negroes is being recorded by the police than actually occurs. Whether such underreporting adds up to more or less than the underreporting of white crimes is not known. Another result of this attitude is that Negro victims often are not receiving equal protection under the law, either by police surveillance or by conviction of the guilty. When white officers ignore or bypass Negro violations of sex, drinking and gambling laws, or dismiss intraracial assaults as "typically Negro," they are probably contributing much to negative attitudes toward the law, to the reluctance of many victims to make official complaints, and consequently to the crime rate of Negroes.

Sellin's review of national prisoner statistics for 1931–1932 showed that Negroes received a lower average sentence in "definite sentence" states, mostly Southern, for homicide, robbery, assault, forgery, larceny and liquor violations, but higher for rape, other sex offenses and burglary. In states with the indeterminate sentence, Negroes had longer sentences than whites for all major offenses.[71] Negroes also had more commitments to prison and served more actual time before release from state penal institutions. The average (median) number of months served before release among all states in 1951 was 25 for Negroes and 20 for whites. The disparity was greater in the Northeast (Negroes 30 months; whites 24 months) and in the West (Negroes 30; whites 19) than in the Northcentral states (Negroes 26; whites 21) or in the South (Negroes 21; whites 17).[72]

Combined with those facts is the knowledge that proportionately about 10 to 14 per cent more whites than Negroes are annually "released conditionally," that is, granted some form of parole, thus always leaving behind a greater number of Negroes among prisoners eligible for release. The increasing number of Negroes in our prisons partly stems from this differential pattern of release. Clearly we cannot use the racial composition of a prison population as an index to the amount of crime committed by different racial or ethnic groups.

An analysis of over 1,400 cases handled without jury in the Philadelphia Court of Quarter-Sessions from 1956 to 1957, involving 21 different judges, revealed no racial differences in sentencing practices. In this analysis by Edward Green, Negroes numbered 1,092 and whites 333.[73] By using the minimum period served, he noted that about one-fourth of each race was sent to prison for 12 months or more; slightly more Negroes (34 per cent) than whites (28 per cent) received sentences of three to 11½ months; and equal proportions of each race (21 per cent) were sentenced to less than three months. Slightly more whites (20 per cent) than Negroes (13 per cent) received probation, more Negroes (5 per cent) than whites (2 per cent) were fined (mostly for gambling and liquor violations), and an equal per cent (3 per cent) had suspended sentences. When the sentences were compared by type of offense, age of offender, and previous criminal record, no significant race differences were noted. Some of the cases involved personal contact with the victim, but the victim-offender relationship was not examined in this study.

Green later selected and analyzed 118 robberies and 291 burglaries from the original study, for which information on race of the victim was available. He found that although there was some variation in sentencing according to the race of the offender and victim, the disparity stemmed from intrinsic differences between the races in patterns of criminal behavior, and not from racial discrimination. The offenses involving black offenders and victims were "relatively high in impulsiveness and low in the elements of repetitiveness and malicious intent,"[74] and therefore resulted in less severe punishment. Severer penalties were imposed in assault cases, including robbery, involving Negro offenders and white victims, because they were crimes of a more serious nature. The strictest sentences were imposed on white offenders who burglarized members of their own race because, Green's findings indicate, they were generally convicted for a greater number of separate offenses.

National data on executions, reported by the Bureau of Prisons, indicate that, regardless of the offense, blacks are more often executed than whites. During the years 1930 to 1966, 3,857 persons were executed in the U.S.: 53.5 per cent were black; 45.4 per cent were white; and 1.1 per cent were members of other minority groups.[75]

When persons are sentenced to death, some have their sentences commuted to life imprisonment by a board of pardons or similar agency. A fundamental question is whether these sentences of execution are carried out equally for whites and Negroes. Research gives a negative answer, indicating that over time and in different states, between 10 and 20 per cent more Negroes than whites are executed.[76] That whites have greater access to private legal counsel may partially contribute to their chances of having a death sentence reduced to life imprisonment.

Among the prisoners sentenced to death for rape in North Carolina from 1909 to 1954, for instance, 56 per cent of the blacks, compared to 43 per cent of the whites, were actually executed. Of all offenders committed to death row for burglary, 26.6 per cent of the blacks, but none of the whites, were executed.[77] C. S. Magnum, who has studied the statistics on executions for all offenses in other Southern states, reports:

For Florida, from August 1928 to December 1938, 56 per cent of the whites and 74 per cent of the Negroes sentenced to death were executed. Comparable percentages for Kentucky, from 1928 to 1938, amounted to 59 for whites and 64 for Negroes; Missouri in 1938, 75 and 83; North Carolina, from 1909 to 1938, 39 and 52; South Carolina, from 1912 to 1938, 75 and 83; North Carolina, from 1928 to 1938, 35 and 67; Texas, from 1924 to 1938, 79 and 83; and in Virginia, from 1928 to 1938, 42 per cent of the whites and 61 per cent of the Negroes sentenced to death were subsequently executed.[78]

There is some evidence that young minority-group offenders from underprivileged homes are the most likely to be condemned and executed. Ten teen-agers were executed in 1954: seven in Georgia, two in New York, and one in Florida. All were Negroes. Between 1950 and 1953, nine teen-agers were executed; seven were black, two were white.[79]

⟨ 19 ⟩

Black Powerlessness in
Policy-Making Positions*

*KARL H. FLAMING, J. JOHN PALEN,
GRANT RINGLIEN, AND CORNEFF TAYLOR*

A recent study of black powerlessness in Chicago examined the extent to which Blacks were excluded from positions of influence in major institutional sectors (Baron, 1968). Their findings indicated that Negroes occupied only 1.4 percent or 285 of the 19,997 top policy-making positions in the Chicago area (Baron, 1968:28). Black representation in Chicago was greatest in the elected public sector, welfare and religious voluntary organizations, and industrial unions . . . There was a virtual absence of Black representation in the policy-making positions of the private institutions such as business corporations, banks, insurance companies, universities, and professional business organizations.

How representative are these findings of Black powerlessness in other metropolitan areas? The authors of the Chicago study suggest that their city is atypical in that it ". . . has proportionately more Negro-controlled businesses, larger than neighborhood operations, than any other major city in the North" (Baron, 1968:28). They then hypothesized that ". . . similar surveys in other Northern metropolitan areas would turn up an even smaller percentage of Negro policy-makers in the business world.

* Abridged from K. H. Flaming, J. J. Palen, G. Ringlien, and C. Taylor, "Black Powerlessness in Policy-Making Positions," *The Sociological Quarterly*, 1972, *13*, 126–133. Reprinted with permission of the publisher and authors.

Our research tests this hypothesis by examining the degree to which Blacks are found in key policy-making positions in the Milwaukee, Wisconsin, metropolitan area. In this study a total of 4,930 policy-making positions in the business, public governmental, academic, and voluntary sectors were identified and the number of Blacks holding such policy-making positions were identified.

METHODOLOGY

At the time of this study, the city of Milwaukee had a population of approximately 750,000 of which 90,000, or 12 percent, were Black. The county was 9 percent Black while the total SMSA population was over 1,400,000, of which 6.9 percent was classified as non-white.

This study, as in the earlier Chicago report, assumes that men who hold power are those who have been elevated to policy-making positions in powerful institutions such as insurance firms, city boards and commissions, universities, and labor unions. Policy-making positions were defined as those which the major goals and orientation of the organization are set. As in the Chicago study, every effort was made to include the total universe of policy-making positions.

Within Milwaukee County four major institutional areas were identified. These were the private sector (business, industry, law, etc.); the public-governmental sector (city, county, and federal elective, appointive, civil service, etc.); academic (school boards, principals, administrators, etc.); and the voluntary sector (labor unions, civic service organizations, etc.) . . .

The criteria for inclusion of organizations differed from the Chicago study in that, (1) the size criteria for inclusion was lowered to allow for the difference in city size, (2) the Milwaukee Labor Council helped formulate more representative parameters for this sub-sector and, (3) a hospital sub-sector, not included in the Chicago study, was added to cover the area of health care.

The collection of data varied somewhat in each of the organizational areas. Data for the public administrative area was already available for the most part. In the area of corporations, a complete list of all Milwaukee corporations was obtained from *Poor's Register of Corporations, Directors, and Executives, 1968*, and *Geographical Index*. Listings of directors, presidents, vice-presidents, and managers were found in *Poor's Register of Corporations, Directors, and Executives, 1968*. Policy-making positions in voluntary associations, labor unions, and universities were obtained from the organizations themselves or from knowledgeable sources. Letters, telephone conversations, and interviews were used to obtain information on the size of the organization. If the organization met the criteria for inclusion in the study, then the names of those persons occupying policy-making positions were obtained.

Of the 4,930 positions surveyed, there were 1,867 policy-making positions in the business sector, 856 policy positions in the public-governmental sector, 553 positions in the academic sector, and 655 positions in the voluntary sector. As in the Chicago study, all policy-making positions were ranked equally. The data thus reflect the presence or possible potential for Negro influence rather than actual exercised power or influence.

FINDINGS

A total of 1,867 policy-making positions in the private sector were surveyed. Included were business and industrial concerns, law firms, banks, stock brokerage firms, insurance companies, and hospitals. Qualifying for the study were 44 Milwaukee-based business and industrial concerns with a thousand or more employees or annual sales of over twelve million dollars and non-locally based firms employing at least 700 persons; sixteen banks with announced assets of at least ten million dollars; seven major insurance companies; 26 law firms with six or more partners or with at least two public-owned corporations as clients; and 24 private hospitals.

Only *one* Black occupied any of the 1,867 key positions in the business sector. The all-but-total absence of Negroes in these critical positions is a major handicap to expanding Black entrepreneurship. At the time of the study, the Milwaukee Negro community did not have representation in major business firms. Only one Black held a major policy position.

As Table 1 indicates, Blacks fared somewhat better in the public-government sector. There, twenty Blacks held 42 of the 856 (4.9%) policy-making positions in the city and county. Of the 121 elected positions only five were held by Negroes. Thirty-six of the 588 appointive positions (6.1%) were held by Blacks. Only two Blacks (1.4%) were found in any city or county administrative post with policy-making potential. Negro representation was strongest in the city where Blacks were 12 percent of the population. Here they held 8.3 percent of the elective and 7.2 percent of the appointive positions.

TABLE 1. *The Percentage of Blacks in Policy-Making Positions in the Public Government Sector*

SELECTED AREAS	NUMBER OF POSITIONS	NUMBER OF BLACKS IN POSITIONS	PERCENT OF BLACKS IN POSITIONS
Officials elected at large	66	1	1.5
City of Milwaukee elected positions	24	2	8.3
City of Milwaukee administration	81	1	1.2
City of Milwaukee appointed Bds. & Com.	387	28	7.2
Milwaukee County elected positions	31	2	6.5
Milwaukee County administration	66	0	0.0
County appointed Boards and Commissions	201	8	4.0
Total	856	42	4.9

The picture of limited Black participation was similar in the academic sector. Table 2 shows that of a total of 553 policy-making positions, Blacks held 21 or 3.8 percent. However, in the highest policy-making positions (public school boards, Board of Vocational and Adult Education, and University Regents) there was no Black representation. Some Black representation was found in the next lower level, positions concerned with the administration of public education (principals, vice-principals, assistants, and central administrators). Blacks were also absent from the 118 administrative positions surveyed in the private academic sector.

Highest Negro representation was found in the voluntary

TABLE 2. *The Percentage of Blacks in Policy-Making Positions in the Academic Sector*

SELECTED AREAS	NUMBER OF POSITIONS	NUMBER OF BLACKS IN POSITIONS	PERCENT OF BLACKS IN POSITIONS
Elementary—Secondary			
Public			
School Board	14	0	0.0
Administration	68	4	5.9
Bd. or Vocational & Adult Education	7	0	0.0
Principals	157	5	3.2
Vice-Principals	80	5	6.3
Assistants	31	2	6.5
Colleges and Universities			
Public			
Regents	17	0	0.0
Administration	23	2	8.7
Deans & Directors	38	3	7.9
Private			
Regents	64	0	0.0
Administration	24	0	0.0
U. Officials, Deans & Assistant Deans	30	0	0.0
Total	553	21	3.8

sector. Table 3 indicates that Blacks were highly visible in programs and organizations primarily concerned with minority groups and poverty problems. Of the 472 policy-makers posts in the voluntary service organizations, 125 or 26.5 percent were held by Blacks. However, the majority of these voluntary organizations, such as the Urban League, or the O.E.O.-funded Social Development Commission, possessed only limited community influence. Blacks were most visible in organizations dealing directly with minority group problems. On the other hand, it is noteworthy that in civic (Association of Commerce, Bar Association, Board of Realtors) as opposed to service organizations, only two of the 121 posts were held by Blacks. Finally, within organized labor, there were no Blacks in the 26 policy-making posts and only two Blacks were found in the 36 regional decision-making positions surveyed.

DISCUSSION

The study supports the hypothesis that Blacks in northern metropolitan areas would constitute an even smaller percentage of potential policy-makers than they did in the Chicago study. Milwaukee Blacks are clearly absent from

TABLE 3. *The Percentage of Blacks in Policy-Making Positions in the Voluntary Sector*

SELECTED AREAS	NUMBER OF POSITIONS	NUMBER OF BLACKS IN POSITIONS	PERCENT OF BLACKS IN POSITIONS
Voluntary Organizations			
Service	472	125	26.5
Civic	121	2	1.7
Labor Organizations			
Regions	36	2	5.6
Local	26	0	0.0
Total	655	129	19.7

policy-making positions with the exclusion being most pronounced in the business sector where only one Black was found in the 1,867 policy positions. This suggests that Blacks in medium to large size northern cities may be even more poorly represented than Blacks in the largest cities.

In reality, Milwaukee Blacks are even *more poorly* represented than the above data indicate. There are two major reasons for this. First, according to Negro decision-makers, Blacks who are appointed to decision-making positions are those who are best known to, and have the widest acceptance in, the White community. More militant Blacks, while they may be known, tend to be distrusted. A second related factor is that those few Blacks who are known and acceptable to White decision-makers tend to be appointed to a much larger number of positions than their white peers. Thus, a limited number of Blacks tend to be repeatedly used and reused as representatives of the Black community. For example, 605 Whites held 814 policy-making positions in the public-government sector while at the same time only 20 Blacks held 42 positions in the same sector. The same pattern of Black duplication was found in the other sectors where a significant number of Blacks were present. Given the level of specialization and professionalism required in our society, this duplication of Black leaders further weakens actual Black participation in decision-making.

Black decision-makers are more likely to be found in civil rights and welfare oriented positions. This pattern dilutes the degree of Black influence even in those areas where Black representation is most frequent. Further limiting Black influence in these sectors is the discovery that a small number of Black representatives "acceptable" to White decision-makers were repeatedly used in "Black slots." These same Blacks were present on numerous committees and boards. As a result, they simply do not have the same amount of time to devote to each issue as do their white counterparts.

A related question raised by this research is whether Blacks must necessarily be represented by Blacks. We can think of a number of reasons why such representation is necessary. In the short run, Whites can possibly obtain more for Blacks than Black representatives can for themselves. However, such paternalism is debilitating at best and devastating at worst. A paternalistic approach prevents the emergence of viable Black leadership. Black leaders can also bring different insights and perspectives to problems. For example, the Milwaukee case provides evidence that Blacks in positions of power have raised issues which Whites in similar positions could not, or would not raise. In the case of open housing legislation, the only Black member of the Milwaukee Common Council in the mid-sixties introduced an open housing ordinance. It was defeated 19–1.

The symbolic influence of visibly signifying to both the Black and White communities that Blacks can legitimately achieve power should also be emphasized. Black attitudes concerning the causes of riots during the sixties emphasize Black alienation from local decision-makers. In Milwaukee, as in other cities which experienced civil disturbances, Blacks felt that decision-makers did not care about the problems of the inner city . . .

The research reported in this paper clearly documents the extent to which Blacks are excluded from the decision-making process in one large mid-western city. We have also described the highly structured pattern of token representation of Negroes in positions that clearly affect the welfare of the Black community, and the exclusion of Blacks from positions controlling economic power . . .

BIBLIOGRAPHY

H. M. Baron, "Black Powerlessness in Chicago," transaction, November 1968, 27–33.

20

Differential Trends Toward Equality Between Whites and Nonwhites*

ERDMAN PALMORE AND FRANK J. WHITTINGTON

There has been considerable doubt as to whether nonwhites are actually moving toward equality with whites in the various sectors of our society . . . Part of the confusion is caused by the fact that no one has systematically applied a standard index of equality to all the various kinds of statistics available in order to measure trends in equality. There have been many studies which summarize the statistics on the status of Negroes at one point in time (U.S. Department of HEW, 1965; Broom and Glenn, 1967; Glenn and Bonjean, 1969; Price, 1968; Duncan and Duncan, 1969; U.S. Department of Labor, 1966; U.S. Office of Education, 1966; Fein, 1965; Siegel, 1965; Farley and Taeuber, 1968; Moynihan, 1965; Pettigrew, 1964) and some of these present trend data in selected areas. But most of the indexes and the comparisons of central tendencies are either not applicable to much of the data or are inadequate in various ways . . .

The purposes of this paper are: (1) to describe a standard index of equality that can be used with ordinal as well as in-

* Abridged slightly from Erdman Palmore and Frank J. Whittington, "Differential Trends Toward Equality Between Whites and Nonwhites," *Social Forces*, 1970, 49, 108–117. Reprinted with permission of the publisher and authors. Copyright 1970 by the University of North Carolina Press. All rights reserved.

terval data and to discuss its advantages over other measures; (2) to use this equality index to measure the differential trends in income, education, occupation, weeks worked, housing, mortality, and marital status; (3) to discuss briefly some of the possible explanations for the differential trends.

THE EQUALITY INDEX

The *equality index* (EI) is simply the positive complement of the older *index of dissimilarity* (Duncan and Duncan, 1955). It may be described in several ways. It is the proportion of the white and nonwhite percentage distributions that overlap each other. Or, it is the proportion of nonwhites who are equal to the same proportion of whites. It can be thought of as the percent of complete equality, because *100* would mean that there is complete identity, or equality, between the two percentage distributions, and *0* would mean that there is no overlap between the two distributions.

$$\sum_{i=1}^{n} Min \, W_i \, N_i$$

means the summation of the smaller of the two percentages, W_i and N_i, where W_i is the percent of whites in the ith category and N_i is the precent of nonwhites in the ith category. Thus, the EI is quite simple to calculate: the percent of all whites in a category is compared to the precent of nonwhites in that category, and the lesser of the two percentages in each category are summed. The index of dissimilarity can be derived from this by subtracting the EI from *100*, or the EI can be derived in the same way from the index of dissimilarity.

Figure 1 shows graphically the curves of the white and nonwhite income distributions superimposed upon one another with the area of overlap shaded. The EI is the measure of the shaded overlap area as a percentage of the total area ur.derneath the two curves. Thus the EI would increase if more Negroes shifted to the upper end of the distribution or

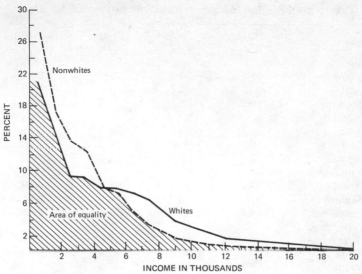

FIGURE 1.   *Percentage Distribution of Whites and Nonwhites by Income for 1967.*

more whites shifted to the lower end, thereby increasing the amount of overlap . . .

A few comparisons of the EI with the ratio of nonwhite to white medians will show how these measures behave differently. In 1967 the ratio of nonwhite median income to white median income was *.60*, indicating that the average nonwhite income was only 60 percent as great as the average white income. However, the EI for that same year was *80* (Table 1), indicating that actually 80 percent of the nonwhites had incomes equal to 80 percent of the whites. Thus, the EI revealed substantially greater equality between white and nonwhite incomes than one would infer from the ratio of median incomes.

For another contrast, the ratio of median incomes indicates that since 1960 the ratio has increased by *.013* (the equivalent of *1.3* EI points) per year which is a faster increase than in any other decade. In contrast the EI shows that the percent of nonwhites achieving equality with whites in income in-

TABLE 1. *Equality Indexes from 1940 to Present by Sex*

	1940	1950	1960	1966–68
Income:				(1967)
Total	57.5	70.7	76.6	80.8
Male	56.9	65.6	69.7	73.3
Female	55.2	75.6	83.3	89.4
Education:				(1968)
Total	56.5	63.2	72.7	74.9
Male	56.3	62.3	70.5	73.2
Female	59.8	65.2	74.0	76.2
Occupation:				(1967)
Total	52.7	59.1	61.3	66.4
Male	57.5	63.4	64.1	67.0
Female	39.2	47.9	55.1	65.9
Weeks worked:				(1967)
Total	*	88.0	88.0	92.8
Male	*	88.8	85.8	90.9
Female	*	90.9	95.0	98.0
Housing:				(1968)
Total	*	58.6	67.1	72.6
Mortality:				(1966)
Total	79.2	80.8	83.3	82.9
Male	82.2	84.0	85.8	86.2
Female	75.7	76.4	79.5	78.4
Marital status:				(1967)
Total	*	88.5	85.3	84.8
Male	*	89.7	85.7	85.1
Female	*	87.2	84.8	84.7

* Data not available.

SOURCES: Edwards, 1943; U.S. Bureau of the Census, 1943a, 1943b, 1953a, 1953b, 1953c, 1963a, 1963b, 1963c, 1968, 1969a, 1969b, 1969c; U.S. Bureau of Labor Statistics, 1969; U.S. Public Health Service, 1953, 1963, 1969.

creased by only 0.6 of a point per year, which is less than half the 1940–50 rate (Table 2). Similarly, the ratio of non-white median years of education to white median years of education shows the same rate of increase in this decade as for any of the preceding periods. However, according to the EI, movement toward equality in education in this decade was

TABLE 2. *Annual Rate of Change in Equality Indexes for Three Periods Since 1940, by Sex*

	1940–50	1950–60	1960–66–68
Income:			
Total	1.32	.59	.60
Male	.87	.41	.51
Female	2.04	.77	.87
Education:			
Total	.67	.95	.28
Male	.60	.82	.34
Female	.54	.88	.28
Occupation:			
Total	.64	.22	.73
Male	.59	.07	.41
Female	.87	.72	1.54
Weeks worked:			
Total	*	.00	.69
Male	*	−.30	.73
Female	*	.41	.43
Housing:			
Total	*	.85	.69
Mortality:			
Total	.16	.25	−.07
Male	.18	.18	.04
Female	.07	.31	−.18
Marital status:			
Total	*	−.33	−.05
Male	*	−.40	−.06
Female	*	−.24	−.01

* Data not available.

less than one-third the rate of increase for 1950 to 1960 (Table 2). Thus, the use of medians often produces different conclusions from the use of EI as a measure of equality and trends toward equality. One measure is not necessarily more accurate or valid than the other, but it is our contention that the EI is more broadly useful . . .

It should be recognized that for certain purposes a comparison of central tendencies is more appropriate than the EI. For example, to compute the per capita amount of money it would take to bring nonwhite incomes up to white incomes, a comparison of mean incomes would provide a closer estimate.

The data presented in this paper all compare equality between whites and nonwhites rather than between Negroes and whites. The reason for this is that much of the census data used are not available specifically for Negroes, and it was decided to use the nonwhite category consistently so that the EI would be exactly comparable from year to year and from one variable to another. When data for whites and Negroes are used, the EI is about one or two points lower than the EI for whites and nonwhites, because more of the non-Negro nonwhites have equality with whites than do the Negroes. However, the differences between using data on nonwhites versus Negroes is so small that the two indexes may be used interchangeably for most purposes. This is true because the non-Negro nonwhite population is so small relative to Negroes (less than 8 percent of nonwhites were non-Negro in 1960).

U.S. Census data were used to compute all the EI. The income EI was computed from a percentage distribution of white and nonwhite income by $500 intervals up to $5,000, $1,000 intervals up to $8,000, a $2,000 interval to $10,000, a $5,000 interval to $15,000, and all over $15,000 in the final interval. The occupation EI was based on the following occupation groups: professional and technical, manager and proprietor, farmers and farm managers, clerical, sales, craftsmen and foremen, operatives, private household, service workers, farm laborers and foremen, and nonfarm laborers. The weeks worked EI was based on the following intervals: 13 or less, 14–26, 27–39, 40–49, and 50–52. The housing EI for 1960 and 1968 was based on the following categories: sound housing with all plumbing facilities, sound housing lacking some or all facilities, deteriorating housing with all facilities, deteriorating housing lacking some or all facilities, and dilapidated housing. The EI for 1950 housing was based on somewhat different, but comparable, categories: sound housing with private bath and hot water, sound housing with private bath and cold water, sound housing with running water but no private bath, sound housing with no running water, dilapidated housing with private bath and hot water, dilapidated housing lacking bath or running water.

The EI for mortality was more complex than the others. It was computed on the basis of the percent of death in ten-year age intervals standardized against the white age structure. It is necessary to standardize the nonwhite deaths by applying the death rate to the white age structure in order to control for differences between the white and nonwhite age structures which, in turn, are affected by differential birth rates. If the age structure is not standardized, the EI is about six to nine points lower because nonwhites have a larger proportion of the population in the younger age categories. This age-standardized mortality EI can be thought of as the percent of nonwhite deaths which occurred at the same age as a similar percent of white deaths, after the white and nonwhite age structures have been equated.

The marital status EI is based on the following categories: married with spouse present, married but separated, married but spouse absent for other reasons, widowed, divorced, and single. Marital status was conceived of as an ordinal variable in the sense of declining degrees of "marriedness" from married with spouse present, through ex-married categories, to the never-married category.

FINDINGS

Table 1 presents the EI for income, education, occupation, weeks worked, quality of housing, mortality and marital status, for 1940, 1950, 1960, and for most recent year in which data are available (1966–68). Table 2 converts these EI to annual rates of change for the three periods since 1940.

These tables show that income had the greatest overall increase in equality with a rise of over twenty-three points between 1940 and 1968 (Table 1). Furthermore, the *rate* of increase has remained stable at about 0.6 of a point per year since 1950 (Table 2). At this rate it would take about thirty years to achieve complete equality of income.

Females started at about the same level of income equality in 1940 but have been increasing at a substantially faster rate than men ever since. By 1967 the women had an EI which was sixteen points greater than the men's. This is probably due primarily to the large proportion of nonwhite women who are employed and now earn substantial incomes. It is not due to any greater equality in education nor in occupation among women because the EI in these areas are almost the same between men and women. In a sense, the high EI for women is somewhat deceptive because more of the white women are living on the greater incomes of their husbands.

Equality in years of education completed shows the second greatest gain, with a rise of over eighteen points. But in contrast to income, there has been a substantial slowdown in the rate of increase between 1960 and 1968. For some reason, the attempts at integration and improvement of education among nonwhites is producing less effect during the 1960s than at any time since 1940. It is true that the absolute amounts of education among both whites and nonwhites are still rising, and the gap between whites and nonwhites is still shrinking, but the rate at which this gap is closing has slowed to about a quarter of a point per year.

Duncan (1969) found in a regression analysis of school years completed that the increased equality seems to be related to both increasing similarity between whites and nonwhites in background variables and to a decrease in residual differences due to "color" which may be taken to measure decreases in discrimination.

By contrast with the slowdown in the education EI changes, equality in occupation shows a faster rate of increase in this decade compared to the previous one. The women especially have shown a fast increase with a gain of over ten points in the past seven years. The fact that women show greater rates of increase in each decade is related to their low occupational equality in 1940 (39.2). This low level of equality in 1940 was due primarily to the concentration of nonwhite women in the occupation of private household workers. Fifty-eight percent of the nonwhite women were in this category in 1940 compared to only *11* percent of the white women. By 1967, the percentages in this occupation were less than one-half as great. Since the women's rate of increase in occupational equality is over three times as high as the men's, the amount of equality among women will soon be substantially higher than among men, if this rate of increase continues.

Nathan Hare (1965) earlier noted the decline in progress toward occupational equality during the 1950s. He also found that the higher the educational level, the greater the equality in occupations. Our analysis shows that movement toward equality in the 1960s has again stepped up, now progressing at a rate even higher than in the 1940s. Perhaps this is a result of the earlier high increases in educational equality.

The EI for weeks worked assumes that the smaller percentage of nonwhites who work 50 or more weeks per year represents the greater amount of unemployment among nonwhites. While there was a mixed pattern in this index between 1950 and 1960, with the men showing a decrease and the women showing an increase, there have been consistent increases for both sexes in this decade. The EI for women in 1967 was so high (*98.0*) that for practical purposes it might be said that complete equality in number of weeks worked has been achieved by women. However, it is true that more of the nonwhites with less than 50 weeks of work were unemployed during part of the year while more of the whites with less than 50 weeks of work did not want work when not employed. Thus, the unusually high EI in weeks worked is somewhat deceptive in not reflecting the distinction between voluntary and involuntary lack of employment.

The housing EI shows a fairly steady improvement from 1950 (the first census in which comparable data were collected) to the present. In 1968 almost three-quarters of the nonwhites had housing rated as equal in quality to three-quarters of the whites'. Thus, the quality of nonwhite housing has improved steadily, even relative to white housing, despite the evidence that segregation has increased during this period, especially in southern cities (Farley and Taeuber, 1968). Apparently the migration of nonwhites to the cities and their general economic gains have enabled nonwhites to substantially improve the quality of their housing despite continued discrimination and segregation.

The mortality EI shows a small increase for men and a small decrease for women since 1960. This decrease among women is not due to increased mortality among nonwhites, but reflects the somewhat larger decline in mortality among white women than among nonwhite women. In other words, while early mortality decreased among both groups, it decreased faster among the white women. Thus, it appears that in the area of health and longevity, progress toward equality between whites and nonwhites has come to a virtual standstill in this decade.

Finally, the EI for marital status shows a consistent decline since 1950. On the other hand, the rate of decline has slowed almost to a standstill since 1960, which may indicate that the EI will soon begin to rise. The Moynihan Report (1965) documents the many factors related to the decline in family stability among Negroes, such as high rates of unemployment, poverty, high rates of mobility from rural areas to city slums and within city slums, etc. Presumably, if these factors were reduced, family stability would increase and the EI for marital status would climb.

DISCUSSION

It is clear that nonwhites have made substantial, though somewhat uneven, progress toward equality in the economic areas of income, occupation, and weeks worked, as well as in education and equality of housing, which are largely dependent on economic status (Figure 2). Thus, those who claim that the economic gap between whites and nonwhites is increasing or that "the black communities are becoming more and more economically depressed" are incorrect, at least on the national level. Despite a slowdown in the rate of change toward equality in education, progress continues to be made on all of these fronts. In most of these areas, complete equality

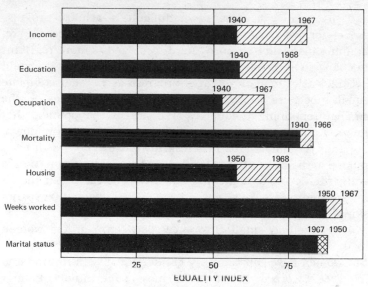

FIGURE 2. *Changes in Equality Indexes Since 1940*

could be reached in thirty to forty years at present rates. Progress toward equality in education has slowed so that it would take ninety years to achieve full equality. Faster progress would require extensive adult education for nonwhites.

On the other hand, it is also clear that in the social variable of marital status and in the socio-environmentally related area of mortality, there has been almost no movement toward equality in this decade. Mortality had shown small increases in equality up to 1960 and perhaps with the advent of such public health programs as Medicare and Medicaid, movement toward equality in this area will soon be resumed. The deterioration in marital status shows signs of leveling off and may begin to climb if the economic gains begin to have a delayed effect on marital status.

It might be argued that a basic reason for the slowdown in movement toward equality in education, as well as a reason for the lack of progress in mortality and marital status, is the fact that all these EI are in the mid-seventies or higher and that it may become more difficult to achieve progress the closer we move to complete equality. Perhaps the remaining inequality is more "hard-core" and is more resistant to change. On the other hand, one might argue that it should become easier to achieve rapid progress as we near complete equality because we could concentrate our resources on the smaller remaining inequality. We are of the opinion that there is no necessary reason why progress must slow down, but that the amount of progress toward equality is directly related to the amount of attention and resources our nation is willing to devote to achieving equality. The facts that the EI for income and weeks worked are also high, but have not slowed, support this view.

There are only small differences between men and women in the indexes for education, occupation, and marital status. But women have substantially greater equality in income and in weeks worked, while men have substantially greater equality in mortality. We believe these sex differentials can be explained by one general principle: greater equality among the inferior category. Thus, women generally make less income and, therefore, constitute the inferior category in this dimension and have a higher income EI. Women work less weeks per year and are "inferior" in the sense of having less of this variable and so have a higher weeks worked EI. In mortality, men are the inferior category because they have less longevity and, therefore, have the higher EI. We believe the reason this principle holds is that the inferior category has a constricted range and variation because they have less of the given variable, and thus there is less room for as much discrepancy between whites and nonwhites within that category. This principle also applies in other areas as shown by the fact that white and nonwhite incomes are closer to equality among the aged than among younger persons (Orshansky, 1964). In this case, aged persons are in the inferior category with less income than others . . .

The reader should be aware that the aggregated data on which these EI are based can show only main trends and that detailed analysis of the various reasons for changes at various levels of the distributions is a massive and complex task which has begun in only a few areas. Another use of the EI would be to compute the equality between sexes, between different age groups, between different regions of the country, between countries, etc. We believe there are vast bodies of data to which the EI could be applied to reveal important practical and theoretical information on the present degree of equality and trends toward or away from equality between many types of groups and social categories.

BIBLIOGRAPHY

H. R. Alker, Jr., and B. M. Russett, "On Measuring Inequality," *Behavioral Science*, 1964, *9*, 207–218.

L. Broom and N. Glenn, *Transformation of the Negro American* New York: Harper & Row, 1967.

O. D. Duncan, "Discrimination Against Negroes," in B. M. Gross (ed.), *Social Intelligence for America's Future*. Boston: Allyn & Bacon, 1969; pp. 352–374.

O. D. Duncan and B. Duncan, "A Methodological Analysis of Segregation Indexes," *American Sociological Review*, 1955, *20*, 210–217.

A. M. Edwards, *Comparative Occupation Statistics for the United States*, 1870–1940. Washington, D.C.: GPO, 1943.

R. Farley and K. E. Taeuber, "Population Trends—Residential Segregation Since 1960," *Science*, 1968, *159*, 953–956.

R. Fein, "An Economic and Social Profile of the Negro American," *Daedalus*, 1965, *94*, 815–846.

E. Ginzberg and D. L. Hiestand, *Mobility in the Negro Community*. Washington, D.C.: U.S. Commission on Civil Rights, 1968.

N. Glenn and C. Bonjean (eds.), *Blacks in the United States*. San Francisco: Chandler, 1969.

N. Hare, "Recent Trends in the Occupational Mobility of Negroes, 1930–1960: An Intracohort Analysis," *Social Forces*, 1965, *44*, 166–173.

D. P. Moynihan, *The Negro Family: The Case for National Action*. Washington, D.C.: GPO, 1965.

M. Orshansky, "The Aged Negro and His Income," *Social Security Bulletin*, 1964, *27*, 3–13.

T. F. Pettigrew, *A Profile of the Negro American*. New York: Van Nostrand Reinhold, 1964.

D. Price, "Occupational Changes Among Whites and Nonwhites, with Projections for 1970," *Social Science Quarterly*, 1968, *49*, 563–572.

P. M. Siegel, "On the Cost of Being Negro," *Sociological Inquiry*, 1965, *35*, 41–57.

U.S. Bureau of the Census, *U.S. Census of Population: 1940*, Vol. 2, *Characteristics of the Population, Part 1, United States Summary*. Washington, D.C.: GPO, 1943a.

U.S. Bureau of the Census, *Vital Statistics of the United States, 1940, Part 1*. Washington, D.C.: GPO, 1943b.

U.S. Bureau of the Census, *U.S. Census of Population: 1950*, Vol. 2, *Characteristics of the Population, Part 1, United States Summary*. Washington, D.C.: GPO, 1953a.

U.S. Bureau of the Census, *U.S. Census of Housing: 1950*, Vol. 1, *Part 1, United States Summary*. Washington, D.C.: GPO, 1953b.

U.S. Bureau of the Census, *U.S. Census of Population: 1950, Subject Reports, Marital Status*. Washington, D.C.: GPO, 1953c.

U.S. Bureau of the Census, *U.S. Census of Population: 1960*, Vol. 2, *Characteristics of the Population, Part 1, United States Summary*. Washington, D.C.: GPO, 1963a.

U.S. Bureau of the Census, *U.S. Census of Housing: 1960*, Vol. 1, *Part 1, United States Summary*. Washington, D.C.: GPO, 1963b.

U.S. Bureau of the Census, *U.S. Census of Population: 1960, Subject Reports, Marital Status*. Washington, D.C.: GPO, 1963c.

U.S. Bureau of the Census, "Marital Status and Family Status: March 1967." *Current Population Reports*, Series P-20, No. 170. Washington, D.C.: GPO, 1968.

U.S. Bureau of the Census, "Educational Attainment: March 1968," *Current Population Reports*. Series P-20, No. 182. Washington, D.C.: GPO, 1969a.

U.S. Bureau of the Census, "Income in 1967 of Persons in the United States." *Current Population Reports*. Series P-60, No. 60. Washington, D.C.: GPO, 1969b.

U.S. Bureau of the Census, "Housing Units by Condition and Plumbing." Unpublished preliminary release, 1969c.

U.S. Bureau of Labor Statistics, *Handbook of Labor Statistics*, 1968. Washington, D.C.: GPO, 1969.

U.S. Department of Health, Education and Welfare, *White-Nonwhite Differentials in Health, Education and Welfare*. Reprinted from Indicators. Washington, D.C.: GPO, 1965.

U.S. Department of Labor, *The Negroes in the U.S. Bureau of Labor Statistics Bulletin*, No. 1511. Washington, D.C.: GPO, 1966.

U.S. Office of Education, *Equality of Educational Opportunity*. Washington, D.C.: GPO, 1966.

U.S. Public Health Service, *Vital Statistics of the United States: 1950, Vol. 3.* Washington, D.C.: GPO, 1953.

U.S. Public Health Service, *Vital Statistics of the United States: 1960, Vol. 2, Mortality, Part A.* Washington, D.C.: GPO, 1963.

U.S. Public Health Service, *Vital Statistics of the United States: 1966, Vol. 2, Mortality, Part A.* Washington, D.C.: GPO, 1969.

PART V

THE HUMAN COST OF RACIAL DISCRIMINATION

N o *discussion of racial discrimination is complete with just census percentages, statistical models, and theoretical arguments. We can never forget that the victims of this process are human beings, and its cost is needless suffering and shattered dreams in the richest nation on earth. This section presents three selections that outline this human cost of racial discrimination.*

There are many ways to respond to injustice and blocked opportunity. Four common alternatives are described in the following articles—distrust, escape into drugs, additional striving, and violence. Selection 21 reports on national survey data from the University of Michigan's Survey Research Center. It shows that there has been a sharp drop in trust of the federal government in recent years among black Americans. Considering the continued effects of racial discrimination after a generation of the Civil Rights Movement, the assassinations of the Kennedys and Martin Luther King, and the policies of the Nixon Administration, such an indication of growing black alienation should not come as a surprise.

Kenneth Clark, in Selection 22, presents the views of Harlem drug addicts in their own moving words. Taken from Clark's classic volume, Dark Ghetto, *these self-descriptions offer a vivid picture of the ravages of racism. Ridgely Hunt, a reporter on* The Chicago Tribune, *provides in Selection 23 an account of a particularly tragic— but far from uncommon—story of a young black man of unusual promise. Virgil White's response to his situation, a continuing search for a better life, ends in futility as he becomes yet another victim of the big city ghetto's internal violence.*

21

Blacks' Trust in Government Falls Sharply[*]

*INSTITUTE FOR SOCIAL RESEARCH,
UNIVERSITY OF MICHIGAN*

Distrust of government has grown alarmingly in the last eight years among the American electorate—and the continued growth of this distrust could create a generation of cynical Americans and plunge this country into a cycle of discontent.

These dire warnings emerge from the findings of a Center for Political Studies research team, directed by Arthur Miller, which analyzed political trust from 1958 through 1972. Miller, Thad Brown, and Alden Raine, in a paper entitled "Social Conflict and Political Estrangement, 1958–1972," report that in 1972 attitudes toward the federal government continued to deteriorate much as they have since 1964. Perhaps the most startling finding in the 1972 election study, however, is that between 1968 and 1972 blacks' trust in government deteriorated four times as rapidly as that of whites (Figure 1).

RACIAL DIFFERENCES

The study reveals the significance of racial differences in political trust over the last fourteen years. In 1958 blacks,

[*] Abridged slightly from "Americans' Trust in Government Falls Sharply, Blacks Rapidly Lose Faith in Political System," *Institute for Social Research Newsletter*, Spring–Summer 1973, *1*, pp. 4–5. Reprinted with permission of the publisher.

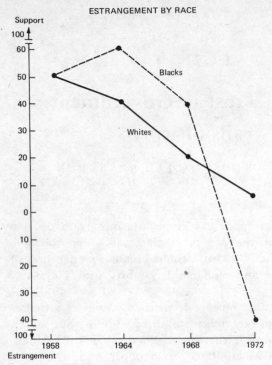

FIGURE 1.   *Election Study Results, 1958–1972*

despite a history of discrimination and economic and social deprivation, expressed levels of trust identical to those of whites. By 1964, as Lyndon Johnson was swept into office and the civil rights movement was cresting nationally, black trust in government soared to an all-time high. During the same period, whites were growing increasingly distrustful of government's expanding role in the area of civil rights.

After 1964 both black and white attitudes toward the government began the precipitous decline. Blacks moved from positive political attitudes to what the report describes as a "profound sense of political estrangement," at a time when whites, many threatened and disturbed by the race riots of the mid-sixties, also expressed increased alienation from government. With President Richard Nixon's election in 1968, the pace of whites' plummeting trust in government was slowed while cynicism and distrust took an even firmer hold of the black community.

INDEX PREPARED

Since 1958 the election study has measured trust in government through answers to five basic questions which are then combined into a composite index of trust-distrust. Questions asked of the respondents were: 1) how much they can trust the government in Washington to do what is right, 2) whether the government in Washington is pretty much run by a few big interests looking out for themselves or for the benefit of all the people, 3) if the government wastes the money we pay in taxes, 4) whether or not the people running the government are smart people who usually know what they are doing, and 5) whether or not the people running the government are a little crooked.

To determine how cynical or trusting a group is, the study directors compiled an Estrangement Percentage Difference Index (PDI) by computing the number of cynical responses given to the five questions and then subtracting the percentage of persons in the most cynical category (4–5 questions answered cynically) from the percentage in the most trusting category (0–1 questions answered cynically). The resulting percentage difference denotes the preponderance of one type of response over another for a given point in time. Values can range from +100 (most trusting) to −100 (least trusting).

ELECTORAL PROCESS

In addition to these five trust questions the election study asked about people's confidence in elections, political parties, and in the responsiveness of congressmen.

In 1964, the results show, blacks had more confidence than whites for all three areas, but as with trust, confidence in these specific aspects of the electoral process waned considerably after that point with an especially sharp drop among blacks between 1968 and 1972. Only whites' confidence in elections showed any stability during this period and that, the researchers explain, may be due to the fact that "discontent with leaders and parties has not yet reached the critical level where it becomes generalized to the institution of elections."

One of the primary aims of the 1972 election study analysis was to determine whether trust in government was being eroded more noticeably in any subgroup of the population than another, thus paving the way for deep and perhaps explosive social conflict. The evidence on race is clear—while both black and white attitudes have become increasingly cynical, blacks have become especially estranged from the federal government, national leaders, the election system, and the political parties. But how about persons of different social classes or of different generations? Are there signs of new social cleavages?

SUPPORT VARIES

When the study examined trust among the different social classes, using measures of both income and occupation, the results were generally what one would expect—the persons benefiting most from the system are least cynical (although trust has declined since 1958 among all income and occupational levels). There were, however, several notable exceptions to this link between system rewards and trust. Among blacks, for example, persons in professional occupations had become more cynical by 1972 than the blue collar workers, and by 1968 and on into 1972 upwardly mobile blacks, those whose social status was higher than that of their parents, were considerably more cynical than blacks whose status had not changed. Among whites there was no difference in levels of political support for those who were upwardly mobile than for those who were stationary . . .

Creating trust will not be an easy task in a period when the events surrounding Watergate are once again shaking Americans' faith in their government, their leaders, and the political process. Anger and discontent are important ingredients to a democratic political process, the study directors note, for they provide the impetus to "throw the rascals out" when a new election arrives. But a deep cynicism about the relevance and basic integrity of government can have a deadening effect on the processes of government. Indeed, cynicism has already taken a toll: voter turnout, for example, has been falling steadily since 1960 and in 1972 was at its lowest point for any presidential election since 1948 . . .

(22)

Harlem's Drug Addicts Speak*

KENNETH B. CLARK

My first bit—I did five years, and I feel that was unjustified because I feel that if they had given me some kind of break from the jump—probation—then I might have done something for myself. I would have been, you know, still in the street, but under their supervision. But they didn't do that. What they did was just send me upstate, and I stayed up there six or seven months before I saw the streets again. I was eighteen years old when I went up there, and it was the first time I had even been arrested in my life. I think it was wrong. If they had given me some probation, like they are giving the white kids, understand, I might have been able

* From K. B. Clark, *Dark Ghetto: Dilemmas of Social Power*. New York: Harper & Row, 1965; pp. 93–97. Reprinted with permission of the author, Harper & Row, Publishers, Inc., and Victor Gollancz Ltd. (British rights). Copyright 1965 by Kenneth B. Clark. All rights reserved.

to have the same advantages that he did. Maybe I would have gone out and got a job, and I would have worked from then until now, you know. But I wasn't given that chance. I was black, so I was sent away. And I was told it was for my good. I was sent away for six or seven months for *my* good. I was sent to a place where there was only criminals, and the only thing I could learn up there was how to be a better criminal than I was. You know, they haven't done anything for me. All they did for me was tell me I was a slave. That's the best way I could put it, brother.

—*Drug addict, male, age 26*

You have to survive . . . if you don't have the proper education that you should have, and you go *downtown* and work, they don't pay you any money worthwhile. You can work all your life and never have anything, and you will always be in debt. So you take to the streets, you understand? You take to the streets and try to make it in the street, you know what you have out here in the street you try to make it. Being out in the street takes your mind off all these problems. You have no time to think about things because you're trying to make some money . . . I've been trying to make it so hard and trying to keep a piece of money. I'm trying not to work like a dog to get it, and being treated any sort of way to get it. How to make another buck enters your mind. As far as bettering the community, this never enters your mind because it seems to me, well, I'm using my opinions—to me the white man has us locked up. The black man is progressing, but slowly. The only solution I see to it, I mean, if you are actually going to be here awhile, you have to stay healthy and not die, for one thing. The other thing is while you're here you want to live the best you can. And since Whitey has all the luxuries, I mean, he has it all locked up, you want to get a piece of it, so you have to make some kind of money so you can get it. You can't get what he's got, definitely, but you can get enough to make you feel comfortable. So you're always scheming how to, you know, how to make some money.

—*Drug addict, male, age about 37*

I took one cure down to Manhattan General, if you want to call that a cure. I went in there for about three, two and a half weeks. And all the other cures were in jail—in and out of jail.

So, why is it, when you get the cure and come out, that you go back to it?

I wish I could answer that for you. I really wish I could. I don't know. I couldn't give you a good answer to it.

Do you have any skills?

In the trade or working? Yes, I have them. I've been working in the garment center. I've worked on trucks. I've worked as a dishwasher, you know, all those things. But my only skill is pressing.

If you could get a job, what type of a job would you like to get?

Any kind—any kind. If I can get work—any kind to start me working, you know, to get in the bracket of a clean life, a working life. For frankly, I haven't done that type of thing in quite a few years; it's not easy to get back into it. People think it is, but to me it is not. I haven't been able to, and I have put forth, you know, I have put forth an effort to try to get it. I have, but most people don't think so. I know within myself. I've been down to the Department. I've been down to the employment agency, I've been in the penitentiary and out for about three weeks now, and I've been down to the employment agency four days, four times. Each time when I go down there, well, I sit down there all day and they tell me, well maybe tomorrow they'll have something.

I've asked for truck driving, I've asked for dishwashing, and I've asked to work in the hospital—anything. But . . . when they mention anything about a previous job, I haven't worked in so long, you know, and tell them about things I've been in and out— if I mention the penitentiary I'm always the last one. And you know how many there are before—they have clean records. You know they will come before me. And if I mention anything about dope, that's out. You know that.

—*Drug addict, male, age 34*

And if you're just filling up, being bored, it's a hell of a thing being bored and lonely in the midst of millions of people.

—*Drug addict, male, age 30*

I was just born black, poor and uneducated. And you only need three strikes all over the world to be out, and I have nothing to live for but this shot of dope.

I have nothing to shoot at. All I have to look forward to is a thrill and it's in a bag, and they run me up on the roof to get that. I don't have any place to turn, but I imagine you have. I'm poor and all I can look forward to is what I can get out of this bag. That's the only thrill in life for me, you know. I've never had anything, no opportunity, you know, to get any money, no nothing. All I can look forward to is what I can get out of this bag, and that's nothing really.

When I started I was fourteen years old, and that's twelve years ago. Drugs were much different then. For a dollar a cap poor people got rich. I started back where a man could shoot dope—hey cook that up for me, Eddie. Can you cook? Okay, hit me, man. I started back when I was fourteen years old in 1951, you understand, and I've been using dope ever since, except for the time I spent in the penitentiary. I figure if Whitey gives me half a chance you know, when I came through school, I could have done something more than this, you know. I know it. But I didn't have the chance because, like I say, I had those three strikes against me.

I'm not really blaming him, you know, the younger ones, but all Whiteys are associated with their race, and I blame them all because there isn't anything else I can do, you know, but shoot dope.

Well, I don't think anything can be done to correct it. Me, because I'm too far gone on it, you know. But, I mean, for my brothers and sisters, you know, people that are coming up younger than I, you know, they can do something. Give them a better education and better job opportunities.

Because I've been in this so long, this is part of my life. I'm sick now, I'm supposed to be in a hospital. They tried to admit me into the hospital three days ago, but knowing that it will be detrimental for me to stay out here, I stayed anyway because I'd rather have this shot of dope than go into anyone's hospital.

There's nothing I can do, you know. What the hell else can I do? I can't get a legitimate job, but anything else I do they say is against the law. And as long as I stay in this, I'm going to stay in dope, because everyone that's doing something against the law is in dope.

Your environment, I read somewhere, is just a mirror of yourself, you know. So what can I do?

I mean, I have to get my thrills from life some way. I can't lay back. I think I can enjoy working, and raising a family, like the next man, but this is all they left me. I can't work, so I must steal. And mostly the women who will accept me are thieves, or in the trade. And I mean, they're not thinking about raising a family. I mean, they think about what would be good for them, you know. The relief won't take them, so if I had a woman she would have to go out and turn tricks. I have to go out and steal to support my habit. So what can we do but shoot dope for enjoyment. They have left us nothing else.

Work, work, some kind of work program setup where a man can work and get ahead and support himself. Then he can go to some type of school at night, you know, to learn some type of trade, because in jail you can't learn a trade. You know, they tell you that you can, but you can't. If you go there, it's just a house of brutality, you know, that's all I've ever found. A bunch of people—I don't know how the administration thinks, but I know the guards that are head over you—all the fellows are interested in are confining you there, working you, making sure you obey, not the administration's orders, but their orders, you know.

So you can't learn anything in jail, you know. All you can do there is learn to hate more. You can't learn a trade or anything. All you learn there is how to stay out of the police's way as much as possible, even if it means ducking work. You duck work—you stay away from the law, because you know the more that you stay around them, the more they see you, the more they want to whip you. I know that, because I started going to jail when I was a kid.

I don't think I could be rehabilitated, you know, not now, in this society. Maybe if I see something better offered. But I hope that in the future they offer kids, or my sister's kids, or someone's kids, a better opportunity than they offered me, because they didn't offer me anything. I either accepted a porter job for the rest of my life regardless of how much education I had, or went to jail. In fact, I think jails were built for black men. You understand? If you look at the population up there, the black man is more popular in jail than the white man. The black man makes parole less frequently than the white man; the black man gets more time than the white man; and the black man goes to the chair more often than the white man. Whitey gets all the breaks in this world.

—*Drug addict, male, age 26*

The fact that the kind of creative sensitivity reflected in these testimonies has been made alien to the larger society is one of the major tragedies of the ghetto and the society as a whole.

(23)

Requiem for Virgil White*

RIDGELY HUNT

As far as the gangs were concerned, Virgil White was too good to live, and so they killed him. They caught him one night in the yard of the Ryerson School on Chicago's West Side and blew him apart with a shotgun. He died six days later, on Oct. 21, 1971, at the age of 18.

Virgil wasn't the first black kid to die in Chicago's gang wars, and he certainly won't be the last. Frequently such killings don't rate a mention in the newspapers; there are simply too many of them. But a peculiar excellence in Virgil's life instilled the elements of special tragedy in his death. Because Virgil, though a true child of the city jungle, had caught a vision of the stars. That did not make him a saint. He had had trouble with the police. He had two illegitimate children by two different girls and was awaiting his third. But he . . . had escaped, for one brief and disastrous week, to the Canadian wilderness and had seen the deer.

But a black can't escape forever from his ghetto, and it's a dangerous place to live, a perpetual combat zone where children are beaten on the way to school and parents are terrorized by nightly gunfire in the streets. The gangs do that. Recently they caught the little boy who lives next door to

---

* Abridged from Ridgely Hunt, "Requiem for Virgil White," *Chicago Tribune Magazine*, January 23, 1972, pp. 33–35, 37, 43–44, 48. Reprinted courtesy of the *Chicago Tribune*.

Virgil's house. They slashed his face with a razor and slit his nose open and broke it, probably to make him and his friends join their ranks. The gangs maintain a constant and merciless recruiting campaign. And what they cannot accomplish with beatings and razors, they bring to pass with guns, with which they are plentifully supplied.

"I handled a case last year," says Policeman David Ferguson, "in which this woman's windows were shot out at least four or five times because her son was a member of the Black Souls, and he was being harassed and his home was being harassed by the Four Corner Hustlers, and they shot out her windows four or five times. The woman had an eight- or nine-room apartment, and she had to keep her family gathered right in the center of it. She couldn't use the kitchen or the living room. They were living like war refugees, the whole family sleeping in the same room in the middle of the house."

Ferguson is himself a black man, large of body and large of mind, who fills his home with birds and gerbils and in his spare time studies for his degree in biology. As a member of the Police Department's Gang Intelligence Unit, he tries to defend people like Virgil and his family from the gangs. But the gangs constitute a vast legion, and the Gang Intelligence Unit, having fallen into disfavor, has been drastically reduced, so Ferguson must reckon with defeat as well as victory.

"This woman had a son who was a member of one gang," Ferguson continues, "but he had to live in the neighborhood of another gang. I know this seems sort of silly. You say, 'If you're living in the neighborhood of one gang, why do you belong to another gang?' Well, the kid may go to school in a neighborhood where the other gang is predominant. So consequently he's forced to join that gang in order to get safely to and from school. But then he's coming home into a neighborhood where another gang predominates, and so he's at odds with them. It becomes a toss-up. Where do you want to get beat: at home or at school? You've got to make a choice."

Virgil tried to make a third choice: He would not join any gang. It was a courageous decision, and it killed him.

Virgil lived with his mother, his stepfather, and five

brothers and sisters at 614 N. Monticello Avenue . . . It's a pleasant, tree-shaded block of one- and two-family homes, most of them being purchased by their occupants. They have a block club, and every Saturday they get together to clean their street and hold a weenie roast. But to the gangs, the 600 block of North Monticello represents neutral territory, ripe for conquest. At the time of Virgil's murder, two gangs were competing for this prize: the Black Souls and the Supreme Gangsters. Each was determined, by intimidation and beatings, to recruit every youth on the block.

It would be difficult to compile an inventory of all the juvenile gangs in Chicago. Some of them pursue worthy goals—the maintenance of a social club, perhaps, or an athletic organization—and hence never come to the official notice of the police. Others are too small to constitute much of a threat. But about 100 gangs are big enough and bad enough to engage the attention of the Gang Intelligence Unit. Of these the seven worst are the Mad Black Souls, the Supreme Gangsters, the Vice Lords, the Latin Kings, the Black P. Stone Nation, the Disciples, and a motorcycle gang called the Hell's Henchmen. The Souls and the Disciples are more accurately called "nations" since they have gang-offshoots in several neighborhoods.

These gangs engage in a wide variety of criminal acts ranging from petty shakedowns to the most barbarous assault. They extort money from members and nonmembers alike. To insure fidelity of the new recruit, they involve him in crime. "It's a dirtying-up process," says Ferguson. "A member will be given a gun and told to go out and shoot at a member of a rival gang. This way he is put in a position where he cannot testify against other people because he's as dirty as they are."

It became fashionable, until quite recently, for the white community to support some of these gangs with money and publicity. Huge foundations, private philanthropists, clergymen, and even the government outdid each other in pledging their aid and encouragement in the belief that the gang leaders might help bring the black race to the promised land.

The black community, understandably, was outraged by this benevolence, having long served as the gangs' primary victims . . .

"The gang is like a big, monstrous machine," says Ferguson. "It's like a cancer, really. It has to grow or it will die because there's always a threat of outside usurpation of its territory or loss of prestige."

But on the 600 block of North Monticello, the gangs met unaccustomed resistance in the person of Virgil White. Virgil was big for his age—200 pounds and all muscle—and he was a natural leader with a deep sense of responsibility. He had once warned his 8th-grade classmates that, it they elected him class president and continued to misbehave, he would call a meeting of their parents. They did, and he did. Later, he was part of the "inner-city" contingent enlisted in the Chicago Children's Choir, widely considered one of the finest children's choirs in the country, and after his voice changed, he continued as a junior leader because of the extraordinary respect he commanded among the younger members.

Inevitably, Virgil became the center of opposition to the two gangs fighting to take over his block. He didn't seek the role. He told the gang leaders that his friends could join if they wanted to. But he wouldn't join, and while he held out, so did his friends. To the gangs he represented a fortress that must be captured or destroyed.

In this hazardous position, he received comfort and support from his mother, Mrs. Mildred Flenory, a woman of remarkable energy and courage. Even now despite the murder of her son, despite the gangs' anonymous phone calls that disturb her day and night, she remains defiant.

"I'm not scared of them," she insists, "I just wish I could see them. But I'm not scared of them. It's just that I've got other kids, I've got little kids that go to school around here. I mean, I know they do kill. I found that out because they killed my son. But I'm not scared because if one walks up on me, he might kill me, but he's going to be in my arms when they find me because I'm going to hold on to him. He's going to have to stand away from me because I'm going to be determined to hang on till they find us together. But my kids, they're just too little to defend themselves."

Her house, for which she and her husband are paying $189.40 a month, is a shrine to the middle-class values espoused by white society. The front yard is bordered by flowers, and in its midst, on a wrought-iron standard, is set a sign that says "Flenory." Her second-floor apartment contains all the middle-class appurtenances: drapes and carpets and upholstered furniture and even a cocktail cart with glasses and a bottle of Cinzano. In the center of the living room windows stands a tall and ornate lamp. And she struggled for every stick of it.

"I got it piece by piece from the bargain basement at Sears," she says. "And I started buying it long before I started buying the house. All this in the dining room is floor-sample stuff. I know a lot of people over there at Sears because I shopped a lot in the bargain basement. That's the only way I could get my kids' clothes. You know, you have to catch the things on sale. And my bedroom suite, I got it the same way. Now the stove and my refrigerator, I got them during the riot; you know, the sale was on. Like Sears got a big sale on now. That's the only time that I would buy my stuff, when the specialty sales would come on . . .

"My husband has a lovely boss man, John Musser. He's one of the most wonderful persons you could ever meet. He has helped us out in every way possible. He helped my husband get my ring when we got married. He helped my husband get the house . . . He helped us out a lot. I don't think we could have made it without him. My husband works at Chicago Oxwelding Company. Him and Mr. Musser started out with just the two of them. He's been working for him for about 15 years now. He has all-around-the-clock shifts now."

With a little help, the Flenorys built a secure home for their children. They made it a point to give parties for their children's friends and thus keep them off the streets . . .

Virgil was the eldest of the six children. He slept in the basement where he had his phonograph for entertainment and foam rubber in the windows for protection from flying glass in case the gangs shot at him.

"He never bothered anybody," his mother says. "He never cursed, he didn't smoke, he didn't drink. He didn't go out at night at all unless he was going to visit a girl. He didn't go to any of the dances and things that the young boys would give because he didn't trust the fighting and things that were going on, usually after they would get to drinking—unless I had parties here at the house. He would always be wanting to play the music for that. And he had his own tape recorder. He'd usually be sitting right here with his ears plugged up, you know, listening at a tape or something or other. That's usually what he would be doing when you'd find him. He'd be sitting here or in the basement with this thing in his ear, listening to some record of some sort. That mostly was Virgil's life."

Officer Ferguson knew Virgil fairly well, having often visited the neighborhood at Virgil's request in an effort to relieve the pressure from the marauding gangs. He also knew Virgil's mother.

"My impression of her was a working woman who was trying to do something for her kids," he says. "You could see the way she fixed up this recreation room in the basement. She had to have these kids' interest at heart because she took them off the street and gave them some place where Virgil and his friends could meet. Now whether he and his friends at one time planned something down there that wasn't quite kosher when they were meeting is something that I don't know. But I know that the guns were found down there."

The incident of the guns—that was Virgil's one serious brush with the law, and in a sense, that, too, led to his death.

Undeniably Virgil was hiding guns in the basement. "The police came here," Mrs. Flenory remembers. "Some of the gang, they say somebody called them and told them that Virgil and them had guns. And they found guns. But after they found them, he went to court, and they threw it out. He had to pay $200."

"I talked to him then," says Ferguson, "and he said that the guys had asked him to hide these guns in the basement because they were scared. They were getting pressure from both sides—from the Souls and the Gangsters. They were caught in a pincers. I told him that this was silly. So he said that he wasn't personally getting involved in it and he had just let the guys keep the stuff in his basement. I believed him because I know the kind of pressures that develop in a situation like this where you're the only guy that's got a basement that's fairly accessible. And a guy has to live in a neighborhood. They're going to badger him and say, 'Gee whiz!' you know, 'Man, you've really changed! You don't care about us any more.' "

So Virgil hid his friends' guns out of a sense of loyalty. They had by now formed a loosely knit gang of their own called the Black Angels, designed for self-protection. And until the police confiscated them, they had guns. Mrs. Flenory did not entirely approve of all this.

"They had their own little group in this block to keep the boys off of them; I guess that's what they were trying to do," she says. "So I talked Brody [Virgil's nickname] into not having a gun, and I'm very sorry that I did that because I think that if he had had something to shoot back, I don't think the boys would have run him down like they did. Because they knew he didn't have nothing. He said, 'Well, Momma, if you don't want me to have a gun, I won't carry one.' That way they caught him out without anything."

It is arguable that private citizens, especially teen-age boys, should not undertake to defend themselves with firearms, but as Ferguson observes: "It depends on whose ox is being gored. If you're being shot at, then sometimes it might seem pretty reasonable to try to do something to protect yourself. From where we sit, as policemen, we cannot allow this sort of thing to go on."

But the blacks do not place great faith in the ability of the police to defend them. "The gangs be standing on the corner every night," says Mrs. Flenory. "You call the police, you know what time the police come? Two or three hours after they gone. The police promised to help Brody and them, and I don't think they did as much as they promised they would do."

Ferguson was in fact doing the best he could for Virgil and his friends, but after the Gang Intelligence Unit was reduced to 63 men, he could devote only a limited time to the 600 block of North Monticello. "You see, the difficulty where you have reduced manpower," says Ferguson, "is that you've got the same area to cover but with fewer men. I used to be able to stay right on top of a situation. Now maybe I wouldn't see the kid this week, and then something else would come up, and I would have to go on to another area where something more important was happening—more dangerous—and I might not get back to see these kids—you know, stay on top of this—for maybe a week or two weeks. Things can develop, and by the time you can get back, they can be out of hand."

If Mrs. Flenory has little faith in the police, she has less in the courts. She doubts that her son's killers will be adequately punished, and on the record, she is probably right.

"They got the fellow," she says. "They know who did it. Why don't they do something to him about it? I mean, if you kill somebody in self-defense, you got a right to fight for your life. But just to walk up and kill a person because he don't want to join a gang, and then the jury turn them loose to go out there and kill somebody else—I really don't think it's right. And then, if they turn him loose to kill somebody else and I go out there and kill him, they'll put me in jail. Because they got the money. They're robbing and stealing people, they got the money to get out."

But the courts are impaled on a dilemma. They must punish crime, and yet humanitarianism revolts at the prospect of a 20-year sentence imposed on a 16-year-old kid.

"There's going to have to be a recognition of the fact," says Ferguson, "that because of the youth of the individual, that does not necessarily mean that that individual cannot be thoroughly rotten. There's kids out in the street who are 16 or 17 years old where there would probably be some very grave doubt as to the possibility of rehabilitation. There are some kids that honestly deserve a decent chance—deserve a break.

But I don't think by any means you can say that every kid out there, just because of his tender years, is necessarily capable of rehabiliation because some of these kids are really hardened cases.

"I wouldn't like to be put down as coming out against the Juvenile Court authorities. But I would say this, that I would like to see some of the people who deal with these cases actually trying living in the areas where these situations take place. And I think that possibly it might change their outlook. There's nothing like coming face to face with a guy on a Saturday night when he's in the midst of his cups and he's feeling like he owns the world. He's a lot different guy than the guy who stands chastened before the judge on Monday morning . . .

"In so many of these cases, we'll see the same kids that go away and they'll stay away maybe six months, and they come back out and they're right back doing the same things again. In some cases they're victims who were forced into it by circumstances and by gang pressures. In other cases they are themselves the leaders. With many of these kids, it's very important that something be accomplished with them the first time they're picked up because, if they're arrested and they spend maybe six months away, then they come back out on the street. This increases their prestige with their other associates, and they usually come back with a kind of braggadocio attitude of: 'Yeah, they had me down there but they couldn't do anything with me. I'm back bigger and better than ever.' The more times a guy has been in jail and been back out, the greater his prestige is with that gang out there in the street because to them it means, 'They couldn't handle me.' There are kids walking the street today that have shot people in front of witnesses and killed them, and either witnesses were intimidated and the kids got off in court completely free or the kids, for some reason or other, served very short sentences."

Virgil's mother has not found much comfort in her encounters with either the police or the courts. She recalls the time when Virgil and his cousin, Darryl Coleman, were picked up for a curfew violation.

"Darryl and my son were standing on the corner. All the police had to do was tell them, 'Look, it's 10 o'clock; you go on home.' But they take them all the way to the station, call me up—I'm sick—I got to go down there to get him because he's standing on the corner at 10 o'clock. They kicked him in the back. I asked them, 'Why did you kick him in the back?' He said, 'I didn't kick him that hard.' And then they say, 'Well, you're supposed to trust policemen.' And he was on the corner. All they had to do was say, 'You go on, boy, it's 10 o'clock,' and brought him home. They didn't have to kick him.

"They picked my other son up for curfew right in front of his door. He said, 'My mother's right up here.' He was sitting on the porch. They took him down to the Audy Home, and I was out looking for him. I didn't sleep for a whole week, looking in every hole everywhere. They beat him up in the Audy Home down there. And I asked the judge about it. The judge say, 'Well, some of the kids need beating up.'

"When they took Virgil to jail, after he give the policeman the guns, they put him in the cell with some old boys, and *they* beat him up, knocked him all into the wire till they had to take him out of the cell.

"So if the kids go to jail, they're coming out bad. They stay there, they're coming out bad. And then they want the mother to tell the child, 'Don't you carry a gun' or 'Don't you carry a knife.' And if they catch him with one, they're going to take you to jail, and they're going to fine you . . .

"Then they say if you get bitter, it's wrong. But my child wasn't doing nothing, and they killed him. And they'll turn that fellow right back loose on the street."

Mrs. Flenory wants justice, instant and severe. Indeed, many city dwellers, both black and white, would like the police to impose a sort of martial law in the streets—bust heads, clamp down hard, anything to end the killings and beatings.

"That's very simplistic," says Ferguson, "because there just are no simple answers. We have to set an example of law because these are young people in the formative years, and if we go out and start stomping people and shooting guys on the street like in the old days, then how can we ask them to obey or respect the law?"

The law demands obedience not only in the street but in the courtroom, where gang members are peculiarly difficult to convict.

"We build individual cases when we can get the cooperation," says Ferguson, "but many times—well, there are a couple of attitudes that are taken by the people who are involved in these things. One of them is, 'Don't tell the police anything; we'll handle this ourselves . . .'

"And then the other situation is that there is a conspiracy of silence because many people are afraid to speak and tell the police because so many times we've had it happen that a kid goes to court, and whether he's found guilty or not, he still is eligible to make bond, and he's back on the street, and he's intimidating the witnesses, the people that have to bear witness against him.

"Some of these fellows are extremely dangerous, and they do have a tendency to do dangerous things, especially with the intimidation of witnesses. A guy who's arrested now has the right to make bond. I mean, that is his constitutional right. He goes right out. Now, he may not do it himself, but he'll go and tell his gang members, 'Okay, go lean on this guy and see that he doesn't show up in court.' And many of these kids, when they go to court to testify, they have really done some soul-searching because they've received threats on everything from themselves to their families, their little brothers and sisters, their mothers.

"It's not unknown for these guys to kick open a door on a family that's sitting at the dinner table and really blast through the house with shotguns. This has happened. Sounds like something out of the 1920s, I know. We had a little boy, 3 years old, who was killed in an instance like that over on the West Side in the Vice Lords' territory."

The danger from the gangs greatly restricts the life of

every resident in the black jungle. Mrs. Flenory laments these restraints upon her children.

"They don't get to go to much of the things that I would like for them to go to, to participate in their young lives, because the kids just won't let them have no fun, not unless we give something at home. And then when I give it at home, the kids come around here and then we've got gangs of police all out in the street. You can't hardly even give a party at home for the kids because the other boys are going to find out; then you've got a bunch of boys that you didn't invite. You know, you try to give out invitations to make sure you get the ones that you want to come, but some kind of way they get wind of it, and they come later on during the night. I try to end it between 11 and 12, but sooner or later they come around, and they drive down through the alley, shooting. They drive down the street, and they show the kids the guns. I really don't know what you do about it."

When she allows her children out of the house at all, Mrs. Flenory tries to make them walk in groups of two or three for mutual protection. If darkness overtakes them away from home, they must stay where they are for the night or come home in a cab. Her 15-year-old son Gary has been forced to drop out of school because of the danger from the gangs. So has the boy who lives downstairs. Mrs. Flenory plans to send Gary to California, as she once sent Virgil for a year, to escape the perils of Chicago's streets. Her eldest surviving son, David, has quit school at the age of 16 despite his mother's protests.

"I can't make him go to school," she says. "He says he's scared to go to school. He's determined to kill somebody if they bother him. So what do I tell the kids? My daughter, she's so nervous she can't even sleep. She has hemorrhages. She's scared to sleep because her bed is in the living room window, and she sleeps to the foot of the bed because she thinks somebody is going to shoot through the window. So what do I do with them? I've got six kids. I've got to keep them. But what can I do?"

A white family might simply move to a safer neighborhood,

but as a matter of practical reality, most blacks can live only in certain restricted areas of the city, and all of these are equally infested by gangs and equally dangerous. Many blacks can't face this reality.

"I've talked to people so many times," says Ferguson, "and they said, 'As soon as we get enough money together, we're going off of this West Side and go on the South Side.' You know, as if this was really Mecca. And in your mind you say, 'Oh, God, another one!' And you've got to tell these people: 'Look, you might as well face the future and do the best you can here because things are no better on the South Side. In fact, they're probably even worse because there you've got a number of gangs that are heavily entrenched.' And it's really a heart-breaking thing because sometimes they're doing the best they can. They're out there beating their brains out, trying to make it for their kids, and they live in dread every day that they come home that their kid is dead, he's shot, or he's got an eye put out or something like that. And they live for the day when they can get enough money together and move off the West Side and get to the South Side. And then the horrible realization comes on them one day that things are no better out south than they are out west, that all over the city it's the same thing. It must make these people feel like they're really trapped."

Mrs. Flenory knows full well that she is trapped . . . Her only choice is to stand her ground, to protect as best she can her children who survive, and to cherish the memory of her child who is dead. She always felt especially close to Virgil.

"I don't think I ever whipped Virgil but once or twice," she says, "and that was when he was very little. He never was any trouble. And he never had any trouble with the police until we moved over here—with the guns. He always tried to help things on his own. We'd confide in each other like sister and brother, but when it would come to things that he thought that I would worry about, he wouldn't say too much to me about it. Even the night he got shot, he didn't want them to call me. He gave the police his auntie's number for them to call her instead of me."

Perhaps no one will ever know for certain how Virgil spent the last hour before he was shot. Mrs. Flenory believes he went out to see his girl friend, who lived one block south on Monticello. He had abandoned his studies at Malcolm X and was working at Ryerson Steel.

"Usually after he got home from work and ate and had his bath," says Mrs. Flenory, "he would walk down there to see his girl friend because of course she was expecting, and I wanted him to spend as much time with her as possible because I know how it is with girls when they're expecting; the boys usually try and steer away from them, you know."

Virgil's girl friend was also endangered by the gangs. Earlier that night, they had caught her brother and beaten him unmercifully.

"The only time that they could catch Virgil was when he was going to his girl friend's house. And I think that night the reason they caught him was, the same night they had jumped on her brother and beat him up. His girl friend was going to the store. So I think he was following her to see that she made it to the store okay. And she heard the shot when the boys were shooting at Brody, and evidently Brody ran over near the trailers to try to hide from them, and they slipped up on him from behind."

Ferguson has pieced together a different account. The beating of the girl's brother had inspired new warfare between the gangs. Virgil's friends, afraid that they would be caught in the middle, asked Virgil to arrange a peace treaty. "Now this is strictly second-hand," says Ferguson, "but this is what I gathered out on the street: At the time that he was shot, he was conducting some kind of peace negotiations at this school. And something went wrong somehow, and he was killed."

They shot him in the back at 10 o'clock on a Friday night and left him for dead in the school yard. By rights, he should have been dead. The shotgun pellets tore through his chest, destroyed his right lung, and paralyzed him from the shoulders down.

Several people heard the shooting, but none reported it.

One girl was standing so close that she herself was wounded in the arms and legs. She ran home to her mother, who dug out the pellets. Neither one dared to notify the police. In a neighborhood like that, even the most common acts of Christian charity or civic duty can become unbearably dangerous.

So Virgil lay alone in the school yard, mortally wounded and calling for help, and no one came. At length he pulled out his address book and, on a blank page, wrote his final message, "Greg and Chap Dog killed me." [It should be noted that he wrote "killed me" instead of "shot me." He knew he would not survive.] Shortly thereafter, the police arrested two youths named Greg Vincent and James Chapman and charged them with aggravated battery. When Virgil died six days later, the charge was raised to murder.

At about 4 o'clock in the morning, a woman passed nearby and heard Virgil's cries for help. She reported him. The police reached him an hour or two later. They took him eventually to Cook County Hospital, and there his mother found him.

"I've heard so much about the County," she says, "but they were really beautiful out there. They tried everything possible. They worked with him around the clock. They had nurses around the clock, they had doctors around the clock, and they were really nice. I just wish there was some kind of way that I could let them know how I felt, the care that they really gave him. It really was very nice . . .

"They had all kind of machines that they could get to try to get that lung to working again. One lung was busted or something, and the doctor said they patched it up. The shotgun blast tore up the spine, and the bottom part of his body was completely shot. He wasn't passing any urine. And they said, by the body being tore up so bad, the good lung didn't want to take over.

"When I would go in, the first day after they operated on him, he would hold his hand up like that, as if to say, 'Momma, everything's going to be okay.' I think he still stuck it out to the end. He'd throw me a kiss, and while he was laying there, he would tell me—he couldn't talk, but he would tell me—'Momma, I love you.' But he had a bad hurting in his chest. . . ."

And presently he died.

They held Virgil's funeral in Hyde Park's First Unitarian Church, the same church where he had often sung with the Chicago Children's Choir. Christopher Moore, the choir's director, officiated. The choir sang two spirituals and the Sanctus in Paradisium from Gabriel Fauré's Requiem. The church was crowded with friends, both whites from middle-class Hyde Park and blacks from the jungle. Virgil's girl friend was there and fainted during the service. She and Virgil had planned to marry as soon as he could save enough money.

Virgil himself had once delivered a funeral oration in that same church.

As a result of his ties with the Children's Choir, he had been chosen to take part in a canoe trip in the wilderness of Canada and northern Minnesota. On that trip, another boy named Dale Carey had lost his footing on a rock beside a river and had fallen into the rapids. They did not recover his body until many days later. The disaster might well have demoralized the expedition had not Virgil rallied the members with his usual calmness and leadership. As always, his was the strength on which everyone else relied.

So it was considered appropriate that Virgil should speak at Dale's funeral. His remarks were tape-recorded . . .

In the beginning, one hears Virgil's leather heels, clicking across the marble floor to the lectern. Then Virgil's voice rises like an insubstantial spirit from the loudspeaker:

"To me, this was something I had never done. Everybody has walked on the streets of Chicago, on paved sidewalks, but not everybody has actually went through the woods. Everybody canoes in, maybe, Lincoln Park, but never 10 to 12 miles a day to get somewhere, maybe like the boys did that made our country.

"We all, it seems, were so enthusiastic about the whole thing. We tried our hardest to go the farthest, to make it, because we felt it was doing something. No more wars or nothing. When I say 'war,' I mean there was no war on the streets. The only thing we had to worry about there was the mosquitoes eating us. . . .

"They taught us how to row, how to get where we wanted to go and how to get the most out of the little that we had. We carried 15-feet canoes weighing maybe 75 pounds. We carried 65-pound packs on our backs across half-mile portages. We rowed day and night to get somewhere, to make it.

"And I know, to Dale—to all of us—it was something we had never done. Like I say, everybody has rowed in Lincoln Park, but nobody has ever rowed across a lake, a big lake, almost the size of Lake Michigan maybe, against the current, against the wind, rowing hard to get to the other side, to make it. And after you made it, after you're on the other side, you look back, you look behind you to see where you've been, see where you came from, and you say, 'I did that.' You don't do that in Chicago.

"I felt safe there because I knew I could walk through the woods without having to turn around and duck and dodge to keep someone from hitting me in the head with a brick or a bat. I felt safe because I knew that there weren't—I just felt safe. It's like a peace.

"Mothers and fathers holler about, 'Be quiet! I'm trying to rest!' Out there at night, you can't explain the peace, you can't explain the quiet. At night it got so we had to talk to ourselves all night until daybreak before we could go to sleep because it was so quiet. We walked outside the tent and looked up at the stars. Here in Chicago you may look up there and see one or two, but out there—a cluster. The sky was so clear that all you could see was white—clusters. It's something that I've never seen before, and I've traveled around with the choir. But way out there, it was something new, being a bigger person, a healthier person, and to come back and say to you what it was.

"Dale, it seems, took it in a larger way. He was always off by himself, looking, trying to find . . ." Here the tape becomes indistinct for a moment, and then Virgil resumes . . . ". . . sleeping in a tent, and the next thing you know, somebody is crying: 'There's something outside. I'm scared. I'm scared.'

I was scared too, but I wouldn't let nobody know it because someone had to be brave since everyone else was crying. I guess I had to be brave, but we all kind of stood up for each other. One day I was in a boat by myself and couldn't get to shore; they pulled me in. We all do the same for each other. The only thing we had to rely on was ourselves and what Jim and Ned taught us. And we helped each other out.

"What I'd like to say is, the country we were in wasn't dangerous at all. Everybody can understand an accident. They happen all the time. It was peaceful country, beautiful country, something I believe none of us had ever seen and really experienced. It gave you a chance to take a new look on life and see what the peaceful side is, away from the war, the guns, the scream of the sirens, away from the fog and pollution. It gave you a chance to stop and really look and see what things are.

"Everybody's been to the zoo and seen bear behind a cage, and everybody has seen a deer. But how many ever really stood maybe five feet away from it when it don't see you— just stand there and look at it, in the wild? It's not tamed or nothing. Just seen. And you say, 'Man, that's really something!' Go to the zoo and look at the cage. It's not the same.

"I'm talking about things that are for real. There's not much in this world that I feel today, from my own experience, that I believe is real. Everything is man-made. The only other thing in those woods I think I believe is real is a baby because that is something you can put together yourselves. You can't go to the store and buy one. Maybe some day they'll make that, too.

"And I'd just like to say that all this meant to Dale was something to do with peace. And I know that his greatest moments were when he went into the woods. That's where his thoughts were at peace."

Here Virgil ends, and all that remains is the sound of his heels as he walks away into the silence.

PART VI

PROPOSED REMEDIES

RACIAL *discrimination in the United States is a complex web of social processes. The previous selections all contribute evidence for the* structural *bases of these processes. The model of psychological reductionism, with one or more white bigots who as individuals racially discriminate against other Americans, is obviously insufficient. Worse, this too-simple but popular view of the problem leads us badly astray in our search for viable remedies to eradicate the phenomenon from American life.*

Structural processes, clearly, require structural remedies. The simple psychological remedy of changing anti-black attitudes first in order eventually to change institutional structures even turns out to be questionable psychology, not to mention sociology. For social psychological research has repeatedly demonstrated that attitudes are often most effectively altered by first changing social structure.[1] The new social environment typically elicits new behavior that is inconsistent with the old attitudes; and this creates a powerful pressure for attitude change. It is, then, a social psychological perspective as well as a sociological one that leads us to emphasize structural remedies in this final part of the volume.

The first three of the following selections provide concrete examples of proposed remedies that attempt to restructure institutional arrangements that presently discriminate against black Americans. Hardly exhaustive, these three varied proposals will, hopefully, stimulate the reader to think of further possibilities that would serve to counter the racist processes previously described in this volume. In Selection 24, Lester Thurow illustrates how an incentive system could be established for upgrading impoverished workers. Either through direct grants or tax credits, employers would be funded directly in proportion to their ability to raise an individual worker's income over a five-year period. Note how such a scheme would attack a variety of previously discussed black problems—unemployment, underemployment, and discrimination in pay and promotion.

Selection 25 describes a new design for elementary and secondary public education in urban areas. The Metropolitan Educational Park would draw its students from a wide attendance area across central city and suburban boundaries; thus it would greatly enhance both racial and social class desegregation. Both its advantages and disadvantages are discussed. The Metropolitan Educational Park idea needs federal incentives, too, and it has already received positive attention in Congress.

The Negative Income Tax, described by James Tobin in Selection 26, also requires federal enactment. And it, too, like Thurow's employment upgrading plan and the educational park, involves an attempt to shift the economic incentives away from its support of present discriminatory structures toward the support of new, more promising institutional structures. Tobin emphasizes that the negative income tax could not only significantly raise the floor of American poverty, but it could create financial incentives for remaining in the labor force and maintaining intact families where disincentives often operate today.

The volume concludes with a summary analysis of institutional racism by Robert Friedman. He describes four different types of discrimination against black Americans —structural racism, procedural racism, systemic racism, and ideological racism. Friedman cites numerous concrete examples of these various processes. And the reader will find his analysis helpful in organizing the documentation of racial discrimination provided throughout this book. Friedman's ideas, published here for the first time, also provide a useful model for designing further structural remedies for the elimination of America's most serious domestic problem.

An Incentive System for Upgrading Impoverished Workers*

LESTER C. THUROW

To give Negroes on-the-job experience, either direct grants or tax credits would be given to private firms, nonprofit institutions, state and local governments, or departments of the federal government, based on the amount by which they were able to raise an individual worker's income over a five-year period.

ELIGIBILITY REQUIREMENTS

Any individual whose income is below the maximum covered by the subsidy system would be eligible, with the following exceptions: (1) full-time students; (2) part-time students who do not work full time; (3) those who are within two years of their last year of full-time schooling or within two years of their last year of part-time schooling and part-time work; and (4) individuals over sixty-five years of age.

The first three restrictions are designed to solve the problem of entry into the labor force. Subsidies should not be given to individuals whose incomes are low because they are receiving training or entering the labor market. The two-year

---

* From L. C. Thurow, *Poverty and Discrimination.* Washington, D.C.: The Brookings Institution, 1969; Appendix I, pp. 191–196. Reprinted with permission of the publisher and author. Copyright © 1969 by the Brookings Institution, Washington, D.C. All rights reserved.

requirement should be waived for individuals from families with an income below the poverty line. The program would then have an impact on the problems of poor teen-agers not otherwise possible. Persons over sixty-five are eliminated because training is not the proper answer to their problems.

The program should not be limited to heads of households, but should be open to everyone, since limitation to heads of households will create the same problems as exist in the current welfare system. Such a limitation would encourage male desertion and the creation of female-headed households. To overcome the problem of females who are returning to work, a two-year work requirement should be instituted like that for teen-agers. To be eligible for the program, a married woman must have worked full time in the labor force for two years unless she comes from a family where the family income is below the poverty line. This would allow the program to have an impact on poor females without giving a big subsidy to white middle-class wives who are returning to work after their children leave home or go to school.

MAXIMUM INCOME LIMITS

Subsidies should be provided to encourage increases in income for all individuals who are now earning less than $4,000. This sum is high enough to allow the head of a family to lift his family out of poverty, but is still significantly below the median income for families with a year-round worker ($9,314 in 1967). Since the amount of subsidy per dollar of income increase will fall as income rises, the upper limit is not tremendously important. Most of the subsidy will be given for increases in income below the $3,000 level.

THE TIME PATH OF THE INCOME STREAM

Since calculating the increase in income eligible for a subsidy as the difference in income between the year previous to entry into the program and the fifth year of the program would encourage large income increases in the fifth year and low incomes in the first four years, the subsidy must depend on the average income over the five years. It is still desirable, however, to encourage an upward trend in income, since most income increases will not be reversible. Thus a weighted average should be calculated, with the fifth year weighted more heavily than the first year. I suggest the following set of weights:

Year	Weight
1	0.10
2	0.15
3	0.20
4	0.25
5	0.30

Income in the fifth year would thus be three times as valuable as income in the first year. To prevent firms from playing the system by juggling increases in income into a favorable pattern, there should be a requirement that the maximum annual increase in income be no greater than twice the minimum annual increase in income. This will force income increases to be spread over the period, but will still encourage firms to keep employees for the full five years. Wage payments in later years are more valuable to the firm than wage payments in early years. It is hoped that after five years the workers will be so integrated into the firm that very few will be discharged at the end of the program.

DEGREE OF PROGRESSION IN
THE INCOME SUBSIDY

Since the utility of increasing very low incomes is presumably greater than the utility of increasing relatively high incomes, a strong degree of progression should be built into the subsidy system.

For the first $1,000, 4 percent of the total subsidy should be given for each $100 increase in incomes; for the second $1,000, 3 percent; for the third $1,000, 2 percent; and for the fourth $1,000, 1 percent.

Thus of the total subsidy 40 percent would go for income increases from $0 to $1,000, 30 percent for increases from $1,000 to $2,000, 20 percent for increases from $2,000 to $3,000, and 10 percent for increases from $3,000 to $4,000. This kind of progression in the income subsidy payment constitutes a bonus to employers as an inducement to reach hard core groups and to make the initial hiring decision.

THE SIZE OF THE SUBSIDY

How large a subsidy should be given for raising an individual from an income of zero to a weighted average income of $4,000? If increases in income were constrained so that the maximum annual increase could be no more than twice the minimum annual increase, the smallest amount of income that would create a weighted average of $4,000 over the five-year period is $16,848. The time stream of annual incomes would be the following:

Year	Income
1	$1,053
2	2,106
3	3,159
4	4,212
5	6,318

Although this would be the minimum, most firms would pay considerably more, since it is doubtful that union and labor market restrictions would allow wage adjustments precisely tailored to the subsidy system.

To put the subsidy into perspective, the training costs of current government programs should be observed. Unofficial figures suggest that current Job Corps costs are about $5,000 per man (initially they were much higher) and that total costs under the Manpower Development and Training Act are about $6,500 per man-year of training, with costs per enrollee about $1,600; however, most programs do not last one year. These figures indicate that a rather large subsidy could be given without exceeding the costs of current programs, especially since the costs of the subsidy system are related to actual benefits while the costs of current programs do not necessarily result in any benefits. Thus there are no government risks of failure in the subsidy system. If failure occurs, there are no budgetary costs.

On the basis of these figures, I would suggest $5,000 as the proper subsidy for raising one man's income from $0 to an average of $4,000 over the five-year period. Five thousand dollars is less than one-third of the minimum possible income that can produce the maximum subsidy. In most cases the actual subsidy would be much less, since most individuals do not start at the zero income level. The subsidy could also be adjusted as experience is accumulated.

POTENTIAL COSTS

To obtain an idea of the maximum cost of such a program, I have calculated the subsidies that must be given over a five-year period if every individual in the labor force were brought up to an income level of $4,000. However, this is an overestimate of the actual costs, since not every individual is eligible and not everyone would be brought up to that level in five years. Based on the 1965 distribution of income, $64 billion would be needed. If a rough correction for program eligibility requirements is made by eliminating teen-agers, the elderly, and women who do not work full time, the costs fall to $40 billion, or $8 billion per year. More precise calculations could be made when and if a specific program has been agreed upon.

ENFORCEMENT

The income concept used for enforcement and for calculating the subsidy should be based on the personal income reported on the tax form. Enforcement then would require only a computer check of the income tax files to find income in year zero and the succeeding five years. To be eligible for the program the individual must file an income tax form in year zero, but withholding statements are available for all those who worked during the year.

No particular training programs should be required of industry or government. Any technique that allows increases in individual incomes would be acceptable. The subsidy would be based solely on ability to increase the incomes of the workers. It is not a subsidy for training labor but for increasing incomes. If this could be done without training or by upgrading other workers and creating vacancies, so much the better.

SPECIAL HANDICAPS

Should the subsidy differ for different groups of individuals, depending on the handicaps they face? Should a black worker with little education and a criminal record receive a larger subsidy than a worker with fewer handicaps? With progression built into the subsidy system, special categories would not need to be established. Workers with the most handicaps have the lowest incomes. The subsidies for increasing incomes would be largest for the lowest income groups. Thus the handicapped could be favored without appearing to discriminate in their favor.

TIMING OF PAYMENTS

The subsidy could be paid in annual installments, with the requirement that the books balance at the end of a five-year period.

JOB MOBILITY

If a worker changed jobs voluntarily, he would be eligible for another five years of subsidies with a new employer, but his initial income would be the last income which he received from the previous employer. Thus the new employer could receive subsidies only to the extent that he is able to raise the worker's income above its level with the previous employer. The old employer, of course, would receive a bonus based on how much he was able to raise the worker's income level. This provision is necessary to prevent immobility in the labor force and create competition for the workers in the program. Private industry risks from job mobility should be covered in the size of the subsidy rather than by preventing job mobility.

If a worker should be fired for not working satisfactorily during the five-year period, no subsidies would be given to the firm. This is a risk which the firm must bear. If a worker was fired because of a slack economy, the firm would be eligible to receive the subsidy coming to it for the time the worker had been employed, if it agreed to rehire the worker at the end of the recession and actually did so.

THE LAZY

What should be done about a worker who participates in the program for five years, quits his job, and then enjoys a period of idleness and poverty? Should he be eligible for the program again? I suggest that he be allowed to enter the program again, but not with the same employer. This would prevent sweetheart deals between the employee and the employer.

DEPRECIATED SKILLS

What should be done about workers who have been earning good incomes but whose skills become obsolete because of technical progress? How long a period of poverty should they be forced to endure before being eligible for the program? One year of low income should be necessary for program eligibility. This would guarantee that skills were really obsolete and that the costs of technical change were not simply being transferred to the federal government. In special cases where large numbers of workers become technologically obsolete, the Secretary of Labor could certify their eligibility.

CONCLUSIONS

There are as yet unrealized problems that would emerge during the detailed staff work in trying to design a practical system of income subsidies, but the problems are worth solving.

(25)

The Metropolitan Educational Park

THOMAS F. PETTIGREW

Public schools in the United States remain largely homogeneous both in terms of race and social class. In small cities and towns the remedies for public school separation are well known—district-wide redrawing of school lines within a district, the pairing of schools, careful placement of new schools, alteration of feeder systems, and conversion of more schools into district-wide specialized institutions.

As noted in Selection 15, the problem is most intense in the large central city, brought about basically by: (a) the antimetropolitan manner in which our school districts are drawn and operated; (b) the growing racial and class ecological divisions between central cities and their suburbs; (c) the depletion of the central city's pool of middle-class white children by large parochial and private school systems; and, finally, (d) the cynical and willful planning by major school systems to achieve maximum racial and class segregation. Here the techniques for heterogeneous schools in smaller localities are mere palliatives at best and counter-productive at worst.

One is led to consider new ways to structure our public schools in metropolitan areas which are not based on antimetropolitan, "neighborhood school" assumptions. Actually, these four basic reasons for the growing intensity of big city race and class segregation of schools provide the form and direction for future efforts. Thus large educational complexes drawing from wide attendance areas will be essential. These attendance areas will generally have to include both central city and suburban territory in order to ensure the optimal stable racial mix. The sites for these facilities must not only be convenient to the mass transit network but must also be on racially "neutral turf." Such locations would avoid immediate public labeling of the school as "white" or "black."

Racial specifications are by no means the only criteria for future remedies. Public schools in our largest cities have lost their former preeminence as the innovative educational leaders. Smaller communities are now the pacesetters. Thus the plans for the future should accent and facilitate innovation. Indeed, future public schools should possess facilities which could rarely be duplicated by expensive private schools if they are to compete effectively for the children of advantaged parents. Such arrangements, of course, will cost considerable money; thus a final criterion must be significant federal support of capital costs.

Several designs would meet these criteria; but let us consider one design as illustrative. Arranging our major cities with educational parks, each of which serves both inner city and suburban students, offers one basic plan—*the metro-*

politan park plan. Each park would be located on "neutral turf" in an inner-ring suburb or just inside the central city boundary, and it would be so placed that the same spoke of the mass transit system could bring both outer-ring suburban children into the park and inner-city children out to it. The attendance area of each park would ideally cut out a metropolitan pie-slice containing a minimum of 12,000 to 15,000 public school students, with the thin end of the slice in the more dense central city and the thick end in the more sparse suburbs.

But what incentive could generate the metropolitan cooperation necessary for such a plan? A number of systems have considered educational parks, but they usually find the capital costs prohibitive. Moreover, many systems are currently hard-pressed for expansion funds—especially as referenda for school construction bonds continue to be defeated throughout the nation. Federal funding will obviously be needed, though it must be dispersed in a more careful and strategic manner than the everybody-gets-his-cut, "river and harbors bill" principle of the 1965 Elementary and Secondary Education Act. As long as alternate federal funding for capital costs is available, many school systems—particularly those in bad faith—will not choose to join a metropolitan park plan. Therefore, future federal construction grants must involve more than one urban district and the consortium must always include the central city (note that any one park would not require the entire metropolitan area to join the proposal); must require racial and social desegregation—and, hopefully, integration—in every school involved (metropolitan involvement makes this requirement feasible); and must exclude alternate routes for federal building funds (though if the first two criteria are met, the proposal need not adopt the metropolitan park plan as the model).

A 15,000-student, $50- to $60-million park, 90 percent of it paid by the federal government, would be a powerful inducement. But is such federal funding possible in the near future? Nothing like the Vietnam war costs, of course, will now become available for the domestic scene. Yet a $2-billion-a-year school construction program—enough for building roughly 40 parks annually—is not unlikely during the late 1970s. Here lies both a great opportunity and an equally great danger. If the money is distributed in the easy fashion of the 1965 Education Act to individual school districts, the antimetropolitan effects could be disastrous for both race relations and public education. Federal building money spent in such a manner would further insulate aloof suburbia and institutionalize *de facto* school segregation in the inner city for at least another half-century. School construction money is likely to be made available by the federal government. The vital question is: What will be its form and effects?

The educational park idea is not a panacea; there can be elegantly effective and incredibly ineffective parks. Yet ample federal funding combined with the nation's planning and architectural genius should be able to set a new standard and direction for public schools. This combination has successfully been applied to public facilities ranging from interstate highways to magnificent airports. Now the combination should be applied to the benefit of children.

From high-rise structures to multiple-unit campuses, educational parks themselves can be planned in a variety of ways. The most widely discussed design would involve a reasonably large tract of land (80 to 100 acres as a minimum) and no fewer than 14 or 15 schools serving grades from kindergarten through high school. One educator has visualized a campus design for 18,000 students consisting of two senior high, four junior high, and eight elementary schools. In general, an educational park resembles a public university. Both include a variety of educational programs for a large group of students of varying abilities. And like public universities in our major cities, some parks could consist of high-rise structures and some could develop a more spacious campus atmosphere with numerous buildings. Hopefully, the metropolitan park could usually follow the campus model since sufficient space would generally be obtainable at suburban-ring locations.

Apart from offering racial remedies, the metropolitan park

concept has a number of distinct advantages. First, there are considerable savings that accrue from consolidation; centralized facilities, such as a single kitchen, need not be duplicated in each of the park's units. Savings on capital costs, too, would accrue from simultaneous building of many units at one location. These savings, however, do not necessarily mean that the total construction and operating costs would be less than those for the same student capacity spread out in traditional units. The advantage is that for essentially the same cost, metropolitan parks could boast significantly better facilities than traditional schools. Consequently, each child would be receiving far more per educational dollar in the metropolitan park.

The improved centralized facilities of the park should maximize innovations and individualized instruction. It is difficult to institute new approaches to learning in old settings. A prime finding of social change research is that new norms are easier to introduce in new institutions. The metropolitan park offers a fresh and exciting setting that should encourage new educational techniques and attract the more innovative members of the teaching profession. In addition, the park presents a rare design opportunity for building innovation into the physical and social structures of the schools. This, of course, includes the latest equipment for aiding the teacher and the student. Centralization enhances this process, for example, by providing efficient concentration of all electronic information storage, retrieval, and console facilities. The accent should be on individualized instruction as the unifying and positive theme—a theme far more possible in the park design than in the present model of scattered "little red schoolhouses."

Concentration of students also allows wider course offerings. Specialized classes, from playing the lute to seventeenth-century English literature, become economically possible when the students electing them are gathered from units throughout the park. Moreover, concentration makes possible some remarkable facilities that can be shared by all of the park's units—e.g., an Olympic-size swimming pool, extensive auditorium and theatrical equipment, etc. These special facilities could far surpass what is now available in all but the most affluent districts, become a source of student and community pride, and provide a competitive status advantage over private schools. They also would be used efficiently, in contrast to the minimal use that expensive facilities receive in single-site schools.

The metropolitan park offers unusual opportunities for an effective liaison with a local university or college. But direct contiguity is not necessary to develop a mutually beneficial coordination.

Recall that an important cause of public school segregation in many central cities is the enrollment of large percentages of white children in parochial schools. This fact suggests closer cooperation between public and parochial schools. The metropolitan educational park could facilitate such cooperation under optimal conditions. Most parochial systems are currently in serious financial condition. Tapping into the park's superior facilities should prove attractive. Roman Catholic educators point out that those items that cost the most—the physical science laboratories, gymnasium, and stadium—tend to be least related to the "moral training" that they believe to be the distinctive feature of their schools. Scattered-site schools, public and parochial, make "shared time" and other cooperative arrangements awkward at best. And when parochial students come to take their public school class as a group, such segregation often reaps its usual harvest of intergroup tension and hostility.

An idea from Vermont introduces a more promising possibility. At the time of planning a large educational park, Roman Catholic educators are provided the opportunity of buying an adjoining plot of land and constructing a new facility of their own. As long as the land price is consistent with its true value, no constitutional infringements appear to be involved. The new parochial facility need only concentrate on housing courses directly needed for "moral training." Parochial pupils would be free as individuals, not as separated groups, to cross the park's grass, not urban streets, and attend physical education, science, and other public school courses when they fit their particular schedules. The Vermont Plan offers construction and operating savings to hard-pressed parochial systems; and it offers a greater race and class student balance to hard-pressed public systems.

Cost efficiency, educational innovations, more individualized instruction, wider course offerings, special facilities, and coordination with universities and parochial schools—all of these advantages of the well-designed metropolitan park are features that parents, white and black, would welcome in the schools of tomorrow. This is politically critical, for desegregation efforts of the past have seldom come as intrinsic parts of a larger package promising an across-the-board improvement in education for *all* children.

In addition to the natural resistance to change, four major objections have been raised to the park concept: (1) excessive capital costs; (2) the phasing out of existing schools; (3) the problem of impersonalization in the large complexes; and (4) the loss of neighborhood interest and involvement in the school. Each is a serious objection and deserves comment.

The park *is* expensive, and major federal funding is necessary. Furthermore, mistakes in design and location could be disastrous. A park is an enormous commitment of resources, and, if poorly conceived, it could stand for years as a major mistake in planning. This is precisely what would happen if parks were operated totally within central city systems, for demographic projections prove the folly of building parks for a single central city system as a desegregation device. It is for this reason that the parks of the future must be *metropolitan* in character.

Present schools were expensive, too, and raise the problem of phasing out existing facilities. For many urban districts this is not a problem; they already have overutilized schools with double shifts and rising enrollments or old schools long past their usefulness. But some urban districts have many new schools and would be hesitant to join a park consortium. The program, however, is a long-term one. Hopefully, by the early 1980s most of the nation's leading metropolitan areas would boast one or more parks; these in turn could serve as models for completing the park rings in the decade.

Metropolitan parks, then, could be phased in as older facilities are phased out. Such a process would be ideal nationally, but there will be special problems in localities with "planned *de facto* school segregation." If racial progress is to be made in these cities, recent structures will have to be converted to new uses—perhaps to much-needed community centers.

The third objection to parks centers upon the impersonalization of organizational bigness—"the Kafka problem." Indeed, much of the park's description—15,000 students, a staff approaching 1,000, the latest electronic equipment—has a frightening Kafka ring; and one can easily imagine how an ill-designed park could justify these fears. But such a prospect is not inherent in the park plan; nor is bigness a park problem alone, for many of today's huge urban high schools accommodate many thousands of students in a single unit and arouse the same uneasiness. In fact, imaginatively designed parks could act to counter the urban trend toward ever-larger public school units. *Smaller* schools at each level can be economically built as units within the park; and careful planning can afford a reasonable degree of privacy for each unit while still providing access to the shared facilities of the park.

Some critics are particularly concerned about the park's loss of neighborhood interest and involvement. The criticism assumes that most urban public schools today are neighborhood-based, and that they generate considerable neighborhood involvement. Serious doubts can be raised about both assumptions; we may well be worrying about the loss of someting already lost. In any event, there is no evidence to indicate that only a neighborhood-based school can generate parental concern, or that there is a close and negative association between the size of the attendance area and involvement.

The criticism does raise an important planning issue: How can the park be initiated and planned to heighten parental and community interest? Certainly, the special facilities, the university liaison, and cooperation with parochial schools could help generate community pride and interest. So could smaller schools and a park school board of parents with wide authority short of taxing power. Furthermore, widespread use of the park for adult education, community affairs, etc., would also contribute to public involvement; indeed, the special facilities of the park lend themselves to such adult use more readily than does the typical school today.

Finally, one might ask how such a metropolitan educational park plan fits with other such widely discussed possibilities as "decentralization" and "community schools." First, it should be noted that decentralization and community control are typically advanced either apart from integration considerations or as outright alternatives to integration. Yet there is an obvious need in such large and unwieldy systems as New York and Chicago to decentralize authority, as well as a general need to increase parental and community involvement in public education.

Similar to compensatory education, however, these possibilities acquire force and meaning when they *accompany* the drive for integration rather than substitute for it. Thus, effective decentralization need not take the form of isolated social class or racial islands but should assume the metropolitan pie-slice shapes described earlier as ideal attendance areas for educational parks.

In summary, then, those who say there is nothing we can do about the educational segregation of our major cities are fortunately wrong. This is not to say that desegregation progress will be easy, or even that we will do what is necessary to achieve such progress. But it is to say that it potentially *can* be done for a significant number of urban Americans, white and black.

26

The Negative Income Tax*

JAMES TOBIN

The reduction of inequality in earning capacity is the fundamental solution, and in a sense anything else is stopgap. Some stopgaps are useless and even counter-productive. People who lack the capacity to earn a decent living need to be helped, but they will not be helped by minimum wage laws, trade union wage pressures or other devices which seek to compel employers to pay them more than their work is worth. The more likely outcome of such regulations is that the intended beneficiaries are not employed at all.

A far better approach is to supplement earnings from the public fisc. But assistance can and should be given in a way that does not force the recipients out of the labor force or give them incentive to withdraw. Our present system of welfare payments does just that, causing needless waste and demoralization. This application of the means test is bad economics as well as bad sociology. It is almost as if our present programs of public assistance had been consciously contrived to perpetuate the conditions they are supposed to alleviate.

These programs apply a strict means test. The amount of assistance is an estimate of minimal needs, less the resources of the family from earnings. The purpose of the means test

* Abridged from J. Tobin, "Improving the Economic Status of the Negro." In T. Parsons and K. Clark (eds.), *The Negro American*. Boston: Houghton Mifflin, 1965; pp. 462–469. Reprinted by permission of the author and of *Daedalus*, Journal of the American Academy of Arts and Sciences, Boston, Mass. Fall 1965, *The Negro American*.

seems innocuous enough. It is to avoid wasting taxpayers' money on people who do not really need help. But another way to describe the means test is to note that it taxes earnings at a rate of 100 per cent. A person on public assistance cannot add to his family's standard of living by working. Of course, the means test provides a certain incentive to work in order to get off public assistance altogether. But in many cases, especially where there is only one adult to provide for and take care of several children, the adult simply does not have enough time and earning opportunities to get by without financial help. He, or more likely she, is essentially forced to be both idle and on a dole. The means test also involves limitations on property holdings which deprive anyone who is or expects to be on public assistance of incentive to save.

In a society which prizes incentives for work and thrift, these are surprising regulations. They deny the country useful productive services, but that economic loss is minor in the present context. They deprive individuals and families both of work experience which could teach them skills, habits, and self-discipline of future value and of the self-respect and satisfaction which comes from improving their own lot by their own efforts.

Public assistance encourages the disintegration of the family, the key to so many of the economic and social problems of the American Negro. The main assistance program, Aid for Dependent Children, is not available if there is an able-bodied employed male in the house. In most states it is not available if there is an able-bodied man in the house, even if he is not working. All too often it is necessary for the father to leave his children so that they can eat. It is bad enough to provide incentives for idleness but even worse to legislate incentives for desertion.

The bureaucratic surveillance and guidance to which recipients of public assistance are subject undermine both their self-respect and their capacity to manage their own affairs. In the administration of assistance there is much concern to detect "cheating" against the means tests and to ensure approved prudent use of the public's money. Case loads are frequently too great and administrative regulations too confining to permit the talents of social workers to treat the roots rather than the symptoms of the social maladies of their clients. The time of the clients is considered a free good, and much of it must be spent in seeking or awaiting the attention of the officials on whom their livelihood depends.

The defects of present categorical assistance programs could be, in my opinion, greatly reduced by adopting a system of basic income allowances, integrated with and administered in conjunction with the federal income tax. In a sense the proposal is to make the income tax symmetrical. At present the federal government takes a share of family income in excess of a certain amount (for example, a married couple with three children pays no tax unless their income exceeds $3700). The proposal is that the Treasury pay any family who falls below a certain income a fraction of the shortfall. The idea has sometimes been called a negative income tax.

The payment would be a matter of right, like an income tax refund. Individuals expecting to be entitled to payments from the government during the year could receive them in periodic installments by making a declaration of expected income and expected tax withholdings. But there would be a final settlement between the individual and the government based on a "tax" return after the year was over, just as there is now for taxpayers on April 15.

A family with no other income at all would receive a basic allowance scaled to the number of persons in the family. For a concrete example, take the basic allowance to be $400 per year per person. It might be desirable and equitable, however, to reduce the additional basic allowance for children after, say, the fourth. Once sufficient effort is being made to disseminate birth control knowledge and technique, the scale of allowances by family size certainly should provide some disincentive to the creation of large families.

A family's allowance would be reduced by a certain fraction of every dollar of other income if received. For a concrete example, take this fraction to be one third. This means that the family has considerable incentive to earn income, because its total income including allowances will be increased by two-thirds of whatever it earns. In contrast, the means test connected with present public assistance is a 100 per cent "tax" on earnings. With a one-third "tax" a family will be on the receiving end of the allowance and income tax system until its regular income equals three times its basic allowance.

Families above this "break-even" point would be taxpayers. But the less well-off among them would pay less taxes than they do now. The first dollars of income in excess of this break-even point would be taxed at the same rate as below, one-third in the example. At some income level, the tax liability so computed would be the same as the tax under the present income tax law. From this point up, the present law would take over; taxpayers with incomes above this point would not be affected by the plan.

The best way to summarize the proposal is to give a concrete graphical illustration. On the horizontal axis of Figure 1 is measured family income from wages and salaries, interest, dividends, rents, and so forth—"adjusted gross income" for the Internal Revenue Service. On the vertical axis is measured the corresponding "disposable income," that is, income after federal taxes and allowances. If the family neither paid taxes nor received allowance, disposable income would be equal to family income; in the diagram this equality would be shown by the 45° line from the origin. Disposable income above this 45° line means the family receives allowances; disposable income below this line means the family pays taxes. The broken line OAB describes the present income tax law for a married couple with three children, allowing the standard deductions. The line CD is the revision which the proposed allowance system would make for incomes below $7963. For incomes above $7963, the old tax schedule applies.

Beneficiaries under Federal Old Age Survivors and Disability Insurance would not be eligible for the new allowances. Congress should make sure that minimum benefits under OASDI are at least as high as the allowances. Some government payments, especially those for categorical public assistance would eventually be replaced by basic allowances.

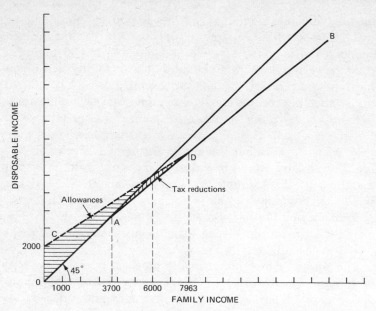

FIGURE 1. *Illustration of Proposed Income Allowance Plan (in dollars) (Married couple with three children)*

Others, like unemployment insurance and veterans' pensions, are intended to be rights earned by past services regardless of current need. It would therefore be wrong to withhold allowances from the beneficiaries of these payments, but it would be reasonable to count them as income in determining the size of allowances, even though they are not subject to tax.

Although the numbers used above are illustrative, they are indicative of what is needed for an effective program. It would be expensive for the federal budget, involving an expenditure of perhaps fifteen billion dollars a year. Partially offsetting this budgetary cost are the savings in public assistance, on which governments now spend five and six-tenths billion dollars a year, of which three and two-tenths billion are federal funds. In addition, savings are possible in a host of other income maintenance programs, notably in agriculture.

The program is expensive, but it need not be introduced

all at once. The size of allowances can be gradually increased as room in the budget becomes available . . . First of all, there is room right now. The budget, and the budget deficit, can and should be larger in order to create a tight labor market. Second, the normal growth of the economy increases federal revenues from existing tax rates by some six to seven billion dollars a year. This is a drag on the economy, threatening stagnation and rising unemployment unless it is matched by a similar rise in federal spending or avoided by cutting taxes. With defense spending stable or declining, there is room both for increases in civilian spending . . . and for further tax cuts. Gradually building an allowance system into the federal income tax would be the best way to lower the net yield of the tax—fairer and more far-reaching than further cuts in tax rates.

I referred to programs which make up for lack of earning capacity as stopgaps, but that is not entirely fair. Poverty itself saps earning capacity. The welfare way of life, on the edge of subsistence, does not provide motivation or useful work experience either to parents or to children. A better system, one which enables people to retain their self-respect and initiative, would in itself help to break the vicious circle.

The proposed allowance system is of course not the only thing which needs to be done. Without attempting to be exhaustive, I shall mention other measures for the assistance of families without adequate earning capacity.

It hardly needs emphasizing that the large size of Negro families or non-families is one of the principal causes of Negro poverty. There are too many mouths to feed per breadwinner, and frequently the care of children keeps the mother, the only possible breadwinner, at home. A program of day care and pre-school education for children five and under could meet several objectives at once—enriching the experience of the children and freeing the mother for training or for work . . .

[Much] Negro poverty in the South reflects the inability of Negroes to make a livelihood in agriculture. As far as the traditional cash crop, cotton, is concerned, mechanization and the competition of larger-scale units in the Southwest are undermining the plantation and share-cropping system of the Southeast. The Negro subsistence farmer has too little land, equipment, and know-how to make a decent income. Current government agricultural programs, expensive as they are to the taxpayer, do very little to help the sharecropper or subsistence farmer . . . Obviously there will be a tremendous burden on educational and training facilities to fit people for urban and industrial life. And I must emphasize again that substantial migration from agriculture is only possible, without disaster in the cities, in a booming economy with a tight labor market.

CONCLUSION

By far the most powerful factor determining the economic status of Negroes is the over-all state of the U.S. economy. A vigorously expanding economy with a steadily tight labor market will rapidly raise the position of the Negro, both absolutely and relatively. Favored by such a climate, the host of specific measures to eliminate discrimination, improve education and training, provide housing, and strengthen the family can yield substantial additional results. In a less beneficent economic climate, where jobs are short rather than men, the wars against racial inequality and poverty will be uphill battles, and some highly touted weapons may turn out to be dangerously futile.

The forces of the market place, the incentives of private self-interest, the pressures of supply and demand—these can be powerful allies or stubborn opponents. Properly harnessed, they quietly and impersonally accomplish objectives which may elude detailed legislation and administration. To harness them to the cause of the American Negro is entirely possible. It requires simply that the federal government dedicate its fiscal and monetary policies more wholeheartedly and single-mindedly to achieving and maintaining genuinely full employment. The obstacles are not technical or economic. One obstacle is a general lack of understanding that unemployment and related evils are remediable by national fiscal and monetary measures. The other is the high priority now given to competing financial objectives . . .

Negro rights movements have so far taken no interest in national fiscal and monetary policy. No doubt gold, the federal budget, and the actions of the Federal Reserve System seem remote from the day-to-day firing line of the movements. Direct local actions to redress specific grievances and to battle visible enemies are absorbing and dramatic. They have concrete observable results. But the use of national political influence on behalf of the goals of the Employment Act of 1946 is equally important. It would fill a political vacuum, and its potential long-run pay-off is very high . . .

The needed spending falls into two categories: government programs to diminish economic inequalities by building up the earning capacities of the poor and their children, and humane public assistance to citizens who temporarily or permanently lack the capacity to earn a decent living for themselves and their families. In both categories the nation . . . has the chance to make reforms which will benefit the whole society.

27

Institutional Racism:
How to Discriminate
Without Really Trying*

ROBERT FRIEDMAN

Let us begin with an example. Economic depressions do not occur because individuals desire or plan them. When I seek to protect my savings by withdrawing them from the bank, I do not intend to hurt anyone, least of all myself. But when others in the community decide similarly, the bank fails and we all lose. Trying to understand the perfidious coordination that resulted in our mutual impoverishment, we sense the presence of social laws no one passed. Folk wisdom decrees that if the outcome is bad, then it must have been caused by bad men. Conversely, if the men responsible seem good, then the outcome cannot be bad. But the equation is inadequate; phenomena like economic depressions teach us that social disasters can occur without anyone seeking harm.

Yet the dictates of folk wisdom have dominated thought about racial relations in the United States. The degree of racial inequality is seen to be a direct measure of the pervasiveness of bigotry and conscious discrimination. It follows that equality will result if only prejudice and intentional discrimination disappear. This analysis is increasingly incapable of accounting for what is happening in America today.

* This paper was specially prepared by the author for inclusion in the volume.

Even more frequently we observe patterns of black-white inequality which no one seems to have planned, or desired. The reduction of prejudice and legal discrimination over the past decades has not produced the across-the-board increases in equality folk wisdom would have us expect. In short, racial inequality seems to be becoming less dependent on individual choice. Rather than looking to the individual for the source of racial inequality, we must look to those forces which coordinate and direct individual attitudes and behavior in modern societies. Racial inequality, like economic depressions, must be explained in terms of the processes of human organization, their invisible laws and unique characteristics.

If societies were no more than collections of people whose encounters and actions, like those of molecules in a gas, were governed only by chance and the particular makeup of each particle, then one could simply sum individual actions to determine the social results. However, people in societies do not usually approach one another as whole organisms. Instead, common goals lead the way to collective action which, in requiring cooperation, impose certain fairly stable relationships upon members of the collectivity. In time, common definitions of goals and the division of labor dictated by social roles develop into a system of exchanges which binds one to another. The members of the society come to resemble, more than particles in a gas, atoms in a crystal. Each person is oriented to others in a way that makes all individual action depend on the "relevant environment." The structure of the crystal assumes a significance quite apart from its substantive makeup. So do systems of social organization assume independent life. It is only crystalline structure that differentiates a diamond from common graphite; so too, the structure of social systems can determine whether, given the same human raw material, a society is egalitarian or not.

The patterns of human relationship which force a collection of individuals into a working society—*the role or social structure of the society and its system of values and goal definitions*—are what we shall call institutions.[1] It is this system that ties the actions of one member to the actions of others.

Most American institutions were born and developed on segregated turf. Indeed, it was not until after 1915 that there came to be substantial numbers of blacks in the Northern United States. This means that blacks were not present in the North at precisely the time when institutions were most sensitive to demands upon them. Later migrations of blacks encountered a functioning institutional system with its built-in biases. Both geographic and demographic differences due to differing regional and historical background provided buffers which made institutional insensitivity to new needs all the easier to maintain. At the same time, the growing interdependence of dominant institutions made the failure of one to respond to black needs sufficient to prevent blacks from full participation in and benefit from virtually any. The normal devolution of institutional purpose inhibited the re-examination and questioning of institutional policies and norms developed by prejudiced men who had long since died or been replaced. Institutional pathology militates against basic changes in institutional configuration. And so, early patterns continue to maintain inequality even as the members of institutions become less anxious to preserve that inequality. "Maintenance of the basic racial controls," comment Louis Knowles and Kenneth Prewitt,

is now less dependent upon specific discriminatory decisions. Such behavior has become so well institutionalized that the individual generally does not have to exercise choices to operate in a racist manner. The rules and procedures of the large organizations have already prestructured the choice. The individual only has to conform to the operating norms of the organization and the institution will do the discriminating for him.[2]

Where causation is so diverse, it becomes futile to speak of racism in terms of intent. When we speak of institutional racism, then, we mean *any action, policy, ideology, or structure of an institution which works to the relative disadvantage of blacks as compared to whites, or to the relative advantage of whites as compared to blacks.* When the options allowed by the structure and function of institutions are exercised by one race so as to limit the choice of another, such operations constitute racism. Thus racism may be overt or covert, conscious or unconscious, intentional or unintentional, attitudinal or behavioral. It may be the result of malice or the best of intentions; it may be based on the direct apprehension of the race of a person or group, or it may be based on criteria only peripherally related to race; it may be the result of no more than apathy, ignorance, and inertia. And it is a phenomenon distinct from prejudice which denotes negative racial attitudes.

The mechanisms which produce racial inequality follow the lines of institutional development, co-opting over time those processes innocent of their perfidious purposes. It is not enough, then, to identify the institutional faces of racism. We must demonstrate the course of institutional diffusion racism has taken and show how blind social processes contribute to racial inequality.

We shall analyze four forms of institutional racism in America today: (1) *structural racism*, (2) *procedural racism*, (3) *systemic racism*, and (4) *ideological racism*. The most direct manifestation of institutional racism lies in the patterns of black participation in American social structure. Call it *structural racism*. These patterns in turn are governed by institutional policy and procedure—*procedural racism*. Both forms, characteristic of individual institutions, occur within the context of the social system as a whole. Composed of persons affected by other institutions and defined in terms of its functional relation to the whole social system, each institution becomes dependent upon the nature of its interaction with other institutions. As a social system matures, sets of institutions become so attuned to one another that the network begins to operate as a distinct subsystem, presenting a relatively unified face to the rest of the social system. We call these subsystems, such as government, business, education, and housing, *sectors*. The institutional mechanisms which sustain inequality have found their way into the differentiations of social purpose which define the interaction of these sectors. A third level of institutional racism can be identified in the interaction of these sectors as it limits black choice. This *systemic racism* is less obvious and more indirect than at lower levels, representing a deeper penetration of racial patterns into the path of American institutional growth. Finally, we may identify *ideological racism* that governs sectoral interaction much as institutional policy governs the patterns of black inclusion.[3]

LEVEL I: STRUCTURAL RACISM: HORIZONTAL AND HIERARCHICAL

Black participation within dominant institutions occurs within two chief structural modes: *horizontal* and *hierarchical*. The first involves the total exclusion of blacks from white institutions and their benefits, resulting in the development of parallel but subordinate institutions. The second is based on separation according to function and results in white-dominated institutions in which blacks fill defined institutional roles. Subordination is accomplished in the horizontal case by the dominant white institution's control of some sort of access on which the subordinate black institution depends; it is exercised in the hierarchical case by white occupation of controlling positions. Each of these structural modes acts to bias institutional policy, action, and effect. *Three factors are thus important to consider when evaluating institutional participation: (1) the manner of separation, (2) the means of subordination, and (3) the probable bias this structuring produces.*

The horizontal structural mode is most evident in business, the real estate industry, and professional institutions. Black business has grown to fill a void left by denial of services, and its constriction by small potential markets and the inaccessibility of credit prohibits large capital investments. Consequently, black entrepreneurs are overrepresented in the provision of services and underrepresented in manufacturing and the supply of goods. M. S. Stuart remarks:

"[The] American Negro has been driven into an awkward, selfish corner, attempting to operate racial businesses—to rear a stepchild economy. This is not a preference. Yet it seems to be his only recourse. It is an Economic Detour . . ."[4] Even so, the market on which the business is based is vulnerable to white expansion into ghetto markets.

A similar parallel structure is apparent in real estate where separate sources of housing, real estate brokers, and financial institutions serve the two racial groups. As the executive vice president of the National Association of Real Estate Boards (NAREB) said in 1945, "Colored real estate dealers have their place in the real estate field . . ."[5] And separate professional schools, institutional bases, professional associations, and clienteles have characterized black participation in most professions.

Once the black person enters into the dominant institutional structures, separation is achieved hierarchically. Subordination, of black interests is achieved by confining the black member to peripheral roles which leaves policy-making to those whose ties are to another community. If one ranks occupational categories according to average yearly income, the picture of hierarchical separation becomes clear. *In 1959, for each increase of $1000 in salary, black participation in the job category fell by 4.5 percent. By 1969 the percentage had fallen to 3.8 percent, due mostly to high-level gains. But the correlation remained constant at −.837, indicating that the relationship of black employment level was still strong.*[6] The general pattern is observed in business firms, civil service, the armed forces, and labor unions.

In some institutions both structural modes are apparent. School attendance betrays a horizontal pattern, while teaching and administration manifest hierarchical subordination.

While these structural modes characterize institutional structure well, change has occurred over the past decade. And this change has itself been patterned. *Horizontal separation has been breaking down fastest, especially where the criterion for segregation has been explicitly racial* (as in the professions and business) and not based on secondary criteria like economics and geography (as in real estate and schooling). The basis of horizontal subordination grates more harshly on American egalitarian ethics than does separation accompanied by differences in skill. In addition, horizontal change is faster because its remedy does not require substantial retraining. *Modification of hierarchical separation has tended to occur more frequently in newer institutions and in those characterized by relatively high educational levels.* Thus the electronics and aerospace industries have better desegregation records than rails and textiles; and the Air Force has more blacks than the older Navy.

The significance of structural subordination of black people is found in the relegation of a racial group to the margins of American institutional life and the limited provision of institutional benefits. But it is also found in the attitudinal and behavioral warping it produces in both racial groups, the racial blindness it induces by condemning different races to live in different worlds.

Gordon Allport suggests that interracial contact will result in positive attitude change only if the individuals participating are (1) of equal status in the situation, (2) striving for similar goals, (3) cooperatively dependent, and (4) operating with the sanction of authority.[7] Translated into institutional terms, these conditions become requirements: that there be enough members of both races that the mixture is perceived and neither group feels isolated or lost; and that both groups are represented proportionately at all levels so that there are no clear hierarchical differentials by race which create status, goal and dependency differences.

It is common to view prejudice as the necessary precursor of all discrimination. It should be clear from the above, however, that prejudice is the product of racist institutional structure, as well as its creator. Insofar as institutions structure black participation within them in contradiction of the Allport criteria, they mediate black-white conduct in such a way that racial hatred and distrust are the inevitable results. We suggest as a crude rule of thumb that an institution risks encouraging prejudice and discrimination to the degree that black participation within it falls below 12 percent (the current percentage of the nation's population that is black) in each occupational category. According to this criterion, virtually every American institution qualifies as racist.

LEVEL II: PROCEDURAL RACISM

In biasing institutional policy as well as individual attitudes and behavior, structural racism enhances its own survival. Yet the morphological patterns could not sustain themselves without the policies and procedures of institutions which dictate the limits of black participation. Compared to this procedural racism, structural patterns seem passive.

Some faces of procedural racism reveal themselves readily, but others draw cover from the complexities of institutional life. Time, organization, abstraction, and a plurality of other concerns intervene to endow institutional acts with unintended effects, some of which work to the relative disadvantage of black people. Since institutional procedure tends to be keyed to relatively objective traits of persons, rather than dealing with individual human beings in their totality, policies which is effect discriminate against blacks may be predicated on other (though ultimately derivative) grounds. Thus, unequal treatment may result from primary distinctions based on race *qua* race, or from secondary distinctions based on economic or educational status which are affected by race.

The institutional procedures most directly responsible for the patterns of black participation are those concerning inclusion and exclusion of black people. We identify six categories of this sort of restriction—three forms of "primary" restriction, and three forms of "secondary."[8]

The most blatant form of procedural racism is aimed at excluding blacks from institutional roles purely because of their color. Member boards of NAREB have a long record of excluding blacks in this manner. Labor unions have used exclusion by constitutional provision,[9] the establishment of segregated locals,[10] collusion with employers, long-standing refusal to accept blacks into apprenticeship programs, and informal agreements not to sponsor or vote for black applicants.[11]

Often where blacks are admitted into an institution, they occupy marginal jobs from which they may be fired during times of high unemployment to allow for continued white employment. This "discriminatory retrenchment" is partly responsible for the fact that since the early 1950s increases in unemployment have hit the black community twice as hard as the white. The establishment of "auxiliary" locals which are subject to jurisdictional raids in hard times is a similar process used by unions.[12]

With increasing pressure toward reducing exclusion, camouflaging the actual situation has come to play an important role. "Tokenism"—the inclusion of a few well-trained, middle-class blacks in visible positions—often obscures exclusion, both from outsiders and insiders.[13] The size and differentiation of large institutions allow even sincere nondiscrimination promises at high management levels to devolve into active discrimination at the strategically important lower levels. Herbert Hill argues that the willingness of the AFL-CIO to attest to egalitarian principles contrasts sharply with their reluctance to end discriminatory patterns,[14] a fact which caused the first chairman of the AFL-CIO Civil Rights Committee to resign in frustration.[15] Another type of camouflaging is found in the shifting of a few black workers from job site to job site on federally financed building projects, giving the illusion of equal employment through "checker-boarding."[16]

Secondary forms of restriction are less obviously racist than primary forms. Thus the nepotism common to the selection, promotion, transfer, and referral of union members is not predicated on racial considerations but works as effectively as the grandfather clauses of old to keep unions lily-white.[17] Less indirectly, institutions exclude blacks from membership on the basis of characteristics determined by the action of other institutions. By charging high initiation fees, unions reduce black membership by virtue of the race's relative poverty;[18] by advertising only in major (white) newspapers, employers virtually assure low black response; by stressing educational requirements, employers exclude blacks because of educational deficits.

The increasing reliance placed on "qualifications" in hiring has introduced a great new source of techniques for excluding blacks. In general, the more qualifications to be met, the more easily and covertly members of a race traditionally denied the chance to qualify can be further denied. Such screening can be innocent or malicious. Thus we note that since 1964 the pressure to integrate unions has resulted in a proliferation of apprenticeship tests in an obvious attempt to limit black membership,[19] while a well-meaning effort to improve the quality of police can result in the raising of qualifications and the diminution of black officers.[20]

In providing services, the dominant institutions of our society also treat the races differently. There are three varieties of primary procedures which result in the provision of different service: (1) the denial of service, or its rendering only on a completely separate basis, (2) the misrepresentation of the costs and prerequisites of service, and (3) less effective service. A prime example of the first category is the NAREB, which only admitted its responsibility to serve blacks *at all* in 1945.[21] Since then the service provided by realtors to black people has been separate and unequal. In 1961, for example, the U.S. Commission on Civil Rights reported that only 3 of 60 realtors in Palo Alto, California, would sell homes to blacks in white neighborhoods.[22] Financial institutions, insurance companies especially, refuse to extend loans to black people for homes in white neighborhoods and frequently in black neighborhoods.[23] Similarly, employment agencies tacitly identify jobs as "white" or "Negro," and act accordingly.[24]

Misrepresentation of the costs and prerequisites of service is another source of unequal service. Instead of explicitly refusing to sell homes to black homeseekers, realtors may tell the black would-be buyer that no homes are available, quote different sales terms, or show homes on different terms. (See Selection 6.) Financial institutions more often require security deposits from blacks, more often have blacks sign land contracts for their deeds, lend money for shorter periods, charge higher rates of interest, and require larger monthly payments.[25] Unions often fail to treat members equitably in terms of seniority privileges, lay-offs, promotion, transfer, recall rights, distribution of overtime and desirable work shifts, and eligibility for vacation and welfare plans.[26] School systems often distribute supplies, books, facilities, and maintenance so that predominantly black schools get less.[27]

Secondary procedures which deny black people equal benefit from institutions supplement the primary ones. Zoning practices of suburban governments limit black residential mobility by requiring large lot sizes, limiting buildings to single family houses, excluding housing whose floor area or cost falls below a given minimum, thereby raising prices beyond the means of most blacks.[28] Building codes may be similarly invoked, as the testimony of a Philadelphia builder indicates: "If I sold just one suburban home to a Negro, the local building inspectors would have me moving pipes ⅜ of an inch every afternoon in every one of the places I was building."[29]

Economic differentials are often translated into differences in the administration of justice. Because blacks can less often afford to pay bail or hire their own attorney, they must show up in court in prison clothes which tend to bias juries, and proceed to be defended by often inexperienced and overworked public defenders or court-appointed attorneys. Cultural clashes—modes of speech, dress and behavior—add to the relative disadvantages of blacks in the halls of justice.[30] Other deprivations of service based on secondary criteria can be noted in virtually every American institution.

Two major trends in procedural racism emerge. *First, the forms of procedural racism tend to be most numerous in those institutions where the determination to resist racial change has been most intense* (e.g., union exclusion and housing discrimination) *and where practices are most subject to public view* (e.g., business employment and government). Institutions, it seems, share with insects a basic insight: Great fertility can overcome a high mortality rate. *Second, the sixties witnessed an increasing reliance on secondary forms of exclusion and differential service.* The opening of the apprenticeship detour, the proliferation of tests, the raising of employment standards, the increase of screening techniques, strict reliance on geographical districting—all point to this trend. As black demands have become more strident, our analyses of the problem have become more sophisticated, fair employment practices commissions more numerous, egalitarian sentiment more widespread, and more direct and blatant discriminatory practices increasingly unworkable.[31] Such pressures have led to disguised and more intricate techniques as often as they have to more equitable ones. This retreat to the more distant trenches is not necessarily a measure of deviousness. Secondary supports for racism were always around; their increased role often reflects nothing more than the elimination of direct techniques.

The existence of these two trends leads to a significant conclusion: *Insofar as challenges to racism focus on specific procedures on a case-by-case bias and emphasis is placed on the genesis of racist procedures rather than simply on their results, one can expect procedural fertility and trench warfare to make victories pyrrhic.*

LEVEL III: SYSTEMIC RACISM

Structural and procedural racism are adequate explanations of racial inequality only to the extent that individual institutions and sectors are independent of one another. The increasing presence of secondary forms of procedural racism belies the existence of this independence. We must investigate the interaction of the major institutional sectors—government, housing, business, education—in order to determine the role of "systemic" relations in sustaining inequality.

The degree and nature of sectoral interdependence is constantly changing. Around the turn of the century, when college and even high school education was a scarce commodity, employment patterns were far less dependent on educational profiles than they are today. Similarly, as recently as thirty years ago the rural and Southern nature of black residence precluded employment, not metropolitan segregation.

Consider, for example, the impact of racial housing patterns in metropolitan areas on black occupational distribution, educational achievement, and political power. There is perhaps no other sector of American life where whites and blacks are so completely separate as in their places of residence. Karl and Alma Taeuber calculated that for 1960, 86 out of every 100 nonwhite families living in our central cities would have to move to another block in order to achieve random distribution,[32] a pattern that has increased during the past decade.[33] (See Selections 3, 4, 5, 6, and 7.)

Four patterns of black metropolitan residence emerge. The first involves the concentration of black people within the central city of a metropolitan region, and within particular areas of that city.[34] The second includes the growth of core cities which resemble the central city in almost every way save age, history, and the fact that the Bureau of Census regards them as suburban. Thus, for instance, Oakland, Berkeley, and Richmond have come to encompass roughly half (49.1%) of the black population of the San Francisco Bay Area, as compared to San Francisco's 30.3 percent.[35] Together the four core cities contain 79.4 percent of the Bay Area's black population, leaving those cities 21.7 percent black and the remainder of the nine Bay Area counties 2.7 percent black. The core city-suburban boundary represents not only a racial dividing line, but also a socioeconomic gradient. Since 1950, average city economic and educational levels have fallen relative to suburban levels.[36]

Though census statistics imply that suburban blacks are residentially "integrated," the large majority are not. A study of San Francisco housing patterns concludes: "The fact is that most minority families living in the suburbs are in enclaves as ghettoized as are the residential locations of minority families in our central cities."[37] *City* magazine estimates that two-thirds of Philadelphia's black suburbanites and 41 percent of Denver's reside in such enclaves.[38] In 1968 there was a higher percentage of black people in poverty in the suburbs (28%) than in the cities.[39] The rise of these "suburban black belts" constitutes the third major pattern of black residence.

The final form of racial residential patterning involves the token sprinkling of wealthy and highly educated blacks in the more exclusive suburbs. Since the numbers are small and there is little threat of racial takeover, this form of "integration" is analogous to tokenism in business.

There is a widespread misconception that racial segregation is the offspring of economic segregation. Although, on the average, black people make less than whites, there is a considerable overlap in incomes which, save in the case of suburban sprinkle, does not find residential representation. The Taeubers compared hypothetical segregation indexes based solely on economic criteria to actual patterns and found that there was no significant stable relationship between them. In a majority of the cases, economic criteria could account for no more than 30 percent of the racial separation.[40]

Concentrating black residence in defined areas has direct consequences. (See Selection 9.) It increases the ease with which the white community can ignore black Americans and the effects of the social system in this regard; it raises the cost of housing to black people by restricting access; it limits black mobility; and it increases white prejudice.[41] More important, perhaps, residential patterns provide the geographic context in which the economic, educational, and political institutions of the modern metropolitan area must operate.

A study of housing and job patterns in the San Francisco Bay Area concludes: "A direct cause and effect relationship exists between territorial separation of the population on the basis of ethnic grouping and their social stratification in terms of income and occupations."[42] Indeed, new jobs are precisely in those areas where black people are denied residence. Eighty-three percent of the 550,000 new jobs added in the Bay Area between 1958 and 1968 were located outside the four core cities where 80 percent of the region's black population lived.[43] And projections suggest that 63 percent of the new jobs in the next decade will be located outside the four core cities.[44] Moreover, many of the new suburban jobs are entry jobs like manufacturing and transportation— ones that require few initial qualifications—while new core city jobs are largely white collar.[45]

It is important to realize that insofar as "suburb" connotes primary dependence on the central city, many "suburbs" have ceased to exist. Five of the nine Bay Area counties employ over 80 percent of their residents within county lines, and every county provides jobs for a majority of its residents.[46] Commuting provides no immediate answer. Not only is it prohibitively expensive and time-consuming, but the design of the systems militates against reverse commuting by blacks. Primary emphasis has been placed on highway development which puts the poor at a disadvantage. Furthermore, rapid transit systems, like the Bay Area Rapid Transit System, are usually designed to carry the white suburbanite to his core city job and are often inadequate for reverse commuting.[47] New geographic barriers have thus risen to maintain old employment patterns.

Moreover, residential segregation is becoming increasingly responsible for maintaining a segregated school system. (See Selection 15.) As long as residence remains the basis for school composition, the educational system will continue to map socioeconomic and racial separation into educational inequality. (See Selections 14, 15.)

In concentrating the black population, residential segregation funnels black political power. At the same time, by over-concentrating the black vote in certain areas, residential segregation can often act to minimize the effect of the black vote. (See Selection 19.) Donald Canty, editor of City, notes: "Concentration of blacks and minorities greatly simplifies exploitative gimmicks such as gerrymandering and contains their power at a level well below the point where important political decisions are made."[48]

The concentration of the bulk of black people and other minorities within the core cities will tend to increase minority political power within those bounds, but county boundaries may well serve to insulate whites and their institutions from the demands of black constituents as no other mechanism could. Since many government functions are financed by local taxes, black core city residents are being left with a political domain at the same time the tax base is eroded by the flight of wealthier whites and industry to the suburbs. The increase in suburban vested interests meanwhile militates against tax sharing, school integration, or similar metropolitan cooperation.

In the next decade our metropolitan areas will grow and most new housing will be built in suburbia. In such growth and in the ever-present intra-area movements lie the potential for integrating metropolitan regions and thereby educational, business, and political institutions. Yet it is likely that the housing patterns established in the last thirty years of unparalleled expansion, Northern black migration, and massive governmental financing will not be changed for decades to come. In such a situation the promise of equality is vested in the capacity of other sectors to effect institutional equality despite residential barriers. The National Committee Against Discrimination in Housing's study of the New York Metropolitan Area concludes:

The only rational solution lies in comprehensive metropolitan-wide planning and programming which embraces all of the economic, social and political factors affecting community life: housing, education, training, employment, health, transportation, cultural amenities, economic development, and—above all—human dignity.[49]

LEVEL IV: IDEOLOGICAL RACISM

Forged early in the development of an institution and only reforged during periods of crisis, institutional ideology plays a central role in determining the structure and function of institutions. Through it the institution defines, explicitly and implicitly, its social function and relationship to the rest of the social system. Because it is embodied in no particular action or structure, the basic ideology guides the formation of policy but remains relatively impervious to changes as long as they are not systematic.

I go to the employer and ask him to employ Negroes, and he says, "It's a matter of education. I would hire your people if they were educated." Then I go to the educators and they say, "If Negro people lived in good neighborhoods and had more intelligent dialogue in their families, more encyclopedias in their homes, more opportunity to travel, and a stronger family life, then we could do a better job of educating them." And when I go to the builder he says, "If they had the money, I would sell them the houses"—and I'm back at the employer's door again, where I started to begin with.[50]

The late Whitney Young's experience as related above is neither uncommon, nor is it the mere dodging of responsibility. Rather, the circularity derives from the interlocking of institutional ideologies. It is this interlocking of the orientations of the real estate industry, business, labor unions, the school system, and government that causes the interaction of sectors to subordinate black people.

Reviewing her interviews with Chicago realtors, Rose Helper observes: "The interviews indicated to me that the respondents' racial practices are the logical outcome of a group of related ideas, values, beliefs, and principles—that is, the racial real estate ideology."[51] The cornerstone of this ideology is the belief that when an individual buys a home, he buys a neighborhood, a school, and a government as well, and that the realtor is therefore responsible for the character of the community. The major index for determining the quality of a neighborhood is the value of property. And in the field of real estate, the concept of value has become inextricably bound up with the principle of homogeneity. Homogeneity of educational, economic, ethnic, even temperamental characteristics of residents has come to be seen as the primary determinant of residential area value and stability. Real estate appraisers translate the homogeneity doctrine into monetary terms, invert the causation, and transform the doctrine into a self-fulfilling prophecy.

As race becomes subject to the homogeneity guideline, the general real estate ideology becomes specifically racist. Neither the NAREB nor the American Institute of Real Estate Appraisers have ever recognized economic, educational, or social distinctions among black people to the extent that these characteristics balance the racial determinant. Until 1950, Article 34 of Section III of the NAREB's Code of Ethics—the "Homogeneity Article"—specifically prohibited sales to black people of housing in white neighborhoods, based on the belief that this would lower property values.[52] Though the article was changed in 1950 because it was becoming embarrassing, an interpretation of the change printed at the time in *Realtor's Headlines*, NAREB's newsletter, illuminated the dodge: "While the qualities of property and its utilization are subject to the provisions of the article, any questions as to its habitation is subject only to local determination in accordance with local practice."[53] Thus realtors were urged to follow traditional practice.

The hold the real estate ideology exerts over the housing industry is all the more exceptional as repeated studies suggest that the homogeneity principle is based partly on myths. Luigi Laurenti, for instance, found in a study of 1.3 million homes in seven major cities that in only 15 percent of the instances where blacks entered a white neighborhood did property values actually fall. In 41 percent of the cases, property values stayed within 5 percent of control group prices, and in 44 percent the values actually rose.[54] Nor are white attitudes as negative to having black neighbors as the ideology assumes.[55] (See Selection 8.)

As long as blacks live in areas geographically distinct from white areas, the small size of government jurisdictions, insofar as they are independent, tend to increase racial inequalities. Yet the American political commitment to local autonomy is old and fundamental. Alexis de Tocqueville

noted that "in general the prominent feature of the administration in the United States is its excessive decentralization."[56]
Though it is over 130 years since de Tocqueville toured the
United States, history has vindicated his judgment. Parochial autonomy is still defended in an age where economic,
political, and social systems obviously transcend county
boundaries. Nowhere has the effect of America's small town
origins been more obvious than in the field of education. The
image of "the little red schoolhouse" is central to the ideological focus of segregationists on "the neighborhood school"—
as discussed in Selection 15.

Once the institutional ideology of our school system has
mapped residential separation into educational equality,
business ideology takes over, transforming educational inequality into economic differentials. Corporation managers
increasingly see themselves as professionals whose decision-
making is guided by "scientific" considerations and the
dictates of "economic rationality."[57] Explicit sets of qualifications for hiring and promotion replace individual discretion
in the belief that such objectivity will surely pick out the
best men for the right positions. This set of beliefs sees the
intrusion of noneconomic criteria into decision-making as
contrary to the best interests of the corporation and, indeed,
of society as a whole. Yet the fact remains that under such
hiring criteria, most black applicants, having been denied
access to the prerequisites, are excluded from decent jobs
by the "objective" criteria.

The institutional ideology that excludes blacks from labor
unions derives from particularism almost completely opposite to the universalism that excludes them from large
corporations. The belief among union members is that first
and foremost unions exist to protect their interests: to shield
them from unemployment, to maintain the status of their
occupation, to provide them with a desirable social peer
group. To the extent that these objectives militate for a
relatively closed and exclusive membership, they tend to
keep predominantly white unions white.

Adherence to the homogeneity doctrine produces residential

segregation; governmental localism exacerbates differentials in community welfare; school boards' commitment to geographical districting converts geographic inequality into educational discrepancies; business' faith in economic rationality excludes blacks because of the educational system's shortcomings; and the contained self-interest of labor unions makes traditional social lines an employment barrier. The interlocking of institutional ideologies constitutes an especially "vicious circle." Note that because racist elements are embedded in the most intimate conceptions of social role and principles of institutional operation, these ideologies are not only not recognized as racist but are legitimized as fundamental institutional orientations. The blindness to alternate orientations that ideology engenders leads institutions to deny responsibility for their contributions to the vicious circle. The cry *de facto* has become an eloquent sociological indicator of our times.

However convinced institutions are of the validity of their ideological orientations toward other sectors, the fact remains that there are alternatives. The homogeneity doctrine is largely a self-fulfilling prophecy, though the laws of the market will certainly reserve the most desired residential areas for the wealthy. The determination of the scope of jurisdiction at various levels has been an ongoing one in American history; the federal government's metropolitan sewage grants have shown that metropolitan cooperation is possible given proper incentives, and certainly the establishment of regional governments is not unthinkable. Segregation in schooling need exist only insofar as redistricting, building plans, feeder arrangements, busing, and the existence of specialized district-wide institutions are not used to reduce intracounty segregation, and concepts like that of the metropolitan educational parks are not utilized to reduce metropolitan segregation. (See Selection 25.) There is evidence which suggests that job qualifications for many positions are inflated, and little evidence which indicates that job training and retraining could not produce black employees with adequate skills.[58] (See Selection 24.) Finally, in an expanding labor market, union self-interest need not lead to black exclusion.

That a racist interlocking of institutional ideologies exists does not mean it has to exist. Each institutional sector has the capability—and the responsibility—to break the vicious circle.

ACROSS THE GREAT DIVIDE

In the mid-sixties, Governor Andrew Brimmer of the Federal Reserve Board argued that while the upper two-fifths of the black population were making rapid progress toward equality, the poorer three-fifths were, at best, maintaining their position.[59] In 1970 he found these trends continuing. "Within the Negro community," he concluded, "there appears to be a deepening schism between the able and the less able, between the well-prepared and those with few skills."[60] Occupational patterns, income distribution, and educational trends all manifest the growing schism.

Brimmer's findings, generally ignored, undercut unqualified optimism regarding the progress of our society toward equality. The trends are unexpected; and they have thus far remained unexplained largely because they can only be accounted for in terms of current institutional configurations of racism.

The deepening schism marks not the segmentation of the black community, but the widening of a division that has existed almost from the time black people began migrating north. For, while almost all blacks were poor, they were not homogeneously so. There existed a relatively well-defined black middle class as early as the 1940s.[61] What made the black middle class distinct, however, was not the small income differences but the fact that its position rested on an identifiable institutional base. Composed primarily of black professionals and the owners and managers of black businesses, the "black bourgeoisie" owed its existence to the parallel institutional structures which evolved as a result of horizontal exclusion.

Now the horizontal modes of separation and subordination in business and the professions are breaking down. The number of black businessmen employed in black businesses shrank by one-fifth from 1950 to 1960. The four years from 1964 to 1968 saw the number of black students in predominantly white colleges double. And in the professional world, far from being excluded, "qualified" blacks are sought after. Even housing restrictions for affluent blacks are lifted as they take part in the suburban sprinkle. This skimming off of the black middle class into dominant institutions raises black salaries to white levels, but it scarcely affects the nature of the work of those involved.

The pattern of the changes in structural racism, the deterioration of horizontal subordination, and therefore of hierarchical subordination at the highest levels, has been shaped by the nature of the attacks on procedural racism. The aim of policy has been to promote "equal opportunity"— color blindness—in the procedures by which institutions determine membership. In a country that has come to believe, by and large, in the equality of the races and in meritocratic hiring and promotion, the principle of equal opportunity fits nicely. In fact, economic rationality demands no less.[62] Parallel institutions whose separation was based on differences in color bore the brunt of the attack. High-level integration was speeded by the more liberal complexion of the professions and newer businesses.[63] But by concentrating only on primary forms of discrimination, the equal opportunity approach rarely challenges those subtle forms of procedural racism that stemmed from sectoral interdependence, accepting the lack of qualifications as an adequate justification for racist structural patterns. It affects only the already qualified and does little to change the forces which keep most of the black community unskilled and unqualified.

Meanwhile the systemic forces which impoverish the lower-class segments of the black community have gathered strength. Where there had been only one circle—a vicious one, there·are now two—one benign, the other all the more vicious for its invisibility. The increasing isolation of blacks in core cities and suburban ghettos concentrated those blacks who could not escape where they were least likely to reach entry level jobs, interracial schools, and effective political power. At the same time, the growth of skill barriers and the increase in sectoral interdependence made it harder than ever for the poor and unskilled to break into the mainstream of American society.

For those blacks who were not already as qualified as their white countrymen, the equal opportunity emphasis on color blindness not only did not help but actually retarded their progress. By underlining qualifications and merit, the approach strengthened the interlocking of institutional ideologies. In stressing process rather than end-state, the forces of change allowed procedural fertility and systemic interactions beyond the field of vision to undercut isolated victories. And by indicating a case-by-case, prove-discriminatory-intent approach to remedying inequality, equal opportunity militated against systematic changes. As Leon Mayhew concludes from his study of the Massachusetts Commission Against Discrimination:

Equal treatment harmonizes rather closely with the individualistic strain in American values. The standard of equal treatment demands that each actor be treated equally by every other actor. However, it does not demand that the system as a system treat everyone alike. Thus the businessman bears no collective responsibility for the effects of inequality beyond his control . . . Because of its individualistic emphasis, the implementation of the equal treatment standard fails to uproot the collective structural sources of unequal participation.[64]

Color blindness becomes a more general pattern-blindness; microscopic preoccupation with interpersonal relations obscures macroscopic social inequalities. Each depositor does what is best for himself, and banks continue to fail. Everyone looks at the parts; no one takes responsibility for the whole; and three-fifths of the black community stagnates in the backwaters of "progress."

HOW TO GET WHAT YOU WANT

The hope of effective challenges to racism as it is presently institutionalized in the American social system lies not in a policy of equal opportunity but rather in one of equal results. We must design strategy in terms of end-state rather than process out of a healthy respect for the devious paths of institutional life. No less a strategist than General George Patton presents our conclusion: "Never tell people *how* to do things. Tell them *what* to do and they will surprise you with their ingenuity."[65]

To be successful, any challenge to racism must encompass three general goals: (1) *It must effect the inclusion of black people into institutions in the same proportion that blacks are represented in the population of the country as a whole.* An institution whose black participation falls below 12 percent prolongs racial inequality. (2) *It must encourage the delivery of services in equal quantity and quality to all racial groups.* As long as black people receive less, they will give less. (3) *The challenge must engender a metropolitan base for all institutional operation.* Given the nature of present metropolitan segregation, there does not exist a geographic boundary for any type of action that does not have racial implications. In short, the first step to an egalitarian society is looking like one. Process follows morphology.

Just as the design of the physical environment defines a set of boundaries for our lives, so the structure of our institutional systems—social, economic, educational, political—affects the decisions of living. The social structure that houses our lives affects the way we act and interact and even what we believe.

We must become the architects of our social system. Social, economic, political structures must be rearranged, reordered. "Unseeing forces must give way in critical areas to seeing forces; . . . the blind forces of the marketplace . . . must give way to overall, deliberately chosen objectives."[66]

NOTES

Part II: Housing Discrimination: A Critical Illustration

1 K. E. Taeuber and A. F. Taeuber, *Negroes in Cities.* Chicago: Aldine, 1965.
2 *Ibid.,* p. 2.
3 Leon Mayhew, *Law and Equal Opportunity: A Study of the Massachusetts Commission Against Discrimination.* Cambridge, Mass.: Harvard University Press, 1968.
4 U.S. Bureau of the Census, *Current Population Reports,* Series P-23, Nos. 38, 42, 46 (*The Social and Economic Status of Negroes in the United States, 1970, 1971, 1972*). Washington, D.C.: GPO, 1971, 1972, 1973.

The Housing Problem and the Negro

CHARLES ABRAMS

1 There is no single price reaction to minority infiltrations. Prices may remain constant, fall, or rise and depend on a complex of factors, including the social and economic status of a particular minority at a particular time; its numbers in relation to the numbers in the majority group; the latter's social and cultural level; the minority's capacity for social improvement and assimilation; the size of the city and the physical condition of its neighborhoods; the particular pattern of minority distribution; the nature of the then current minority stereotype; the type of social and educational leadership and maturity in the community; and the relationship between the groups in employment. Shortages may intensify competition for dwellings and increase values. Whether values rise or fall may also depend upon the ability of the newcomers to bid up prices. Nor do values automatically collapse because the minority happens to be of a lower economic status. A minority family may be of lower economic but higher social status, and vice versa. See Charles Abrams, *Forbidden Neighbors.* New York: Harper & Row, 1955; pp. 285 ff.
2 "If a neighborhood is to retain stability," said the FHA manual, "it is necessary that properties shall be continued to be occupied by the same social and racial classes." (Section 937) Among "adverse in-

fluences" was "infiltration of inharmonious racial or nationality groups." Protection against "adverse influences" included "prevention of inharmonious racial groups." (Section 229) "Presence of incompatible racial elements" (Section 225) and "the social class of the parents of children at the school will in many instances have a vital bearing" on whether the neighborhood is "stable." The neighborhood will be less desirable if there is "a lower level of society or an incompatible racial element . . . in such instance it might well be that for the payment of a fee children of this area could attend another school with pupils of their same social class." (1936 Manual, Section 266; 1938 Manual, Section 951) FHA advocated not only deed restrictions but zoning to bar the wrong kind of people, and it included stables and pig pens in the same categories as sections occupied by the wrong kind of race. (1936, Section 284 (3f)) It advocated the use of hills, ravines, and high-speed traffic arteries to discourage the wrong kinds of parents and children (1936, Section 229; 1938, Section 935), and even prescribed and urged the use of a racial covenant form in which it left the space blank for the group excluded to be inserted.

3 Violation of the rule exposed a member board to expulsion. Supplementing its official code, the association issued a brochure in 1943 entitled "Fundamentals of Real Estate Practice." This classed the Negro seeking an education with strange company:

"The prospective buyer might be a bootlegger who would cause considerable annoyance to his neighbors, a madame who had a number of Call Girls on her string, a gangster, who wants a screen for his activities by living in a better neighborhood, a colored man of means who was giving his children a college education and thought they were entitled to live among whites. . . . No matter what the motive or character of the would-be purchaser, if the deal would instigate a form of blight, then certainly the well-meaning broker must work against its consummation."

Residential Segregation in the Mid-Sixties

THEODORE G. CLEMENCE

1 Karl E. and Alma F. Taeuber, *Negroes in Cities*. Chicago: Aldine, 1965.
2 U.S. Bureau of the Census, *Current Population Reports*, Series P-20, No. 151, April 1966.
3 U.S. Bureau of the Census, *Current Population Reports*, Series P-23, No. 21, January 1967.

Black and White Attitudes Toward Race and Housing

THOMAS F. PETTIGREW

1 In a follow-up item, however, only 6 percent thought that "Negroes are born that way," compared to 66 percent who believed "changes are possible" (Campbell & Schuman, 1968).

2 Bradburn *et al.* (1970, p. 248) have shown how previous integrated
experience, as a child and as an adult, are related to selection of an
integrated neighborhood in which to live. Thus, 44 percent with both
experiences chose integrated neighborhoods, compared to about 32
percent with one; only 18 percent of those who had not had previous
interracial experience as either a child or as an adult chose an integrated neighborhood.

3 This is particularly true of the newer cities in the South, such as
Atlanta and Miami. There still lingers a trace of the old master-slave
quarters pattern in such older southern cities as Macon, New Orleans,
and Charleston, South Carolina, giving them slightly lower indices
of residential segregation by race. (Taeuber & Taeuber, 1965).

4 One rigorous study of race and housing conducted in 1956 in Chicago
concluded that for roughly equivalent housing, nonwhites had to pay
about $15 more a month than whites (Duncan & Hauser, 1960).

Part III: Discrimination in Employment, Education, and Income: The Barriers to Status

1 T. F. Pettigrew, *Racially Separate or Together?* New York: McGraw-
Hill, 1971; chap. 7.

2 Social psychologists have shown that this misperception enhances
antiblack feelings and actions of middle-class whites, because it leads
to the unfounded assumption that all blacks have values that conflict
with those of the middle class. *Ibid.*, chap. 12.

3 These and other census data cited are drawn from U.S. Bureau of the
Census, *Current Population Reports*, Series P-23, Nos. 38, 42, 46 (*The
Social and Economic Status of Negroes in the United States, 1970,
1971, 1972*). Washington, D.C.: GPO, 1971, 1972, 1973.

4 Rashi Fein, "An economic and social profile of the Negro American,"
in T. Parsons and K. B. Clark (eds.), *The Negro American.* Boston:
Houghton Mifflin, 1966; pp. 114–115.

5 "A Markov model" refers to an ahistorical chain concept introduced
by the Russian mathematician, A. A. Markov. A Markov chain is a
chance process having the special property that its future can be
predicted just as accurately from knowing its present state as it can
from knowing both its present state together with its past history. The
model has proven particularly useful in understanding social mobility
across generations—as in the Lieberson-Fuguitt article. The model
when applied to mobility predicts that a man's social status can be
predicted as well from knowing his father's status as it can from
knowing the status of his father and his earlier ancestors as well. One
can fully understand the major points of Selection 13 without understanding this model. But the interested reader may pursue the subject
further: Patrick Billingsley, "Markov Chains," in D. L. Sills (ed.),
International Encyclopedia of the Social Sciences. New York: Macmillan and Free Press, 1968, vol. 9, pp. 581–585; and J. C. Kemeny
and J. L. Snell, *Finite Markov Chains.* New York: Van Nostrand
Reinhold, 1960.

6 Francis Tucker, "White-Nonwhite age differences and the accurate assessment of the 'cost of being Negro,'" *Social Forces*, 1969, 47, 343–345.

7 Andrew Brimmer, "The Negro in the national economy," in J. P. Davis (ed.), *The American Negro Reference Book*. Englewood Cliffs, N.J.: Prentice-Hall, 1966; pp. 266–271.

8 H. L. Browning, S. C. Lopreato, and D. L. Poston, Jr., "Income and veteran status: Variations among Mexican Americans, blacks, and anglos," *American Sociological Review*, 1973, 38, 74–85.

9 J. C. Coleman, C. C. Berry, and Z. D. Blum, "White and black careers during the first decade of labor force experience: Occupational status and income together," *Social Science Research*, 1972, 1, 293–304.

10 O. D. Duncan, "Inheritance of poverty or inheritance of race?" in D. P. Moynihan (ed.), *On Understanding Poverty*. New York: Basic Books, 1969; pp. 85–110.

11 *Ibid.*, p. 103.

Housing Segregation and Racial Inequality in Southern Cities

W. CLARK ROOF

1 The following assumptions are required: (1) linear, additive relationships among variables; (2) one-way causation, i.e., each successive dependent variable is presumed to be caused by some of the previous variables but not by any which appear after it; (3) negligible measurement error; and (4) variables not included in the causal system are presumed not to be producing confounding effects which systematically distort underlying relationships among the model variables. Admittedly, there may be violations of these assumptions since "feedback" effects are indeed likely. Yet such "feedback" effects, even though present, are assumed to be secondary to the major direction of causal influences.

2 In general we may write a prediction equation for each pair of variables that are *not* linked directly by a causal arrow; usually, these predictions take the form of the absence of correlations or the disappearance of higher-order partial correlations. With Model I shown above, the following predictions are made:

$$
\begin{aligned}
r_{12} &= 0 \\
r_{14.3} &= 0 \\
r_{15.34} &= 0 \ (\text{reducing to } r_{15.3} = 0) \\
r_{16.345} &= 0 \ (\text{reducing to } r_{16.3} = 0) \\
r_{24.3} &= 0 \\
r_{25.43} &= 0 \ (\text{reducing to } r_{25.3} = 0) \\
r_{26.345} &= 0 \ (\text{reducing to } r_{26.3} = 0) \\
r_{35.4} &= 0 \\
r_{46.5} &= 0
\end{aligned}
$$

Since a simple chain model is postulated, r_{36} may be stated in terms of the cross-products of the intervening variables connecting the two end variables. This gives the prediction:

$$r_{36} = r_{34}r_{45}r_{56}$$

The predictions, along with the three exploratory hypotheses, may be examined empirically, and on the basis of this examination the adequacy of the model can be judged.

Employment Discrimination on the Government Job
U.S. COMMISSION ON CIVIL RIGHTS

1 O. G. Stahl, *Public Personnel Administration* (5th Edition). New York: Harper & Row, 1962; p. 118.
2 *Ibid.*, p. 109.
3 *Ibid.*, p. 120.

Patterns of Occupational Mobility Among Negro Men
OTIS DUDLEY DUNCAN

1 U.S. Bureau of the Census, "Lifetime Occupational Mobility of Adult Males: March 1962," *Current Population Reports*, Series P-23, No 11, May 12, 1904.
2 Peter M. Blau, "The Flow of Occupational Supply and Recruitment," *American Sociological Review*, 1965, *30*, 475–490; Otis Dudley Duncan, "Occupation Trends and Patterns of Net Mobility in the United States," *Demography*, 1966, *3*(1), 1–18.
3 The reader should note the departure from the conventional pattern of presentation by color—white and "nonwhite." In the population under study, estimated at 39,969,000 men aged 25 to 64 years in March, 1962 (all civilians in this age group plus some 718,000 members of the armed forces who were living off post or with their families on post), there were 3,514,000 Negroes; 459,000 other nonwhites; and 35,966,000 whites. Classifying the "other nonwhites" with the whites hardly disturbs the latter category of the "nonwhite" group when that group is to be studied primarily for the information it conveys about Negroes.
4 It should be stated that the terms "over-" and "underrepresentation" refer merely to the relative size of the percentages of Negro and non-Negro men in a category, without regard to whether that situation is desirable or not. Reference to "higher" and "lower" categories, moreover, is simply a convenience in discussing the occupation groups as arranged in Table 1, where the ordering corresponds only very roughly to a socioeconomic ranking of occupations.
5 Nathan Hare, "Recent Trends in the Occupational Mobility of Negroes, 1930–1960: An Intracohort Analysis," *Social Forces*, 1965, *35*, 41–57.
6 Beverly Duncan, *Family Factors and School Dropout: 1920–1960*. Ann Arbor: The University of Michigan, 1965; Otis Dudley Duncan, "Discrimination Against Negroes," *Annals of the American Academy of Political and Social Science*, 1967, *371*, 86–103.
7 Peter M. Blau and Otis Dudley Duncan, *The American Occupational Structure*. New York: Wiley, 1967.

Negro-White Occupational Differences in the Absence of Discrimination
STANLEY LIEBERSON AND GLENN V. FUGUITT

1 For a general elementary discussion of Markov chains see: John G. Kemeny, J. Laurie Snell, and Gerald L. Thompson, *Introduction to Finite Mathematics.* Englewood Cliffs, N.J.: Prentice-Hall, 1956.
2 Beverly Duncan observed, e.g., that growing up in a broken family means from 0.6 to 1 year less schooling for a boy. See her *Family Factors and School Dropout: 1920–1960.* Ann Arbor: University of Michigan, 1965; p. 8.
3 See the discussion of problems in the measurement of discrimination in H. M. Blalock, Jr., "Theory, Measurement and Replication in the Social Sciences," *American Journal of Sociology,* 1961, *66,* 346–347.
4 Otis Dudley Duncan, "The Trend of Occupational Mobility in the United States," *American Sociological Review,* 1965, *30,* 491–498; Natalie Rogoff, "Recent Trends in Urban Occupational Mobility." In Paul K. Hatt and Albert J. Reiss, Jr. (eds.), *Cities and Society.* New York: Free Press, 1957; pp. 432–445.
5 U.S. Bureau of the Census, "Lifetime Occupational Mobility of Adult Males, March, 1962," *Current Population Reports,* Ser. P-23, No. 11, May, 1964.
6 Otis Dudley Duncan and Robert W. Hodge, "Educational and Occupational Mobility: A Regression Analysis," *American Journal of Sociology,* 1963, *68,* 644.
7 Gosta Carlsson, *Social Mobility and Class Structure.* Lund: C. W. K. Gleerup, 1958; chap. vii.
8 U.S. Bureau of the Census, "School Enrollment, and Education of Young Adults and Their Fathers: October 1960," *Current Population Reports,* Ser. P-20, No. 110, July, 1961.
9 Paul M. Siegel, "On the Cost of Being a Negro," *Sociological Inquiry,* 1965, *35,* 41–57; and Nathan Hare, "Recent Trends in the Occupational Mobility of Negroes, 1930–1960: An Intracohort Analysis," *Social Forces,* 1965, *44,* 166–173.
10 The discrepancy between this index of 38 and the index of 40 reported in Table 2 is due to the fact these data are for non-whites rather than Negroes only and because the data for whites here are based on a 5 per cent sample.
11 The differences between the two indexes cannot be used to determine the percentage of the actual 1960 index which is not explained by formal educational attainment. The indexes, taken pair-wise, are not simply additive. For formulas on the minimum and maximum restrictions, see Stanley Lieberson, *Ethnic Patterns in American Cities.* New York: Free Press, 1963; p. 39.
12 Leonard Broom and Norvel Glenn, *Transformation of the Negro American.* New York: Harper & Row, 1965; p. 84.

The Racial Integration of the Schools
THOMAS F. PETTIGREW

1 D. J. Armor, "The Evidence on Busing," *The Public Interest*, Summer 1972, 90–126.
2 Walter Shapiro, "Black and White Together Is Still the Point," *The Washington Monthly*, June 1973, 32–42; Godfrey Hodgson, "Do Schools Make a Difference?" *Atlantic*, March 1973, *231*, 35–46.
3 T. F. Pettigrew, E. L. Useem, C. Normand, and M. S. Smith, "Busing: A Review of the Evidence," *The Public Interest*, Winter 1973, 88–118.
4 D. J. Armor, "The Double Double Standard: A Reply," *The Public Interest*, Winter 1973, 119–131.
5 Marshall S. Smith, "Agreement and Disagreement: A Final Word." Unpublished manuscript, Harvard Graduate School of Education, March 1973.
6 Harry Singer, "Effect of Integration on Achievement of Anglos, Blacks, and Mexican-Americans." Unpublished manuscript, Department of Education, University of California, Riverside, 1972; pp. 25–26.
7 James McPartland, "The Segregated Student in the Desegregated Schools: Sources of Influence on Negro Secondary Students," *Report No. 21*, Department of Social Relations, Johns Hopkins University, 1968.
8 Pettigrew et al., op. cit.
9 I. S. Hendrick, "The Development of a School Integration Plan in Riverside, California: A History and Perspective." Unpublished manuscript of the University of California, Riverside, and the Riverside Unified School District, 1968; p. 201.
10 Pettigrew et al., op. cit.
11 James Coleman et al., *Equality of Educational Opportunity*. Washington, D.C.: GPO, 1966; p. 332.
12 Pettigrew et al., op. cit.; and T. F. Pettigrew, "The Negro and Education." In I. Katz and P. Gurin (eds.), *Race and the Social Sciences*. New York: Basic Books, 1969.
13 Coleman et al., op. cit., p. 333.
14 S. K. Bailey, *Disruption in Urban Public Secondary Schools*. Washington, D.C.: National Association of Secondary School Principals, 1970.
15 G. W. Allport, *The Nature of Prejudice*. Reading, Mass.: Addison-Wesley, 1954; chap. 16; T. F. Pettigrew, *Racially Separate or Together?* New York: McGraw-Hill, 1971; chap. 12.
16 Coleman et al., op. cit., p. 333.
17 Christopher Jencks and Marsha Brown, "The Effects of Desegregation on Student Achievement: Some New Evidence From the Equality of Educational Opportunity Survey." Unpublished manuscript, Harvard Graduate School of Education, 1972.

The 1960s: A Decade of Progress for Blacks?
REYNOLDS FARLEY AND ALBERT HERMALIN

1 Whenever possible, data for Negro and white populations have been used, but for some of the earlier dates statistics are available only for the white and nonwhite populations. In 1960, 94 percent of the non-white population identified themselves as blacks (U.S. Bureau of the Census, 1961, Table 44).

Part IV: Discrimination in Crime, Politics, and Other Areas

1 Ann H. Pettigrew and T. F. Pettigrew, "Negro American Health," in T. F. Pettigrew, A Profile of the Negro American. New York: Van Nostrand Reinhold, 1964; pp. 72–99.
2 Ibid., pp. 136–156; and T. F. Pettigrew and R. B. Spier, "The Ecological Structure of Negro Homicide," American Journal of Sociology, 1962, 67, 621–629.
3 The absolute numbers of criminal executions by race do not, of course, by themselves prove racial discrimination. But carefully controlled research on the point is convincing. See M. E. Wolfgang and Mark Riedel, "Race, Judicial Discretion, and the Death Penalty," The Annals of the American Academy of Political and Social Science, May 1973, 407, 119–133.
4 P. B. Johnson, D. O. Sears, and J. B. McConahay, "Black Invisibility, the Press, and the Los Angeles Riot," American Journal of Sociology, 1971, 76, 698–721.
5 G. D. Lowe and H. E. Hodges, "Race and the Treatment of Alcoholism in a Southern State," Social Problems, 1972, 20, 240–252.
6 Joint Center for Political Studies, National Roster of Black Elected Officials, Vol. III. Washington, D.C.: Joint Center for Political Studies, May, 1973.

Crime and Race
MARVIN E. WOLFGANG AND BERNARD COHEN

1 Crime in the United States: Uniform Crime Reports, 1967. Washington, D.C.: U.S. Department of Justice, 1968.
2 Philip H. Ennis, Field Surveys II: Criminal Victimization in the United States. Chicago: National Opinion Research Center, May 1967.
3 Albert J. Reiss, Jr., Field Surveys III: Studies in Crime and Law Enforcement in Major Metropolitan Areas. Volume I. Ann Arbor: University of Michigan; especially pp. 29–65.
4 Attorney General's Survey of Release Procedures: Probation, vol. IV. Washington, D.C.: Department of Justice, 1939.
5 Ibid.
6 Herman B. Canady, "The Negro in Crime," in V. C. Branham and

S. B. Kutask (eds.), *Encyclopedia of Criminology*. New York: Philosophical Library, 1949; pp. 267–277.

7 Walter R. Chivers, "The Negro Delinquent," in *National Probation Association Yearbook*, 1942; pp. 46–59.

8 John Dollard, *Caste and Class in a Southern Town*. Garden City, N.Y.: Doubleday, 1957.

9 Harold Garfinkel, "Research Note on Inter- and Intra-racial Homicides," *Social Forces*, 1949, 27, 369–381.

10 Edward Green, *An Analysis of the Sentencing Practices of Criminal Court Judges in Philadelphia*. Ph.D. thesis, University of Pennsylvania, 1959.

11 A. H. Grimke, *The Ultimate Criminal*, The American Negro Academy Occasion Paper no. 17. Washington, D.C.: The Academy, 1915.

12 Guy B. Johnson, "The Negro and Crime," *The Annals of the American Academy of Political and Social Science*, 1941, 217, 93–104.

13 Ira DeA. Reid, "Race and Crime," *Friends Journal*, 1957, 3, 772–774.

14 Edward B. Reuter, *The American Race Problem*. New York: Crowell, 1927.

15 Thorsten Sellin, "Race Prejudice in the Administration of Justice," *American Journal of Sociology*, 1935, 41, 212–217.

16 A. L. Wood, "Minority Group Criminality and Cultural Integration," *Journal of Criminal Law and Criminology*, 1947, 37, 498–510.

17 Gunnar Myrdal, *An American Dilemma*. New York: Harper & Row, 1944.

18 *Field Surveys V, A National Survey of Police and Community Relations*, The President's Commission on Law Enforcement and Administration of Justice. Washington, D.C.: GPO, January 1967, p. 14.

19 *Ibid.*, p. 15.

20 For instance, Ennis, *op. cit.*, Chapter VI.

21 *Task Force Report, The Police*, The President's Commission on Law Enforcement and Administration of Justice. Washington, D.C.: GPO, 1967, p. 146.

22 *Ibid.*

23 *Ibid.*, footnote 27.

24 *Ibid.*, p. 146.

25 *Ibid.*, p. 147.

26 *Ibid.*

27 *Ibid.*

28 *Ibid.*

29 *Field Surveys IV, The Police and the Community, Volume 2*, The Presidents Commission on Law Enforcement and Administration of Justice. Washington, D.C.: GPO, October 1966, p. 111.

30 Donald J. Black and Albert J. Reiss, Jr., *Field Surveys III, Studies in Crime and Law Enforcement in Major Metropolitan Areas, Volume 2*, The President's Commission on Law Enforcement and Administration of Justice. Washington, D.C.: GPO, pp. 133 ff. Also see: Albert J. Reiss, Jr., "Police Brutality—Answers to Key Questions," *transaction*, July-August 1968, 10–19.

31 Black and Reiss, *op. cit.*, p. 136.

32 *The Police, op. cit.*, p. 180.

33 William A. Westley, "Violence and the Police," *American Journal of Sociology*, July 1953, *59*, 34–41.
34 *Field Surveys V, op. cit.*, p. 185.
35 *The Police, op. cit.*
36 *Field Surveys IV, Volume 2, op. cit.*, p. 127.
37 *The Police, op. cit.*, p. 183.
38 *Ibid.*, p. 184.
39 Irving Piliavin and Scott Briar, "Police Encounters with Juveniles," *American Journal of Sociology*, 1964, *70*, 206–214.
40 *The Police, op. cit.*, pp. 183–184.
41 *Field Surveys IV, Volume 1, op. cit.*, p. 89.
42 *Field Surveys III, Volume 2, op. cit.*, p. 88.
43 *Ibid.*
44 *The Police, op. cit.*, p. 180.
45 Nathan Goldman, "The Differential Detection of Juvenile Offenders for Court Appearance." Ph.D. thesis, University of Chicago, 1950.
46 *Field Surveys IV, Volume 2, op. cit.*, p. 248.
47 Press Release, "Civilian Complaint Review Board Report." Bureau of Public Information, Police Department, City of New York, July 1968. Especially Appendix F, p. 1.
48 *Field Surveys V, op. cit.*, p. 186.
49 *Ibid.*
50 *Ibid.*
51 *Field Surveys IV, Volume 2, op. cit.*, p. 231.
52 For a detailed discussion of police problems and recommendations for improvement, see: George Edwards, *The Police on the Urban Frontier*. New York: Institute of Human Relations Press, The American Jewish Committee, 1968; and James H. Scheuer, *To Walk the Streets Safely: The Role of Modern Science and Technology in Our Criminal Justice System*. Garden City, N.Y.: Doubleday, 1969.
53 Garfinkel, *op. cit.*
54 Johnson, *op. cit.*
55 Our discussion of discriminatory practices in jury selection comes mainly from: Michael O. Finkelstein, *Appellants' Brief in Support of the Grand Jury Challenge*. U.S. Court of Appeals for the Second Circuit. Docket Nos. 32327, 32328 and 32326. *U.S.A. v. Charles T. Bennett, et al.*, pp. 1–51.
56 For instance see M. O. Finkelstein, "The Application of Statistical Decision Theory to the Jury Discrimination Cases," *Harvard Law Review*, 1966, *80*, 338. For non-statistical accounts of discrimination in jury selection the reader may consult: S. W. Tucker, "Racial Discrimination in Jury Selection in Virginia," *Virginia Law Review*, 1966, *52*, 736–750, and R. S. Kuhn, "Jury Discrimination: The Next Phase," *Southern California Law Review*, 1968, *41*, 235–328.
57 W. S. Robinson, "Bias, Probability and Trial by Jury," *American Journal of Sociology*, 1950, *15*, 73–78.
58 Edwin M. Lemert, "The Grand Jury as an Agency of Social Control," *American Sociological Review*, 1945, *10*, 751–758, p. 753 cited.
59 *Appellants' Brief, op. cit.*, pp. 3–19.
60 The probability is 1.1×10^{-146}. This is the mathematicians' method

of designating the number described by a decimal point followed by 145 zeros and the number 11.

61 *Appellants' Brief, op. cit.,* pp. 15–16.

62 Hugo Adam Bedau (ed.), *The Death Penalty in America.* Garden City, N.Y.: Doubleday, 1967; p. 411.

63 *Ibid.,* p. 413.

64 Ohio State Legislature Research Commission, *Capital Punishment,* Staff Research Report No. 46. Columbus, Ohio: The Commission, January 1961.

65 *National Prisoner Statistics, No. 20, Executions, 1958.* Washington, D.C.: Federal Bureau of Prisons, February 1959.

66 Bedau, *op. cit.,* p. 511.

67 Florida Civil Liberties Union, *Rape: Selective Electrocution Based on Race.* Miami, 1964.

68 "Preliminary Analysis of Rape and Capital Punishment in the State of Arkansas 1945–1965," by Marvin E. Wolfgang. Unpublished manuscript.

69 E. M. Lemert and Judy Rosberg, *The Administration of Justice to Minority Groups in Los Angeles County.* Berkeley and Los Angeles: University of California Press, 1948.

70 Henry Bullock, "Significance of the Racial Factor in the Length of Prison Sentences," *The Journal of Criminal Law, Criminology, and Police Science,* 1961 52, 411–417.

71 Thorsten Sellin, "Race Prejudice in the Administration of Justice," *American Journal of Sociology,* 1935, *41,* 212–217.

72 *National Prisoner Statistics, 1951,* "Prisoners Released from State and Federal Institutions, 1951," Washington, D.C.: Federal Bureau of Prisons, 1955.

73 Edward Green, "Judicial Attitudes in Sentencing," *Cambridge Studies in Criminology,* vol. XV. London: Macmillan, 1961.

74 Edward Green, "Inter- and Intra-Racial Crime Relative to Sentencing," *The Journal of Criminal Law, Criminology, and Police Science,* 1964, *55,* 348–358.

75 "Executions 1930–1966," *NPS Bulletin,* Bureau of Prisons, 1967.

76 For one of the most recent studies, see Marvin E. Wolfgang, Arlene Kelly, and Hans C. Nolde, "Comparison of the Executed and the Commuted Among Admissions to Death Row," *The Journal of Criminal Law, Criminology, and Police Science,* 1962, *53,* 301–311.

77 Elmer H. Johnson, "Executions and Commutations in North Carolina," in Bedau, *op. cit.,* p. 462.

78 C. S. Magnum, *The Legal Status of the Negro.* Chapel Hill: University of North Carolina Press, 1940.

79 Sara R. Ehrmann, "The Human Side of Capital Punishment," in Bedau, *op. cit.,* p. 512.

Part VI: Proposed Remedies

1 T. F. Pettigrew, *Racially Separate or Together?* New York: McGraw-Hill, 1971.

Institutional Racism: How to Discriminate Without Really Trying
ROBERT FRIEDMAN

1 Admittedly, our definition of "institution" is broad. The realm we have described as institutional subsumes Parsons' four categories of roles, collectivities, institutions, and values. Talcott Parsons, *Structure and Process in Modern Societies*. New York: Free Press, 1969; p. 171.

2 Louis Knowles and Kenneth Prewitt, *Institutional Racism in America*. Englewood Cliffs, N.J.: Prentice-Hall, 1969; p. 143.

3 This four-level breakdown of institutional racism is the result of crossing two distinctions: the structure-process distinction suggested by Parsons with its implications that norms govern morphological patterns, and the subsectoral, supersectoral distinction with its implication of dominance. Talcott Parsons, et al., *Theories of Society: Foundations of Modern Sociological Theory*. New York: Free Press, 1961; vol. I, p. 31.

4 M. S. Stuart, *An Economic Detour: A History of Insurance in the Lives of American Negroes*. College Park, Md.: McGrath, 1940; pp. xxiii, xxiv.

5 Rose Helper, *The Racial Policies and Practices of Real Estate Brokers*. Minneapolis: University of Minnesota Press, 1969; pp. 236–237.

6 From regression analysis based on Peter Blau and Otis Duncan, *The American Occupational Structure*. New York: Wiley, 1967; p. 27. And U.S. Bureau of the Census and U.S. Bureau of Labor Statistics, *The Social and Economic Status of Negroes in the United States, 1969*. Washington, D.C.: GPO, 1970.

7 Gordon Allport, *The Nature of Prejudice*. Garden City, N.Y.: Doubleday, 1958; p. 297.

8 We borrow from Bloch's suggestion of three forms of discriminatory hiring: (1) total restriction, (2) partial restriction, and (3) discriminatory retrenchment. Herman Bloch, *The Circle of Discrimination*. New York: New York University Press, 1969.

9 Herbert Hill, "Racial Practices of Organized Labor—The Age of Gompers and After." In Arthur Ross and Herbert Hill (eds.), *Employment, Race and Poverty*. New York: Harcourt Brace Jovanovich, 1967; p. 392.

10 Julius Jacobson, *The Negro and the American Labor Movement*. Garden City, N. Y.: Doubleday, 1968; p. 364.

11 Hill, loc. cit.; and Ray Marshall, *The Negro and Organized Labor*. New York: Wiley, 1965; p. 109.

12 Hill, loc. cit.

13 Knowles & Prewitt, op. cit., p. 173.

14 Herbert Hill, "No End of Pledges; Continuing Discrimination in the Construction Unions," *Commonweal*, March 15, 1968.

15 Herbert Hill, "Black Protest and the Struggle for Union Democracy," *Issues in Industrial Society*, 1969, *1*, 1, p. 21.

16 *Time Magazine*, April 6, 1970, p. 92.

17 Jack Star, "A National Disgrace: What Unions Do to Blacks," *Look Magazine*, November 12, 1968.

18 Whitney Young, *To Be Equal*. New York: McGraw-Hill, 1964; p. 40.

19 Knowles & Prewitt, op. cit., pp. 21–22.
20 George Strauss, "How Management Views Its Race Relations Responsibilities," in Ross and Hill, op. cit., p. 277.
21 Helper, op. cit., p. 189.
22 Ibid., p. 292.
23 Ibid., p. 167.
24 John F. Kain (ed.), *Race and Poverty: The Economics of Discrimination.* Englewood Cliffs, N.J.: Prentice-Hall, 1969; p. 82.
25 Helper, op. cit., pp. 45–46, 169; and Davis McEntire, *Residence and Race.* Berkeley: University of California Press, 1960; pp. 190–191, 229.
26 Jacobson, op. cit., p. 364.
27 Charles E. Wilson, "Racism in Education." In Barry Schwartz and Robert Disch (eds.), *White Racism: Its History, Pathology, and Practice.* New York: Dell, 1970; pp. 309–310.
28 Lawrence Sager, "Tight Little Islands: Exclusion, Equal Protection, and the Indigent," *Stanford Law Review*, April, 1969, *21*, p. 767; and National Committee Against Discrimination in Housing, *Trends in Housing*, June/July, 1968, p. 8.
29 Kain op. cit., p. 25.
30 Knowles & Prewitt, op. cit., pp. 71–73.
31 Marshall, op. cit., pp. 105–108.
32 Karl Taeuber and Alma Taeuber, *Negroes in Cities: Residential Segregation and Neighborhood Change.* Chicago: Aldine, 1965; p. 23.
33 U.S. Bureau of Census and U.S. Bureau of Labor Statistics, op. cit., p. 10.
34 U.S. Commission on Civil Rights, *Racial Isolation in the Public Schools.* Washington, D.C.: GPO, 1967; p. 12.
35 Hal Dunleavy and Associates, "Population, Housing and Jobs," in National Committee Against Discrimination in Housing and United States Department of Housing and Urban Development, *Project California D-8, Phase 1 Report.* Unpublished paper, 1971; p. 13.
36 U.S. Commission on Civil Rights, op. cit., p. 20.
37 Dunleavy, op. cit., p. 3.
38 "The Suburbs: Frontier of the 70s," *City*, January/February, 1971, *5*, 1, p. 123, 142.
39 Ibid., p. 13.
40 Taeuber & Taeuber, op. cit., pp. 84–85.
41 Commission on Race and Housing, *Where Shall We Live?* Berkeley: University of California Press, 1958; pp. 35–38; and Allport, op. cit., pp. 228–229.
42 Dunleavy, op. cit., p. 12.
43 Ibid., p. 24.
44 Ibid., p. 46.
45 Ibid., p. 43.
46 Ibid., Table III.
47 "Partial Report—Regional Transportation Improvements," in NCDH and HUD, op. cit.
48 "Suburbs . . .", op. cit., p. 50.
49 National Committee Against Discrimination in Housing, *Jobs and Housing: A Study of Employment and Housing Opportunities for*

Racial Minorities in the Suburban Areas of the New York Metropolitan Region. New York: March, 1970, p. 4.
50 Young, op. cit., p. 18.
51 Helper, op. cit., p. 56.
52 Ibid., p. 217.
53 Eugene C. Conser, *Realtor's Headlines*, 1958.
54 Luigi Laurenti, *Property Values and Race: Studies in Seven Cities.* Berkeley: University of California Press, 1961; pp. 51–52.
55 The belief that other people are in fact prejudiced can lead to increased discrimination. Kenneth Lenihan found that while two-thirds of the residents of one small city said they were not opposed to having a black neighbor, only one in five was willing to sell for fear of his neighbor's opposition. Such pluralistic ignorance can be manipulated to justify real estate practice. Quoted in T. F. Pettigrew and Kurt W. Back, "Sociology in the Desegregation Process: Its Use and Disuse." In Paul Lazarfeld, et al., *Uses of Sociology.* New York: Basic Books, 1967; p. 705.
56 Alexis de Tocqueville, *Democracy in America.* New York: Knopf, 1945; p. 86.
57 Strauss, op. cit., p. 273.
58 The programs of the National Alliance of Businessmen suggest just the opposite. NAB, "Guidelines for Introducing the Hardcore Unemployed to a Productive Job," Pamphlet, 1969.
59 Andrew F. Brimmer, "The Negro in the National Economy." In John Davis (ed.), *The American Negro Reference Book.* Englewood Cliffs, N.J.: Prentice-Hall, 1966; pp. 251–336.
60 Andrew F. Brimmer, "Economic Progress of Negroes in the United States: The Deepening Schism." Unpublished speech delivered before the Founder's Day Convocation at Tuskegee Institute on March 22, 1970, p. 3.
61 E. Franklin Frazier, *Black Bourgeoisie: The Rise of a New Middle Class in the United States.* New York: Free Press, 1957; pp. 45, 49.
62 Leon Mayhew, *Law and Equal Opportunity: A Study of the Massachusetts Committee Against Discrimination.* Cambridge, Mass.: Harvard University Press, 1968; pp. 261–263.
63 Professional acceptance of equal opportunity varied, of course, with the more liberal professions desegregating first. For example, academic associations had never been formally segregated, while real estate boards still resist.
64 Mayhew, op. cit., p. 263.
65 George Patton, *War As I Knew It.* Boston: Houghton Mifflin, 1947; p. 357.
66 NCDH, *Jobs and Housing . . .* , op. cit., p. 163.

Index

75 76   9 8 7 6 5 4 3 2 1